CONVERSATIONS
WITH
ARCHITECTS

CONVERSATIONS WITH ARCHITECTS

PHILIP JOHNSON
KEVIN ROCHE
PAUL RUDOLPH
BERTRAND GOLDBERG
MORRIS LAPIDUS
LOUIS KAHN
CHARLES MOORE
ROBERT VENTURI &
DENISE SCOTT BROWN

BY JOHN W. COOK
AND HEINRICH KLOTZ

FOREWORD BY VINCENT SCULLY

LUND HUMPHRIES LONDON

For Phyllis and Gertrud

PHOTO CREDITS

Chalmer Alexander, 2-26, 2-36. Wayne Andrews, 5-9, 5-10. Morley Baer, 7-5, 7-8, 7-10, 7-11, 7-12, 7-13. Hedrich-Blessing, 4-1, 4-10, 4-11. Peter Bromer, 5-5. Orlando Cabanban. 4-3, 4-6, 4-15. Louis Checkman, 5-19. Dalwadi P.M.. 6-13, 6-15. John Ebstel, 6-31. Alexandre Georges, 1-2, 1-6, 5-22. Steve Hill, 8-8. Anwar Hosain, 6-14. Steve Izenour, 8-13, 8-14. Donald Luckenbill, 3-18. Joseph Molitor, 1-20, 3-3, 3-5. Robert Perron, 3-22. George Pohl, 8-11. Gottscho-Schleisner, 5-2, 5-4, 5-7, 5-11, 5-12. Franz Stoedtner, 1-25. Lee Tabor, 2-32. William Watkins, 8-10, 8-12. Kurt Wyss, 6-1.

Published in the United States of America in 1973
by Praeger Publishers, Inc., New York

Published in 1973 by
Lund Humphries Publishers Limited
12 Bedford Square London WC1
SBN 85331 353 9

© 1973 by John W. Cook and Heinrich Klotz

All rights reserved

Made and printed in the United States of America

CONTENTS

	Foreword by Vincent Scully	7
	Introduction	9
1	PHILIP JOHNSON	11
2	KEVIN ROCHE	52
3	PAUL RUDOLPH	90
4	BERTRAND GOLDBERG	122
5	MORRIS LAPIDUS ALAN LAPIDUS	147
6	LOUIS KAHN	178
7	CHARLES MOORE	218
8	ROBERT VENTURI DENISE SCOTT BROWN	247
	Glossary	267
	Index	268

FOREWORD

I am glad to have been asked to write this Foreword because I think this collection of interviews represents one of the most successful attempts to get architects to talk that I have seen to date. I don't quite know how it got that way, but it must somehow be due to John Cook and Heinrich Klotz. They seem devoid of theoretical preconceptions most of the time. This has got to be their strength. Somehow the architects seem to open up for them and to talk with an admirable and most uncommon lack of hypocrisy themselves.

And I do like very much the freshness of what the architects have to say here. Only the Venturis are their usual stern selves, as strict and systematic as always in their remarks. But they have been made to talk so much during the past five years or so that they have probably stiffened in their didactic role. They should now be allowed to build and not to speak—as Robert Venturi tells us flatly enough in these pages.

The "inclusive," realistic school of design which the Venturis have so far best defined is delightfully represented here by Charles Moore. His account of his struggles with F.H.A. housing restrictions, and with the parking fanatics who dominate the New Haven Redevelopment Agency, illuminates at once the mortal shame of America's housing policy and the outdated mentalities of those who implement it at the local level. Kevin Roche, whose Knights of Columbus Building is Moore's formidable neighbor across New Haven's Oak Street Connector, produces not only his usual sane and civilized discussion of his method of design (though how science-fiction stupendous some of his offspring are!) but also an eloquent and memorable portrait of Mies van der Rohe as he knew him as a wordless teacher. Mies appears in Bertrand Goldberg's clear and useful remarks, as well, in a somewhat more *gemütlich* guise —and he turns up just about everywhere in one way or another. It is clear that Mies was the true father of this generation, even for the architects who have most reacted against him. And what an ideal father figure he makes; bulky, unflappable, and always right, a real prewar man with a big cigar. In this he is rivaled only by Louis Kahn, in a sense his successor as an architect-parent. Yet Kahn is wholly American, highly verbal but obfuscatory with his words, awkward and rather solemn when he is expounding theory, but flashing and mellow when the wholly intelligent, utterly lovable human being breaks through and shows us where the flesh of reality ultimately resides.

In the interview with Philip Johnson, I find Cook and Klotz unnecessarily tedious —with their bits about travertine and Hitler and all. But everybody baits Johnson, and he asks for it and usually comes dancing through it with a fine, brittle Balanchine-like rigor—as he does here. Paul Rudolph is good and serious in these pages, acknowledging his education under Gropius —and his sources of inspiration and his heroic intentions—and then being properly concentrated on his megastructures by the interrogators. How much the pure breath of the 1950's still comes through in Rudolph's words—all the best of the first, immediately postwar generation of American artists, a fated mixture of Tennessee Williams and Franz Kline.

I like so much what all these people have to say about themselves that I hesitate to say that I like the interview with Morris Lapidus best. And I am not sure now that I really do. But it is awfully good, and the most unexpected and even endearing of them all. Lapidus emerges as a wholly unassuming, intelligent, and good man. It is a moot and perhaps irrelevant point as to whether or not he is a good architect as well, especially in his late hotels, and the interrogators are not quite subtle enough themselves to resolve the question. I am not certain that our generation can resolve it. But they do make us see how excellent Lapidus's early storefronts were, and we cannot help but be tickled later when he gets his guests at the Fontainebleu in Miami Beach all in the same musical comedy together. He is the environmentalist *par excellence*.

Only when more Puritan virtues appear in his Firm toward the last does interest in Lapidus wane, and by that time we have been alerted to some fundamental qualities of architecture and to some general considerations about humanity which our theories had perhaps been too hermetic to allow us to perceive before.

These interviews turn up no new Le Corbusier with a grand if rather shivery scheme to reorder the world. What emerges in the end, and hopeful enough in view of the complexity of the country's human and environmental problems as a whole, is the normal American pluralism and pragmatism in, if not its strongest, at least not its weakest phase (though with the usual European Grandaddy), manifested in what may be the last generation of architects to enjoy the extraordinary prestige as artists and thinkers with which Romanticism endowed them. Still, the thought processes of people who can make and imagine things will always be of intense critical interest, and Cook and Klotz permit some of that to come through in these pages. They don't really add it all up, which is probably to the good. The structure is for elsewhere. Here the life is best.

Vincent Scully

INTRODUCTION

Having provoked the architects interviewed in this book to talk frankly about their ideas and intentions, we believe that the results reveal something more about their creative process, prejudices, and motivation than can be read from concrete, steel, and glass.

American architecture today is represented, in a pluralism of styles, by many voices speaking simultaneously. This pluralism, symptomatic of the era, is illustrated in the opinions of these architects, who exemplify the variety of established directions. The order in which they appear and the length of the conversations were determined not by their relative importance but by the relationships among their architectural styles.

We do not discuss the entire oeuvre of each architect, of course, but probe selected aspects in an effort to explore how they work and to define their personal characteristics. In order to approach each architect as a unique personality, we studied his work before the conversation took place. Primarily emphasizing his achievements, we nevertheless asked some similar questions of each architect, with the intention that conflicts and similarities would emerge to evoke comparisons. Every conversation stands on its own, but each one is best understood in relation to the total collection.

What an architect says about his buildings may not be how people experience them or how history will define them, but the reasons he gives for the way he builds are a vital part of the story of how our human environment is being created.

It is significant to us that three of the twentieth century's greatest architects died while this book was being put together: Mies van der Rohe, Walter Gropius, and Richard Neutra. With their deaths, the era of a dominant style—the International Style—gave way to a scene of complexity brought about in large part by the men who speak here. No one trend rules, and no single father figure reigns.

After World War II, as the influence of the International Style began to break down, architecture became increasingly independent of European prototypes. Previously, modern architecture in America had reflected the influence of Europeans who emigrated, like the Viennese Rudolph Schindler and Richard Neutra, working in California, the Bauhaus chieftain Walter Gropius, and Mies van der Rohe. The succeeding generation of native American architects, identifying less with European teachers, has introduced indigenous styles.

Although Philip Johnson worked closely with Mies in the 1950's, he later made a conscious break and formulates an interesting and elegant eclecticism. Louis Kahn grew up in the American Beaux Arts tradition of the 1920's and '30's, but he transposes the old into a new vocabulary that has been the springboard for younger architects like Robert Venturi and Charles Moore. Many will be surprised that we have included Morris Lapidus, an architect who is relatively unaccepted by his colleagues. His early career and Florida hotels exemplify a world of popular taste, and his openness and humor provide insight into the merchandising mentality determining much of today's architecture. Although Bertrand Goldberg is not widely acknowledged, he has introduced new technological forms in his Chicago high-rise buildings, which have been seen as dramatic images but as yet not understood as new structural possibilities. The case is entirely different with Paul Rudolph and the Irish-born Kevin Roche. Paul Rudolph, the creator of soaring concrete monuments, explores new megastructural forms. Kevin Roche, an architect of super-scale corporation structures, describes a sequential planning method illustrating the genesis of his work. (We regret, however, that he prevented the inclusion of some of the critical and controversial material about his buildings.)

Robert Venturi and Charles Moore take exception to the monumentalizing gestures of their contemporaries, calling for more acceptance of reality and less grand scale through their pop vocabulary and anti-heroic forms. Venturi and his wife, Denise Scott Brown, insist on the life of the man-made landscape as given and include it in their requirements. Sober and thoughtful, they counter the Goliaths. Charles Moore asks the architectural environment to express a fuller register of man's feelings, especially humor and irony.

There are many architects we could not include, of course, because of space and time, and others who we felt had adequate exposure. Naturally, the exciting avant-garde movements across the country would constitute at least another volume. These eight architects define one spectrum within the contemporary scene, representing a significant part of the modern American architectural tradition. Our questions to them seek to reflect domestic as well as European responses to that tradition.

We thank Beverly Kelsey for transcribing the tapes and Jeannie Rittmueller and James Kennison for editing assistance. We are grateful for the invaluable help of our editor at Praeger Publishers, Brenda Gilchrist, and for their patience with endless details, Helen Strodl and Cherene Holland.

J.C.
H.K.

New Haven, Connecticut, 1973

1 PHILIP JOHNSON

JC: Mr. Johnson, let us first turn to one of the most celebrated buildings of your later works, after you had dismissed the Miesian credo, the Kline Biology Tower [*Fig. 1–1*].

PJ: Is it really celebrated that much? Well, I guess it's certainly one of my favorite buildings.

JC: It is sited on the top of that hill so that nobody can ignore it!

PJ: Oh, yes, the setting is perfect. There couldn't be any better site, up on that hill.

HK: Now, that doesn't mean that we are in favor of it in every respect.

PJ: You aren't? Well, you are European. And the Europeans don't like my later works, not one of them. You are still thinking in terms of Gropius.

HK: Don't you think that Gropius was one of the major architects of this century?

PJ: Who is he? By all means, who is he?

HK: Well, I have objections against

your selection of materials, for instance. Don't you hesitate to use travertine?

PJ: Michelangelo used travertine!

HK: Hitler, too—it was his favorite material.

PJ: Well, does one dismiss a material because Hitler used it?

HK: For the Europeans, or at least for Germans, even material can acquire a certain meaning—travertine, for instance, reminds us of a fake monumentality.

PJ: Oh, does it? I never thought of that.

JC: At the Kline Tower, you use red sandstone.

PJ: Yes, for the slabs in between the columns.

JC: You call them columns?

PJ: You might call them pilasters—and of course I used the brick facing.

JC: Now, when one looks carefully, the Kline Tower is actually a copy of the Seagram Building [*Fig. 1–2*], in spite of the surface differences.

PJ: Well, that's right. You are the first who observed that. Yes, that's right! It's a very similar model; it even has the "risalit."

JC: You mean that center part that sticks out, which corresponds to the rear of the Seagram Building?

PJ: Yes, that's right.

HK: Well, there is, of course, that very strong difference between both buildings—instead of Mies's flat curtain wall, you introduced that very plastic, massive façade, a dramatic happening on the surface . . .

PJ: Not only on the surface! Look at the columns down below [*Fig. 1–4*]. The building ends up with those columns; the pilasters are carried all the way down; they really support the building; they are the feet of the building! What's wrong with that?

HK: O.K.—You create the impression that those columns support the building. However, it's the skeleton frame—the inside, which you faced with that dramatic façade. It's actually the Seagram Building that you covered up with columns, pilasters, and sandstone slabs.

PJ: Yes, that's right, except when you use the word "façade," you give it a pejorative meaning.

HK: One enters the building by going through a monumental colonnade. Every column is stretched upward throughout the façade [*Fig. 1–3*]. The surface of the col-

1–1. Kline Biology Tower. Yale University. New Haven, Conn. 1966. Philip Johnson and Richard Foster.

1–2. Seagram Building. New York. 1956–58. Mies van der Rohe and Philip Johnson.

1-3. Kline Biology Tower. View up façade.

umn melts into the wall of the window jamb. It's a smooth transition from column to wall, and suddenly it's not a column any more.

PJ: It becomes a waving wall, something that might have been done in Spain in 1914.

HK: Gaudí!

PJ: Gaudí, very conscious. The first time I did those pilasters, whatever they're called, I did not reverse the curve. Then I asked, "Why worry about separating the pilaster from the wall? Let's make it an undulating wall." You're right to point out the inconsistencies, but they didn't bother me at the time. I was too busy with this part today and that part tomorrow. The building that is most like my building, strange to say, is Eero Saarinen's CBS [*Fig. 1–5*], which has a diamond column that is fake. I think the base of that building keeps on going down into the earth too

1-4. Kline Biology Tower. Columns at entrance.

1–5. CBS Building. New York. 1965. Eero Saarinen and Associates.

far. My [Glass] house [*Fig. 1–6*], for instance, is not an indoor-outdoor house. It is not on the same level as the ground. There's a very bad step, intentionally bad, to hold you in, and the same thing with the rail. Those two items keep you from being in a Miesian building.

HK: That is a very classicistic attitude.

PJ: It is classicistic, by all means.

HK: You want to differentiate?

PJ: Yes, from the ground.

JC: So plinths are necessary?

PJ: Plinths were very necessary for me. I doubt if they are now.

HK: You don't object to the columns as a tired, used-out form?

PJ: Heavens, no. Maybe I do now, but I certainly didn't at the time. But I started the other way around. I started from the undulating façade up above, and then the bridges, which look like small balconies [*Fig. 1–3*]. Those are empty, you know. That third-dimensional undercut was what I was after. It's really a façade feature. And I said, "What do you do with these rounded forms, these half-columns, when you come toward the ground?"

HK: So, you were not designing from the ground up, but from the façade down.

PJ: "How would you take that undulating wall to the ground?" I said. I came

1–6. Glass House. New Canaan, Conn. 1953. Philip Johnson.

1–7. CBS Building. View of entrance.

down the Miesian way; I emptied it out, rather than—well, the worst building in the world, no doubt, is Wallace Harrison's steel building in Pittsburgh, where the building just keeps right on going. Well, I think the CBS Building is just as bad; you don't know when you've hit the bottom.

HK: Down below, Saarinen used the sides of his triangular columns as portal jambs, door jambs [*Fig. 1–7*]. It is interesting that you object so much.

PJ: My classicism!

HK: Rushing into the ground.

PJ: I have this old phrase that every building has five edges. One of them is against the ground. Well, that's no edge.

HK: The ground itself is no edge.

PJ: No, you've got to *do* something.

HK: Then you need postament?

PJ: I'm not sure if you need a socle of this kind or that kind. This [Glass House] is pure classicism.

HK: The Wiley House in New Canaan —the whole lower story is a socle [*Fig. 1–8*]!

PJ: It's a contradiction to the upper story. What I don't like about the Wiley House is that the bottom and the top don't meet; it's like not having a bottom on a building. It is not inevitable. It floats. Nothing must float.

JC: And you noticed that when it was finished, or just now?

PJ: It's the first time I ever thought of it, right now, right this minute. I just thought, "Now I know what is wrong with it." This building [Glass House] can't go down into the ground because it is held by that brick band [socle]. Nowadays, a lot of buildings go right down into the ground. They just keep right on going; they don't stop.

HK: To me, your objection is very interesting. I have a different feeling about that. To me, the Saarinen building is good because of that . . .

PJ: Ah hah!

HK: . . . because there is no interruption.

PJ: You don't particularly like the reversed socle, do you? The depression? One of my own principles is, "Never go down into a building."

HK: But Saarinen designed it that way. You are led to go down.

PJ: Never. You have to, but that's not good.

HK: The steps lead you down.

PJ: I know, but that's wrong!

HK: You hate that.

PJ: Oh, as a classicist!

HK: Does one have to go up? It is a marvelous understatement, to go down.

1–8. Robert Wiley House. New Canaan, Conn. 1953. Philip Johnson. Photo: Ezra Stoller © ESTO.

PJ: That denigrates the building. It can't be a very important building if you have to go down into it.

HK: I object to the monumental.

PJ: I certainly hear this every day. I still want to be monumental.

HK: You want to be monumental? You still want to?

PJ: All architects do, I don't care what the hell they say. All architects essentially want to be monumental.

JC: What do you think of the termination of the CBS Building at the top?

PJ: I think it's the same problem. It doesn't really stop. The Seagram Building does. That was Saarinen's point. He said, "I want to build a simpler building than any that's ever been built, including the Seagram Building." You see, the Seagram Building was the building to beat for him, naturally. I don't want any top or any bottom. The corners, for instance, are execrable; the two diamonds fit together in that terrible flat [*Fig. 1–9*] . . .

JC: You put a hollow concave corner here in the Pavilion where the arches meet [*Fig. 1–10*]. You have, actually, the same problem.

PJ: Yes, but I could have filled that in the way Saarinen did. It's not a corner, nor is it even logical with the rest of his grammar to me. He should have spread those apart. Mies's corners are the greatest: the Seagram Building. Here [Glass House] I spent more time on the corners than I did on the whole house. I failed in one place, but I ain't going to tell you. I still don't know what I should do. Mies didn't like this corner. He said, "You come see the Farnsworth House; I will show you how to turn a corner." And it is beautiful —by keeping the column away from the corner.

HK: He was here?

PJ: Many times. But he hated this house. We got into a terrible fight, late one night, and at two o'clock, he said, "Philip, take me somewhere else to sleep." He had slept over here the night before. I said,

1–9. CBS Building. Detail.

"Mies, you must be joking. It's two o'clock in the morning." He said, "I don't care; get me out of here." And he never came back.

HK: That was the end?

PJ: No, I saw him again, and he apologized the next morning. We had had quite a lot to drink. But I had to find a friend of mine who would take him in. He never would come near this house. You see, this was before we built the Seagram Building.

HK: Let's go back to Kline.

PJ: My top of Kline is the same as the top of the Seagram, exactly. And for the same reasons.

JC: And it houses the services. I wanted to ask about the sandstone slabs, which look like balconies [*Fig. 1–3*]. They are not functional; they simply add dimension to the façade. Dimension. Shadow. Show. At night, the lights are supposed to be on.

PJ: You mean those bulbs behind each slab, which have no other purpose than to add effect? I put the lights in later. That was not part of the essence.

JC: Why did you put in the lights? In order for the building to be admired at night?

PJ: Well, the owner said, "Why don't we do something to light it?" And I said, "If you want to, you can put little bulbs in behind there." I never thought they'd do it. They did.

HK: The slabs turned out to be the shadow walls for the lights. Your only intention was to give the façade . . .

PJ: Third dimension!

JC: Day and night.

PJ: Of course, that was Frank Lloyd Wright's main objection to modern architecture—flat-chested.

JC: You put these slabs in just for an aesthetic sensation?

PJ: Of course, that's why you do everything.

JC: So even if a form is not useful at all, you put it there saying, "Look at me, I'm a slab and nothing more"?

PJ: Yes, that's right.

JC: The slabs are on the same horizontal line as the spandrels.

PJ: The spandrels are on the same horizontal line as the slabs. Again, it's the Seagram Building. The Seagram Building has an opaque spandrel, and the glass on the same level where the floor goes. So does the Kline Tower. The slab represents the spandrel, but it's deeper in this building, because it's the science building. You see, I get absurdly functionalistic. The slab has that width because the ceiling to floor in a

1–10. The Pavilion, Philip Johnson estate. New Canaan, Conn. 1962. Philip Johnson. Corner detail.

1–11. Seagram Building. H beams.

laboratory is much more than it need be in a regular building. We're back to proportional thinking.

HK: The sandstone horizontal on the outside projects the thickness of the ceiling?

PJ: Yes, floor and ceiling.

HK: Which is very thick, of course, because of the machinery.

PJ: Yes. I say I get into silly functionalism now and then, but then I go back. Actually, a façade is a plaid. It's a series of horizontals and verticals, whether it's shadow, change in material or fenestration. There are many ways of expressing it, but every façade that has a repetitious background, like an office building, has to be a plaid. So it's the relations, isn't it, of the vertical to the horizontal.

Now, you can do the vertical, like the Seagram Building, with its exquisite shadows, caused by those H beams [*Fig. 1–11*]. The discovery of that H in 1947 is a turning point in façade design. That H column, which makes that shadow, was an absolute revolution, you see, because it gave you your third dimension. It gave you an incredible shadow. You wouldn't have gotten it with many mullions sticking out flat because of the undercut. Mies said he studied it by hanging various shapes out the windows and looking at them. But the application of a common, ordinary H beam was a turning point for the third dimension in façade design.

And what do the Miesians do? They copy everything but the most important thing. The Bunshafts [architect Gordon] of this world use just a plain mullion. Then it's just a sheet of glass again. The Seagram Building is not glass. Unless you are looking right at it, you get mostly the light of the front of the H and the black of the interior of the H. I think it is the work of genius. My only interest being I was still Miesian enough. You're right, a pure Miesian building. Now I remember, I was still just doing Mies, but instead of an H beam vertical, I took these enormous pilasters and made it into an undulating wall. The verticals had enough shadow; then the horizontals, their shadow came with the change of materials,* setting them out and causing the shadows.

JC: You are called the one who brought elegance to modern architecture.

PJ: Yes, I don't mind that.

JC: Is the Kline Biology Tower "elegant"?

PJ: Well, that's a very rich building in comparison to university buildings. It's no richer than any nineteenth-century university building. It doesn't pay any attention to the usual economies of façade design that is required of any tall building.

JC: Do you mean it is rich because of the budget?

PJ: No. In the material. The budget would naturally go up with that.

HK: It is certainly not a plain façade.

* Johnson refers to the sandstone slabs.

PJ: It's a plaid. The word "façade"! You still have a prejudicial reaction to the word "façade"?

HK: Yes, you are correct. In this case, I intend to use it in a pejorative sense. However, I might change my mind.

PJ: I know you are struggling . . . *Facadenarchitektur* is the worst thing you Germans can say about any building.

HK: Because of the arbitrariness. It is not only freedom; you can be arbitrary. You can apply anything to a wall. Your free-hanging sandstone slabs, for instance, are very arbitrary.

PJ: Ooo! Expensive, too! The most important part is that little cut.

HK: It's that very sharp cut in the sandstone horizontal, separating the half column from the slab.

PJ: But it is cut in exactly the wrong place. If the slab was to hang, it should be strong at the hanging point. And it is weakened there by the fact that the column comes around a little further and there's that little V cut which is the most important thing in the building. Otherwise, there would be no vertical.

HK: This becomes very expressive on the small side of the building, where the columns are in the wall.

PJ: Where there are no windows. Of course, that's the best part of any building, where there are no windows.

JC: As far as façade design is concerned, even in the Seagram Building there is a fake façade [*Fig. 1–12*]. On the north side, Mies simulated the grid design on that solid marble wall, and that's fake.

PJ: Totally fake. That's a solid wall.

JC: Why fake the windows on the solid wall?

PJ: Because Mies had an idea of a glass building with a certain rhythm of mullions. While he was working on that, the engineers said the building would fall down in the wind. So we put a sheer wall there. We didn't need the plaid. That's solid concrete, the most expensive part of the building. I received a letter recently from an architect

1–12. Seagram Building. Fake façade on the north side.

who asked, very sensibly, "Why wasn't it plain, like the U.N. building?" He commented that it is just a piece of marble, that you don't have to decorate it with those mullions. I must say it never crossed my mind. It seemed most logical to Mies and me that the building all look the same. And you don't really notice it. That solid wall even goes around the corner of one window bay. That happened just before the construction started because the air conditioning people said we didn't have enough vertical risers. And Mies said, "Okay."

JC: He was after something like the Lever House . . . ?

PJ: Oh, my God!

JC: . . . a continuous grid façade on all sides?

PJ: Oh yes, sure. His logic, you see, was a very flexible kind of logic. Take, for instance, Mies's famous remark that until he got a bay size, he wouldn't work on a building, a 3 by 5 bay. Then he could work, be-

1–13. Amon Carter Museum of Western Art. Fort Worth, Texas. 1961. Philip Johnson. Photo: Ezra Stoller © ESTO.

1–14. The Pavilion, Philip Johnson estate.

1–15. Sheldon Memorial Art Gallery. University of Nebraska. Lincoln, Nebraska. 1963. Philip Johnson. Photo: Ezra Stoller © ESTO.

cause a column is a column is a column. All right, you get this rhythm of columns every 27 feet in our Seagram Building. However, in the dining room of the Four Seasons, the central column is just taken out. All right, you say, "Take it out," but what happens to the beam? The beam should get twice as deep! But we couldn't make the beam twice as deep because of the ceiling. On the outside, the size of the spandrel had to be kept. Oh boy, so you see, I lost all respect for honesty, the logic of buildings. The only way to build logically is to build the way the cheap people build. They would never do that, leave out a beam! Look at the Glass House. Look at that chimney. That chimney goes right through the beam [*Fig. 1–6*]!

JC: Do you still like this house?

PJ: I never think of it. I just live here. I wouldn't live any other way.

HK: Mr. Johnson, this conversation gives me the impression that it is difficult to attack you, to pin you down.

PJ: Because I'm not consistent myself. However, you *have* pointed out the inconsistencies in the waving walls and the columns of the Kline Tower.

HK: I don't object to a waving wall, as such. I question with you the whole façade idea. You still are an art historian. I wonder if you are able to build without being so much aware of the *history* of architecture.

PJ: It would have been different. I remember the headline in a show I did, "You cannot not know history." It's just part of us, whether it is self-conscious in my case or unconscious, but I exaggerated terribly in the interim [architectural] period. In the Fort Worth Museum [*Fig. 1–13*] or in this building down here [Pavilion, *Fig. 1–14*] it became *spielerisch* [playful] to a degree that borders on irresponsibility.

HK: Your Pavilion is almost a toy. However, I think that there is some humanity in it, in that you are able to play, and not only to build monumentally.

PJ: All right, but then let's add that it is better kept as a toy than enlarged to a Nebraska Museum [*Fig. 1–15*], let us say. Does the *spielerisch* idea become a sin when it becomes a monumental statement in a city? I don't know. I'm not sure.

JC: Play is also in the Kline Tower—those slabs, for instance.

PJ: That is a much more serious statement. It is not quite as absurd as a Yamasaki [Minoru] or even Johnson in Fort Worth.

HK: I think you mentioned once that you wanted to build a "Parthenon of science."

PJ: Did I? I hadn't thought of that.

HK: The Kline Tower standing there on the top of a hill as a symbol of science! Of course, it's far from being a temple, but is it a symbol?

PJ: That is what I meant it to be.

HK: You wanted more than a functional box. You wanted to make the building state its meaning. You wanted to show how powerful science can be, and you did that with these huge columns.

PJ: Actually, I didn't. That is your interpretation.

HK: But that's the way I experience it.

PJ: But, you see, I was after a plaid because I used the same motif in all three buildings. I was much more modest in my ambitions. It was merely to get an expressive façade design that could be applied to vertical buildings and horizontal buildings. You see, the spacing is entirely different in Geology and Chemistry [buildings in the Kline Tower complex]. I was really after a vernacular, not after monumentality. The height, yes, and the siting, yes! I wanted to say, "Science at Yale." If I had built *six* buildings, then the general vernacular of the columns, with the steeple being the Kline Biology Tower, would have made more sense. You see, one wears out one's welcome at these universities. Whitney Griswold [former president of Yale] died, and that was the end of that. That's always the way. I wasn't thinking in monumental terms. Though I probably always believe in monumentality.

HK: One enters the Kline Tower through your enormous colonnade [*Fig. 1–4*].

PJ: Yes, I like that.

HK: How do they [the columns] affect people? Or didn't you think about that?

PJ: To me, I'm afraid it was a technical problem of façade design. The brick wall between the columns is near the front.* That reduces the size of the column. Except which one? The corner has to go around much further. It takes care of that devilish question, which I don't think Saarinen solved, of how to get around the corner, easily, pleasantly, but firmly. The bigger the columns in the center, the bigger the corner column becomes. That narrowing of the two ends—I narrowed the two ends for the same reason it was done in Rockefeller Center. It makes a narrower front to Hillhouse Avenue. It certainly wasn't very original of me, but it gave me an extra corner. Any corner breaks the number of those columns. It breaks the bay; it narrows the building. Now, to get

* He created quarter-columns instead of half-columns.

back to your problem, the monumentality at the bottom. I really didn't realize it. I wonder how I could not have. Now, as you read back, it is very monumental.

HK: This colonnade is one of our major objections. There are, in our opinion, not only fake details like the plinths of these columns [*Fig. 1–16*], but there is also an exaggerated scale which alienates the individual, which diminishes him.

PJ: Ah, well, that's a good criticism. I'm just on the other side. I think it's wonderful; it's fun to be small. I mean, I love Bernini colonnades. You may not. It's a difference in taste on monumentality. I don't think there's a European who *would* like it. That's one reason that Kevin Roche and I get along well.

HK: Being European, this kind of monumentality reminds one immediately of Stalin and Hitler.

PJ: Or the Leningrad Embassy [by Peter Behrens and Mies]? Mies didn't deny those times. He was very proud of the Leningrad Embassy.

JC: The problem for architecture today is to create an environment which responds to human values rather than the architect's quest for immortality.

PJ: Of course, that humanist argument

1–16. Kline Biology Tower. Plinths.

against monumentality is Frank Lloyd Wright's. He resented our work because it was monumental. He resented this house [Glass House] because the ceilings are too high. Of course, Mies himself liked low ceilings. I took Mies to the Wiley House and he said, "Philip, why did you make the ceilings so high?" I laughed and answered, "It's about two feet too *low!*" Mies is also of that generation, in spite of his own classicism, you see. He's not late enough in the nineteenth century. He would have preferred Karl Friedrich Schinkel; I would prefer Henry Hobson Richardson.

In the 1870's, in this country, in the great county courthouses, Indiana for instance, a ceiling under 18 feet was unthinkable. That's what I like! I was with a lot of people in the McKim, Mead, and White Municipal Building in New York City. They said, "Oh, it's too Russian, too monumental, isn't it?" I said, "I'm sorry, it's wonderful." All built of granite. You look out the fourteenth-story window, and the reveal of that jamb is a piece of solid granite, none of this thin stuff we use now. That, in itself, is worth the price of admission. I don't care if it's Russian, or what it is. But we carry a big, bad ballast on monumentality. The library at New York University is going to be very, very unpopular because it doesn't have the in-and-outness of today. It has no slanted wall, no glass at all. It has symmetry, which is of course considered to be very bad.

HK: Not necessarily.

PJ: It's not forced symmetry, but . . .

HK: Symmetry is almost a special feature of modern American architecture.

PJ: Is that so?

HK: Take, for instance, in my opinion, the fascist ground plan of Stone's [Edward Durrell] Albany campus. Note the symmetry of recent American embassies, or, on a much higher level, the ground plans of the great Louis Kahn.

PJ: Of course, he's an old Beaux Arts man. Take the towers of the Richards Laboratory [see Fig. 6–27]. They're just decoration, but they're very strong and very, very beautiful. But Kahn, of course, is a total phony, a worse phony than I am. Well, we are all phonies. Wait until you get into some of Kevin Roche's work. But the tricks Roche goes through to get his windows 3 or 4 feet back from the façade—the tricks are unbelievable. But if it works, who cares? It's just marvelous. I think his Ford Foundation is his least good building [see Fig. 2–24]. That's an early building, but his work is going to be, I think, stupendous.

JC: Do you think the Knights of Columbus Tower [see Fig. 2–23] . . .

PJ: I hate it.

JC: . . . is competing . . .

PJ: Of course not—oh, no.

JC: . . . with your Kline Tower?

PJ: Of course not; it's down at the bottom of the hill. I think it's the worst building he ever built. I mean, those towers have no connection with the ladder.

JC: By "ladder" do you mean the floor beams?

PJ: Yes. And of course there's the *plan.* Have you ever seen the plan of those floors? You have to get to them because they're fire stairs. The whole plan. I like that—that he can do just plain *that.* It's probably the most expensive office building per floor in the world.* But it's going to be dedicated by sixteen cardinals and five bishops, and the Pope will probably come over too. It will be a great show. I think that's splendid, but the building isn't good enough for that. He can do better—and he will.

JC: You said that the NYU Library was going to be unpopular. What about your Boston Public Library?

PJ: The Boston Public Library was designed about six years ago. It's just going up now. That's my most controversial building because it's the most enormous, I

---

* Knights of Columbus cost approximately $30 per square foot.

mean, out of scale. It's the most small-making, makes people look small. It's not a human building. You see, I've always been violently antihuman because of Frank Lloyd Wright, who thought that any ceiling higher than six feet three inches was unnecessary and not cuddly enough.

HK: You're an aestheticist, as well.

PJ: Of course. I always thought that was what architects were for.

HK: You believe that an architect has to be an artist. The setting and landscaping here [New Canaan] is a very aesthetic environment.

PJ: "What's wrong with that?" I always say!

HK: Every piece of the earth, of the ground we are standing on, is tastefully arranged.

PJ: Yes, it's a carpet. This lawn is very expensive carpet material.

HK: I'm sure. We are in a surrounding which is somehow dissociated from everyday life. And all your architecture, as far as I understand it, makes this aesthetic statement. Yet I don't think your architecture relates to the street.

PJ: Oh. The Boston Public Library and the New York University Library are street buildings, street-creating buildings. Kline isn't, you see. Kline is a building out in nowhere.

HK: And the Glass House.

PJ: Oh, this is a country house!

HK: I wonder how you would build a housing project?

PJ: Well, I'm doing that now—Welfare Island.

JC: Is that a housing project for low income families?

PJ: All housing is for low income. It's all very virtuous.

JC: How do you approach a welfare housing problem, being an aesthete?

PJ: I figure out what the streets should be. The opposite of Corbusier's is the simplest way to put it. The isolated block in the park—fuck that! The point is, what do you do when you step *out* of that building of Corbusier's, I mean, Unité or anywhere, you're just dead! Now, here I'm getting human, too.

HK: Very surprising.

JC: You say the Unité is antihuman?

PJ: Oh, I think so, but it's also antiarchitectural, antistreet architecture! You see, you can't deny the street—but to Corbusier the street was just something to carry trucks to the building. The roof was important to Corbusier. *I* think the roof is something to pretend doesn't exist—I think he was wrong on several questions. He was a terrific sculptor, you see. I think Marseilles may be one of the greatest buildings of all time . . . if you don't go there too often. But under *pilotis* is one hell of a place to be unless you want to pee! It's just a great big place where you go in a corner. Just terrible. But that enormous building floating on those beautiful feet . . . Who could do feet like that? Well, Mies and I just take the columns and run them on down. How silly and cheap can you get? Of course, Corbusier could only do it once. It was too expensive, but who cares how expensive it was? How expressive to have those feet! And that fantastic roofscape! But all those things don't have much to do with the problems.

JC: Would you be more receptive to the Peter and Alison Smithson [British architects] solution of streets in the air, where people gather on an exterior level outside the building?

PJ: I'm very much against that, for the simple reason that I don't think there are enough people in the world to take care of the streets we have. I love Mulberry Street [Greenwich Village, New York City], especially during the Feast of San Gennaro, when you simply cannot move. Now, unfortunately, Mulberry Street was much better in 1890 than it is now. It's been emptied of its folk. Those old pictures of the Jewish Lower East Side were teeming with people. How about that? Venice is good for only one reason—that the little streets are impassable and intolerable for sleeping. Try living back in the town—the stench, the lye, ugh, the noise of being only 6 feet across the street from the other windows. What would you do if you lived there? You'd go to the piazza, wouldn't you? So you do. Americans don't do that because they have television, and they have decent quarters. So how then can a street be small enough? How can a crowd be enough? And you put them on the fourth floor. That's not where the action is—on anybody's fourth floor! The action is where the girls are with the loosest blouses, wiggling their asses. They don't do that on the fourth floor. No, sir! Always go to the ground floor.

JC: Would you call those dead spaces?

PJ: I sure would! And all two-level towns agree with me. You go to Hartford just once! Whoever goes up to that place in Hartford?* And that's easy compared to other two-level cities. All these English two-level cities make me tired. They're all theory, you see.

Now, I'm a fine one to talk. I'm building a two-level town, but only because it already exists on two levels. It's the only town in the world that does. That's Minneapolis. Minneapolis is so goddamn cold and so goddamn hot. It's exactly the same climate as the middle of Siberia. It goes down to forty below zero and stays there. Well, then you don't go outside; you don't want to cross the street. So they've erected a series of bridges on the second floor in regular buildings, and they have a hell of a time getting back down to the ground. But, in good weather in Minneapolis, people will not cross the street. They go indoors, go up an escalator, across, and another escalator down. That's habit, and people are creatures of habit, so I took advantage of that. I took the center block in Minneapolis, between two department stores, and there I have an escalator world. So I'm not always against two levels.

---

* Johnson refers to Constitution Plaza, Hartford, Connecticut.

JC: Has anything started there?

PJ: Demolition.

HK: How will it look?

PJ: Very monumental! Ha, ha. It's on the street. Boy, I love streets.

HK: I was not referring to the antagonism between monumentality and street architecture. I was talking about aestheticism versus . . .

PJ: Humanitarianism?

HK: . . . versus sensitivity to the given environment.

PJ: You see, to me, my way of approaching the town is pure aesthetics. There is the aesthetics of a street where the whores walk—the *Strich*. What do you call it in English?

HK: Isn't there a word for *Strich* in English?

PJ: There's no such thing. The Kurfürstendamm in the 1920's, before you were born, was the greatest *Strich* that the world had ever seen. Every other person was a whore. Berlin in the 1920's was something! And the Kurfürstendamm was a street! Goddamnit! The only problem was the Kurfürstendamm didn't have any end, but there was a certain block where everybody turned around and walked back.

HK: And you would like to have a certain emphasis at the end?

PJ: Oh yes, in my housing I do have ends. I want to make a place. I'm doing a town of 20,000 people.

JC: Welfare Island.

PJ: Yes. Of course, an island is God's gift to any architect because you have your orientation all settled. You just look out your window: Oh, I see water! It's just like my bluff here [Glass House]. This house could not be possible without that granite garden wall. This house is a Chinese box in a box in a box in a box. It starts with the coffee table. That is the first unit, and that has never changed. A carefully designed living room that is outlined by the edge of the white rug. The white rug is a raft. The living room is the next box, and the living room sits in a bigger living room,

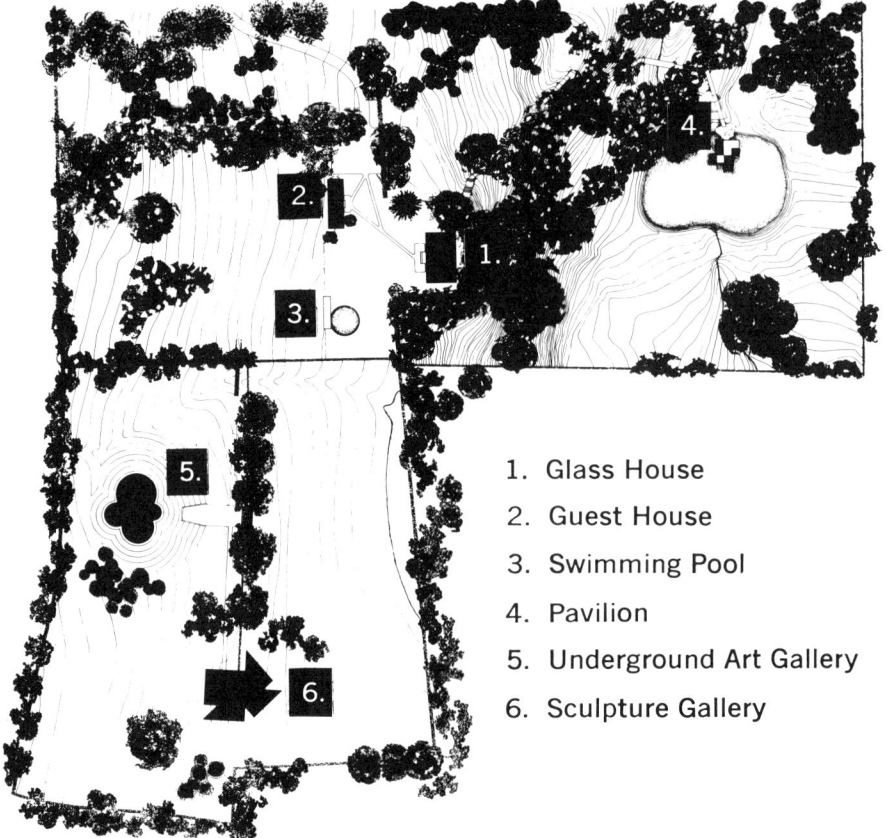

1–17. Philip Johnson estate. 1949–71. Plan.

which is outlined, interestingly enough, by the Poussin, the cupboards, the chimney. And then you jump to the kitchen, the sculpture, and the plant. That's the next envelope. *That* envelope sits in the Glass House. The Glass House sits on the lawn, which is stopped by the lawn grass and by the parking space. But this grass carpet again is another microcosm, which is held by the edges of the woods, which are, of course, the wall and the woods and the woods and the woods. So it's a set of enclosed things within things. [*Fig. 1–17*]

JC: As your house has been photographed over the years, the arrangement of the furniture has never changed.

PJ: Never. It's not supposed to change. No, it's the Miesian principle. Mies never knew that. I told him how he did furniture in the Tugendhat House, and he said, "Yes, that's right. I do arrange furniture like architecture." Today, however, I arrange furniture like the gallery,* in clusters, everything movable [*Fig. 1–18*].

JC: You became an architect when you were thirty-four or thirty-five, after you were already an architectural historian. What were your first architectural designs?

PJ: My first building was a thing copied naturally from Mies's Barcelona Pavilion. It was in my first year, the usual problem given beginning students, to do a pavilion in the woods.

HK: That means that you started immediately with the International Style.

PJ: Pure Mies! I am the first Miesian. But my very first house wasn't built until 1940. I brought Mies first to the atten-

* Underground gallery at New Canaan.

tion of the Americans, you see.

HK: And also to many Europeans.

PJ: Yes. It was silly, the way they denigrated Mies. Of course, it was the International Style people who hated him most because he used silk, you know, marble. Yes, he was not living well when I first met him. Breuer was my teacher, and I learned more from him than from Gropius. I graduated from college in 1930. There was no architectural school that anyone could go to.

HK: You mean you never went to any architectural school until . . .

PJ: Until 1940.

HK: And where did you go to school?

PJ: Harvard.

HK: When Gropius and Breuer were there. Then you didn't have any of that old Beaux Arts ballast?

PJ: No, never had any. My start you see was with Hitchcock [Henry-Russell].

HK: Did you meet Hitchcock in Europe?

PJ: I met him in Paris in 1930. Then we wrote the book *The International Style*. Well, *he* wrote the book!

HK: You are too modest.

PJ: Not true. Not at all modest. It just happened that way.

JC: Looking back to your beginnings, it's surprising to observe your move away from Mies's sobriety toward your decorative arch façades of the late 1950's.

PJ: The British call it my "ballet school" period. The British are the most bitter critics, you know.

JC: We have noticed, surprisingly enough, among your *first* designs for the Glass House [1949] that you proposed brick façades with large arches. Later, when you moved away from the Miesian influence, were you creating new forms or getting back to your original love?

PJ: The romantic, yeah . . .

JC: Do you feel that you're being more yourself in the Pavilion on your pond, or the arcaded interior of the bedroom in your guest house?

PJ: At the time, I thought it was more Johnson than the cold Miesian.

JC: You purposely were looking for a new individual expression?

PJ: Individual? Sure. There is no point in staying a Miesian *Schüler* [disciple], although I think it's perfectly all right, mind you, to do pupil architecture. It's natural.

JC: Well, you did things Mies never did.

PJ: Then I did it unconsciously, because I was very consciously trying to understand Mies.

JC: Later, there was a conscious break. Do you recall why you felt strongly about getting away from these pure Miesian forms?

PJ: Well, I was just growing up kind of late.

JC: It's important to document this transition, it seems to me. It's such a distance away from Mies. Would you say there are stylistic reasons, psychological reasons, perhaps frustration, that drove you away from Mies?

PJ: I always called it boredom.

JC: Why would you be bored with it?

PJ: Why, wouldn't anybody?

JC: You were very successful at it.

PJ: Yes, I was a good Miesian. But then to go *on* doing it, you see. . . . Unlike Mies, I'm too romantic a person perhaps to want

1–18. New Canaan Art Gallery. New Canaan, Conn. 1965. Plan.

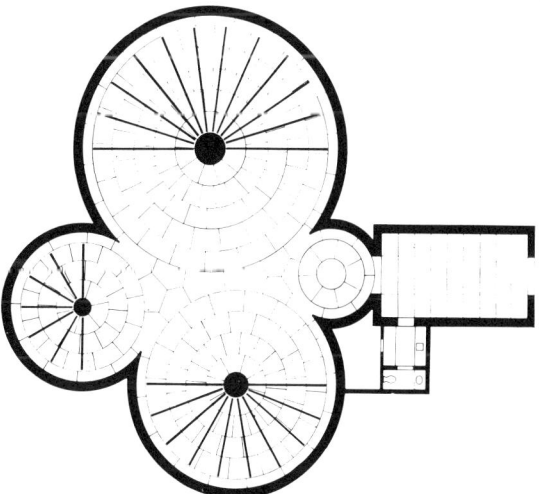

to do anything *again*. I should think Mies would have got so bored with himself he wouldn't have been able to design these buildings.

JC: Were you looking for a new form, an original form?

PJ: I never believed in originality. I thought Mies was right about that. Better be good than original. So that's why I defended my use of classical motifs.

JC: But Mies himself was always original.

PJ: Mies never got anything from anybody else. He was adamant; he was *sui generis*. He was a success because of what he did for the American steel fabrication system. For him, that was no accident because *bauen* [to build] means the technique of our time, the technological expression of our day. He didn't even think he was an artist. He felt that he was making forms that anybody could use. Why didn't everybody build that way? He thought we were all crazy. Not only my generation, but the next one. He thought we were all going to pieces.

JC: How did you feel about it when you started using arches?

PJ: I didn't feel I was original with that arch when I first worked on it, because I wanted to see how many corners I could turn, how plastic the sculptural qualities of it were. I was more interested in that than I was in following along with modern architecture.

HK: At that time, the so-called brutalist movement didn't make any impression on you.

PJ: Not to me. I never liked concrete as a material.

HK: Do you perhaps remember what brought you back to sculptural qualities?

PJ: Well, I remember a luncheon in Rome with Frank Lloyd Wright at the Scarlini. We went from one room to the other; there was this enormous thick wall through which they had cut an arch. He hit the side of the jamb and said, "You see, Philip, the third dimension!"

HK: But Wright was always thinking in those terms.

PJ: That's why he hated me, you see, and the whole International Style. He called it flat-chested, like a woman with a flat chest. It was just something unhuman to build these flat buildings. But it had been in my mind and Hitchcock's mind that the third dimension, the shadow, was coming in in the 1930's. I was so convinced that everything had to be two-dimensional that I . . . was very amused to discover this whole third dimension business.

HK: Weren't you one of the first to move away from that flatness?

PJ: Maybe. But other architects went about it differently. No, I was never an avant-garde man. It never interested me.

JC: You have said that one cannot not know history. Then one must ask, "If you're going to practice a kind of historicism, it has to be selective." Were you looking for forms that were aesthetically appealing or for a historic model with which to realize the third dimension? Or did you want to originate a new form?

PJ: No, I didn't.

JC: What were your sources for selection?

PJ: Oh, I got the feeling—everybody does this, of course, whether he admits it or not. You take a strong modernist like James Stirling, whom I admire enormously, you see. He has a whole file of pictures of back alleys in Liverpool, Mendelsohn's [Erich] great ridge for silos, *Wie Baut Amerika?* [*How Does America Build?*], that great book, or Corbusier's interest in ocean liners. We all get things from other visual impact. With me, it was certain periods of history.

HK: You were not interested in the machine?

PJ: My God! That was absurdity. Think of J. J. P. Oud's *The Bauhaus Book*. He thought it was absurd to compare the ocean liner to the Parthenon.* I never liked

---

* Oud objected to Le Corbusier's comparison of the Parthenon to an ocean liner.

machines just for machines' sake, even back alleys for back alleys' sake.

JC: Do you tell the story about lunch with Frank Lloyd Wright in Rome because that is the turning point for you?

PJ: Yes. Yeah. I don't know why, but it just sticks in my memory as the time when I realized what he meant by the third dimension.

JC: Would you say that your arch façades are an outgrowth of that?

PJ: I think that that was my struggle to get out from under Mies. I let myself go in my own fashion for history. Why be a pupil of one international style when you have the *récit* of the world's history to draw from?

JC: Did you make a conscious decision to move to a particular period in history?

PJ: No.

HK: What would you call it, Romanesque?

PJ: No, not Romanesque, but *Rundbogenstil* [round arch style]. It wasn't Romanesque in any sense. I never understood Romanesque architecture. I still don't. I'm much more interested in romantic Romanesque. It's entirely different.

HK: It's of course quite a step at a time when everybody thought that the arch was not possible any more.

PJ: I know, but that's another thing that I have, a Peck's bad boy feeling, you know. I wanted to be the bad boy of *some* kind. I was bad enough when I introduced Mies to this country. Everybody thought that was horrible. It was still worse when I did my arches. I remember Arthur Drexler [of the Museum of Modern Art] was going to do a book on me, and at that time I was working on the museum in Nebraska. And he took one look at it and he said, "How do you expect me to write an article about somebody that would do something like *that?*" That was the worst building, from everyone's point of view. That was the time when they stopped publishing my work. They still don't. I mean, you get to be an older architect; it's nothing new. And that was the end.

HK: You mean as soon as you introduced the arches.

PJ: Absolutely cut off from all public outlet.

JC: Are you *out* of the arch period?

PJ: Oh, Lord, yes.

JC: You still feel positively about the Nebraska Museum and the Pavilion here at New Canaan?

PJ: That's right.

JC: Are these the highest achievements of your arch period?

PJ: The only two. The Amon Carter Museum at Fort Worth I think missed by being set into that travertine frame. The arcade doesn't go around the building like the portico of the Loggia dei Lanzi or the Feldherrnhalle in Munich. Actually, what's good in Fort Worth is the terraces, not the building. But I spent more time on *them,* now that I think back on it. I spent more love and energy, whatever it is, because of the position. The way it sits there on that hill is the important part; the siting is more important than the porch.

But what an entrance! From the park, from the street, from the back, everywhere! And it includes a view of the city from that porch. That's where I set up the building. On the site, I made them set up an enormous scaffolding to a height where I would be on the ground floor. I climbed up there and looked. That was my study for the building. Of course, all architects are different, but I give more attention than other architects to materials on the one hand and to siting on the other.

But now I resent the arch period very much. We now have a greater freedom in the treatment of masses. Take, for instance, my Art Gallery [New Canaan], where those four circles of space merge and you get those interior cuts. That's the only thing that interests me.

JC: You mean those sharp edges which jut into the space?

PJ: Yes.

JC: Before you discovered this freedom,

1–19. Asia House. New York. 1959. Philip Johnson. Early design.

why did you begin again with arches?

PJ: Well, I always liked the *Rundbogenstil* of Perseus, but that's too simple an answer. It has to do with the whole idea of the continuity of the wall. A series of arches keeps the architrave going, keeps the wall going, and doesn't cut into it. You get a tenseness in an arch, a continuity, that you don't get in a Greek temple colonnade. The arch connects the columns in a pulling way that a series of columns does not.

Nebraska is totally fake, structurally. I just filled in the arches and made pilasters out of the columns, except in the entrance hall, where they became really structural. So I had a system. I was trying to invent a system that would carry me through an entire building, take care of unpleasant functional requirements, and still give me a dignified building. I think I was on the wrong track. But what is wrong with the building doesn't make any difference if it makes an *interesting* building. That's all I wanted.

But you should have seen my first version of the Nebraska Museum. There were three units, three buildings under an enormous trussed roof, which was a Mondrian-Miesian setup. The idea of separating the roof from the building was an old theory of mine, this business of pulling apart elements. The buildings under the roof were boxes, just blank pieces of marble, and the entrances were related into a Mondrianish central court. But the commissioners hated it. They said, "That doesn't look like a museum," because of the great trussing that carried the roof, suspension-bridge columns with wires going off. Under the guide-wire suspension roof that hung from these trusses were these blocks that expressed the functions of the museum, which should have been a good idea, now that I think of it more carefully. In the podium, I put all the things we didn't know what to do with. It's the same as Mies's Crown Hall of the IIT campus [Illinois Institute of Technology, Chicago]. So I did a quick switch and did the one which is there now.

HK: Obviously, your commissioners thought that travertine arches were appropriate for a museum . . .

JC: And you started to be dissatisfied with the arches as soon as you saw a way to model the surface of a façade?

PJ: That's right.

JC: The flat surface no longer satisfied you.

PJ: This happened to everybody, of course, the third dimension bit; the whole skin idea of the International Style began

to annoy me.

HK: Corbusier introduced the flat segmental arch along with his new treatment of masses in the houses of Neuilly. It was the first domestic arch in contemporary architecture.

PJ: I introduced it in an entirely different sense. "Very historical, very decorative," anyone would say. All I was doing was decorating a block wall.

JC: Was that purely decorative?

PJ: Oh, yes. It was obviously decorative.

JC: And you were not interested in having the exterior define the interior?

PJ: Actually, Nebraska denied entirely any differentiation of interior spaces. What I had there was taken more from Schinkel's Berlin Museum than from the normal way of pulling apart functions and expressing them.

JC: In this arch period, you were returning to a historical preference.

PJ: One I've never forgotten, still haven't, I guess, of the romantic period, the early nineteenth century.

JC: It is evident in your early proposal for the Asia House [Fig. 1–19].

PJ: That's when the first word came from the English magazines that I had proposed a new Art Nouveau.

JC: You have an arch sequence on the top.

PJ: That's right.

JC: Without a cornice.

PJ: Yes, there wasn't any top on it.

HK: It's very interesting that the final result, however, is a Miesian façade [Fig. 1–20].

PJ: No, a Bunshaft façade.

JC: Now, that's an interesting distinction . . .

PJ: Oh, yes, Bunshaft isn't Mies!

JC: . . . because you have criticized architects who copy Mies but did not understand his H beam. Now, in the Asia House, when it's finally built, you have done the same thing for which you criticized other architects.

PJ: I did, that's why I call it my Bun-

1–20. Asia House. 1960.

shaft period.

JC: Why did you?

PJ: Cheap. The second version, you know, has some dignity to it, still Miesian perhaps, but I saved only $50,000. But Mr. Rockefeller said, "I want to save $50,000." Mr. Rockefeller liked glass buildings.

JC: Do you mean that the client wanted such a façade?

PJ: That's right.

JC: And he did not like your arch façade?

PJ: Oh, no. That wasn't modern. He

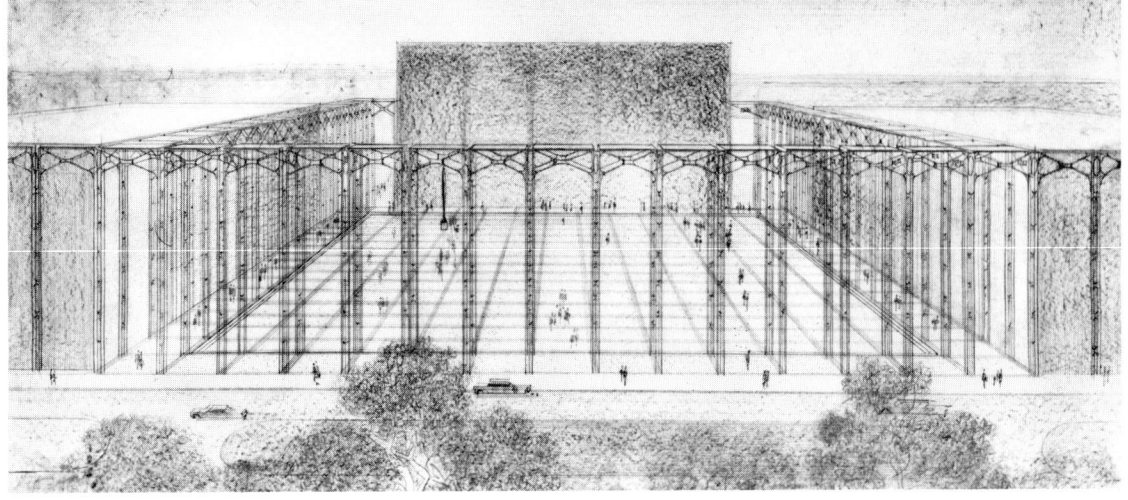

1–21. Proposal for Lincoln Center. New York. 1958. Philip Johnson.

used money as the reason, but I can't believe that for him $50,000 was the reason.

JC: Do you remember in which way he objected to your first proposal?

PJ: It really wasn't modern. He wanted more glass.

HK: He didn't object to any special details?

PJ: No. He just had an impression. It looked nineteenth-century.

HK: But he said, "This is not modern."

PJ: That's right.

HK: And then you came up with the second proposal?

PJ: Too expensive.

HK: And then he finally gave in?

PJ: Why wouldn't he? That was the cheapest façade you could build.

JC: Did you have any problem building the final façade?

PJ: Oh heavens, no. How could you? It's stock, right out of the book.

HK: At that time, in 1959, you were already aiming at a new concept, whereas your commissioner still wanted the stock glass façade.

PJ: Still dragged me back to Bunshaft. Bunshaft represents the accepted style of our time. That's one of the secrets of Bunshaft's success. Now he's moved on to heavy things, but it's still right in the line of acceptance. He and I dislike each other very much. A very famous dividing of the ways was written up in one of the magazines when I had a meeting of six architects at my house to discuss where we were all going: Saarinen, Bunshaft, Rudolph, Mies, Johansen [John], and myself. We met for two days at my house. No reporters, no wives.

It was before Saarinen's last building, CBS [started 1961]. There we really disagreed. The six of us hardly spoke after that. You see, each of us was showing what was currently on our minds, sketches or anything else, and the rest of us would jump on him!

JC: You didn't call on Louis Kahn?

PJ: No, he hadn't appeared yet.*

JC: When you called the five other architects to your house, was this the time when you were making designs for Lincoln Center?

PJ: No, long before that.

JC: Do you recall what inspired you to propose those concrete arcades, which look like Art Nouveau decoration in the early Lincoln Center drawings [*Fig. 1–21*]?

PJ: Precast. I was fascinated with precast. I knew it wouldn't be built, but that

* One of Louis Kahn's first major buildings, the Yale University Art Gallery, is dated 1951–53 [*see Fig. 6–2*].

1–22. Lincoln Center Complex, New York. Left: New York State Theater. 1964. Philip Johnson. Center: Metropolitan Opera House. 1966. Wallace K. Harrison of Harrison and Abramovitz. Right: Philharmonic Hall. 1962. Max Abramovitz of Harrison and Abramovitz.

wasn't the point.

JC: You were after something.

PJ: Oh, certainly. It would have at least been a center.

JC: But now you are just as unsatisfied with the results as we are?

PJ: Oh, it was terrible. The only thing that was left from my plan was the placing of the buildings [*Fig. 1–22*]. They are where I put them, but they're not unified. The space leaks out everywhere.

HK: Were you first asked to do the whole thing?

PJ: No, that was why my first plan was thrown out. When I walked in with *that*, all the architects said, "Well, Philip is trying to kill us all," which of course I was.

HK: And now you have a temple façade there! How far did the commissioner go in altering these plans, these proposals?

PJ: The commissioner didn't; the other architects did.

JC: Did each have judgment on the others?

PJ: Yes, until the end, when Harrison built the opera house. We were tired by then. The result is that your own judgment gets warped. So I got quite interested in solving this cheap façade idea. *I* know that the outside of my theater is no good, but by then I was *so* sick. It's a great deal better than the *others*, though, but that's not saying anything. What I had to do was to follow the 20-foot rhythm of the building

1–23. New York State Theater. Lincoln Center. New York. 1964. Philip Johnson.

across [Philharmonic Hall], and by then I didn't *want* to follow a 20-foot rhythm. We'd all agreed years before to stick to it, and the only person who broke it was Bunshaft. And he was right. That's the best building there from the outside—the Vivian Beaumont Theater. But, since I had to follow these others, I made my baroque temple, or whatever it is.

HK: The State Theater has that temple colonnade. There you are traditionally classicist [*Fig. 1–23*].

PJ: Oh, yes.

HK: So, you agree that you identify with a classicism by using the post and beam as if they were column and architrave.

PJ: Free standing columns!

HK: I would say posts. You call them columns.

PJ: I always call them columns.

HK: And the strip up above, you call it an architrave?

PJ: Oh yes, very classical.

HK: It doesn't fit, of course, into the concept of classical proportioning.

PJ: No, it doesn't. I don't think it's a successful adaptation of the classical motif. I'm not sure it's possible, and that's why I revolted. I think that's the end of my arch period, if you want to call it that.

HK: If I understand you correctly, in your arch period you wanted to achieve a new plasticity. In the early 1950's, when everyone else was still involved in the International Style, Corbusier was beginning to search for massiveness, for a new plasticity, getting away from plane surfaces and flatness. Your problem must have been similar. You must have asked yourself how to get the plane moving again.

PJ: It probably was a cul-de-sac because that never became anything, and I gave it up. But now, the way we get away from the flatness is by the undulating walls, the shapes that do our work for us. So I was probably in a total cul-de-sac, and I don't know. I revolted, as anybody would. I'd been a Mies pupil until I was almost forty, which is pretty reactionary, late. Mies didn't remain a Behrens student until he was forty. But you can't use that analogy. You couldn't have a better school to grow up in than Mies.

HK: A moment ago, we discussed the first design for the Asia House in New York [*Fig. 1–19*]. You proposed a façade which ended at the roof with a slender, slightly plastic arcade. That was in 1959.

PJ: Yeah, that's when I was doing those things. The arch was the same at the top as my Pavilion [*Fig. 1–14*].

HK: The first design for the Asia House was the beginning of your arch period. This is the moment when you turned away from Mies, and we were very surprised to notice that you were drawn to the great American architect of the nineteenth century, to Louis Sullivan, especially his Guaranty Building in Buffalo, which seems to resemble your first Asia House project.

PJ: You're absolutely right. Guaranty in Buffalo! It is exactly! Gaudí, of course, was in there, too, but the front plane, and then these three long inserts, got into the frame, which is more like Sullivan's Gage Building, a very narrow building on Michigan Boulevard, Chicago, which has a plane base. I never could come to peace with Sullivan's way of hitting the ground, with the glass going up and cutting across the columns. So I made the first floor solid with only the door, and then I depressed the glass, and ended with an arcade, instead of with Sullivan's heavy cornice, but there was Sullivan in it.

HK: Had you been looking at Sullivan's buildings around that time?

PJ: I spent a whole summer in 1932 with Russell [Hitchcock] in Chicago, looking up Sullivan. Obviously, it stayed with me. It lies around, for the very good reason that Sullivan was faced with the same problem I was: What do you do with a façade along a city street? I suppose my final solution was the very worst. It was minor Bunshaft.

HK: It's not that bad.

PJ: Oh, it's not that bad, and it's quite interesting. I like the white and black.

HK: It's the best Bunshaft in New York.

PJ: Oh, ha, ha, ha. I was trying to break away from the flat and get some character, but still carry the street, and it seemed to me the only way was depressing the windows into a deep column, which was Sullivanian. Before Sullivan in New York, as far as history is concerned, the buildings are Gothic, and they are terra cotta, which you no longer can buy. But the spandrels and windows are all set back. The shafts out in front run all the way up, and are connected at the top. It was one skyscraper solution or façade solution of the high period which was viable, I thought.

JC: You're very much aware of formal effects.

PJ: Very. To me, architecture is all about form, in spite of Mies.

HK: You consider an architect as an artist. Many would deny this, maintaining that an artist and an architect are not necessarily identical. In Germany and France, an architectural school is incorporated into a technical university, rather than in the art and architecture school of an American university, such as Yale. Where does architecture belong? You seem to be saying that architecture has little to do with engineering or technique.

PJ: Well, you see, not with what we're talking about, because what we're talking about is the way a building finally looks. There's a great *deal* to do with techniques, just as designing the house has to do with designing the kitchen, but it's nothing worth *discussing* because you get technologists of kitchens that do better than architects, anyhow. And, to talk about architecture as a technical matter, or a social matter, or a participatory democracy matter, is not the point to me. So I don't really know how to discuss it any more because, really, the old boys are winning. I've been asked to do an article for the *Architectural Record* on the relation of the present attitude toward functionalism to the 1920's. You see, I get a feeling of *déjà vu*, whereas by far the majority of writers, as it appears at least in the magazines, are for participatory democracy and socialism in the broad sense, and architecture as a technique of satisfying the needs of the masses. This is exactly what Mies was up against when he did the Afrikanerstrasse [Berlin] in the 1920's. Gropius thought "Wohnungen für das Existenzminimum" ["housing for minimal existence"] was a perfectly good phrase, and Mies's answer was, "Well, if my buildings are too expensive for the workers, why don't you give the workers some more money?" which I think is the most delightful way. It's like saying, "Mies, why do you build all your buildings of glass when it gets so hot behind the glass?" Mies says, "Well, why don't you air condition the building?" I find it a delightful way to slice through it. Of course, the fact is that it costs a little something to air condition. Are we so poor in this culture? Which, of course, is the right attitude, and that was the big fight of the 1920's, when they threw Mies out of the local CIAM [Congrès Internationaux d'Architecture Moderne] chapter for using silks. So, today, we have it, but in slightly different things. We don't have *Neue-Sachlichkeit* [new objectivity]; we don't have *Maschinenarchitektur*, that wouldn't interest anybody; but we have this vast participatory democracy, community, boards . . .

HK: Co-op cities.

PJ: That's right. And I asked one of the Negro architects who was here the other day what he did all the time. He says, "I go to meetings." Every single night. Every *single* night. He's bankrupt, by the way. In other words, he doesn't fit into our culture, but he thinks the only thing to do with architecture is to meet with these community people every single night of his life. Well, I still think architecture is more than that. And I resent deeply that the U.S. Government is influenced by this ideology, putting post offices into the ground floors of business buildings. I'm a nineteenth-century man, I guess. In *my* day, the post office was the pride and joy of the city. And where is the new one? I look at it out of my window. It's the ground three floors of the big skyscraper on Third Avenue.

So, somehow, my attack on functionalism is about "business functionalism," which says, "I'll do whatever the client says, instead of standing up for art." But the client demands this kind of functionalism because this *Weltanschauung* is permeating our society. Fortunately, in the German Weimar Republic this did not happen. Then, of course, it went too far with Hitler, who was, unfortunately, an extremely bad architect. The only thing I really regret about dictatorships isn't the dictatorship, because I recognize that in Julius's time and in Justinian's time and Caesar's time they had to have dictators. I mean I'm not interested in politics *at all*. I don't see any sense to it. About Hitler— if he'd only been a good architect!

HK: Mussolini didn't object to good architecture.

PJ: At *first*. He built the Casa Fascismo in Como, a perfectly fine building. And lots of *Terza Roma* is good, but you can't talk about it because it was done by Mussolini. But, if you go to Rome today, you'll find that the *Terza Roma* was much better than what's been done in the Republic, in the same area, since the war. So let's not be so fancy pants about who *runs* the country. Let's talk about whether it's good or not.

JC: The so-called Architectural Resistance today among the students . . .

PJ: Oh, yes, attack Skidmore, Owings, and Merrill for cooperating with the apartheid government of South Africa. Oh, the kids. Very simple: Do away with architectural schools. They have no more meaning; they never had any meaning.

JC: Is there a commission which you would refuse?

PJ: Of course not. I'd work for the devil himself.

JC: Are there ethical standards an architect must reflect?

PJ: There are building standards. I disobeyed them in the Epidemiology Building at Yale [*Fig. 1–24*]. That's a sin against the Holy Ghost. The *real* sin is to build something that stands there and says

1–24. Laboratory of Epidemiology and Public Health. Yale University. New Haven, Conn. 1965. Philip Johnson with the office of Douglas Orr.

"Philip Johnson" on it and it isn't right.

JC: Not that Hitler may have commissioned it.

PJ: No! Whoever commissions buildings buys me. I'm for sale. I'm a whore. I'm an artist. What did Michelangelo say when Julius locked him up? What the hell difference does it make who locks whom up? It's what you *do* when you get locked up that...

JC: When you build, let's say, two toilets, one for black, one for white, does it matter?

PJ: My dear man, I was brought up in the South. It's always had separate facilities. My habits and everything condition me to do what my client says. It never crosses my mind. *Now* it would, of course. Now, of course, I'd object because of all the publicity, but it never crossed my mind when I was a kid that there was anything wrong when I saw two sets of toilets. It seemed very silly.

JC: But now you would?

PJ: But now I have to. I'm influenced by public opinion. I gave up the commission I had from the Governor to do the office building in Harlem, for the simple reason that I was convinced it wasn't very good politics for a white man to do a building up there. As it turned out, I was more than right because the blacks won't even let a black architect do a commission there. Wasn't it political pressure more than moral pressure? I don't give a damn who builds a monument for blacks. Who cares?

HK: You only care if the building is "good."

PJ: Is good... yes, of course. The sins that I've committed are all my own. They are all against my own integrity as an artist, and I've done plenty.

JC: You've indicated, too, that you have a desire to build for Washington, for the...

PJ: The emperor, whoever he's going to be. *Architect du roi.* I'd love to build the Vice President's house, for instance, which is up for grabs now. Say, give us a couple of million, but it would never happen.

JC: And you wouldn't care who the Vice President was.

PJ: Agnew? How could it be worse?

HK: But you still would build his house. But maybe you could influence Agnew by your architecture.

PJ: Tish-tosh. I don't think people influence people by architecture.

HK: Mies...

PJ: Yes. Mies was a moralist. He was Muthesius's student.

JC: I've got to hear this again. You have said that you don't believe architects influence people by architecture.

PJ: I don't think they influence their *moral* life. I think to gather in Chartres Cathedral is an experience that makes all of us atheists want to be Catholics, just to enjoy it more. When I'm in Chartres, I wish that I could have been born and *brought up* a Catholic, I wish I could have had twenty years' background in the Catholic faith, because I think I would enjoy it even more. But even as an atheist, or whatever the heck I am, not *that* bad, just the same, I have an overwhelming feeling that's almost unbearable, just walking in Chartres Cathedral. Well, that's to me what architecture does. I mean, I could have a black heart and be cheating at cards all day, but I would still get this feeling. You don't have to be a *good* person to enjoy Beethoven. I mean, the *maffioso* can enjoy Beethoven.

JC: Why not!

HK: Do you prefer to build for a dictator or for democracy?

PJ: Well, I prefer democracy because it's a little easier, I think, but maybe not. A dictator might be a friend of mine. I'd prefer a democracy for a simple reason: that I would get a better chance. In the pluralistic system, there's more chance of finding a patron. A dictator says either yes or no. If you're on the outs, you're out. Why did Mies leave Germany? He didn't give a damn who was running the government, but Hitler liked pitched roofs. That's why he left Germany. He didn't leave in 1933. He stayed till 1937, after all.

JC: It's not only the younger architectural students who would object to . . .

PJ: What do you think the youth were saying in 1925? That Mies was the invention of the devil, and should be put in jail for using silk and matching marble slabs. He's book-matched his marble! Shocking! That's the way you *hang* marble, by the way! Mies was terribly hurt by it. He couldn't understand why people all hated him. He went on book-matching it. Until the end. We all book-match marble. But Mies was able to stand all that, and I hope some of us can stand it now. The battle, believe me, is the same. They were all Communists in those days. It's not popular now to call yourself that. Now, it's the New Left, which is much more respectable, and really much sweeter, because they don't carry guns so much. Not as aggressive. But Hannes Meyer was a Communist, and was a damned good architect, and the more I see of Hannes Meyer the greater man I think he was. But I don't like what he *said*. There has been much criticism even recently about his design for the League of Nations building, for instance, an article in *Architectural Design* on how much better Corbusier's proposal was. I'm not so sure, but Meyer presented it in the worst way he could, an isometric, a totally meaningless design.

You see, in those days I hated Hannes Meyer because I thought that the shit of the *Neue-Sachlichkeit Weltanschauung* [new objectivity as world view] had something to do with architecture. The only mistake I made was to try to think that somehow the political opinion had something to do with the architecture. Not true at all! At that time I was just antifunctionalist, you see. I was never anti-Marxian. Who cares who runs a country! I still believe *that*. I loved Stalin. He was splendid because I thought he was going to build something. I felt as a youth that anybody that built was good. Of course, Hitler was a terrible disappointment, putting aside the social problem . . .

HK: But you hoped that he might . . .

PJ: Of course. I think it shows in my article perhaps, written for a Jewish magazine in 1940.

JC: I can understand your thinking as an architect, but how does your citizenship relate to your architecture?

PJ: It's disconnected. Totally disconnected. Of course, with whom *hasn't* it been? Michelangelo did run into trouble in Florence, but what did he do? Did he stay and fight? He went to Rome. He believed, I suppose, that he was doing his duty. Nationality didn't exist then.

JC: But Mies is considered sometimes a hero for coming to the States.

PJ: Mies was no hero at all. That's just a myth. You can't like Mies and think he was a Nazi, you see. That wouldn't fit the American dream. Everything has to fit into the myth in this country, doesn't it? But he remained a *stiller Deutscher* to his death. He never told anybody. But the Americans, of course, created Mies in their own image, which was a revoltee against Hitler. He wasn't. He was a revoltee against a law that said he had to put pitched roofs on his buildings. He was *so* innocent! You have no idea how innocent that man was! He said, "Why should I move?" He wasn't a man that moved. He was a man of Berlin; he lived in Berlin. Certainly, he was no Nazi, but he wasn't a democrat either. He was nothing. He was a Catholic. And he just sat there until there weren't any more commissions. He saw that if he submitted a building, it would be turned down.

JC: This generation is going to want to force you into a sociological or political camp.

PJ: All right. I can put on the coloration.

JC: So we have you on Welfare Island now.

PJ: Welfare Island has been an old dream of many architects, building on a large scale.

JC: How many people?

PJ: Twenty thousand. It probably won't

get built, but the study has been fun. In New York, things have a habit of not getting built.

JC: We have called your house at New Canaan "Utopian."

PJ: Utopian. In other words, nonexistent. Robertson [architect Jacquelin], a very bright Yale man, says it is the only estate in America with a modern house on it.

JC: Will you be able to transfer some of the qualities of this environment to Welfare Island?

PJ: No. We're in a different era.

HK: In other words, it's a project for the poor.

PJ: All black. It doesn't say that, but . . .

HK: So is there money to build these houses?

PJ: Government money. All subsidized.

JC: Are you seeking an environment which inspires people, improves them?

PJ: Reactionary! I never improved anyone. To entertain, yes. To excite, yes. Not to improve.

JC: Let's say that excitement is improvement. It's better than boredom.

PJ: Well, if you're a *maffioso* numbers racket man, it would be hard to improve you, but I hope to amuse you. So the numbers man will stand on this corner and not on that. I've just the place for the *maffioso* numbers game man.

HK: So, instead of killing someone, he might do something, he might even play.

PJ: Oh, nonsense. That's improvement. He'll go on killing his people, but I hope to amuse him in between.

HK: You're very Nietzschean.

PJ: Well, he's my God.

JC: But you have admitted that you are a moralist.

PJ: That's it. And Nietzsche was. *Was ist vornehm?* [What is superior?] Remember those chapters in *Der Wille zur Macht*? In other words, *vornehm* to him was good. He wouldn't dare use the word "good," but what he thought was good—aristocratic! In other words, his highest values of conduct. He had the highest, you see, but he would have denied it if you had accused him of it because he was as objective as hell. He was a moralist. So you can't help being a moralist, as much as I pretend I'm not.

JC: What are your hopes as a moralist at Welfare Island?

PJ: Oh, it's to create an ambience that will excite people beyond the normal street corners of today. You see, I've no money, so I'm not using money or materials or apartments or interior space. There isn't a penny to create interior space, so just give that up. Create *outside* interiors. That's right. Because all architecture is interior architecture. Remember, the piazza in front of San Marco.

HK: The greatest saloon on earth, as Napoleon called it.

PJ: Who called it?

HK: Napoleon.

PJ: Of course, he built the last part of it. Good old Napoleon. All right, a dictator. Have to be careful about these dictators. But he built! Unless, of course, you have a religious order running the world, like those who created the Mexican baroque. It doesn't make much difference who is doing the dictating as long as somebody . . .

JC: Or the Jesuits, Loyola.

PJ: Loyola, my God, of course! The Jesuits, what an organization! Anyhow, I like building organizations. I don't give a damn about Attila. I don't give a damn about the Church or the organizations with their dictators. The only one military dictatorship that I know of that was great was Akbar's, which we don't study at all for some reason. One of the greatest builders of *all* time. The Moguls only built for thirty years and then went on. They only built a town to use as a camp for twenty years, but yet they built of stone. I want to know more about those people. Why is there nothing published of the impetus to build of the Moguls? The Indians are not interested in writing it because they resent the

Moguls. They were sort of the Hitler of their period. But there's no sympathetic person left. There's no Mohammedan that can write. In Islam, there is no historian who can put all this together. And yet, if you want great buildings, you get the Mogul buildings and carry that all the way through the Islamic world, and you'd have a building thing that would make Europe look like small potatoes, indeed. And we spend our time on the thirteenth-century church. And if you wander through the Indian plains and see those Mogul cities, Tuklahabad, which is in the suburbs of Delhi—no one has ever heard of it—I went there, and I went back to my hostess and said, "You've got to find out about Tuklahabad." Finally, one little scholar wandered in. He had written an article in the most obscure journal in the world, had it with him. But, you see, it's a sin. Who has eyes for Mogul architecture? There's no preparation, as there is in Carolingian and the baroque. Tuklahabad is part of Delhi, practically, just outside. And there was a whole city that Akbar himself built, lived in for thirty years, and walked away. Just left it. And all the explanations don't make sense. There was no more water or something. He just went away. They all did it, all the time. Whole *cities*, in red sandstone.

But what were we talking about? Oh, the impetus to build. How do we know? It's easier to understand it as we get nearer home. The impulse to build has not existed in this country except in the Civil War period. But then it fades away. Even today, there is no impetus to build, except in business, and that pride is disintegrating. You see, there's no Sam Bronfman [late president of Seagram] now, who builds a Seagram Building. Who wants to spend twice as much for a skyscraper as you have to?

HK: Just allowing the piazza in front...

PJ: Was a great gesture. He lost $1 million a year income on that. If you built a bank on that piazza now, you'd get $1 million. He asked me, "Would that hurt the building?" I said, "Mr. Bronfman, it would ruin the building." He said, "I won't do it." That's a piece of Medici greatness that we don't have now.

HK: Are there really no commissioners like that any more?

PJ: None. He's the last, the last. I'm building a building for Lehman Brothers now. They're as rich as any bankers, but what did they do? They tied themselves up with a real estate speculator, and gave him the job of running me.

HK: So you can't talk directly to the commissioner any more.

PJ: No, can't talk to the commissioner because he said, "Well, you speak to the speculator." They call themselves developers now, naturally. It's pejorative to use the term "speculator" now. They are, of course. It's all filtered down through that man who says, "It's expensive to put that frame around that window."

JC: Could you tell us something more definite about Welfare Island?

PJ: There I am interested in the quality of life of the people in our century with no money. To keep the quality of the insularity of the island is the main point.

HK: What do you do with the cars?

PJ: You transfer to a minibus, like the World's Fair.

HK: Before you get on the island?

PJ: No, you cross the bridge, and the street goes right into the garage. So there are no cars except for trucks. But you see, I'm not trying to do away with traffic. Traffic is generating to life. That's why I'm against all modern city planning which says that the city should distinguish between the service deck and the pedestrian deck. To me, that's death to the city. The point is: *all* on one level. The life of the slums in New York which made them so beautiful was that the pushcarts couldn't get through the streets because there were so many bazaars. Istanbul today. The wrecking of Istanbul was due to Atatürk.

He put in those great 100-foot-wide streets right through town. He totally ruined it; changed the scale. So I'm keeping a pedestrian scale. I think that is the fundamental thing: pedestrian scale with the trucks rather looming up. Well, they loom up in Pisa, too.

The island will be very dense. In fact, had I been allowed, I would have built them as dense as a slum in Venice. But that's inhuman, of course, so I didn't.

JC: In a television interview, many years ago, you said, "What every man really needs is a tree outside his window."

PJ: Oh, is that printed somewhere?

JC: No, I heard you say that on television.

PJ: Well, I'll be goddamned. That's *still* my point. Yes, sir. You can see a tree out of every window. It is dense, but my density isn't inhuman, to use an unfortunate word. It's about the density of a nineteenth-century block in New York. In fact, more dense because there are twelve stories instead of six. The streets are winding.

JC: Are all these residential? Are there commercial areas?

PJ: I haven't got to the commercial. In the residential district, the street bends. You want to go and see what's around *there*. Some of the apartments bridge the street several times, so that you go through little tunnels. I've kept an 1889 church, which makes a little square. Down to each bank are pedestrian roads. The only vehicular road is in the middle. The waterfront is all promenade, like a Greek village, a chain of lights, and a walk, 12 feet wide and 4 miles long. It's for people and bicycles.

JC: There is not much money, so you don't create splendid forms?

PJ: No splendor. This is a little town, and there's no place for monumentality, in the old sense, at all.

JC: There is going to be a town center?

PJ: Oh, that's where I spent all my time. It's a dumbbell plan going across the island.

On the Manhattan side, it's a square: three-sided square with water on the fourth side. Then there's a glass-covered arcade 75 feet high and very, very narrow and 20 feet wide that crosses over to the other side of the island where there is a harbor; a little slip like the old slips in New York. Steps that go to the water. So that's very different in character from the square at the other end of the dumbbell. You have two centers of interest connected by the arcade, because arcades are no good unless they are going somewhere. And the traffic goes right *through* these squares. There's no attempt to separate the minibuses from the pedestrians because that brings *people*. Whether all this will be developed as a place for New Yorkers to shuttle across on water taxis, or not, I cannot foresee, but it would be ideal to fill the thing full of restaurants and shops, not only the arcade, but the square and the harbor. Within this framework, it could be a town of 20,000 with its own center and the A and P and the school. I put the school right in the center of the town, much against the objections of everybody. I want so much to get the life of the babies, crying babies, right up to the offices. Stacked together. It was done in every old city. The silly idea of separating out, zoning, has ruined our cities.

JC: What are the materials?

PJ: Whatever is the cheapest when I get around to building.

JC: Do you pay attention to color and textures?

PJ: Not yet.

JC: Will you?

PJ: I haven't even considered. If I can get my town plan across, I'm not interested in the architecture. You see, if you are only interested in the architecture, it becomes Le Havre. Perret [Auguste] built that after the war. It's just awful. It's dead.

HK: You mean the concern for pure architecture creates a sterile, lifeless environment?

PJ: Yes. Why should *I* build that?

HK: Do you have any money to build places for pleasure? What do people on an island do?

PJ: Parks, mostly parks. Oh, thousands of parks. There are more parks than there are houses because it's a park island. I kept that. There are 150 acres. The town is 50 acres; all the rest is park. But I have public rooms and all that kind of crap, you know—meeting rooms where these participatory democracy people can get up and yell. I have a Mussolini balcony, which they wouldn't let me call that. I should call it the demagogue's balcony. I don't care. The square I was going to build in Harlem I called the Screaming Square. The Governor thought that was brilliant. Well, that's what this is, but I realize I can't use those words. But that's where the revolution should start. I can see the black and red flags crossing through that square. Although the square is so small, it's hardly worth it. Maybe we don't have street cafés in New York, but this is the place for them. You have this incredible river rushing by, and incredible views of Manhattan, which you wouldn't believe exist.

JC: How do you get to Welfare Island.

PJ: You follow the road to La Guardia [Airport] and turn off to Welfare Island, that's all. Unfortunately, nobody knows this, so it's totally deserted, very mournful, very sad. Not even any condoms and beer cans are lying around. We want to develop it so people will want to live on it. We are getting a subway station.

HK: This sounds as if you have a certain sociological concept.

PJ: I call it an artistic concept. I don't have a sociological concept.

HK: Do you consult sociologists?

PJ: Good heavens, no. *They* don't know anything about how to build a town. It's only artists who know how to build a town.

HK: So you think to consult sociologists shows a lack of imagination on the part of the architects?

PJ: I use structural engineers. I use mechanical engineers. I use housing architects to tell me how big an apartment is because I don't know. How to build a cheap apartment? How would *I* know? I'm not interested. I have people to do that. But *sociologists*—what in heaven's name can they do? I ask the finance people how much rent to charge and if I'm in the ball park.

HK: Well, the sociologists and psychologists said that olive green is the best color to use inside a school. That idea has become so dominant in the past ten years that now even the blackboards in schools are olive green. The olive green classrooms are now just as aggressively boring as the old-fashioned grays and browns.

PJ: That shows you about sociologists. Nobody these days will believe anything that is spontaneous or artistic. Everything is scientific. Sociologists pretend that sociology is a *Wissenschaft* [science], which of course it's not. It's just abracadabra. It is the role of the artist to show what the town should be like. Sociology in architecture is a crutch.

JC: Do you ever read any sociology and city planning?

PJ: I glance through their books.

JC: And you never find anything helpful?

PJ: No. I learned about city planning by walking around the streets of cities. I have seen how people feel and how I feel.

HK: Sometimes little things can mean a lot, like benches.

PJ: Benches. But, you see, a bench is not good without sitting in them. Think of the acres of unused benches in New York parks.

HK: Because they are badly designed?

PJ: No, they're put in the wrong place. They're very comfortable, those benches, marvelous benches.

HK: Sometimes, one wishes for a different kind of bench, not just huge concrete blocks in front of insurance companies where you get hot, wet, or cold.

PJ: Oh, yes, we're doing new kinds of benches for the plaza at NYU. But it isn't the bench that is important. You have to have the people. We designed those blocks in front of the Seagram Building so people could not sit on them, but, you see, people want to so badly that they sit there anyhow. They like that place so much that they crawl, inch along that little narrow edge of the wall. We put the water near the marble ledge because we thought they'd fall over if they sat there. They don't fall over; they get there *anyhow*.

HK: Well, it's the only place you *can* sit!

PJ: I know it. It never crossed Mies's mind. Mies told me afterward, "I never dreamt people would want to sit there."

HK: It is significant that Mies complained about his chairs in the Barcelona Pavilion, which were never used because they looked so . . .

PJ: Beautiful.

HK: *Too* beautiful! That is what is meant by hygienic aestheticism.

PJ: Well, there's no danger. People use it if it's good.

HK: You once said, "It doesn't matter how comfortable a chair feels, it depends on how it looks."

PJ: Oh, that argument, yes. You feel comfortable *if* you like the chair. But actual comfort this one hasn't. I can't sit on one of Mies's chairs. I never *do*.

HK: In one of your articles, probably the best known one, "The Seven Crutches of Architecture,"* you state that functionalism alone cannot create good architecture. Your effort to get away from the International Style, from the Miesian style, appears to have been a quest for a new monumentality. It seems also that you were consciously longing for beauty independent of function. In the same article, you also state, using the words of Nietzsche, a building should express the "will to power," should *be* "will to power."

PJ: Oratory. I read it in German. Then

Perspecta III (Yale Architectural Journal), 1955.

I found an English translation.

HK: Architecture as "will to power," doesn't that mean monumental architecture, as we were discussing earlier?

PJ: *All* architecture is monumental.

HK: I don't think so.

PJ: I know, but . . .

HK: Monumentality can be interpreted in a very superficial and ambiguous way.

PJ: The word smacks of Napoleon and Hitler, and all sorts of terrible things. But what I mean by it is different. As all music is intended to impress your emotions, so all architecture, no matter how small, can be monumental. I'm afraid I used the word wrong, or you used it wrong. Everything I do, my little Pavilion, everything is done for a feeling of monumentality.

HK: Even your Glass House is a monument?

PJ: Of course. It has nothing to do with a house. I live here, but I'd live in a barn. You know, people laugh at me for saying that I'd rather live in a cathedral and go outside to the toilet than live in your comfortable American suburban houses. They become crazy. I don't see why. It would be wonderful to bed down in a cathedral. The toilet functions, you can handle that somehow. It's never important. That's all I mean. I rouse hackles everywhere because no one in this country thinks we should build for monumentality. Monumentality is *vorbei* [passé], as it is in Germany. I use it mainly to . . . just to annoy.

HK: To annoy?

PJ: Yes, to annoy.

JC: Now, wait a minute, you used the term in a positive sense earlier in this discussion. Now, you're using it in a negative sense. It's no longer clear.

PJ: Apparently, it is not clear at all.

HK: As your concepts change, you adapt the word to fit them.

JC: You are referring to this toy, the Pavilion, and to the Kline Biology Tower, both as monuments?

PJ: The Kline Biology Tower, obviously. I use the term in the sense of being anti- or nonfunctional, with other impulses being the important thing. The desire for immortality is the only proper aim. How are you going to be immortal without a monument? I know where I got it—Hitchcock, in his first book on modern architecture in 1929, called any building we went to see a monument. Monument means maybe a house by Choisy [Auguste] or Muthesius. They are all monuments to him as an architectural historian. And if you call them monuments, you can't think that they're just functionalist *objects, Gegenstände*. They are monuments. I mean that very particular use of the word, and I was wrong to use it in any other sense; but in a way it makes me nose-thumbing at the people who say *machina habita;* it puts me in complete opposition by the use of a single annoying word.

JC: It is a polemic . . .

PJ: It's a polemic stance that has nothing to do with any other definition of the word.

PC: What *are* you after, besides thumbing your nose at antimonumentality? There must be something positive which you want to put in its place.

PJ: I think what I mean is . . . What do I mean? That's a good question. Every object, even something as small as this microphone [of the tape recorder], should be designed, and in fact is, as a monument, although they would deny it because that very shaping was done by an idiot who wanted to give it some aesthetic quality. I know what we can use, a very simple word, "aesthetics," which of course has a worse reputation than the word "monument." The reason I use "monumental" instead of "aesthetic" is because I refer to scale and dignity.

From the point of view of eternity, *sub specie aeternitatem,* it's everything you do. I design *sub specie aeternitatem.* If you leave out that desire for immortality, you just get cheap design, or the diagonal line that is "in" this year, rather than a sense of monument—you see, I use the word all the time! Because if you think it's going to live on, if you think it's part of your desire for immortality, everything you do should . . . I am a moralist, of course, like all myth-makers and people who tell people what to do. Although I don't believe in morals, I use them myself. *I* am a moralist; I can't help it. To me, every artist should be conscious of his place in history. He's destroying a piece of the landscape when he builds. Therefore, he'd better be monumental. I use the word now for the lack of another one.

JC: We're afraid of the word "beauty."

PJ: Yes. I'm not, of course. And fortunately the kids are not again.

HK: Let me clarify, in order not to be misunderstood. We are not objecting to all monumentality.

PJ: I know.

HK: We are objecting to the way you express monumentality in certain buildings, sometimes only in certain details. For instance, the Kline Biology Tower again. I object to the colonnade, which has that aggressive gesture of command which, in my opinion, becomes a lie when you use it again. At the same time, it's a dead form. It's worn out. Forms have a life by themselves. When you use dead forms, you become a ruin yourself, and you certainly don't create a monument for eternity. I think you are too much of an art historian, like I am. And art historians are often not able to hate or to love. They just appreciate.

PJ: They are much too catholic in their tastes.

HK: Too tolerant . . .

PJ: That's right.

HK: . . . of everything. At the same time, this is a definition of eclecticism.

PJ: Of course, I'm an eclectic and an art historian. That's my great weakness as an architect.

HK: That's your strength, too, I might say.

PJ: Of course. Don't you see, but that's what makes me a little peculiar in the story of architecture. I'm the only architectural historian that became an architect. I don't know how well I am doing; that's for another historian to say. I get so discouraged. Any person who works in the arts is most of the time in the total depths of despair. Everything I did is so awful, you know.

HK: But you don't believe that. What about your Glass House?

PJ: No, I still like that. I like quite a few of my things.

HK: Some of your buildings belong to the greatest done in this country in the recent past.

PJ: But not very original.

JC: But you have already said that originality is not a goal.

PJ: Of course. We all want to be original in one sense or another, in order to be good, but the idea of borrowing forms doesn't bother me at all. I think the search for originality can lead to things like Johansen's Clark University library [Worcester], which isn't very amusing. On the other hand, the reappreciation, for instance, of expressionistic architecture the last few years has certainly affected me, as it has everyone. It was amusing to see the photograph in the *Time* magazine obituary of Mies. How beautiful the Friedrichstrasse Building looked [*Fig. 1–25*]. I haven't seen that picture every day, and I remember when I first studied it, I said, "How funny that Mies started with these angles." Well, it doesn't look funny any more.

HK: Now it looks up to date.

PJ: Amazing. Today the trend in architecture is to get away from the Miesian box. His earliest high-rise designs are being rediscovered. The use of voids which break open the volume and displace the mass is no longer strange.

JC: Your Epidemiology Building [*Fig. 1–24*] of 1964 remains a box, but seeks an exterior plasticity.

PJ: Well, that was too bad. I should have worked on that building more. That's one of the buildings I'm disappointed in.

HK: It looks too much like a bunker,

1–25. Friedrichstrasse Building. Berlin, Germany. 1921. Mies van der Rohe.

too little like a laboratory.

PJ: Well, I think you are very superficial. I don't mind things that look like bunkers. I mind things that don't look good.

HK: What is the purpose of those rectangular blocks projecting beneath the windows?

PJ: It's so stupid of an architect to do what I did, quickly and with another architect. The windows were designed the same as the Moses Laboratory. Then, all of a sudden, there was no more money, and the president of the university called and said, "Why don't you leave them out." Well, the result was those silly bumps. I shouldn't have done that. They don't mean anything. They're just a hoax.

HK: There, again, is the attempt to make the surface sculptural, to give it life.

PJ: Oh, I know what I was trying to do;

it was to give it third dimension again. I had all sorts of things wrong at that period. What's so shame-making is that Rudolph's old people's home [*see Fig. 3–22*] is the best building he ever built and is right there at the same place. Embarrassing, you know, but you're going to have embarrassments. That was a transition building, and my first proposals were much better than the way it looks now, but I picked the wrong reason. But, when I was working up there on the Kline Biology Tower, the dean said, "Why don't you do this building, too." I don't want to excuse myself, but it's an interesting thing—what *does* happen to an architect. They already had their architect, very bad local architect, and the dean was a very difficult person to work with. The building is what Mies would call a *Schnapsidee* [silly idea].

And then, I didn't follow it through. I didn't do the interiors; I didn't do the shape of the building, but I did the siting. That's the right way to site a building there, but then that's what I'm best at. But the idea of the building was a quickie. I brought the model up a week after he gave me the job, and he said, "That's fine, build it." And, from then on, the other architect took over. If, earlier on, I had known that those windows were too expensive for the job, then I would have redesigned the building, but it was just going out for bids when he found out about that window.

JC: But isn't the building working very well?

PJ: It's not hard to make a building work.

JC: Are you sure?

PJ: I certainly am. Some of the worst buildings work. That's the whole point of my article "The Seven Crutches of Architecture."

JC: But isn't there another point? The Epidemiology Building may be more successful in functional terms.

PJ: That's mighty low terms to be successful.

JC: At least, at the level of functionalism, it meets human needs.

HK: For you, it's not the question if something works or not, if something functions. It's a question of how it looks, if it's enjoyable, if the building is enjoyable as a visual structure in the city.

PJ: All buildings work. That's not an argument. The Parthenon even works. I don't know why, but nothing ever happens to it, I suppose. Rudolph and I have this fight all the time. I say I'm the only functionalist architect around because I'm very careful about my basements, whether you can find your way around, and all that. Rudolph thinks *he's* a functionalist. So, you see how silly the word is. But I think one should ignore it. I learned that from Hitchcock, early on. The only answer is what is the building, in the last analysis, in the end; what came out. In a hundred years from now, the functions will have changed. Look at the redoing of the interior of Renaissance palaces. You leave the outside; you can do what you want. Any building is functionalist. If not, you can always tear out the inside. It's whether it's successful as a form.

HK: So you are conscious of creating monuments for yourself.

PJ: Sounds arrogant. I think everybody does it, whether they say it or not. Frank Lloyd Wright was the clearest about it. Of course, I'm arrogant. It is better to have an honest arrogance than a dishonest humility, but at the same time Wright was tortured with doubts, as every other architect is, I know.

HK: One could ask if other values get lost with such a *summum bonum*. It depends on your primary goal; the question of value hierarchies arises. I sometimes ask myself if you don't sacrifice other values by creating monumental masses like the Kline Biology Tower.

PJ: You're mistaking my original use of monumentality: The Friedrichstrasse sketch of Mies's, which is all glass, is monumental. It has nothing to do with massivity, you see. You're influenced by your own post-Hitler background.

HK: I think I have a right to understand your building as *I* experience it.

PJ: But not my *words*. I have to get my words straight for you.

HK: That is not necessary. I understand what you mean. Nevertheless, I experience that colonnade of the Kline Tower as very massive monumentality.

PJ: That's right. It is.

HK: Okay.

PJ: I think we can leave out the word "monumental" till we find something else. The most *massive* building is, of course, the Kline Tower, but at that time I was most under the influence of my own feeling of Richardson. I still think he's the greatest American architect.

HK: There's a certain distinction to be made. When you approach Saint Peter's in Rome, and you are encircled by the colonnades of Bernini . . .

PJ: You are very small.

HK: Still, there is a possibility to maintain individuality there. But there is also another kind of monumentality, one which diminishes you, and makes you feel out of place. Monumentality can be a hollow and empty roar.

PJ: We've got to stop using the word because, obviously, you have something entirely different in mind from what I've got. So, let's just talk about building. *All* buildings are monuments, so let's just say, "building." In other words, what you feel is that the scale of the Kline Tower is inhuman, more inhuman than the Bernini colonnade, which is human although big in scale. The interior of Saint Peter's—does that also do that to you? Is it okay? What other building, besides the Kline Tower, is too monumental or too massive, too inhuman?

HK: The whole problem for me is that several hundred years have passed since Saint Peter's. And I ask myself if we should still compete with that kind of monumentality. We cannot get rid of this word as a critical tool. We can't simply eliminate it.

PJ: I can. I simply won't use it any more. And I don't see why *we* should bring it up because it's a pejorative word in your prejudicial mind, and it's not in mine. You mean to say that the impetus for that kind of space, as exhibited in the sixteenth century, is not here, so we should not build vast spaces and heavy things. Heaviness is Hitlerian, Mussolinian.

HK: Let's say it could be authoritarian.

PJ: "Authoritarian" is not a word that has anything to do with architecture. Justinian was not authoritarian by building the greatest building in the world in five years [Hagia Sophia]? Of course he was. A more authoritarian government surely never existed. Or the pyramids. Are the pyramids therefore faulty because they are not sweet and nice? You see? I'm trying to get at your thought, not trying to contradict you, because I don't think we're in that much disagreement. But anyone can feel that the Kline Tower is heavy. To me, it isn't. You see, Hitler's post offices and Mussolini's town halls are ugly, not monumental. If you copy a Borromini façade at the post office by Mussolini, it doesn't destroy Borromini; it destroys Mussolini.

HK: Of course.

PJ: It isn't the monumentality that's wrong. It's the architect that's wrong. Baalbek isn't wrong! Let's go back to what the real criticism is of the Kline center: it's dark; it's out of scale. I understand words like that. It's too tall for its square. The cylinders come down in an inexorable way that makes you feel you'll be killed if you go between them, as you would indeed in Luxor. But you don't think Luxor, or maybe you do think Luxor, is too heavy. I don't know.

HK: If it would be built *today,* I *would* object to it.

PJ: Ah, you see, I don't have this prejudice about today. To me there is no today. There are just wonderful things and not-wonderful things.

JC: This would agree with your eclecti-

1–26. Nuclear Reactor. Rehovet, Israel. 1961. Philip Johnson.

cism. Because you borrow forms, you wouldn't feel badly borrowing forms a thousand years old, if you found them aesthetically appropriate for your purpose.

PJ: I don't know how conscious it was, but when I was bouncing from column to column in Luxor, the spatial effect was very peculiar. You can't talk about space. I don't know what you *can* talk about, really. But the intercolumniation isn't much bigger than the column, which is true of Kline. But that's not an unpleasant experience. I wouldn't say it was borrowed and old. Nothing old, nothing new. Whatever you do is new.

HK: Forms are not only beautiful or ugly; they also mean something, especially a colonnade means something. It has meant so many things. I ask myself if it still is possible to use a colonnade after its meaning has been distorted in the twentieth century, where it became a lie, a pretense. Can we still get a meaning and beauty out of it? That is my question. Knowing history doesn't mean that we can use everything that history has to offer. Even an architect may become an antiquarian.

PJ: But not for the same reasons that you adduce. You don't like colonnades. So what?

HK: It's not that simple.

JC: Did you get strenuous objections to your nuclear reactor in Israel [*Fig. 1–26*]? In approaching it from the outside, one comes to these very massive forms, which slant out at the sides in what one could call a terribly ominous, heavy . . .

PJ: Fortress?

JC: I was going to say "bunker," but that is a loaded term.

PJ: Well, no. Oh, I love bunkers. Those things on the north coast of Brittany, my God, Normandy, hmmm . . .

JC: Did the Israelis find problems with these forms?

PJ: They said, "Philip, this looks Egyptian to us," and they can't say anything worse than that. And I said, "Sure, you're all Semites, come on." And there was no problem. I thought you were going to ask another question, "How do you reconcile the court with the . . ."

JC: There your columns are light, almost lifting, and quite a contrast to the massiveness of the exterior [*Fig. 1–27*].

PJ: Nothing wrong with that. If you build a fortress, you can have boudoirs inside.

HK: There's a very different court at Kline Tower, which gives the building a frame [*Fig. 1–28*].

PJ: It's supposed to.

HK: Where do people go? This court is a great gesture, but it's not used.

PJ: Mussolinian, you mean. I know what the next line is.

HK: I never saw anybody walking in the passageway around the court.

PJ: It will never be done. Not necessary.

HK: You simply say it is not necessary for people to use it? Why should people use your architecture at all? They could stay at home!

PJ: Let them. They'll watch television. That's the American way. I mean, we are getting much less public-minded and much more private-minded, but that's another point. Naturally, I'd like to have it used.

1–27. Nuclear Reactor. Interior court view.

The point was, of course, it should be used. But the main building is left out. In the model, the building was there in glass because I didn't know what the building was going to be. So I merely attribute that, not to Mussolinism, but to the fact that they haven't built the other building yet. But that happens to every architect. When that court *was* right, it was at the dedication of the building. The brick part was full of people. The very fact that we're talking only about the Kline Tower and not about the other buildings around, Chemistry or Geology, which are background buildings, is the point. I don't care how many background buildings you build, you'll always be judged by the main square.

JC: Lincoln Center could be another example. What are your objections to your Theater?

PJ: The exterior. Once I was forced into using the rhythm of the building opposite, something must have happened to my brain. These things are very bruising to creativity, if I am creative at all, which I doubt. I'm so art historically conscious I don't know where creation ends and where history starts.

HK: One can be historically conscious and creative at the same time.

PJ: I wonder. The jury is still out on that one. How good an architect can you be when . . .

JC: How spontaneous can you be . . .

PJ: When you know too much? You see, these artists are pretty stupid people, intellectually speaking. Somebody like Lou Kahn, you see, hasn't the foggiest notion what's up and what's down. And that's a very great help. Mies! He wouldn't admit it, but he was a violent anti-intellectual. He said, "I've been reading," so I looked at his library, and he hadn't—only three books, anyhow. Not one of them had left the shelf for years.

We really need mavericks, disgruntled, ignorant—there's a phrase in our office, "Let's get a high school dropout with twelve years' experience." We don't want educators. Education must be canceled. I'm violent on the subject. I'm influenced by the fact that none of the architects I've

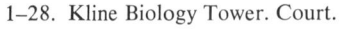

1–28. Kline Biology Tower. Court.

known has ever been to school, including Michelangelo and Bernini.

JC: Do you lament your education and intelligence?

PJ: I do. But it's much too late. No, I don't. I've got to find a niche where the educated person can do something. Where that fits into the history of our time is not important, because somebody will fit it in. I happen to feel that, among the younger architects, there are some very good people coming up. We don't know whether they'll blossom or not yet—like what's-his-name in Toronto, who built Scarborough College—Andrews [John].

JC: Or the Smithsons.

PJ: Oh, no, God help me, there's a case of intelligence ruining architecture! Stirling may or may not; it's too close to tell. What I don't believe is that the future of architecture is Frei Otto. To me he's para-architectural. And Buckminster Fuller is simply not an architect.

JC: But do you think your Pavilion is architecture [*Fig. 1–14*]?

PJ: There is as much Mondrian in it as —what is it?—Greek? I was interested in two different problems. I was interested in moving cubes about, which was in the Boissonnas House here [at New Canaan]; cubes arranged in casual relations. The Pavilion was really just the relating of cubes, or double cubes, or single cubes, or double cubes covered, double cubes uncovered.

JC: Why did you make it underscale?

PJ: Because I think that makes you feel better. Feeling is the only thing I'm interested in, and since I got that feeling at the dwarfs' quarters in Mantua—at the palace of Mantua, the Duke put in a whole suite of rooms for dwarfs, and I felt very big and important in them. It's underscale, so you feel big.

JC: And then you overscale.

PJ: And then you feel small. And there's nothing wrong with feeling small. I like the interior of Saint Peter's. I am very aware of proportions. All architects are.

As Mies said, "The only important thing in architecture, but you can't talk about it, is proportion."

HK: Not only the proportion determines the relation between a building and man, or how a man feels in a space. There are other qualities, for instance, the use of materials.

PJ: Surely.

HK: The choice of materials can create a purely aesthetic environment, which may be aggressive. Take Mies's use of material, for instance, which has long been admired. Now, these materials become offensive. They are too clean, too laboratorylike, too hygienic and sterile. There is always inhumanity in aestheticism.

PJ: But you see, you use "human" as if that was a value of any kind. I don't mind inhuman. Your use of the word "human" sounds to me like Lewis Mumfordism. To Lewis Mumford, architecture was not important if it didn't have a sort of human character. That's why he likes the Bay Region style, which is all wood and lovely overhangs and . . .

JC: Frank Lloyd Wright.

PJ: And, of course, it comes from Wright, but Wright wasn't that way at all. Guggenheim? Human? Nuts. No, the word "human" is one of those words we all agree with, like "motherhood." I'm not against motherhood. Or children! Or honesty! Look! I'm not building for orangutans or elephants. I'm building for people, by the very jobs I get.

HK: How high are your ceilings?

PJ: How high? How high? Well that's a mad . . . That's an interesting point. How high are ceilings? Mies never could understand why I made my ceilings so high. I think that now we're very, very sick of low ceilings. "Human" to me is not a word that we can use in architecture, simply because everything is human. I don't want to talk about humanity and monumentalism as a dichotomy, because I think it's entirely meaningless to what I'm trying to do.

2 KEVIN ROCHE

HK: When Hitchcock and Johnson wrote their book *The International Style*, it was easier to define a well-established architectural language than it is today. Now there seems to be some confusion and arbitrariness in the aftermath of the Bauhaus and Mies. There is a great variety.

KR: Maybe one shouldn't worry so much about that.

HK: It's certainly much better than being dogmatic and working within an established framework of style.

KR: It's obvious that the society is enormously complex. It isn't a simplistic situation, so I suppose it's reasonable to expect this enormous range.

HK: However, it is difficult to make a decision about quality and values in architecture today.

KR: Well, in a sense, quality *should*

have more to do with the ideas and the intentions behind what gets built. It seems to me that the intention behind a building has a great deal to do with its ultimate value to society, if we're going to consider value to society as a measure. Of course, you can also say that there are abstract values which aren't immediately apparent, historic truths which may have some meaning for a later generation. It's hard to judge *that*. I don't mean to consider architecture as simply a social tool, for it's certainly more than that, but that's where it begins, I suppose, for us.

JC: It is important to understand your place in the story of present-day architecture. Part of that understanding is determined, not always convincingly, by the critics. How do you consider yourself in this whole framework?

KR: One doesn't. If you have any sense at all, you just don't.

JC: Do you mean that that kind of self-consciousness is a trap?

KR: Yes. You have other, more important, things to do. We shouldn't be thinking in those terms. We have been so terrifically inadequate to the problems; we have solved them so poorly—*everybody!*

HK: You don't see any hope anywhere?

KR: I do. I see a lot of hope, but performance to date falls very far short of the potential. Architecture is not an isolated activity. It's very much a part, even an appendage, of the general movement of society. Sometimes we architects would like to think that we lead, but of course we don't. Sometimes we can point in certain directions, but society moves very closely behind.

HK: Would you say that society has had much influence on your work?

KR: I regard what's happening as very influential. One has inbred desires of what a physical environment ought to be. You know, It doesn't take too much vision to imagine a better physical world, and one certainly responds to the mood of society on a day-to-day basis. You *must*, because those are the people you are building for.

JC: How do you relate the major sociological problems as they are defined today to your work? What are your priorities?

KR: Well, I tend to think of it more in terms of the instrument whereby the problem can be solved. I mean the governing organization whereby one can get resources to build the stuff, because there's no use talking about things unless you build them. Physical environment isn't created out of words; it's created out of materials. How do you *harness* the forces of society to build portions of the city? It isn't a matter of passing legislation; it isn't even a matter of appropriating funds. It's really a matter of *organizing*.

JC: That sounds like an Establishment answer. An architect must then get into that stratum of society which runs it.

KR: Of course, when you say something is Establishment, I don't know what that really means.

JC: For instance, Philip Johnson has said that he would like to build for the White House.

KR: I wasn't thinking that I'd like to be an architect in the situation of building for the government. I was thinking more in terms of the instrument whereby one can accomplish this work, the organization. Is it an organization of forces, political, economic, and technical forces? And then, how is it structured; how is its objective established; who participates? How does the thing happen? Nobody I know of, nobody, has come up with any real answers, because it is not something that is in the normal scope of administrative politics as we know it today

At the break point of 120 or 130 million dollars, you can still work inside the existing technology; you can somehow buy the money to operate the thing; you can get the computers going. You get the sociologists out on the street, and you do certain things. But when you get up to a billion-dollar project, which is the range of the problems we're talking about, you're in trouble. We did a study for the Harlem River, which is a very brief study, but it identified a project along the Harlem River for about 5 miles, no more than a quarter of a mile deep at its deepest into the Bronx. It required a billion and a quarter dollars just to provide the housing and the overpasses, the parks and the water, the shops and schools. Now a billion and a quarter . . .

JC: Well, that's almost a city.

KR: No, not really, just an appendage, part of New York, you know. As soon as you get into that range, you begin to realize that nothing exists. If the federal government decided to put out a billion and a quarter dollars, everybody would suddenly be faced with the dilemma that there was no existing organization capable of handling a project that large. There are many organizations which might pick it up, but only because they were on the scene, not because they were qualified to do it.

JC: Could one architectural firm handle such a project?

KR: It could, but it would really have to organize from scratch. Not only is there no organization for it, but there is also no precedent, no history, no experience.

JC: What has happened to your Harlem River project?

KR: We were trying to bring it up to a point where we could interest some people in funding it.

JC: You speak of it in the past.

KR: Yes. It subsequently died. What is happening now is that this 5 miles of river front, which is a great natural resource in New York City, is being developed piecemeal. There's a tremendous black-white problem in the South Bronx, where the older residents are moving out to Co-op City or further up the Bronx, and Harlem is cycling into it. The whole neighborhood is going down at a terrifically fast clip. It's going down so fast that it turns out that most of the residents have only been there for ten years. There were three or four generations of families who lived there up to that point. A whole section of the city has gone through a tremendous turbulent change which is not being halted, and there is no way to halt it.

JC: What has to be changed in order to . . .

KR: Somehow, the community has to be stabilized so that it can begin to work itself up again. It has to become a desirable place for people to live. A transient population, of course, is highly destructive in a community, disregarding for a moment the whole problem of what happens to the

2–1. Co-op City. New York. 1968–70. Herman Jessor.

transients themselves, but the effect of the transients on the property is tremendously destructive.

JC: Would you say that Co-op City [*Fig. 2–1*] is the maximum size project we are capable of handling today?

KR: Yes, Co-op City is a very good example of something being done in the old way. I don't know how large a project it is. It's probably under $100 million, but it's using all the old technology, all the old planning ideas. Everything about it is old. At the same time, it's better than any other housing these people have ever had. There's that aspect to it, too, but it's very sad. And here's where you begin to get into the hard nuts of the problem. If one had the cooperation of the labor unions, it would be possible to think in terms of fabricating material in such a way that there might even be some economic advantages even in a pilot program.

HK: Your reference to labor unions is another example of the architect's working in a void; there's little cooperation. However, sociologists want to cooperate, but they find that the architects are not interested.

KR: That might be partly because their information isn't usable. It's the problem of the special disciplines again, those who go their own way. Just as the products of the architect's hands are very often not really usable by the person who occupies them, the sociologist's products seem valuable, but mainly to the person who is doing the producing.

HK: But these special disciplines provide you with material which . . .

KR: It's interesting in itself, but how one can meaningfully apply it to improve the end product, which is ultimately going to be a piece of the environment, is hard to find out.

HK: The relationship of the architect to society is dependent upon different kinds of commissioners. For instance, Skidmore, Owings, and Merrill have the commission for the South African Administrative Center at Capetown. How much should an architect engage himself in a political situation like that? When does he have to turn down a commission? Can he build separate rest rooms for black and white, design for apartheid politics?

KR: No.

HK: You would not?

KR: No, not only as an architect; I wouldn't do it as an *individual*. I think part of the problem is that people put on their hats which say Architect, Carpenter, Psychiatrist, whatever, and they wear these hats, and sometimes in their eyes, sometimes in the eyes of the observer, they don't exist as *people*. It seems to me that the term "architect" is meaningless. What you're dealing with is individuals, varying degrees of ability and talent. On the one hand, the architect may be a brilliant organizer, a brilliant politician; on the other hand, he may be an extremely sensitive and creative molder of materials in light and space. In between that is the whole range of technically capable and technically incapable people, then the people with personal hang-ups, problems, childhood hangovers, emotional difficulties, you know, all that stuff, and the kid who never got out of his Creative Playthings period. You're really dealing with people, you see. You're dealing with people who are relatively mature, relatively immature, and they perform in that way and they live private lives. They have problems; they have children; they get divorced; they go bankrupt; they make too much money; they drink too much; they don't drink enough; whatever: all private, personal opinions and situations. All of this comes all the way out. I always assume that everybody is speaking as a person, first. A profession is just another capability which may or may not have some pertinence to the matter at hand, which is most often just an exchange between people. And, a lot of what an architect does is really on that level of personal involvement, of personal common sense.

HK: Of course, it's possible to get into a conflict between your personal beliefs and your professional deeds.

KR: Of course, people range on many levels of moral commitment.

HK: That means you would reject such an offer as the Skidmore, Owings, and Merrill project at Capetown.

KR: Not only "we would"; we did. We rejected several possible commissions.

HK: Would you tell us the occasions?

KR: Oh, I couldn't. There are lots of times when there are things you wouldn't do. But I can put it on a less obscure basis. The guy who is building speculative building in New York City, the development builder, intends mainly to make return on capital at the expense of the user, the person living in the building. Now, I happen to believe that this is the wrong way to build buildings. As a consequence, 99 per cent of New York City is actually untenable space for apartments and office buildings. Appalling! People in New York live under appalling conditions. They're barely above the worst slum conditions in any city in the world.

HK: Just take the sound insulation, as an example.

KR: Personal privacy, the indignity of the whole thing, grime and dirt and grit and congestion, the containment of space, the lack of view, the lack of open spaces, the lack of clear area, the lack of access to water, the traffic, the noise, the whole sanitary thing—everything about it is wrong. It's largely a product of the way New York grows in our society, and it grows because a man puts out so many dollars and he gets an apartment house built, and the only reason he does it is to get a return on his capital. It's perfectly legitimate, but I just don't happen to think that it's the way to build buildings.

HK: Of course it's legitimate, this speculation within a capitalist economy, as long as land can be privately owned.

KR: That's where you begin to get at the problem. In New York City the whole block system was laid out in 1826, divided into 20 to 25 by 40-foot lots.

HK: What determined those divisions?

KR: These divisions came from the first brownstone houses. They were 25 to 40 feet wide, based on a module that came out of the last century. The speculator acquires a half-dozen brownstones and has a site. Then, fifty years later, someone buys the whole thing, squares off the corner, puts out about $12 million and has got himself a site. He builds whatever he can build on the site, but it's enormously wasteful. If you take any block in New York City that has been developed since the war, and add the number of dollars that has been put into that block, you will get something in the neighborhood of $100 million or more. Now, if you take that same amount of money and think of what you could do on that block as a single project or take the $200 million of *two* blocks and close the street in between, resulting in a block of 1,000 feet on a side, using the crossroads for service, you could provide housing and open spaces and work areas and parking and service and everything else to a much higher degree. One could leave all of the small-scale uses now on the street, mainly because a big part of what gives New York its excitement is this street activity. That tempo and excitement of life has to be maintained. You get service working underground. One has to keep the existing houses on the streets. Then, in the center of the new large block, one could build a building of substantial size.

JC: That, of course, would mean that you would have to tear down every existing building on the former middle street?

KR: In the interior of the new block, yes. Where the streets remain, the scale of the streets will be left untouched. Back from the normal street activity is the substantial bulk which could contain apartments, houses, hotels, etc. You could leave the street alone. There are parts of New York that one would certainly want to retain. And this is a very simple way of effecting an entirely different approach without destroying the city.

JC: This is a kind of rationalism which actually calls for a different system.

KR: That's right, but we have to face the fact that we are now confronted by problems which we've never been confronted with before.

HK: You don't think an architect will have to change the economy before he can build on that scale, do you?

KR: I think that in a place like New York you have to be able to take private capital and channel it through an investment program in which there would be a decent return; then use the money to build in a more organized way.

JC: That would mean it would still be possible within our existing society.

KR: It's not only possible, but it's likely to be the *only* way.

JC: Has this been done before?

KR: No, not that I know of. The thing we have to do in our society is not to put *controls* in the totalitarian sense, but only in certain situations to employ structures for channeling money, which is the energy of this society, into more organized uses in the urban scene. There is really precedent for this in a *sense* in the larger housing projects.

HK: That, of course, would mean that all the previous landowners would have to agree.

KR: No, you'd have to get everybody together to invest money in this kind of project, but this is the first step, and that's all. Then, maybe one determines a sensible grid. The grid that was laid out was the grid for horses, for town houses, and it no longer makes any sense whatsoever. Maybe one decides to have a grid in which there is a cross street every tenth street, something like that. Even if you do *this,* you can still establish a separate pedestrian level. One needs to begin to solve these problems by using existing forces in a different way inside the structure of this society.

JC: The level at which you're speaking, the architect needs to become a reformer.

KR: He also needs to get into the City Planning Commission and Board of Estimate, and into politics and everything else.

JC: Then he's not doing architecture.

KR: Well, again, whatever he's doing, it's important. It's more important than screwing around with some town house someplace.

JC: You end up ultimately frustrated if there are no instruments available in society to handle these projects.

KR: What I'm saying is that even if we had the funds available this minute, we don't have the real experience to solve the problem, even if we had the several billion dollars to build new towns.

HK: New towns have been built. There are some famous examples, but they have been disasters, Brasília, for example. Towns like that apparently don't work for the inhabitants.

KR: Right.

JC: People don't want to live in the artificial setups which work aesthetically but simply don't work as human environments. We don't want to live in a drawing board world.

KR: It's possible to cook a certain dish so that you can eat it. Then somebody takes the ingredients, multiplies the dish 100,000 times in aluminum foil trays, quick-freezes it, and it becomes completely inedible. Yet we eat it every day. You can't take any one situation and multiply it and expect it to solve human problems.

HK: The quantity changes the quality.

JC: Mr. Roche, New York City obviously raises crucial questions for the architect. The Ford Foundation is your major building there, to date. Among the many New York projects you now have in process is the Federal Reserve Bank Building. What problems do you face in this special case? It is a very unusual solution and surely will raise many questions.

KR: I can summarize an illustration of the process in a very abbreviated form. As far as the owner is concerned, this is a very

2–2. Federal Reserve Bank. New York. 1969. Kevin Roche, John Dinkeloo, and Associates. Site plan.

simple problem. They want to build 400,000 square feet of office space, just straight office space; they are desperately in need of space. The requirements are very simple, since they have no desire for anything else but this space. However, they would like to be responsible about it in some civic way.

JC: Do they prescribe what they mean by civic responsibility, or do they just indicate general sensitivity?

KR: No, they just feel something should happen. This is a site in Lower Manhattan [*Fig. 2–2*]. It is approximately 21,300 square feet [area in white] and has an irregular shape surrounded by three narrow streets, Nassau Street, John Street, and Maiden Lane. We are dealing with a block in which there are relatively new buildings, a plaza, and a church which is a landmark. This is the piece of property they have been able to acquire. The build-

2–3. Federal Reserve Bank. Nassau Street view.

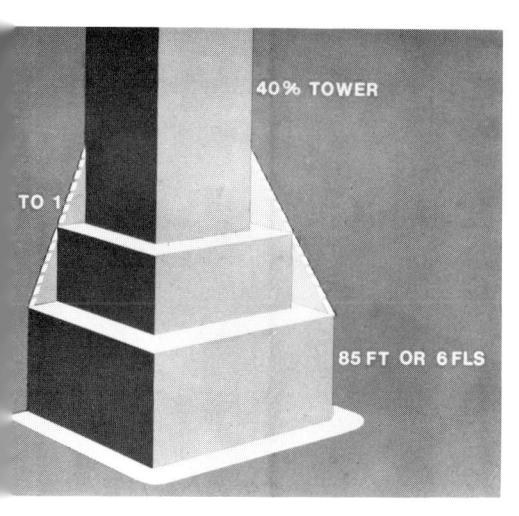

2–4. Federal Reserve Bank. Standard zoning possibility.

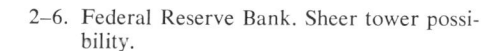

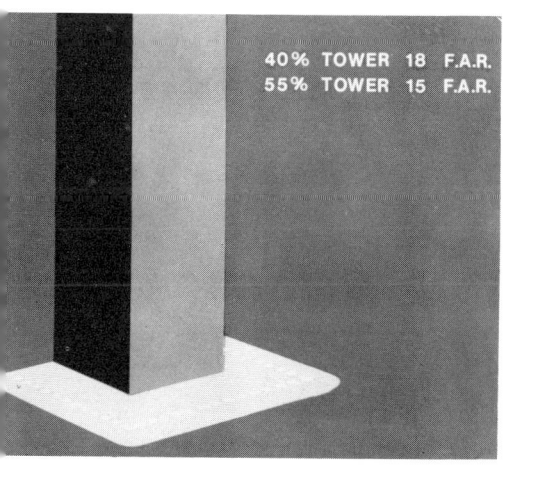

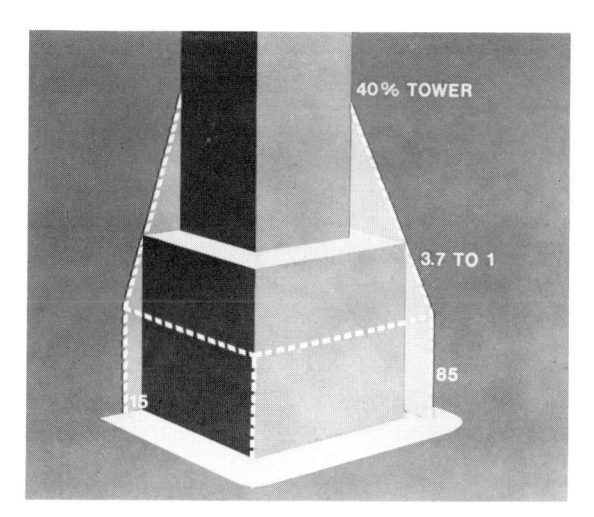

2–5. Federal Reserve Bank. Alternate zoning possibility.

ing is an expansion for the Federal Reserve Bank, which occupies one of the adjoining blocks.

The site has some peculiarities. The problem is to provide the maximum sensible office on a small constricted block, and at the same time achieve maximum public good in terms of open space and proper relationships to other buildings. First of all, the area is very congested. There are street vendors on the sidewalk, which is fine. It is legitimate activity and one would want to encourage it. And there's an extraordinary scene when they close Nassau Street to traffic. Even closed, the population still crowds the whole street [*Fig. 2–3*]. Up to this point, all these people were on the sidewalks. Now, one feels that the public good would have something to do with providing a little bit of space, in this case, on the ground.

How can this be achieved inside existing zoning regulations, regulations which really work best for usual rectangular blocks? Given the existing zoning laws, there were three basic possibilities. The first is called standard zoning [*Fig. 2–4*], and that means that you build right off the property line. You can go up 85 feet and set back, and you get inside a sky-exposure plane, which is an imaginary plane receding at an angle of 2.7 to 1, until you reach a point at which the area of the building is 40 per cent of the area of the site. For this, you

2–6. Federal Reserve Bank. Sheer tower possibility.

2–7. Federal Reserve Bank. Aerial view of standard zoning possibility.

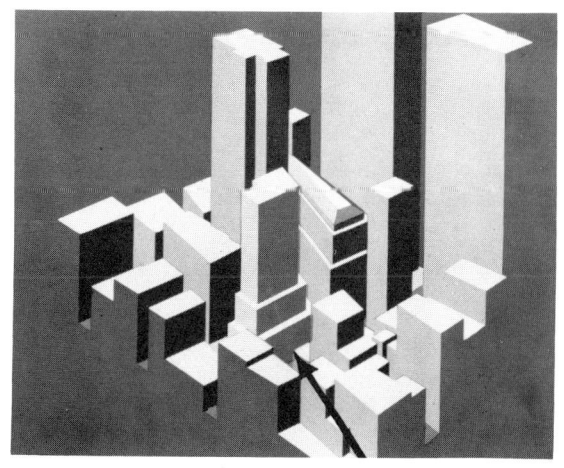

2–8. Federal Reserve Bank. Street view of standard zoning possibility.

2–9. Federal Reserve Bank. Aerial view of alternate zoning possibility.

2–10. Federal Reserve Bank. Street view of alternate zoning possibility.

can build fifteen times the area of the site. Now, in order to encourage the widening of the sidewalks and to set back from the street, there is the so-called alternate zoning [*Fig. 2–5*]. In this, the sky-exposure plane is relaxed and the bulk is increased to a maximum of 18 FAR [Floor Area Ratio]. If you do this, and if you provide the required plaza, you can build eighteen times the area of the site. The third possibility permits a sheer tower to be built by increased lot occupancy for reduction of permitted bulk [*Fig. 2–6*].

So these are the three basic alternatives. Now we apply these general restrictions to our particular site. With standard zoning, we could build a building which consists essentially of three boxes stacked up [*Fig. 2–7*]. The first box is 6 stories high at 21,600 square feet per floor, the second is 14 stories high at 14,000 square feet per floor, and the third is 16 stories high at 8,500 square feet per floor; this makes 15 FAR. This solution does not fully utilize the site potential, for more than half the floors in this building would be too small to be useful. It provides no public space [*Fig. 2–8*] and generates no satisfactory relationship with existing buildings.

JC: What is the total square footage in this proposal?

KR: It would be about 320,000 square feet.

JC: Wouldn't that be sufficient?

KR: Well, it doesn't reach the maximum potential of the site, and it doesn't reach the requirement of the owners, who would like to have about 400,000 square feet. And, also, it doesn't really relate to the other buildings in the area, so there's no reason to build it.

The second possibility would be alternate zoning. It gives maximum bulk for setbacks from the building line and creates a building composed of two blocks [*Fig. 2–9*], one of 11 stories at 14,000 square feet and another of 28 stories at 8,500 square feet. You get in the same dilemma. Here we could realize 380,000 square feet in bulk, but much of it is unusable because the floors are too small. Also, the relationships to other buildings are really not improved very much [Fig. 2–10].

The third possibility would be the sheer tower at 50 per cent of the site [Fig. 2–11]. This would give us the first chance to make a rectangular building [Fig. 2–12]. The other ones were following the lines of the property, which would result in odd-shaped office spaces very difficult to use. In the tower proposal, we could build 34 stories at 10,300 square feet each, still too small a floor.

With this piece of property, and with the existing zoning, we can't build a sensible building. It is apparent that no satisfactory solution is available inside existing zoning, neither in terms of functional requirements nor in terms of public good We could build it right off the street, but we would be compounding an already hopeless situation. If we set it back, we improve things a little bit, but then we've broken the street line. On the one hand you achieve something, on the other hand you don't.

This is the point at which you decide there is obviously nothing productive in the existing situation. If we restate the objectives, perhaps a solution can be developed which will make a variance from zoning ordinances desirable. The first objective which we have to consider is the providing of sensible office space. Sensible office space means a rectangular floor of a large enough area, at least 13,000 or 14,000 square feet [Fig. 2–13]. The second objective, in view of the congestion of the area, is to provide the maximum open space that can be provided, possibly landscaped, and certainly accessible from the street. But, in fact, if one were to follow this objective to its logical conclusion, he just wouldn't build the building at all [Fig. 2–14]. The third objective has to do with relationships of one building to another. It needs to relate to the tall office buildings on the block and to the other large rec-

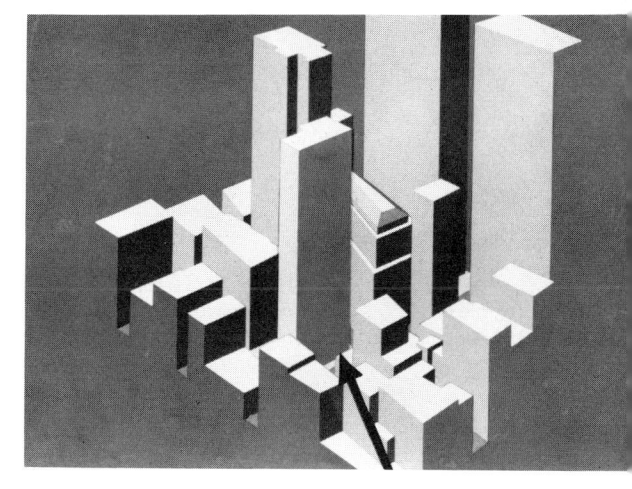

2–11. Federal Reserve Bank. Aerial view of sheer tower possibility.

2–12. Federal Reserve Bank. Street view of sheer tower possibility.

2–13. Federal Reserve Bank. Office space plan.

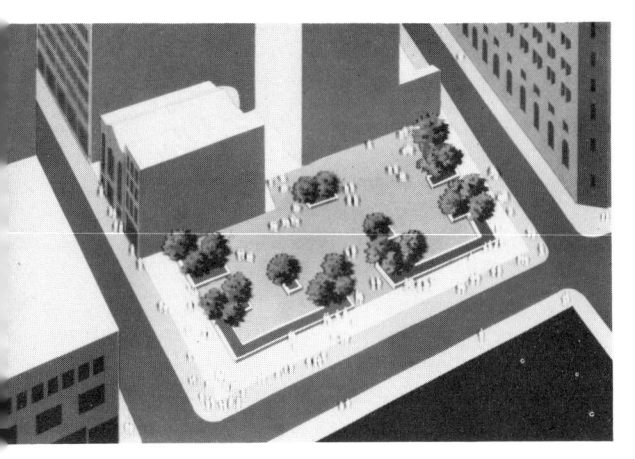

2-14. Federal Reserve Bank. Public space plan.

2-15. Federal Reserve Bank. Proposal in relation to Lower Manhattan profile.

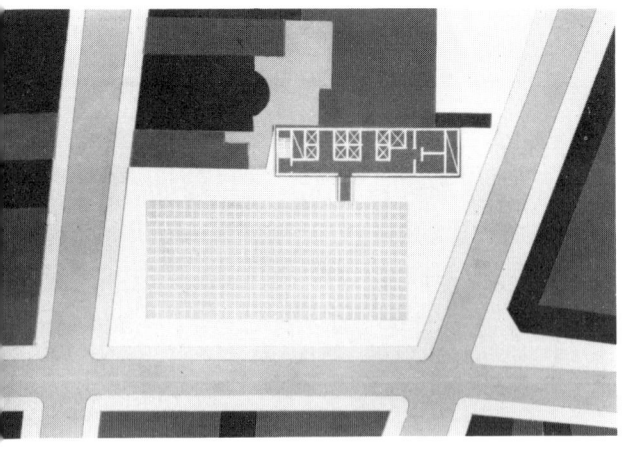

2-16. Federal Reserve Bank. Office space with adjoining service core.

tangular buildings in the vicinity, Chase Manhattan and Marine Midland. That's the containment. If we don't pick up the responsibility for establishing those relationships, then it will never happen in New York. The fourth objective has to do with planned development on the lower tip of Manhattan [*Fig. 2–15*]. These are enormous projects, the two towers of the World Trade Center near Battery Park, the U.S. Steel building under construction, and the existing towers just mentioned. Our building will be surrounded by these monsters. They would place us in a hole. From the occupant's point of view, he would be in a canyon.

Let us reconsider the whole project with new objectives in mind. First, an office building has a core. Then, the rectangular floor space should have a minimum of about 13,000 square feet. We place this floor space in the center of the site [*Fig. 2–16*], but remove the service core and back it up against the service core of the adjoining building, thus providing clear, unobstructed space with maximum window exposure. To do this, of course, we have to violate certain setback regulations, but we'll proceed anyway and see how we come out. The resulting building block would normally look like this [*Fig. 2–17*]. It has some kind of lobby, 20, 30, or 40 feet high. Another objective is to relate the building to the old Federal Reserve Bank across the street. After all, they are occupied by the same people.

Now, here's the point where we make the big step. We say we don't want a lobby down there *anyway*. That's not anything for the public good. Also, we would like to get out of the hole. Let's take the whole building and move it up [*Fig. 2–18*]! Let's move it up to be in line with the cornice of the old building across the street. There the building *starts*. Now, we have space down below which is unobstructed, and a new relationship is established with Chase Manhattan and Marine Midland. The building would be carried on legs 165 feet tall, 11 feet in diameter, and covered with the same stone as the old Federal Reserve Bank. This vertical location is now sufficiently high that, for all practical purposes, the building doesn't exist on the ground, and a public space can be formed [*Fig. 2–19*]. The four columns support beams which enclose the mechanical system [*Fig. 2–20*]. The office block sits on these beams and goes 31 stories high [*Fig. 2–21*]. This is the building we can build. The public space on Nassau Street [*Fig. 2–22*] can be provided in consideration of certain violations of public zoning regulations.

JC: In this abbreviated presentation, you have given us the process out of which this astounding result grew. When the building is completed, the casual observer will not be aware of this background. One first impression will be the strong difference between those very brutalistic legs and the thin glass skin of the building itself.

KR: The supporting system is all concrete. The steel structure rests on this. We proposed reflecting glass as a complete skin on the outside so the structure is isolated from the thermal movement. We are shedding the bulk of the thermal load. We would have three different reflectivities at each floor. The lower section would be 100 per cent reflective. The section above the head would be about 75 per cent reflective. At eye level, the glass would be relatively clear. Every office would be shaded above and below.

JC: How do you treat the space beneath the building?

KR: The plaza could, of course, be designed in many different ways. It's such a small space that one might use a kind of cobblestone similar to the Swiss or Bavarian towns where you get a moving surface.

HK: No concrete?

KR: No. The plaza is accessible all the time from the street. Of course, the relation of the church building to the plaza is important as well. It's the site of the first Methodist church in the United States. The first two buildings burned down, and this is

2–17. Federal Reserve Bank. Possibility.

2–18. Federal Reserve Bank. Possibility.

2–19. Federal Reserve Bank. Final solution of office and public space plan.

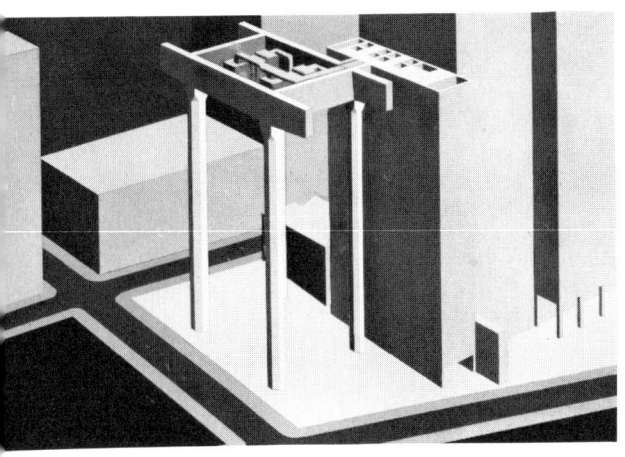

2–20. Federal Reserve Bank. Model of supporting columns.

2–21. Federal Reserve Bank. Model of building on columns.

2–22. Federal Reserve Bank. Public space in final proposal.

their third, built in 1850. It's an historic monument. For the plaza, we will provide a very strong central light, so that late in the afternoon there will be some illumination, even in this space.

HK: A substitute for the sun.

KR: The sun cannot penetrate down onto the street.

HK: Was there any objection from the clients?

KR: The point that you couldn't build a sensible building going the normal way didn't get through at first to everyone. But they finally approved it.

JC: Your buildings distinguish themselves by their unique scale.

KR: Let me explain it this way. I'm fond of thinking of the island of Manhattan, for all of its faults. It tends to be an unguided prototype of where we're heading. The nice things of New York, and the evil things of New York, will simply spread. The island itself has a certain scale because of the technical problems involved in spanning the rivers and all that, not because of any over-all intention. One gets into a scale structure which begins to be in scale with the whole island. It isn't in scale with the little house down on its space, necessarily, but it's in scale with the whole city.

Large projects are the things we have to face if we want to solve the urban dilemma. Because of the volume of these projects, and the scale of them, we will all be required to think in terms of much larger scales, much bolder scales, and of the broader planning purpose and of the subsequent breaking down of these scales until they fit the individual and his measure of space. There are many other kinds of experiments which one would carry out while trying to explore the possibilities of dealing with a larger project and the subdivision of it. A $1 billion project cannot be built on a 4-foot grid; one really begins to think in a different structuring system. It is the beginning of the realization that we are faced with much larger problems, much larger projects.

2–23. Knights of Columbus Building. New Haven, Conn. 1967–70. Kevin Roche, John Dinkeloo, and Associates.

HK: Well, a boldness of scale is obvious in some of your buildings.

JC: For example, the Knights of Columbus Building in New Haven [*Fig. 2–23*] certainly relates to the scale of the highway next to it. You have met the need of the 50-mile-an-hour passenger. But what about the man who approaches your building on foot? You must have done this a number of times and had the overpowering feeling, like everyone else, of being engulfed by the building. One suddenly becomes amazed at the massiveness of the corner piers. What the driver experiences is entirely different from what the pedestrian experiences. For a man walking by, it *is* something like walking under the George Washington Bridge. Is that what you were after? One is overpowered. Does it work at the human scale?

KR: It works very well at the human scale, particularly where people are most involved with the building, which is on the inside. Also, look at the Ford Foundation Building [*Fig. 2–24*]. It has a tremendously large scale on 42d Street, but I don't think you're overpowered by that at all. In fact, very few people are even conscious of it. You have to consider it in terms of the street line before you're aware of the scale of the building. And, in fact, it's a very restful building. It's not aggressive. I hope that, when the Knights of Columbus and the Coliseum are finished, the whole complex will be a contained space [*Fig. 2–25*]. The tower won't have so much of that overpowering effect any more. I simply make a parallel with the Ford Foundation Building, which, in fact, has a much larger scale. The Knights of Columbus Building

2–24. Ford Foundation Building. New York. 1967. Kevin Roche, John Dinkeloo, and Associates. © ESTO for the Ford Foundation.

2–25. Knights of Columbus Building and New Haven Coliseum.

2–26. Oakland Museum. Oakland, California. 1969. Kevin Roche, John Dinkeloo, and Associates.

is really much smaller. Ford is a building which is made of parts. It's not a complete thing. It has, of course, a rather difficult site. It has a very small scale on 43d Street, and an enormous scale in reality on 42d Street. We were relating to buildings which were much, much larger. Take the elevation of 42d Street: All of the buildings on it which have been built since the war have a cutoff at 160 feet because of the zoning; the buildings recess in sections, and 160 feet is the second recess. So we took the second recess as the height for our building. At the same time, we have a very strong shadow [in the façade] which brings the whole street to an end. Let me give you another example as far as scale is concerned. The Oakland Museum really has a very large scale if you see it from the air [*Fig. 2–26*], and the elements which people deal with are actually very large elements. The whole relationship between people and architecture is carried on with very heavy pieces of concrete, heavy bands of concrete, which people sit on. They feel very comfortable. It's a very bold scale. But nobody has ever noticed it or even mentioned it. The step was our basic module and our basic notion. We have a basic 5-inch horizontal module, and the next unit is 20 inches, then 5 feet, and finally 20 feet. We have a grid module, which is worked on the basis of 10 feet. The scale problem in general is funny, because it depends so much on how one deals with it and how one relates to the single piece. When I go to San Francisco, I like to go and stand under the Golden Gate Bridge. It's a very exciting experience! And in a way one isn't dwarfed at all. It has the same quality that you find in nature.

HK: The bridge corresponds in scale to the landscape, to the Bay and the mountains.

KR: It does, in fact. It has tremendous scale, which doesn't really frighten you, because it is a landscape scale.

HK: But is it legitimate to apply the landscape scale to structures in a city?

KR: Well, if you look at an aerial photograph of New Haven, you begin to see a scale of movement of people which is gigantic. That's what has already happened; it is the form of the East Coast.

HK: We have already discussed the scale of the Ford Foundation Building in relation to the street. At the same time, you must have cared about the scale of the interior courtyard and offices in relation to the people who work there. In the brochure for the building, you state that the architecture should provide a setting in which the employees are aware of each other because they can see each other across the court [*Fig. 2–27*].

KR: We were trying to create a sense of community. I can give you an example of things we all experience. Today, there were supposedly 50,000 people on the New Haven Green* while Allard Lowenstein was speaking. He has often spoken to that number of people and more, on television. The television audience has no sense of community. We had it today. The sense of

* Moratorium Day Rally, October 15, 1969.

2–27. Ford Foundation Building. View of offices across the court. Photo: Ezra Stoller © ESTO.

community was generated by the presence of the other people. I felt a very strong sense of community today simply because of seeing the people and being part of a group.

In an organization, the problem of common purpose is critical. A group of people spends working hours dedicated to some purpose. Let's say their purpose is more than just being able to buy a six-pack of beer on Saturday night. Let's say that they are in fact people concerned about making a contribution to the world in which they live. Within the Ford Foundation, they are a part of an instrument which has a lot of money which can, if properly directed, be a fairly substantial contribution to many areas. So, let's make the assumption that we're dealing with dedicated people, who have gone out of their way to join this organization. It's not just another job for them.

Now, we have 300 people with this common aim. It's really very important in that kind of community for each to be aware of the other, for their common aim to be reinforced. I think that the purpose of the organization would be substantially clarified and the things they can do would be more pertinent if they communicated with each other, if they are, in fact, aware of each other. I can illustrate this. They are running parallel programs in many nations, but all of them are run by different groups, different departments. So you might have programs dealing with education or birth control or agriculture in both Southeast Asia and Central Africa. These people in the different departments have never communicated except through the top. I think it is reasonable to suppose that if there were a sense of community in such an organization it would help a great deal.

HK: You want to achieve community through visibility.

KR: We're building a house for them. One of the main purposes is to stimulate the sense of community, and we start with the proposition that this is not just another office building but an entirely new animal. The fact that it is composed to a large extent of office space has nothing to do with its *character*—which has to do with the people in it and their general purpose. The people in a typical New York office building are stacked on different floors. Formerly, the Ford Foundation people were using eleven floors of a typical New York office building. They were stacked on different floors, and had no feeling for what the foundation was. They got off at one floor and that was that. All of the communication was done through the telephone and publications, but that's not really enough, you know. You can't isolate yourself from contact with other people, and it isn't enough just to meet in the cafeteria. The presence of the other person has a tremendous effect on you.

There are probably many ways of solving this problem, if you're given an infinite number of sites and an infinite variety of peripheral problems. But let's consider the problems on 42d Street in New York City. Let me simply give you the presentation I made to the Ford Foundation Board. This is not an ordinary office building in New York which is a product of no concern to the user. An ordinary office building is a product of investment capital, and it is based upon a couple of fairly simple ideas. There is a central core, and there is the office space. The sop that's thrown to the user of the building is that the higher-priced help gets the outside window. You put the mechanical services in the core. You build it as high as the law will allow, and that's what the building is about. And you build another one, and another one, and then you put streets in between, and that's Manhattan. We're going to rise out of the ground, in effect, and the high-priced help will have a view; this works beautifully in theory, until everybody does the same thing. They *all* go to their windows, and they *all* look out and see windows! The office family to which they belong from nine to five previously occupied eleven floors of a speculative office building which did not have a crimson band on the outside, which has nothing to set it apart. There was no way of telling where they were. There was no outer manifestation of their home. This is a contrast to the man who works in a factory and parks in the parking lot; he sees the building as he approaches it and he knows. The place where he works communicates to him in a certain kind of way by its presence. These people, along with many others in New York, had no opportunity to do that.

There is the problem of communication. You take this man in his little office, and he comes to his office in the elevator, and he goes to the toilet, and he may not even *know* anybody on the other ten floors. He may see them in the cafeteria, but that's it. So you have this man, then, in a little compartment with his marvelous view, and all this isolation and all this electronic gear to communicate. This is not what we wanted to provide, not what we wanted to duplicate.

Now, to the problem of the site. Almost all the other buildings on 42d Street were built hastily since the war, for speculative purposes; they are unpleasant, and certainly nothing one would care to relate to. There is, fortunately, on the site another kind of character, which was a phony piece of stage-set architecture but which did have a fairly nice character and made a fairly nice environment, with trees, birds singing, and even some sunlight. There are even places to sit out and enjoy the sun, even in the wintertime. So we wanted to relate to this, instead of the typical 42d Street kind of space.

Traffic is such that you cannot enter from 42d Street, and, of course, we had a building which needed to have a limousine entrance for state heads or ambassadors. The site offered the opportunity for one to approach the building from 42d Street. Crossing the bridge, one sees the building for the first time. We had a unique opportunity, unique for New York, anyway, of approaching a building and driving around it before you get to the entrance [*Fig. 2–28*]. It's rather like having a building in the countryside where one has an approach road.

What kinds of buildings could we have built, given the program? We were not using the full volume potential of the site. We could have built a building nearly two-and-a-half times the volume of our program. But they could not build a building for rental purposes; they could only build it for their own use. So we had a unique opportunity. We could have built a five-story building completely covering the whole site. The plan would have been made up of interior offices and exterior corridors. It would have been a very hard building. Of course, we considered many other possibilities, but we ended up with a solution which creates its own environment.

HK: You gained many characteristics by introducing the court into the building. The employees have a pleasant view, and the public is invited as well; everybody can walk in. The Ford Foundation does not hide its face behind a meaningless façade. You have created the possibility for the employees to see each other at work, by setting the two wings at an angle facing the court. However, it might work adversely in that they not only communicate, but also control each other, even spy on each other. Could one feel watched?

KR: I wish you could spend a day working in the office.

HK: There is almost an ideology of communication in architecture today. Architects are trying to get people together by creating community spaces. At the same time, there should be privacy, even in an office building. If Big Brother is always watching, there may be no privacy.

KR: That really doesn't happen. It's rather like being in your bathing trunks that first day of summer when you're not in such great shape; but the larger the crowd is, the less nervous you are about it, especially if everybody else is in the same situation. You don't feel quite so exposed. I think the best test is to spend some time *in* the building. I've been looking at this building since it opened in terms of how people respond to it, and of course we have all the usual gripes. People feel that the closets aren't big enough. But that's a normal one, which you always get. Or girls: You see their bottoms because there isn't a skirt in front of the typewriter.

2–28. Ford Foundation Building. Site plan.

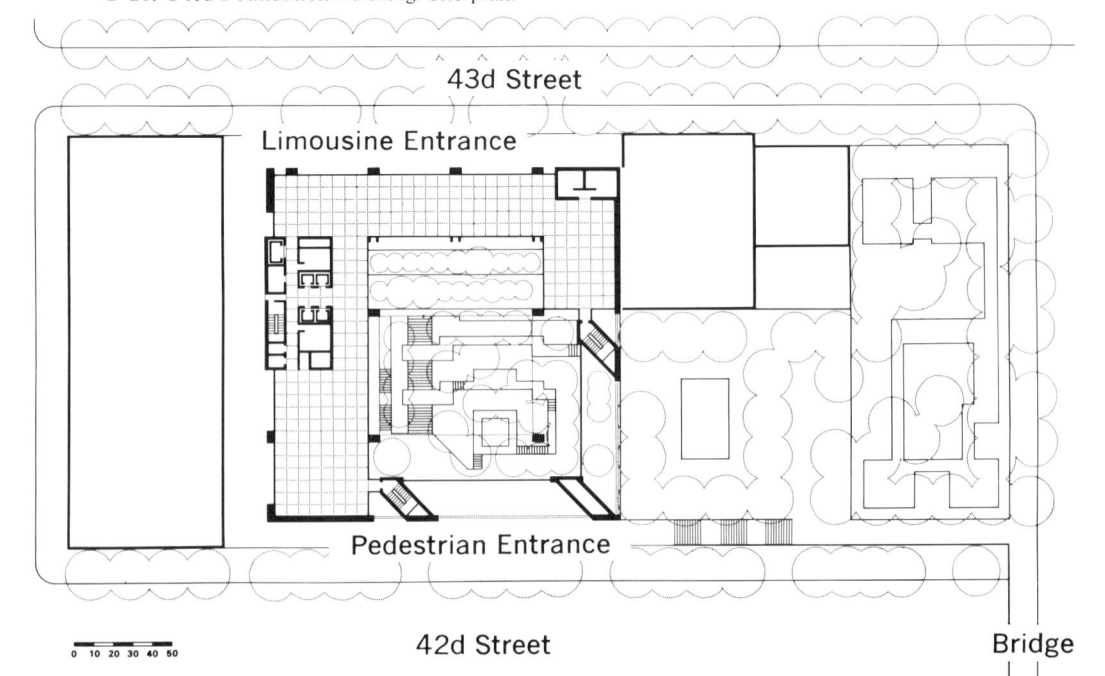

HK: Well, as a man, one wouldn't object, but, architecturally, one might have reservations.

KR: The curiosity of that, of course, is that the only people who fuss about it are the ladies who are slightly older, which is reasonable when you think about it. Everybody has the ability to pull blinds, which he can set anywhere he wants. About three or four girls in the building set their blinds so their legs aren't showing. The rest of the people don't pull their blinds.

HK: Well, it's a minor point, but couldn't such a situation create the pressure to conform? The one who pulls the blinds is considered a separatist.

KR: No. The interesting thing was that McGeorge Bundy [president of the Ford Foundation] didn't pull his blinds the first day. It didn't occur to him. He began to realize, he told me, that he didn't *need* to pull his blinds. Although he treasures his privacy and likes to sit with his feet on his desk, he didn't mind if people saw him doing that. If he takes a nap in the afternoon, he just goes to sleep.

HK: In front of the public?

KR: Yes. He just does, and it's partly because you don't tend to look in; you don't tend to pry on the other person. The distances are such that the aspect of intrusion on privacy doesn't exist.

JC: What happens when an executive or head of state comes to Mr. Bundy's office and doesn't want to be seen, or there is a desire for a private conference?

KR: They've talked a lot about that, but so far it hasn't been a problem. The chairman of the board, Dr. Stratton, elected not to have his office facing into the court at all, so he has a kind of isolation.

JC: So there are possibilities for privacy?

KR: For certain people, yes. But, in a sense, he has a less intimate contact with the workings; being chairman of the board is somewhat different. It was important for the major officers and the president to be with everybody else.

2-29. Ford Foundation Building. Corner of façade. © ESTO for the Ford Foundation.

JC: What happens to the view from the offices which are not on the court? Are they still faced with the old New York view?

KR: This is now the gap between the original intention and the reality of the building as it evolved. I had hoped that we could work with a single loaded situation, where the corridor would always be on the outside, and the offices would all be on the inside. As we expanded the program, it was necessary to put some offices on the outside.

HK: I think the most extraordinary thing about this building is the glass court with the inner garden. That has become quite influential, already. However, one objection to it is that it seems too aesthetic, too perfect, almost hygienic. One misses a bench in there. It's a wonderful landscaped garden, but one doesn't know where to be, how to relax in it.

KR: We had intended benches to go in there. However, Ford has chosen not to put them in because they had a little problem with people working off hangovers there. I would prefer that they work off their hangovers there and let it be.

JC: Is the garden court locked at night?

KR: Yes.

HK: After six o'clock?

KR: I believe it is. Now they're gradually learning to use the building. All the staff officers have changed since the building was designed, so a whole new group of people moved in.

HK: Mr. Roche, the façade of your building, with its hard-edge volumes, seems to be determined on aesthetic grounds. It reminds me of the late sculpture of David Smith. There is that razor-sharp wall at the corner [*Fig. 2–29*].

KR: That big 45° angle? The sun comes around the wall, lights up, and gives a strong wall of light.

HK: So you considered the play of light? The entrance is set behind that shield wall. Were you considering the wind?

KR: One penetrates into the building before going through the door. You're partially in the building before you enter.

JC: You seem to object to a formal analysis. Let me ask the question in a different way. Where would aesthetics begin in your architecture?

KR: Well, I don't know, because I don't really think in those terms. I don't think in terms of separating these things out. Obviously, one has a responsibility to many things, and one has pretensions of being able to control the form of the building once given certain directions.

JC: Does that mean that you're not preoccupied with the textures of materials, the color values, and so forth?

KR: Yes, but not until the reason for the building has been found.

JC: When you used granite in the facing of the Ford Foundation Building, was that a secondary concern?

KR: Its intention was to relate to the city. If you look at the·quality of the shadow in Tudor City, it has a slightly purplish hue, which the city has, even though it is a different material. The original building we designed was to be a weathering steel building. We were working on a system of permanent weathering steel forms which we would then fill with concrete, mainly for strength. The idea is something like the one employed in the St. Louis Arch [by Saarinen], which is a stainless steel form with concrete fill. We'd all have been in a big, rusty pile of stuff, but the board of directors demurred.

JC: They preferred granite! But you could have left bare concrete work.

KR: You could leave the concrete bare, but in New York everything gets so filthy that the surface deteriorates and looks like hell. There is another reason. This weathering steel sheds a red stain, and granite manages to absorb the color.

JC: When you originally preferred the weathering steel surface to the granite, was there an aesthetic judgment involved?

KR: No, because we were initially exploring a method of construction.

JC: Could the aesthetic question then be said to be secondary to the structural?

KR: I happen to be very fond of the steel.

JC: Ah-ha!

HK: Are you the first one who used it?

KR: My partner, John Dinkeloo, developed the use of it in about 1953. The steel existed but had not been used in buildings, and we used it in the John Deere Building in Moline, Illinois, which was started in 1956. Now it's being used very widely.

HK: Your fondness for steel naturally reminds us of the architecture of Mies van der Rohe.

KR: I really came to this country to study with Mies.

HK: You came to the U.S. in 1948. Had you studied architecture in your home country, in Ireland?

KR: Oh, yes. I graduated in 1945, and I had about three years' experience. I had worked in England.

HK: Where did you work in England?

KR: With Maxwell Fry.

HK: Gropius had already gone?

KR: Gropius had left. This was just after the war, and at that time, Maxwell Fry was really the leading office in England. My ambition, of course, like the young kids of that time, was to work with all the leading architects in the world. I started off with Mies and went to Chicago.

HK: From there to Saarinen.

KR: I had plans then to go to [Alvar] Aalto.

HK: Why did you select Aalto after Mies?

KR: It's another end of the scale, in a sense.

HK: Is there any architect whom you consider to be your major teacher?

KR: I guess Eero Saarinen, if anybody. Mies was a very formidable person, of course. He had a tremendous effect on everybody who went anywhere near him.

JC: How long were you working with him?

KR: Less than a year. I couldn't take that much of it.

JC: Why?

KR: Well, when I went there, I had already had some experience.

HK: In other words, you were too advanced; you were not a student any more.

KR: I had had quite a bit of responsibility in the offices I had worked in. I had, I think, an unusual amount of experience for the number of years I'd been out. By the time I got to Mies, I had a sense of what it was all about, and I like to think I was able to learn what he had to say faster than a student who hadn't been around. At least, I learned as much as I wanted to learn. Mies's environment had produced the reaction that either you accepted it as the total solution to everything, as a concept of life, or you had to reject it.

HK: You did not accept?

KR: I couldn't accept all of it. Of course, the problem with all great men is that they are surrounded by people who espouse their views and who have subscribed to them in a much more rigid fashion than the great men themselves, who are flexible.

HK: Was he the kind of person who would impose his . . .

KR: He was just such a strong character that . . . he was a very formidable person, very formidable. Just being in his presence was a little terrifying, in a sense. When he said something about architecture, it had the ring of absolutism.

JC: It was the final word!

KR: It was the final word! Whatever it was, it was the final word! You wouldn't even *dream* of questioning him.

JC: Did he encourage questioning, experimentation beyond his . . .

KR: No

JC: Did he accept that role readily?

KR: It's hard to tell. He wasn't playing a role. He was impenetrable. There was no letup of this quality in him. There was no informal discussion. Or when an informal discussion was carried on, you were standing up and he was sitting down; you were never both sitting down.

HK: Did you have the feeling that he knew a lot other than architecture?

KR: Yes, I think he was very mature; he had a rather varied life, and he pursued it with single-mindedness.

HK: Did you observe whether he had certain conceptions of our society?

KR: I don't remember his speaking about them. What he spoke about was pure, almost pure, technical architecture.

JC: Did he speak often?

KR: His habit, which was very disconcerting, was to come and sit down; this was in graduate school. Then he would light a cigar and then remain perfectly silent for about two hours.

JC: While you worked?

KR: No, while we all sat there.

HK: And who talked?

KR: No one talked. You sat there, and there was absolute silence. He smoked enormous green cigars. You watched, simply watched, as the cigar gradually disappeared. And there would be a few lame attempts at getting a conversation started, through which he would sit impassively.

HK: Nothing to look at?

KR: Nothing to look at. You might be unfortunate enough to have him sit at your board; then everybody would stare bleakly at whatever little crummy thing you had at your board. By the time the two hours were up, you know, you were nearly hysterical; you stared in fear at this stupid thing you had done, being stared at in this way. It was very disconcerting, but its effect was devastating; when he said something, you certainly listened!

JC: Then what happened?

KR: Well, my only reaction after one of these sessions was to go out and get a very strong drink to try to recover.

HK: Now, Saarinen was very different.

KR: Well, he had that quality, too. He was a very active person, but he would sometimes lapse into a total and absolute silence which you couldn't penetrate at all —smoking a cigar.

JC: After all that influence, do you smoke cigars?

KR: I can't stand the damn things! You know, with really extraordinary people, there's a problem, because the whole area around them is filled with their presence; they are of such a strong nature that it can only be tolerable at a distance, not close to them. I think that's true. Their contribution can only be seen as part of a general mix. It can't be taken undiluted.

HK: Did Mies and Saarinen *like* to talk about architecture?

KR: They didn't want to talk about architecture at all.

HK: Actually, were they teachers? I mean, could they teach?

KR: I think Mies was. I had some friends whom I kept contact with, and it took them years to recover. Some of them never recovered from it, even twenty, twenty-five years later. They're still in that same postwar period and still think in the same way.

JC: Do you think of your own work in periods?

KR: I don't really think of them in that way.

JC: Philip Johnson speaks of his own work in certain periods and evaluates them as an art historian.

KR: One tends to look back; when you do look back over a body of work, there are plenty of things which were influenced by that particular moment in time. They can be social influences; they can be influences of other architects, other designers, certain cults going on. When you look back, you see all these fragments of things in the group. I look back in terms of realizing where the mistakes were. I don't mean mistakes in the detail sense; I mean the big mistakes: how we responded to a certain situation when we should have responded better.

HK: Are you unsatisfied in this broader sense with any of your buildings?

KR: One is unsatisfied with it all.

HK: Could you just give us an example?

KR: Well, in a sense, that's very personal stuff. It's like one's little sins, you know, you don't . . .

HK: We observed that Philip Johnson is willing to admit his mistakes. He points them out very carefully, very distinctly; he even talks about details all the time.

KR: Well, I would not think in those terms. I think most architects will admit that most of the buildings they've done aren't very good. You can't look back on your own work and think that it is any good.

HK: But there must be some satisfaction.

KR: There is. But very often I engage in the exercises: *If* you had to do this thing all over again, what would you do? Then you begin to realize how the thing is shaped in part by the circumstances. In many cases, what you end up doing is just guiding a building through the forces which form it. You don't personally form the whole thing because you are not providing the money; you're not providing the labor; you're simply providing a certain amount of direction.

HK: Do you prefer a detailed program from the client or . . .

KR: I prefer the most fluid situation possible because there are enough problems. The problem of trying to make a building is enough in itself without having extraneous, nonrelated things coming up just because of personal whims. So that if you could have a situation in which the conditions have to do only with providing for the definable needs of the occupant, then you have enough to deal with without prejudices or opinions, which are generally not on a very high level. Somebody reads something, God knows where it comes from. The fewer of those things you have, the better, of course. In a sense, the ability to guide a project through the four-year or five-year process from conception to realization takes a great deal of strength and energy and perseverance.

HK: Let's have an example. When you built the Knights of Columbus Tower [Fig. 2–23], what did the client ask for?

KR: Well, they were one of the best clients we've ever had. They didn't ask for anything.

HK: How many square feet did they want?

KR: Well, they had a requirement for about 300,000 square feet.

HK: Did they have a budget limit?

KR: We recognized that it would be the conventional office building limit, the top limit which we set at that time in the neighborhood of about $30 per square foot, I think, which the building came to.

HK: That is quite high, $30.

KR: Well, it isn't now. When the building was started, it was relatively high. It would be comparable to a headquarters building, whereas a conventional building might be $25 to $27 per square foot.

HK: Did the client interfere with the building design? They did not ask for the four towers?

KR: Oh, no.

HK: Did you have any kind of image in mind?

KR: Nothing to do with image at all. I did not see the problem of establishing an image for the Knights. In a conventional office building, one deals with a core and a perimeter of space in idealized form. The dimension needed for the perimeter of space should be in the neighborhood of 30 or 40 feet [Fig. 2–30]. That is to allow the possibility, if you take a 5-foot module, of having offices on the outside wall which are about 15 feet deep; then a 5-foot corridor and again offices on the inside wall which are also 15 feet deep, making a total of 35 feet on each side. Normally, a building which is roughly 150 feet square has a floor area of 22,500 square feet. The core which is required for that building, if it is going to be about 40 stories, will give you a doughnut of space about 35 feet deep.

Now, in New Haven, we were confronted with the problem that we had a site along the highway which had to con-

2–30. Traditional office building. Plan.

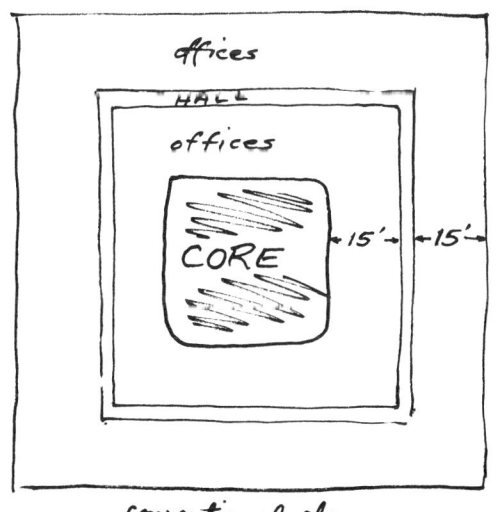

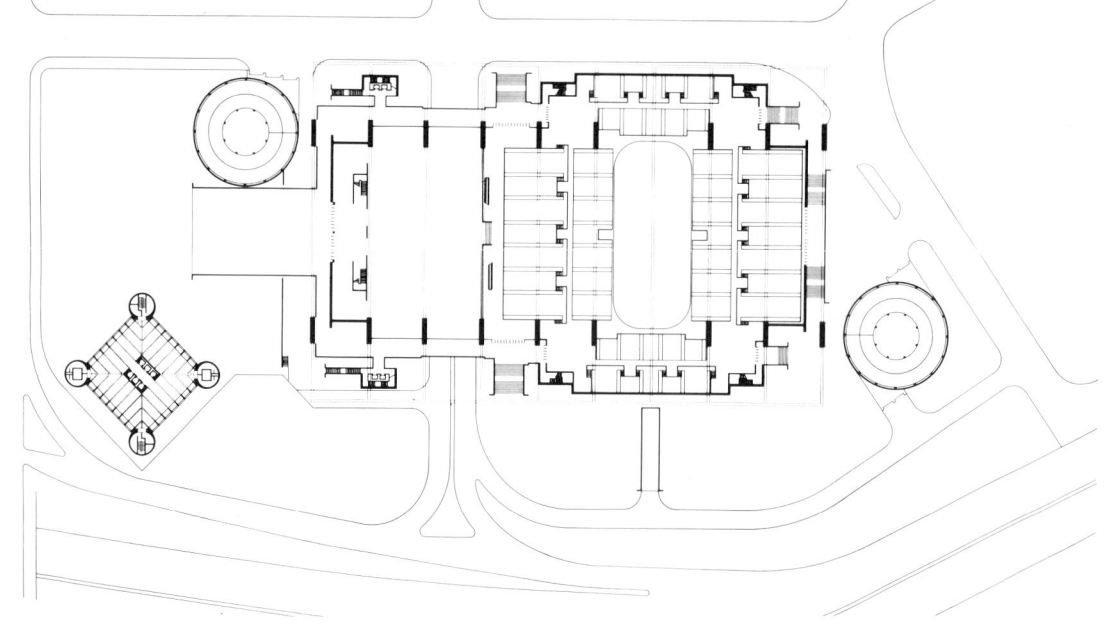

2–31. Knights of Columbus Building. Above: site plan, with New Haven Coliseum. Left: Plan.

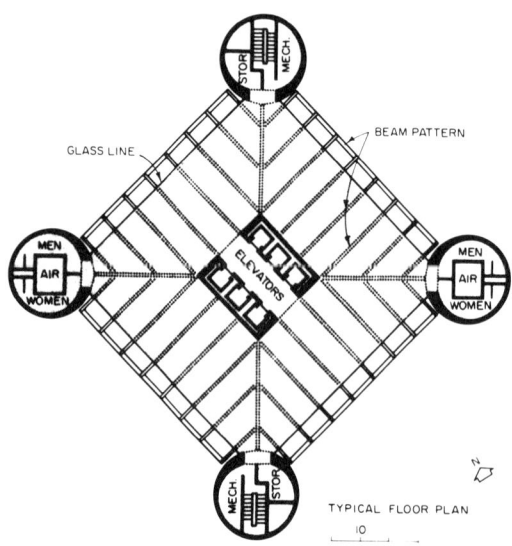

tain a Coliseum and the Knights of Columbus Building. It seemed appropriate for there to be some open space as well in this dense area with Malley's and Macy's and the First National Bank. We could have put the open space toward the highway, of course, but the highway itself was already too open. We felt that a small pedestrian space on the city side would be more appropriate. That idea gave us a very small site for a relatively large building of some 300,000 square feet. So we automatically got into a high-rise building, but we were dealing with a high-rise building that had an area of only about 10,000 square feet per floor, not the 22,500 of this ideal situation mentioned before.

Now, you take a building of 10,000 square feet per floor, and you put a central core in it. By the time you get the elevators, and the corridors, and all that stuff, the space left over becomes about 18 feet wide, which is unusable. The question is, how does one do a tower? Do you do a tower which has a core off to one side, like the Federal Reserve Bank, for instance, or a tower which would have a core in its center? Neither of these solutions seemed to be quite correct, because we were dealing with a building which was sort of in the round at this intersection. There was no appropriate back to it where one could put the core.

It seemed to be a building which would be seen from all directions. And, I think that's justified, particularly if you drive on the highway. You are conscious of the sense of movement around this tower. The problem became how to do a building with a central core and a small floor area which nevertheless had sufficient width within that area. We found the only thing that needs to be in the center is the elevator apparatus [*Fig. 2–31*]. Because they serve traffic, we put the six elevators in the center. That's a square of about 30 feet, a very small core. Now we have a building 90 feet wide. Where do the toilets and stairs go? We put the toilets in two of the outside towers and the staircases in the other two. So we've split up the service core.

Now, what form does this building assume? The concept of cores serving groups of space at certain distances apart, which is the concept of megastructure, began to emerge. In any large structure, the points of access and the utilities will be concentrated at distances up to 200 feet apart. If these points also become the bearing structure, with the clear span in between, we have a perfect multiplication of ground space, which is the essential nature of any urban structure. In a small building like the Knights of Columbus, this idea is expressed; it could be applied to much more extensive structures. This must be the basis for any megastructure design.

Then, we had to decide how to build the four exterior service shafts. The tubular form is very strong and easily allows a slip-form construction method. If we do that in concrete, as we did, we could pour the towers plus the elevator core all in one; we went up very fast [*Fig. 2–32*]. This is an effort to try to explore the potential of a certain aspect of technology. Is it possible that there is a way to combine these materials which deal with bearing and spanning?

Steel is very strong in acting as a beam. If you do the same thing in concrete, it has to be much heavier because it has a tendency to break under a similar load. So steel is best for spanning, but concrete is enormously strong in bearing or in columns. You see the evidence of this in any highway construction: concrete columns and steel spanning. If it makes sense on that level, it makes sense in building construction, too. So we have a concrete column and we span

2–32. Knights of Columbus Building. Towers and elevator shaft under construction.

the steel bearing, the steel spanning structure, between the columns.

Then, because we have bearing structure in concrete, and the major spanning outside, we have no problem in fireproofing this building. We can eliminate the whole fireproofing problem, which allows us to make a simpler expression of the elements which make up the building. We're very straightforward. Everything is bare. There isn't a thing covered in the whole building. It's almost unique in that respect. Now, I believe that this particular system is very usable in a very large, very much higher structure, and would make sense in it. As a structural principle, it could be applied to many other office buildings, but we now have a thing which has a rather strong form which comes out of a succession of decisions, not out of a prior theory.

And, now, we look again at the plan of the city of New Haven, which is, of course, a very great city. In the center is the Green, which is the basis for the grid. Then the Oak Street Connector cuts through the city, and the direction of the grid changes on the other side. Macy's and Malley's build up to a point at the intersection of Church Street and the highway. We pick up that point, and we keep the Coliseum within the downtown grid. Then, with the Knights of Columbus Tower, we make a *transfer* in the grid, which hopefully bridges across to the other side of the city and hopefully minimizes the fracture which the Oak Street Connector initially made.

HK: But do you think the man on the street would notice this? Does it become a visual experience for him?

KR: Well, if you look back at this building from the railroad station, you will begin to see how the relationships are established. If you see the building on the street, you see these relationships, so you're aware of them.

HK: Even if one is close to the tower? Well, one might sense certain relationships in his environment even if he is not aware of them.

KR: That's right, of course, because you don't necessarily have to understand everything to be aware of its being there. From the turnpike, as you drive around, you see the forms again, you're conscious of this building actually changing form. It has, I think, a very lively aspect compared to a rectangular building or a square building.

JC: Right across from your building is the Park Plaza Hotel, which is a Miesian rectangular box. Having seen one view, you've seen it all.

KR: You are never conscious of the hotel's unfolding at all; you're very conscious of the unfolding of the Knights Tower.

JC: You pay a lot of attention to the experience of seeing the building from a moving automobile.

KR: I simply mention that in the sense that these relationships are observable as you drive by, because the highway begins to take the place of the man in the street in seeing the building. From the sidewalk, you hardly see it, but you do see it from the highway.

JC: But the building is something new to the man on the street. We need to talk about that, too, because of this experience of walking into it. But let me ask you: Is the relationship of the building to the grid across the highway better understood by the moving passenger than the man on the sidewalk?

KR: Charles Moore is building an apartment tower across the highway [*see Fig. 7–4*]. When that building goes up, it will be observing the grid on the other side, and then there will be a relationship between these two buildings.

JC: Did he consult with you about this?

KR: No.

HK: Did Moore know that you paid attention to the siting of his future building?

KR: I doubt it very much. He may or may not have. I assumed that whoever was going to build over there was going to work with that grid.

JC: What is your reaction to the criticism that your building competes with the other major towers in New Haven? Was this in your mind?

KR: There couldn't have been anything farther from my mind.

JC: This seems trivial to you?

KR: Yes.

JC: As you look down the Oak Street Connector, you see Paul Rudolph's Crawford Manor [see Fig. 3–22]. Were you building in relation to that tower at all?

KR: That tower didn't exist when we were designing ours.

JC: Did you know it was going to be built?

KR: No, actually I didn't.

JC: So there was no coordinating plan. However, back toward the city is the Neo-Gothic Harkness Tower of Yale University, and Philip Johnson's Kline Biology Tower up on the hill [see Fig. 1–1]. Are you in any way relating to these dimensions of the city with your design?

KR: Hmmm, no—you see, if a layman wants to make public announcements about a building, what does he say? He may decide to talk about one of the peculiarities of it: it's the tallest building, or something. That's something for the layman to grip on to. That has absolutely no bearing at all on the way one designs a building. We have had opportunities to build high-rise buildings in New York, and we didn't do it. For the Ford Foundation, we deliberately chose *not* to build a high-rise building. It's hardly worthy of any serious consideration, because if one were operating on that level he couldn't produce a building at all. This is a consideration which has absolutely no validity whatsoever.

HK: When we talked with Philip Johnson, he considered the question of your tower competing with his Kline Tower. The Harkness Tower, the Kline Biology Tower, are certainly major points in the city. Philip Johnson even interprets as a competitive enterprise the fact that you both use similar dark burned brick for facing. He thinks that you were relating to his building not only in height, but also in material.

KR: I think this is a fortunate accident. Actually, his tower wasn't built when we were designing ours. I would probably have tended to shy away from that identity a little bit, to be very honest about it, but it's a fortunate circumstance because they *do* relate reasonably well. There is, of course, a coincidence of forms as well.

HK: You mean the round columns of the Kline Biology Tower?

KR: But they are forms which are used in an entirely different way.

HK: Yes, those columns are a façade, not part of the structure.

KR: Fair enough. I think that's a happy accident, and I would say one would be lucky to have more accidents; more such accidents would make for a better city. To imagine that New Haven is frozen in its present form is shortsighted. It's obviously growing. We'll need to preserve the central section of the city for its historical importance, but thirty years from now there are going to be a lot of very large buildings in New Haven just by the nature of things, and this can't be stopped. I don't even see why it *should* be stopped. But, in any case, the building comes out of a completely different set of considerations. How it is interpreted by critics who want to denounce it has nothing to do with how the building was *produced*.

JC: This is why it is important for the critic at least to consider your intentions.

KR: The serious historian will consider things in a different light.

HK: As I have experienced the building by visiting it many times, I have never been able to recognize the relationship to the grid on the other side of the highway. I simply didn't see it. People might have entirely different experiences which you never took into account, but it seems to me that these experiences ought to count. When Vincent Scully called it "militaristic" architecture, he had in mind its aggressiveness toward the rest of the city. Although the neighboring blocks of Malley's and Macy's are very large, your tower nevertheless introduces a scale which is not consonant with the rest of the city. By building it you ask for a new city. The tower might be pleasing for the highway driver, but it strikes down the man on the sidewalk approaching it.

KR: All right, let me speak about *that*. When one thinks of the scale of the city, one now has to think of it in terms of the scale that we're dealing with in our everyday lives in the highways and approaches. Modes of transportation have produced structures of enormous scale. The whole highway system is just really gigantic-scale stuff. We're building on the edge of a highway, a movement that is coming from 50 miles away. This ribbon ends or will pass through the city. We're building right on the edge of it, and it has a presence which we cannot ignore; we have to have some relationship to that scale, I believe, because it is, in a sense, the scale of tomorrow.

We deliberately forced this building right out to the sidewalk because we wanted to establish an urban presence as soon as possible for the visitor coming to New Haven. It really produces the same kind of effect as you get when you go into an old walled city in Europe. You go through a narrow gate which is 12 feet wide, and you're forced through it, and you're *in* the city, the heart of the city. We're trying to produce that feeling of a direct urban presence the very moment you walk in. If you remember, before this building was here, New Haven all fell apart. You were on the outer fringes, and you didn't get the urban presence until you got to the Green. I think this building, with the Coliseum, will help to produce that kind of presence. The question of scale in the city of the future—as we get into larger and larger structures—will have to answer the problem of getting from the human scale to the megastructure. You just can't take the human scale or module and multiply it indefinitely; it becomes incomprehensible.

Most New York office buildings are built this way. You start with the person, you go to the next larger object, then the next larger object, etc., and then you have a vocabulary which can deal with those objects on a larger scale. Those buildings on a larger scale in a city ought to be able to relate to *other* larger scale structures, such as bridges, access highways, and other things. You have to begin to develop these scales even to conceive of the megastructures.

JC: There are different kinds of grand scale, an Apollo rocket or an Acropolis.

KR: Well, the Acropolis is very interesting in terms of scale. It has a tremendous acceleration of scale. This, of course, has a

2–33. Model for Knights of Columbus Building and New Haven Coliseum.

little bit to do with why it was built. You suddenly realize that this is, in fact, the home of the gods. Those buildings are, in a sense, not built for people, but for gods, and the people are just allowed to move around them. Here is an example of scale used for an emotional effect, but it is nowhere frightening.

When this project is finished, we hope to have a kind of market place underneath the canopy of the Coliseum, a place where something like a farmer's market can go on [*Fig. 2–33*]. That would really be very exciting, very wonderful.

HK: A second Parisian Les Halles. Everyday life in a public space might need intimate scale. The architect too readily builds grand scale structures when he has to deal with crowds. The Coliseum in Rome is a monumental structure, but it is differentiated by many details. It is somehow broken down into a smaller scale. The same is true of the Acropolis or Chartres Cathedral. They become comprehensible in the detailing. In contrast, the four piers of your Knights of Columbus Building are giant monoliths.

KR: If you really look, it's full of details. You have the differentiation in the beams at the entrance, and in the brickwork a mortarline at every foot.

HK: But these towers are a unit, of course. If you are looking for a historical comparison, you could go back to the revolutionary architects of France who liked huge undifferentiated volumes. I don't object to monumentality as such, but I just ask myself if monumentality used in certain ways is objectionable.

KR: Monumental architecture is something I don't want any part of. I don't believe in it, I don't think it has any part in our society. So it is no concern of mine at all. That is certainly not the intention of the Knights of Columbus Building in terms of design. The intention, in terms of design in this respect, as I described all the other intentions earlier, is really the one of establishing the ability to create a larger scale,

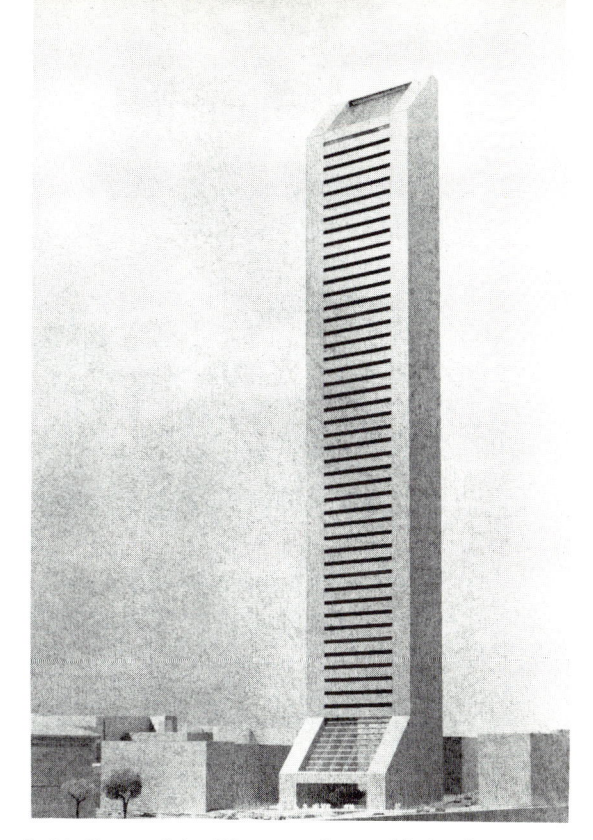

2–34. Proposal for Worcester County National Bank. Worcester, Mass. 1969. Kevin Roche, John Dinkeloo, and Associates. (Under construction.)

and hence larger buildings. You now have the aesthetic tools for making larger buildings. How do we go from this small thing to the next thing? Of course we have to have a scale whereby we can build a whole *city*.

JC: But the old city is still there. Let's say the New Haven Green, the churches on the New Haven Green, which are rather intimate in scale. If you introduce such a new scale, you are actually asking for a new scale for the city as a whole.

KR: We would not do this on the Green. We would only consider doing this in that particular position because obviously this would have been wrong on the Green, much too strong.

JC: In Worcester, Massachusetts, you did a high-rise building right in the center of town [*Fig. 2–34*].

KR: Worcester is another kind of problem. And that's good. It has some parallels, but in New Haven the emerging larger scale structures are already present: this very strong connector highway and the realization that the other buildings on the highway are going to be larger scale buildings. I think the buildings of the future are not going to be built out of 2 x 4s. You're going to have to use larger pieces to put them together.

JC: You're opposing rather vigorously the idea of monumental architecture. Would you be specific about what monumental architecture is for you?

KR: I suppose Washington is a good example of a kind of monumental architecture. It means enormous buildings accessible only by flights of steps, which are terrifying as you approach them; it means snow-white marble, ponderous detail. I don't think our buildings are cold buildings, you see. It depends on how the scale is *used*.

HK: Perhaps you create an effect that you didn't intend to create. Instead of monumentality, one might use a term like "brutalism," which is now fashionable. I would call your tower, if not "brutal," at least "brutalistic."

KR: These are all intellectualizations after the fact and have practically nothing to do with what one is really interested in. What one is interested in and concerned about is finding a means to a future, finding a way to do the things that we must do in the future in the best possible way. That, of course, has to do with the creating of environment, an appropriate environment, which should be stimulating and exciting and keep out the rain, should be restful and happy and whatever. You know all the terms as well as I do.

But, in the process of doing that, you make certain experiments because you want to find out. You have a building to do, and you are thinking about these problems, and you're guided into certain approaches to the problem, in order to see, to test a solution, in a sense, and maybe to make an example. All the buildings which we have done have that quality about them.

HK: I think one thing counts: the relationship between architecture and the human being. You like to walk underneath the Washington Bridge, but I don't. The George Washington Bridge is one example, the churches on the New Haven Green are another.

KR: I equally enjoy the churches on the Green, and so what one ends up with is a variety of experiences, a normal thing. That is, after all, why one goes out west to look at the mountains; it is very exciting.

JC: Well, we're talking about subjective experiences of architecture and how it affects people psychologically. There are many architectural critics who emphasize the aesthetic qualities instead.

KR: They often substitute any superficial aspect as the essence of the building.

HK: But there are many architects who invite such interpretive emphasis; and Paul Rudolph's Art and Architecture Building in New Haven broadcasts its sculptural qualities [*see Fig. 3–3*], and it would be almost unfair to consider the functional aspect first.

KR: It's an easy trap to fall into, of course, but it is disheartening to find that emphasizing these qualities is the only consideration that apparently has any value in architectural criticism.

JC: Edward Durrell Stone is another architect who invites critical interpretation based upon surfaces, textures, and façades. Apparently, for some architects, the visual impression is the major point.

KR: The process of designing a building is really a path which you begin to travel as soon as you possibly can, in terms of the problems. On the path of that travel, you embrace as many problems and try to solve as many of the considerations and aspects of a project as possible. The visual impression is one aspect, and it is only one.

HK: Here in the United States, architects still like to call themselves artists. Of course, that would be a term the European architects coming out of the Bauhaus would hesitate to use.

KR: They would resist it very much.

HK: Johnson and Rudolph think of themselves as artists. What about you?

KR: I wouldn't want any part of it. I think that kind of description is meaningless. I've been accepting the term "artist" in a very narrow sense. If you use it in the general sense of creativity—sure, fine! But, if one uses it in the sense of making decisions which are essentially concerned with visual aspects of a problem, or in the sense of making an architecture which comes solely from stylistic concepts, from Gothic or two-dimensional or three-dimensional or volume principles, then I simply don't want anything to do with it.

HK: And yet, you create architecture which demands visual response.

KR: As I have said, that is one of the responsibilities as one proceeds down the path. The *total* responsibility is much, much greater.

HK: That means that when you get to the visual questions, you could go far beyond a functional solution, even far enough to symbolize a force in society. You would not exclude this possibility from the design process?

KR: Oh, no. One might even search for it. One needs to find out what "role" a building will play in society. We are talking about a democratic architecture, as opposed to the architecture of a monarchy or a totalitarian state. Our architecture must exist for *people*.

HK: But as a pluralistic society?

KR: In a pluralistic society, there are multiple needs. In a society which also has an inheritance of violence, and destruction, and fracture of moral standards, architecture must help stabilize. I don't want to say "restore," because that suggests going back, but you should help create a more stable society. It isn't just the business of being visually pleasant, or exciting, or stimulating, or momentarily titillating, or anything like that. It truly has a role, an organizing role, which produces satisfying results for people who live, and for the few years they have to live.

HK: Does that imply that an architect cannot be revolutionary? Must he accept and affirm the society in which he finds himself?

KR: I would put it in a slightly different way. First, I would say that one has to build a new building. It's a large undertaking, involving a lot of people and a lot of money. In order to accomplish that, an architect has to harness all available energies. And all of the available energies would include our present desires, our idea of the desirable results, and our notion of the desirable end result for the city. So it isn't just expressing what exists; it's taking what exists and using it for a better result.

HK: Normally, the client is not concerned about the city's end result, but merely about his own building. Let's say that a bank wants to be represented as strong and impressive so that a customer might think, "This is a place where my money is protected." But the bank's desires might conflict with the city's scale.

KR: One would try to solve the problem so it didn't have to conflict. We would try to use that intention, as we did at Worcester, in order to build something that had a meaning for the city in the sense that it becomes in fact the center of the city. It becomes the cathedral tower for the city of Worcester, which is down in a hollow surrounded by hills and ringed by superhighways. Today, you can hardly see Worcester from the highway. It has no single visual mark. With our bank building, one can see it again. It assumes the role which the city hall inadequately plays. Our building, standing next to the common, reaffirms the center of the city. On the local scale, we provide the citizens more intimate space by opening the lobby for public use

2–35. Proposal for Worcester County National Bank lobby. 1969.

[*Fig. 2–35*]. So we do two extremes of the scale, and in the process we have satisfied the owner's requirement and have established their role.

JC: That means that the symbol of Worcester is now a bank.

KR: It's private, a private building, yes. It is, however, one of the largest things in the city.

JC: In other words, it should have been the Town Hall, but . . .

KR: Probably it should have been the Town Hall, but it was already built.

JC: So you took what you could get.

KR: You always have to use what's available.

JC: But maybe a bank is a more appropriate town symbol in our present society.

KR: I don't know. Maybe it is. I worried quite a lot about going high with this building. As I said earlier, I'm not a great enthusiast for high buildings, but they have their uses. Worcester was very run down, though it does have a nice quality of density. We are preserving as much of the density of the street as we can. We have a building which occupies, in fact, a minimal amount of land.

HK: You are still thinking in terms of a medieval architect who thought in terms of a cathedral tower which represents the city.

KR: Yes, in that respect.

HK: You build a bank and serve the same desire.

KR: I think of it in visual terms.

HK: It's very interesting that American architects like to think in terms of skyline. I have the impression that too much emphasis is put on the skyline, and it somehow becomes a drawing board venture. Relationships are built up on the drawing board which cannot be realized in the living situation.

KR: That's true, unless you see it from a distance.

HK: There is also a great tendency to use bird's-eye views of cityscapes.

KR: The city of Worcester is surrounded by hills. In the nineteenth century, one naturally went through the town. Anybody going to Boston went *through* Worcester. Now, the superhighway skirts Worcester. The traffic whizzes past, and Worcester suddenly disappeared from the map. In a sense, it's a matter of the existence of a city. By putting a shaft in the center, the city is again established. Everybody coming to or from Boston will see this building, and suddenly Worcester is there again.

JC: Did the client want to have a highrise building?

KR: They hadn't thought about it.

JC: So you gave them the idea?

KR: And they were, in fact, quite surprised when we proposed it. We did have to approach this very carefully.

JC: In other words, they had Worcesterian ideas; they were thinking in terms of Worcester's scale.

KR: They were really thinking of a 20-story building, adjusting to what Worcester already had. They were quite surprised when we proposed a 40- to 50-story building. But here we had the chance to make some kind of statement. What's the strongest punch you can make? I'm sure this doesn't solve the city problems or anything, but it is a first step. And it had a tremendous reception. It's a sudden boost to city pride.

JC: Height makes pride.

HK: One finds the same idea in the thirteenth and fourteenth centuries in Tuscany. The towers of San Gimignano are symbols of family pride.

KR: Yes, it's a fairly primitive approach. I'd say one has to recognize that the whole scale of this country is changing. It's a scale of *movement*. This gets back again to the Knights of Columbus Tower.

HK: But if we say that the car gives the city its scale, it is a lopsided perspective. It could happen that the car will be banned from the city, and other kinds of transportation will be found; your scale will no longer relate to the new situation.

KR: The car may be banned from the city, but it's fairly likely to continue on the freeway.

HK: So the freeway gives scale to the city?

KR: No, I mean in terms of approach *to* the city. When you get to the core of the city, the car should be abandoned.

JC: We have discussed the scale of the tower in Worcester and of the Knights of Columbus Building in New Haven. The Oakland Museum [*Fig. 2–26*] is an extreme contrast in scale to the Knights of Columbus Building. It is indeed a very unusual concept. Could you tell us how you arrived at the final solution?*

KR: Funds had been appropriated by a group of citizens for the building of a museum. They already had an art museum

* Mr. Roche began his description of the museum with a long discussion of the site and the history of the city.

and a collection of African animals being shown in an old Victorian house. There were also some remnants of a cultural history exposition of 1906 in another house. The original attempt was to acquire one block of property and build three separate museums on it because there were separate organizations with separate curators.

Thirty-seven architects were asked to submit proposals. We were fortunate enough to be picked, and we started meeting with people. We discovered almost immediately that there was really no client, in a way. There was no program. Everybody wanted to build a museum, but nobody had stopped long enough to think about exactly what that meant. So it was a unique opportunity. Bond money had been passed in a wave of great excitement, about $6 million. It was the largest bond issue for a museum ever. It was extraordinary.

Eero Saarinen had died in September of 1961, and John Dinkeloo, my partner, and I were interviewed at the end of that month. All of Eero's work had to be completed, and we were wondering what we were going to do next. Then we had this new job. They had intended to invite Eero, but he died; as a courtesy, we were invited. We were completely unknown to them; we had no reputation, so it was very brave of them to select us.

We were suddenly confronted with the question of what a museum should be, and what role it should play in the community. If the situation had been figured out already, we would never have had the opportunity to face the problem from the beginning. Now, the facts were this: It's a very run-down community, still suffering from the fact that it was an overseas base during the war. The city had this honky-tonk aspect to it. It was suffering a depression almost independent of the rest of the United States. It was really a depressed area. And you had these museums that had no artifacts of any value except a few American paintings. They also had no budget for buying works of art.

JC: Did they have a museum director?

KR: They really didn't have a museum director. They had nothing.

HK: In spite of all that they wanted to have a museum.

KR: They wanted a museum.

HK: And they didn't know what to put in it.

KR: Nobody had thought that one through, which was the most fortunate aspect of the whole project. Given the fact that one can define a museum's role in the city, what does one make out of the museum itself? Since this was a bond issue, the citizens themselves were paying for it. It was not given by some wealthy patron. So we felt the responsibility for making it a place where the average person would want to go. Obviously, he would not go to an ordinary art gallery, which appeals to a limited number of people. Also, if one did not give the museum some general purpose and direction, it would be subject to receiving gifts of a thousand snuff boxes or five thousand walking canes or whatever happened to fall to it in the course and chance of time. A director would be forced to accept gifts because a gift is a gift, so they would end up with all this junk, which is an enormous problem.

We began with the natural history of California. The western Pacific watershed area raises a tremendous variety of natural phenomena: the rock formations, the woods, the soil movements, the tidal waves, the earthquakes, the desert, the snow-capped mountains. There's a tremendous variety of wild animal and bird life, and an enormous variety of growing plant life as well as marine life. So here is California, which becomes almost a capsule of what goes on in the rest of the world. So we started with that.

Now, cultural history. The three major Indian migrations came across the Bering Straits through California over a period of five or six thousand years and spread east. All of the Western European cultures progressively came across overland; first, there were the Spanish coming up from the south, and their mission buildings are still in existence; then, there was the gold rush and finally the Oriental movement: the Chinese, Japanese, and Polynesians all coming. So, California is truly a polyglot mixture.

Now, a third peculiarity. California has the strongest traditional painting heritage in the United States. Now, we can bring all these things together. We can now take the child of the man who paid for the museum and show him the range of his natural environment. Then we can show him the impact of both on the art and artifacts which have been produced. So we can relate the fact that all of man's activities are interrelated, interdependent, and all have to do with the land and the environment in which he lives, along with the cultural influences which come in. Suddenly, you can bring to life any object, natural or man-made, in the panorama of everything else. So you have a regional museum which becomes meaningful, and it gives a basis for interlocking these various, separate museums.

The next problem is how to fit the museum into the city plan. In 1868, a park had been proposed on the site we were to use. Since that time, the area had been developed for commercial purposes. We again proposed that this area should be a park. Then, we assumed that seven blocks from the center of town there would be a development of commercial, institutional, and educational buildings, which would eventually culminate in our site. Then we proposed a larger site, four times larger, in fact, than the original concept. We made a master plan connecting our site to the heart of the city.

HK: The connecting area isn't built yet.

KR: Not yet. It may never be built, but at least it gave us a basis for starting to make some assumptions as to how the whole thing might grow.

There were purely architectural problems. We were confronted with buildings

2–36. Oakland Museum. View of terraces.

nearby which are not good architecture, but very formidable, nevertheless. So the problem of relating to them, recognizing the need for some greenery, and interlocking these various museum uses, creating this space to which people would actually come, and making a sort of general-purpose public space, which would not be a big, drafty plaza—all these things came together in the idea of stepping the levels of the museum [*Fig. 2–36*]. You have art on the higher end, then cultural history in the middle, and natural history at the lower end. There are offices related to each of these areas, as well as special gardens, a changing gallery, an auditorium, classrooms, a lecture hall, and a restaurant. A pedestrian street connects these elements, and leads one down to a lagoon, up and down a step, under arbors of blossoming vines into a portico area, and then into a little open court which will be used as an auditorium. You can walk over the entire thing. The Green is an assembly area for outdoor concerts or the like. So, in a sense, the whole thing comes together as a total concept which embodies the problems of use, and function, and city planning, and architectural relations.

Of course, this is all for the enjoyment of the visitor. In a museum, one's attention span is short, especially for children. You really should be able to get out and look at something outside. You can walk out onto a lawn which slopes up away from the window so that you can see more green than if it were level. The light coming off the lawn is soft, and there is no glare.

HK: From your description, one can no longer call it simply a museum. It creates wrong associations.

KR: That's right.

JC: What do they call it?

KR: The Oakland Museum. In a sense, "museum" is still a usable word; it's just that it needs another interpretation.

HK: It's a recreation area.

KR: As I said before, the great advantage was that the situation was flexible, and we could begin at the beginning. People were willing to go along with new ideas. Naturally, there were many who were disappointed when we presented these plans, because it wasn't a big, monumental building.

HK: So there were objections against its appearance.

KR: In the early stages, one of our biggest problems was to bring people along. In 1962, monuments were expected, especially for museums. It was a symbol for the city.

HK: In other words, they wanted to have a nice, big colonnade.

KR: That's right. I suppose that people would say, "Well, where's the building?" Well, if you can imagine the situation, this was rather hard for them to accept.

HK: How did you manage to push it through?

KR: Well, there was a sufficient number of people who liked the whole concept; they felt it was very "Californian," and they liked the relaxed quality.

JC: The exterior walls give it a scale which is not realized in the interior. In the interior, there is a cascading of levels defined by low walls. It becomes a sequence of boxlike frames.

KR: Yes, and everything in it is designed very low, in order to make possible a better view. All these walls are designed to be sat upon. They are all 20 inches high. All over the place, we combined the stairs with side walls, and got miles of seats, rather than getting into the bench world.

JC: And a paradise for children who love to run on walls.

KR: That, in itself, was another subject involving a death struggle with some of the city departments who wanted to put fences up all over the place.

HK: Is there any danger of their falling?

KR: No, everything is so low.

HK: With so many staircases in the entire complex, did you consider the problems for disabled people?

KR: Inside, we have an elevator system which allows one to go from level to level.

HK: We might call this a public garden-museum. Were there any examples from which you developed this?

KR: I would really have to say that it was all ours.

JC: You have created a second focus within the city. Now there is a polarity within the city center. Are the people going there?

KR: Well, it could certainly be the civic center in an entirely new use of the phrase. It's probably working that way. 15,000 people came on each of the first two days, and it turns out that every day they're getting fantastic attendance.

JC: You began your discussion with people in Oakland in September of 1961. The museum opened in late 1969.

KR: We started working in 1962 and made our first presentation to the city planning board in April of that year. Then, we made the first concept presentation of the museum during the summer, and another one around Christmas. The following summer, we made a third presentation. By the time it opened, it was almost eight years.

JC: How was the city as a client?

KR: Very difficult. First, we started with a mayor and city manager who were very, very enthusiastic. We did *not* have a museum commission when we started. At the beginning, we worked with groups of citizens. Later, we had the museum commission. We helped get a charter written, a museum staff appointed, and we helped them select a director. Meanwhile, the mayor had left, the city manager had left, the first director had left, the second director had left, and, finally, toward the end of the thing, there was nobody we knew any more. It has had its difficulties, but at least it's finished.

JC: You get extremely strong reactions to everything you build. On the one side, you were honored in a show at the Museum of Modern Art; on the other side, some critics damn you.

KR: It's possible, truly possible, that architecture should go no further than dealing with the lowest possible desires of people who, in fact, have no education at all in the world of architecture. This is the modern hotel or motel which creates an environment immensely satisfying to an enormous number of people out of *trash*. And there is, in fact, a whole school of architecture headed in this very direction.

There are still things which have true value which require attention and dedication and study, at least to the same extent as the effort which was put into them in the first place. You can't pick up a book by a creative writer and skim through it. Nabokov wrote a book which was just published. He spent six years writing it. It is virtually impossible to read, unless you spend almost six years reading in order to get it. Joyce has that same quality. Unless you attend to the thing, nothing at all comes out.

In a general sense, architecture is a situation in which the viewer who approaches will get varying degrees of satisfaction, depending on the level of education or sophistication or awareness that he brings to it as viewer. It's easy to bring everybody along, if you start with neon signs, or colorful little things of plastic, or psychedelic effects, or whatever. It's easy to bring the masses along to a certain point, and then you go ahead and do the architecture. Having brought the people along, you then do something else. I feel you must go the whole way. You must, in fact, deal with every man. However, it hasn't been in the tradition of modern architecture to do so.

JC: As a reaction to that, an architect like Morris Lapidus builds the New York Americana or Miami Beach hotels. He does what he thinks the man on the street wants but does not find in modern architecture; he makes every man feel like a movie star by putting him in a rather exciting, colorful, and funny environment of kitsch.

KR: I agree that one should cover the whole spectrum of architectural possibilities, but the problem is how to do it, how to cover the whole spectrum of human needs without pandering to the tasteless level of people. You could make an environment that is at once appealing on all levels, but at the same time is not junk, not made out of junk, and has those qualities which survive all periods, and all cultures, and everything else.

JC: You don't want to pander to a tasteless society, and yet you want to speak to everyone.

KR: I think you want to speak to everyone, but in an understandable way which will appeal to him, and which he will enjoy without using the devices such as are used in the motel world. One has to find that vocabulary and, at the same time, carry the environment and architecture along at a much higher level.

JC: Would you explain what you mean by the "higher level" which must be included along with this human attractiveness?

KR: Well, that's the thing that's almost impossible to say. I would really not even try to do it, because that's the seat of your pants that you're really working with. That's the whole instinctive . . . I wouldn't even try to define what the limits were, or what it should embrace, or what its highest objectives were, or anything else, because I don't know. I don't know if I can put it into words. I think that one should have the consciousness, one should have the sense of responsibility, one should have the vision to see the dimension of the problem. One should accept all of this and do the best he can do in response to these realizations. And it has no pretensions of doing anything for anybody; it is just the best assemblage of answers which can be produced out of the given problems.

3 PAUL RUDOLPH

JC: In American architecture today, symmetry is no longer considered anti-modern. In relation to the architecture of men like Kahn, Johnson, and Stone, your buildings display a lack of symmetry. What happens to the "axis"?

PR: I am not interested in symmetry or asymmetry, per se. One characteristic of the twentieth century is that nothing is ever completed, nothing is ever fixed. We don't think of things as being complete within themselves. A building can only be thought of in relationship to a changing setting, and at a point in time. Therefore, the design suggests the past and the future. So the whole idea of the uncompleted building which is going to be expanded in unknown ways is an obsession. I have now lived long enough to know that buildings get torn down, they get burned, they get added on to, their uses get changed, etc., so for me the temple in the park, or aligning a great avenue organized around an axis, is meaningless.

JC: Now, when you propose a project as large as the Stafford Harbor project [*Fig. 3–1*], do you conceive of that as a totality?

PR: Oh, never.

JC: Expandable?

PR: Absolutely. It is only intended to outline a three-dimensional—not two-dimensional—system of organizations which is to be augmented, changed, built upon, elaborated, diverted, etc. The elements which *cannot* be changed are the site and the human needs to be accommodated.

JC: In the drawings of the Southeastern Massachusetts Technological Institute [SMTI; *Fig. 3–2*], there seems to be a fairly complete program around the piazza, focused onto the lake. There is, in the design idea, a completed program.

PR: You call the space defined at the center a "piazza." I would call that a spiraling mall, but I'm being picayune. It is not a piazza at all. It's quite a different kind of space. The usual definition of a piazza would not be encompassing enough to organize a campus of this magnitude. The spiraling mall concept is much looser; it could have an additional spiral or two, be terminated or extended or contracted, whereas a piazza, by its very definition, is fixed and belongs more to the Renaissance.

The central organization of this campus is purposely a moving, or dynamic, one. That's the very nature of what is needed, as I see it. When one gets beyond the spiraling mall, with its defining buildings, walks, terraces, planting, etc., then other architects will take over, and indeed they already have. In that sense, I've thought of it as similar to Thomas Jefferson's University of Virginia, wherein he made a fixed, well-defined, marvelous central core for the campus. But, beyond the core, other architects took over, building very inferior structures. The idea, the central core, must be strong enough as a center of the campus, and other architects will add on to that. But the cohesiveness of the center remains intact.

JC: Transferring that idea to the Art and Architecture Building at Yale University [*Fig. 3–3*], you again designed it for expansion. There was to be another building next to it which would be similar, if not the same. Now if, in fact, that second building is never built, is the A and A Building incomplete?

3–1. Town of Stafford Harbor. Stafford Harbor, Virginia. 1966. Project.

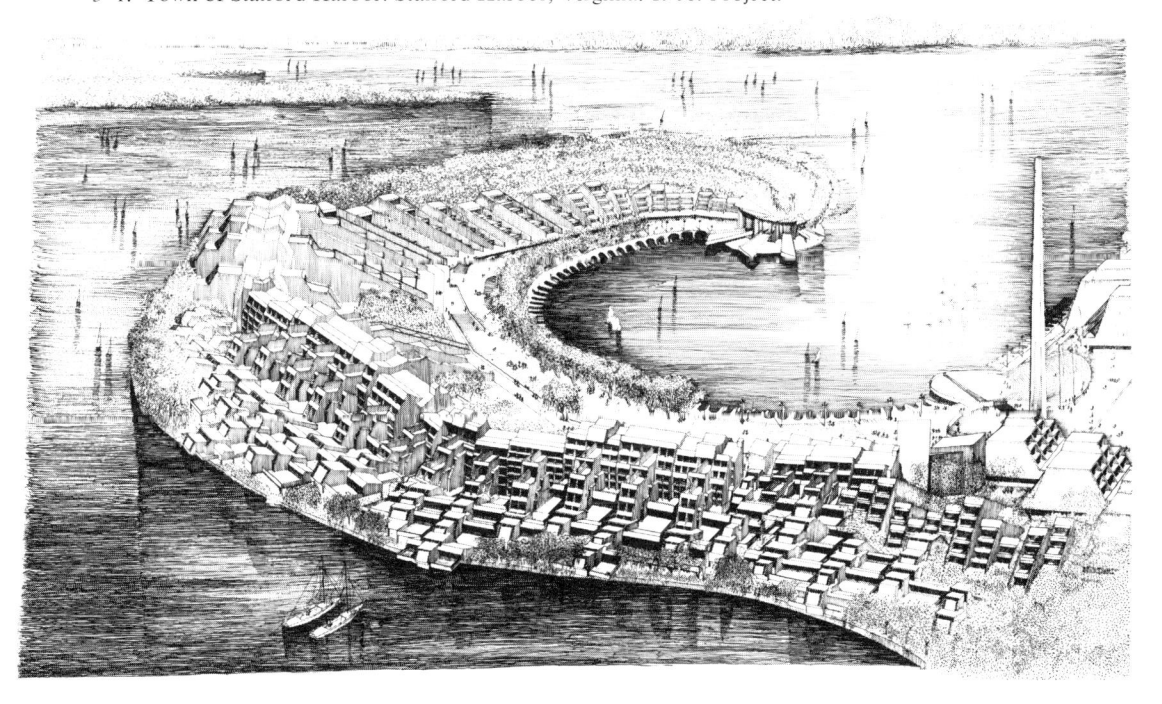

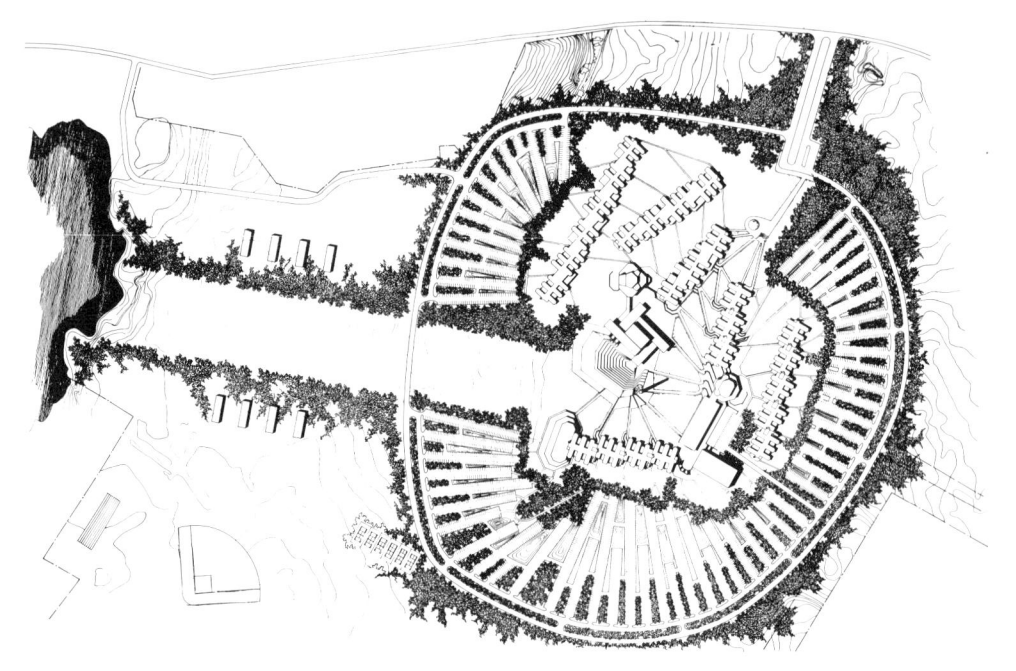

3–2. Southeastern Massachusetts Technological Institute. North Dartmouth, Mass. 1963. Paul Rudolph; Desmond and Lord. Site plan.

PR: Whether the A and A Building is incomplete or satisfying is for others to judge. It is *intended* to be expanded, but I don't think of it as being expanded only toward the *north,* but in all directions. It might be expanded as bridges over Chapel and York streets. The pinwheel motion of the upper floors suggests expansion across the streets. The service core is placed on the north next to two derelict buildings, which would facilitate expansion in that direction. I'd much rather see it expanded across the streets as bridges.

HK: We noticed that not only in the plan of the A and A Building [*Fig. 3–4*], but in *all* your ground plans, you avoid symmetry. You keep the open ground plan of a Bauhaus type, whereas here in the States there is a very definite tendency toward a rigid, symmetrical order. Think of Stone's university plan at Albany [New York] or his Kennedy Center in Washington. There are hundreds of other examples one could mention. To me, it is interesting that only in Russia does one find such a Beaux Arts symmetry, for instance, in the new University of Leningrad. Outside the U.S. and Russia, this is not the case. I wonder about the political implications. Could it be that this tendency toward a symmetry reflects a political desire to establish order, imperial order?

PR: I'm not much interested in trends or fashions, but in what is most appropriate. Symmetry as an orienting device may be most appropriately used where large crowds are involved, such as in an airport, but even there the sun refuses to give its light symmetrically. The open-ended quality of twentieth-century architecture renders mere symmetry impotent in most cases. Well, some of the "major" architects just do not interest me.

HK: Who? Or do you ever criticize other architects?

PR: Well, I'm too old for that. I used to, but I have to be polite now, you see.

HK: Because you belong to the Establishment?

PR: I don't want to belong to the Establishment.

HK: Can you control that?

PR: Since leaving Yale,* I can afford the luxury of being a maverick. Anyway, the Art and Architecture Building is asymmetical because its *site* is asymmetrical. It is at the corner of two streets. Why in the world would anyone want to organize the thing symmetrically? It's conceived from the viewpoint of urban design. It turns the corner. I cannot imagine a symmetrical building placed on a corner.

HK: But it happens.

PR: I don't care what happens. I only care what I want to do.

JC: In terms of the A and A Building . . .

* Rudolph was Chairman of the Department of Architecture at Yale University from 1958 to 1965.

3-3. Art and Architecture Building. Yale University. New Haven, Conn. 1962-63. Paul Rudolph.

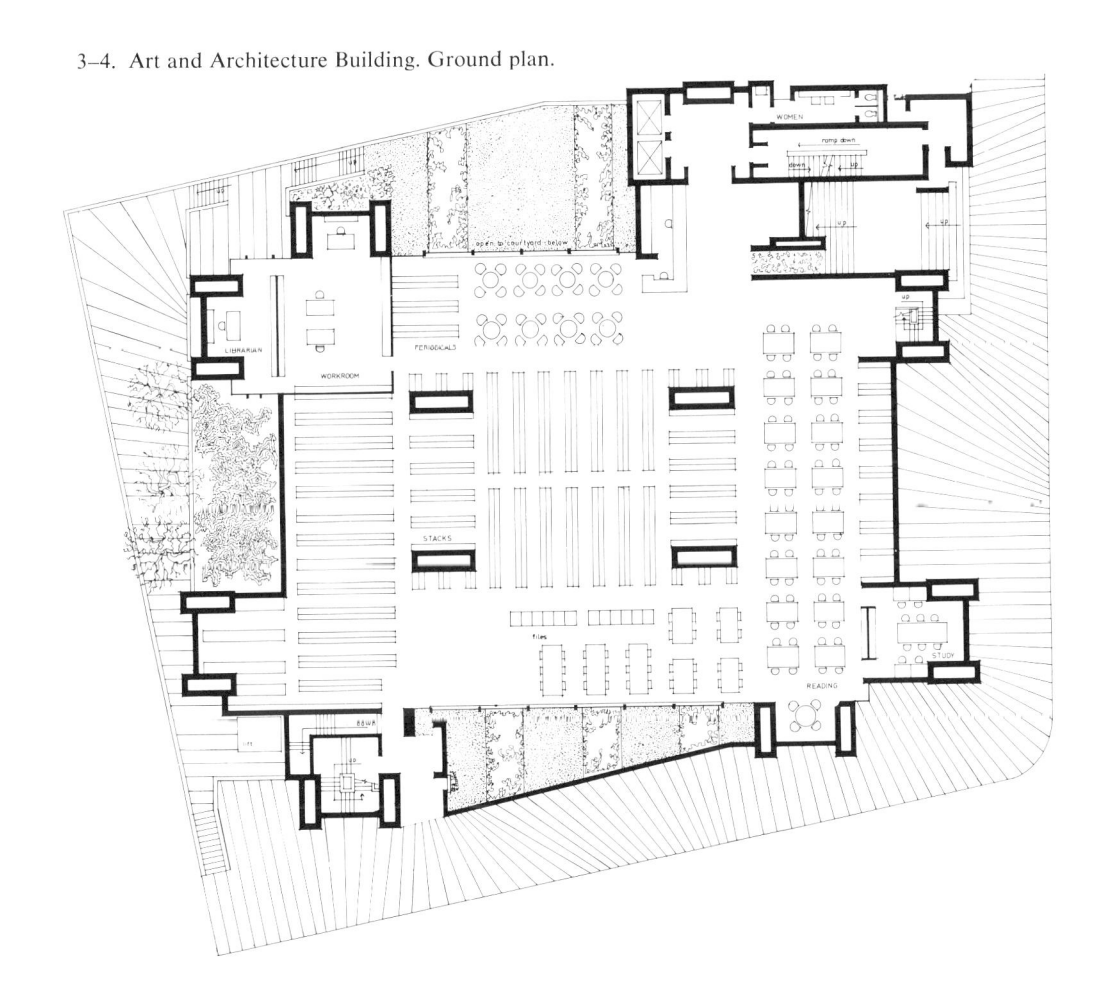

3-4. Art and Architecture Building. Ground plan.

3–5. Mary Cooper Jewett Arts Center. Wellesley College. Wellesley, Mass. 1955–58. Paul Rudolph; Anderson, Beckwith & Haible.

PR: It's really painful for me to talk about it.

HK: Do you always hate the buildings you have done?

PR: No, I don't hate them, but I'm never very satisfied with them. I want to change them. I'm much more interested in the present than I am in the past. I don't really want to talk—I never want to answer critics. I really don't. I only want to be positive. The criticism, finally, never bothers me.

HK: The Art and Architecture Building introduces a new style of building in the United States, a building which stands on the borderline of a whole historical development after Mies and after the International Style. Apparently, you designed it much earlier—in 1958. It was finished in 1963. It is always quoted as being from the year 1963. The original idea, however, goes back to 1958.

JC: There was very little in American architecture at that time which had moved away from the Miesian vocabulary.

PR: Well, for a long time I have felt that Mies was best when building beautiful temples in parks or designing his maximum package fitted to the speculator's site.

Cities cannot, finally, be made of temples or packages. The Seagram Building is a beautiful temple to liquor, but unrelated to the building of cities [see Fig. 1–2].

JC: In your A and A Building, there is a new massiveness, a new texture, new floating spaces. The rectangular box and the flat surface are broken.

PR: Yes.

HK: It would be very interesting to go back to this originating moment, when you broke with all the forms you used before.

PR: It did not begin with the Art and Architecture Building, from my point of view. When I first started, I made guest houses because no one would trust me with the main house. The guest houses were essentially derived from the International Style and adapted to the Florida climate.

The Jewett Arts Center at Wellesley College [Fig. 3–5] addressed itself to the problem of adding a twentieth-century building to a pseudo-Gothic environment. Architecturally, it is lacking; environmentally, it is relatively successful. Wellesley shook me, and I returned to the International Style in my next building, the first Sarasota High School. The second Sarasota High School [*Fig. 3–6*], in 1958, marked the beginning of a more personal and relevant search.

HK: In which respect was it, for you, a new beginning?

PR: If you discount my building for Wellesley, then I would say that the early houses were organized basically on clear structure, simplicity of form, articulation of each part, and what's commonly called "functionalism." The second Sarasota High School was a move from clear form, from clear structure, from linear structural elements defining space, to the organizations of planes in space. It depends much more on the space and handling of light, which really meant planes rather than linear elements, which in turn commenced my investigations of scale.

HK: Also volumes, not only planes.

PR: Right. And, therefore, that building, for me, was more important. But let's face it. All this comes from Corbusier. He, of course, did it all much earlier and much better.

HK: Were you looking around, were you looking for . . .

PR: Always, always. I'm affected by everything I see. I make no bones about it. I haven't invented anything in my life. For instance, the entrance to the Sarasota High School can be traced directly to Corbusier's High Court Building in Chandigarh.

JC: Do you see periods of development in your own work? Is it possible to distinguish stylistic changes from the Sarasota High School Building to your most recent building? I realize that any definition of style is an abstraction that we make, not the architect.

PR: Well, there are certain notions which I can't always explain which are very much a part of what I try to do, and they recur in varying forms. It's been said of me that I don't really know what I want to do, and, therefore, I do many different things, all quite eclectic. That isn't so, and I think I can really demonstrate it.

JC: Can you define some of those notions?

PR: Gropius, my teacher, was a very powerful, but not a very good, architect. He made clear the principles of the International Style, which I adapted to Florida.

3–6. Sarasota Senior High School. Sarasota, Florida. 1958–59. Paul Rudolph. Photo: Ezra Stoller © ESTO.

As time passed, I became increasingly unhappy with the limitations of the International Style, especially with regard to urban design and cities. That is of crucial importance. I have now designed many kinds of buildings, from New England to Florida and as far west as Illinois, and including East Pakistan, Saudi Arabia, and Lebanon. The programmatic and site requirements are very different, technically, climatically, psychologically, etc. I start with the site and environment. However, this can lead to a new eclecticism: a new pseudo-Gothic architecture for a given campus, or a new neo-Georgian for a city hall, etc. Is it any more than movie set making?

Secondarily, the space, interior and exterior, and its psychological effect, is of the utmost importance. The structure is only a means to an end, although each material has its own unique possibilities. In Miesian architecture, the structure is too often an end in itself. No layman has ever said to me, "I want the structure exposed; I want it to be clearly articulated." However, laymen have described very eloquently what space meant to them. I happen to be very interested in what things mean to people, and the symbolism involved. In a nutshell, the principles on which the International Style were based were valid up to a certain point, but they didn't go far enough and didn't face enough different *kinds* of problems. Two of those problems have to do with the psychology of space and the art of urban design, the ability to add to a city.

HK: That means you are not satisfied with building just for needs.

PR: No, never.

HK: You are not satisfied with just exhibiting pure structure for its own sake?

PR: Never.

HK: Beyond the concerns for structure and needs, you want to make a building exciting.

PR: I want buildings to move people.

HK: Do you think an architect has to be an artist?

PR: If an architect isn't an artist, he should not be called an architect.

HK: Sometimes a building might even look more like a work of art than like a building.

PR: You mean sometimes buildings become so *sculptural?*

HK: They become sculptures instead of buildings.

PR: In such cases, the emphasis is wrong. That would be inappropriate, because sculpture is never architecture and architecture is never sculpture. There has to be a balance. Buildings have to be used. One of the definitions of architecture is certainly that a building must fulfill a use.

HK: Nowadays, we respond to the functionalism of the Bauhaus negatively. The tendency is to go too far in the opposite direction. The problem to consider here is that one could neglect the needs while emphasizing design and excitement.

PR: I'm sorry. I don't mean to emphasize excitement per se, because it sounds as if I think architecture can be a substitute for something else. There are certain types of building which need to rise above functionalism.

As far as functionalism is concerned, what works for one doesn't necessarily work for another. The traditional Japanese house worked beautifully for the Japanese. It doesn't even work for the Japanese *now*. And it certainly doesn't work for Europeans or Americans. Functionalism is a very complicated thing.

JC: It can be a crutch, as Philip Johnson would say.

PR: I'm all for buildings that work. It's a question of *what* works.

JC: Walking up Chapel Street in New Haven toward the Art and Architecture Building, one sees that it gives the town another visual emphasis. It is a very self-conscious building. It strikes one as a huge piece of sculpture, and one wonders if it fulfills its everyday needs.

PR: The relationship between everyday needs and spiritual needs is very complex, and they are often at war with each other. Mere functionalism is never enough.

JC: The building is very flexible. It allows the things that have been put in afterward, without destroying it.

PR: The test of any building is how well it can withstand well-intended, and sometimes not so well-intended, changes. The question is: Is this building powerful enough on the inside to withstand all that has happened to it? For instance, plugging up the central exhibition space is alien to the building's organization and indicates contempt.

HK: What was the use of that space?

PR: It varies. The main floor is intended for exhibitions; the fourth floor for architectural drafting; the sixth floor for painting.

HK: The center core of the building is an open, unifying space.

PR: Yes.

HK: The primary need is to have enough working area. Now the students complain that there is not enough space to work but too much space to exhibit.

PR: Well, there is no reason why the exhibition space should not be used as work space.

HK: But then it loses its grandness, the very spatial quality you insist upon.

PR: Does it? Well, I could certainly imagine partitions separating the central volume, which might be retained as exhibition space, from the perimeter space, which might be used for work.

JC: How do you intend to "move" people with your buildings?

PR: I mean it in several different ways. I mean moving emotionally or psychologically. Maybe "moving" is too strong a word. What I really mean is that I regard architecture as important. It changes our lives or modifies them. I feel that one

3–7. Art and Architecture Building. Section drawing.

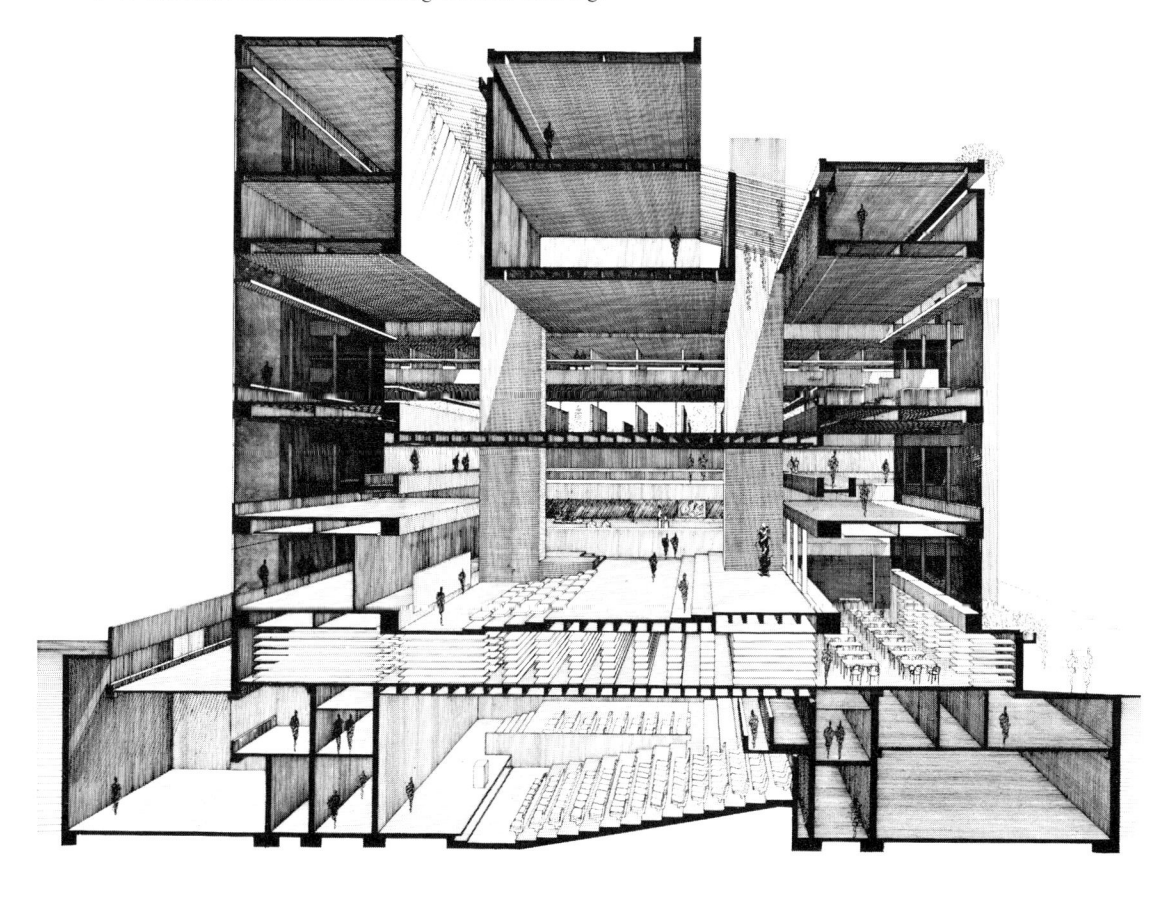

should be aware of *where one is*. The population and communication explosions have made it difficult to know whether you are in Hong Kong or in New York City.

JC: Do you mean that mass population produces anonymous architecture?

PR: Yes, so I want the environment to have character which is related to the varying needs of people as they differ over the globe.

JC: In order to move people emotionally, it seems that for you space is more important than the structure itself.

PR: Oh yes, always. I'm most interested and concerned with the space, but what *defines* that space, of course, varies. Sometimes it is a mass; sometimes it's a plane. Sometimes it's transparent . . .

JC: Aren't you also concerned with the *outside* space?

PR: Oh, yes. When I talk about space, I don't mean merely interior space. It includes the whole urban setting.

JC: The Art and Architecture Building introduces that special quality of organizing exterior spaces with masses.

PR: I'm also interested in space which has a thrust horizontally and vertically [*Fig. 3–7*]. I'm fascinated with the interaction of one thrust of space with another. For example, the A and A Building consists of many wings. Each wing has a strong horizontal thrust around a vertical thrust. So you have a pinwheel. All these spatial thrusts are fascinating for me. You'll find that a recurring thing in my work.

HK: In that space it is exciting to discover the many possibilities to move around. It becomes an adventure to explore the space. But, on the other hand, a stranger can get completely lost. It can be very confusing.

PR: But it's *not* a *public* building! When that building first opened, there were literally thousands of people who came to see it, but it was never intended for that. It was intended for a few students who, presumably, soon learn the purposely secret, labyrinthlike circulation system.

HK: When I came to this country, I stepped out of the plane, came to Yale, walked up Chapel Street, and there it was: a concrete mirage. I walked around it and tried to understand it and was spellbound. There were many entrances, but which was the right one? The large entrance space seemed to demand a festival procession on a special occasion; too important for the daily routine, and the small entrances scattered around seemed to lead to closets rather than to the library. I ended up in the basement and was lost for three days. However, back to my point. One can have lots of associations which are very individual. Many responses are possible.

PR: Sure.

HK: So one cannot pin it down. One of the positive qualities of the building is that it provides a variety of experiences. But it was January when I arrived, and the wind blew through that entrance [*Fig. 3–8*]. It's a great hole opening toward the sky, and it creates a frame for those run-down build-

3–8. Art and Architecture Building. View of front steps.

ings beyond. You have this great view, but there is nothing to see, and the cold wind blows you into the backyard. Did you have something else in mind when you built that great entrance-way?

PR: Oh, yes. You see, I intend for that entrance to lead to a courtyard. The courtyard isn't really formed because the "run-down buildings" next door have not yet been rebuilt. If the next architect is at all sensitive, he will complete the courtyard, thereby adding immeasurably to the whole. Implications in architecture are a twentieth-century must.

HK: It is very significant in American urban architecture that side walls, huge blank surfaces, are left for future additions. The street is marked with blank walls waiting for the building next door. We are always thinking of the next step, and nothing is finished.

PR: Hasn't it always been like that, to a degree? And is it more satisfying when people build their little temples complete within themselves? Things are constantly being rebuilt. I would like to think that, as time goes on, existing buildings would be better understood and, in essence, the basic idea would be carried out. But maybe I'm wrong. I don't know.

JC: In other words, you count on the next generation.

PR: Well, I don't count on anybody, to be quite frank about it. I just hope. We are most limited in what we can do.

JC: If you are that uncertain, then why design with an open-ended attitude? Under the circumstances, one would expect you to work for a totally complete concept.

PR: No, I'd rather imply what *might* be done. The environment constantly changes, as history shows. We are present for a short moment in time and must suggest what is to come.

JC: Yet, one perceives the Art and Architecture Building as a finished product. It is much too unique and self-confident to imagine that it anticipates anything else.

PR: But there are *implications* in the building of what might come.

HK: For instance, there is the implication in the entrance-way to lead into a courtyard that may never be built.

PR: One must think of more than one generation. It is important for architects to think on multiple levels, and for buildings to be read on multiple levels. You can read that building as a thing within itself, but that's not the beginning and the end of it. I could give you a hundred implications for the future in any of my buildings, but I don't really know if any will be recognized. The entrance-way on a cold winter's day can be unpleasant, but the venturi action during warm weather is a plus; so if I were to do it again, I would retain the main entrance as it is, for the important thing to me is to have an entrance of that scale the year round.

HK: If, for instance, you want to get to the library, you are led up that grand stairway to the second floor. This is a "moving" experience, but you have been led in the wrong direction for the library so you have to squeeze into an elevator and go back down. However, one may end up in the subbasement. Next time, you don't try the grand stairway but discover the door to the fire stairs, and then you make it.

PR: This building is for the people who are going to *make* things, if you will. It is not so much for people using the library. They are temperamentally very, very different. Everybody who is going to use that library learns how you get in. But I wanted a *ground* entrance for people who

JC and HK: Create?

PR: Who are going to make things

JC: Like the painters and architects . . .

HK: The other ones, the scholars, can get lost.

PR: There are people who gave me such a hard time that this was *purposely* done.

HK: Congratulations.

PR: Oh, I think buildings should have a sense of humor about them.

JC: There's certainly a lot of humor in the whole building.

3–9. Art and Architecture Building. Alcove window at library corner.

PR: Isn't that clear?

HK: For instance, there is that little alcove window at the corner [*Fig. 3–9*] . . .

JC: In the midst of those masses of concrete.

PR: Yes, yes.

HK: That certainly is a witty, ironical remark. It contradicts that mighty corner.

PR: Yes, yes.

JC: From inside, it makes a very friendly corner. The light there breaks open the box.

PR: I know.

JC: Mr. Rudolph, some of the best of modern architecture has been built for campuses. You have certainly contributed to that scene. The A and A Building at Yale University is one contribution, and, as mentioned earlier, you have planned a whole campus for Southeastern Massachusetts Technological Institute [*Fig. 3–2*].

PR: Yes. The student union and the various buildings around the center are now all under construction, and then I will say goodbye to that campus.

JC: And other architects will step in?

PR: Yes, you see, one has to understand the forces in society. As an architect, you have very little control, and you have to be able to sense what will probably happen. Time is a more important factor in building than the materials used in construction.

HK: To plan and build a campus or a city all by yourself is a very desirable enterprise. However, how can *one* architect guarantee variety? Wouldn't it be better if many architects joined in building a city, so that it would not have the imprint of one individual, in order to avoid monotony?

PR: In the twentieth century, I do not know of a single example where many architects have participated in a given group of buildings where it has ended up being anything viable at all.

HK: Even a small complex like Lincoln Center has indicated that [*see Fig. 1–22*].

PR: The Lincoln Center? Neofascism!

HK: What about the Boston Government Center? Apparently, there exists a general plan by I. M. Pei. Then, many different architects were called in to do different parts. You also have been involved.

PR: The Boston Government Center is beyond the Pei plan.

HK: Kallmann, McKinnell, and Knowles stepped in. Gropius and his group stepped in. Finally, it is difficult to recognize the unity of such a given plan.

PR: There is not much unity, but that is a dilemma of twentieth-century architecture.

JC: But, within the plan, there are some important buildings. You yourself have said that Kallmann's City Hall is one of the most exciting buildings of this century [*Fig. 3–10*].

PR: It's a very good building.

JC: Would you also call this neofascism?

PR: Well, what is a fascist building?

JC: You're the one who brought it up, but let's say "one which dominates."

PR: The Boston City Hall is a magnet, and appropriately so, since its use is at the top of the hierarchy of building types. The superhuman scale and siting insure that it will remain a focal point.

JC: How does the treatment of the surface of concrete affect all of this?

HK: It's your signature, Mr. Rudolph, your dramatic exterior surfaces.

PR: No. We have built of brick, wood, steel, and plastics.

HK: No, you know what I mean. Have you forgotten the Art and Architecture Building? You are talking about your earlier buildings.

PR: They are wood and concrete block.

HK: All right. All right. But what's happening at the Art and Architecture Building?

PR: The aggregate of the concrete is exposed.

HK: Yes, exposed and striated! And you continued to use it. Think of the Endo Laboratories or the Christian Science Center, for example.

PR: Poured-in-place concrete buildings are becoming more expensive, but also I want buildings to be lighter in feeling. I can't explain this completely.

HK: The new Government Center in Boston?

PR: Well, that was designed five or more years ago.

HK: But it is now being built, and it still has that signature.

PR: Yes, that's true, but seriously . . .

HK: You are now getting away from it?

PR: Yes.

JC: Do you oppose that signature?

3–10. Boston City Hall. Boston, Mass. 1963. Kallmann, McKinnell, and Knowles.

3–11. John W. Chorley Elementary School. Middletown, New York. 1964–69. Paul Rudolph and Peter Barbonne, associate architects.

PR: I don't oppose it . . .

HK: It's not interesting any more.

PR: Every material has its own intrinsic values and uses. And I'm interested in *every* material, not just one. It's wrong to think that I'm only interested in concrete. Yes, I built some buildings in concrete and probably will build some more. Today, I'm working on twenty projects, and I think only three of them are concrete. I might add that there is also another aspect to be considered. I'm fascinated with the idea of how to make a building a *dominant* in the city scale. I used to think that it could best be accomplished by making it relatively heavy and solid. I now explore ways to make it very light in terms of steel construction and still make it dominant. I happen to be working on a new government center for New Haven. And it is very, very different in feeling from the Boston Government Center. Poured-in-place concrete

3–12. John W. Chorley Elementary School.

3–13. Richard C. Lee High School. New Haven, Conn. 1966. Kevin Roche, John Dinkeloo, and Associates.

is a continuous material; it is a plastic. That's the essence of it. But a steel frame is the exact opposite. I haven't worked with steel frames so much, but I'm beginning to. So please don't think of me as just a concrete architect.

HK: Why do you want to make a building dominant? Why should it stand out? Why shouldn't it stay modest?

PR: There are certain buildings that *should* stay modest. For instance, I did a school. I hate that school.

JC: Now, wait a minute! We're talking about the Chorley Elementary School building [*Fig. 3–11*]. It is marvelous.

PR: You're too gentle with that building.

HK: Now you are your own worst enemy.

JC: Your school is not dominant. It stays within the scale of the landscape. It does not reflect adult wishes but adjusts to the play world of the child. It allows freedom and does not restrict the child to one place. It is light and inviting [*Fig. 3–12*]. Why shouldn't an elementary school be more like a kindergarten than a detention home? How can you hate it?

PR: I don't really hate it, I . . .

HK: Do you know the high school by Kevin Roche at New Haven [*Fig. 3–13*]?

PR: Yes.

HK: It is the opposite of the Chorley School.

PR: I know.

HK: It impresses the child coming to the school out of the slums. It wants to impress. It creates a very authoritarian environment. In some ways, it implies that every child in it is a vandal. Your school treats the child in a rather friendly manner.

PR: He feels at home.

HK: So why do you hate it?

PR: Well, it's appropriate, and it accomplishes what I intended. I don't think every building needs to be dominant, but a city hall needs to be dominant.

HK: Why can't you like the Chorley School, even if it is not dominant?

PR: Too sweet. Too sentimental.

HK: You really want to impress people!

PR: No. I want what is appropriate.

HK: But that is an excuse. Every architect wants to be appropriate.

PR: I know.

HK: Everybody says, "I am appropriate," and then they go on building what

3-14. Model for Lower Manhattan Expressway. New York. 1967. Paul Rudolph.

they want. In your case, you want to impress, to create dominant architecture.

PR: Let me put it differently. There are certain building types which I feel more sympathetic to than to others.

HK: In other words, you would rather build a city hall than a school?

PR: Yes. That's all I really mean. I guess . . . well, I would like to think that there are ways of making a building like the Chorley School sympathetic to the child, without reverting to forms which become by their associations so sentimental. I think I relied there too much on associative values.

JC: Why would it be sentimental?

PR: Well, all those pitched roofs. Isn't it picturesque?

JC: Why not let a building be picturesque? However, there is a photograph which makes it look like something after an earthquake [*Fig. 3–11*].

PR: That I would like much better. It would have been better if the hill had been steeper so that the villagelike aspect could have been grasped from one point of view.

It was my intention to have each segment of the ceiling painted a different color, but for economic reasons we had to paint it all white. That hurts it. I wanted it to be like an Arabian tent. I wanted it to be very festive and to transport the child into another world.

JC: Comparing your school again with the one by Kevin Roche, one should not forget that his is a high school and yours an elementary school.

HK: And one is in the woods and the other next to a city slum.

JC: You both studied educational needs and came up with entirely different solutions. But, it seems that not only the different settings determined the results—of primary importance is the attitude of the architect.

HK: It appears as if, subconsciously, the two of you began with opposing predilections concerning the idea of a school. Depending, perhaps, on your own school experience.

PR: That might be. They certainly are different!

HK: Your proposal for Stafford Harbor seems to achieve a compromise between the two desires: to build dominant buildings and to maintain an intimate scale [*Fig. 3–1*]. The total form of the megastructures, the step-pyramid shape, makes them dominant, but the organization and detailing of every single dwelling unit within the whole provide the intimate scale. So you get variety.

PR: I would not call it a compromise, but addressing oneself to the possibilities of "dominant" architecture, which usually means superhuman scale and "intimate" scale. The manipulation of scale is an architectural obligation. It is necessary that architecture be read from a distance in one way and, as you approach it, in yet another way. As you come closer, you turn the doorknob and perceive in yet another way. All architects have always been obsessed with this problem, and so am I.

HK: Now, in relating your buildings to

the new traffic systems, would a sixteen-lane highway affect scale?

PR: Of course, of course. We know very little about that. Sixteen-lane highways are new. That's a fascinating problem.

HK: So the scale of the building has to change.

PR: Exactly.

JC: I would like to know more about your study of the Lower Manhattan Expressway for the Ford Foundation [*Fig. 3–14*].

PR: The study is still in a very early stage. It might take a year or so before I come up with a final proposal.

JC: But your general idea already has shape. I think it's a very unusual idea to consider the street itself as a building. That means there is no separation any more between a group of streets and the buildings that stand on the street. You incorporate everything into one structure.

PR: Yes.

HK: That's certainly new.

PR: I sit here and look at this view of the East River Drive from my apartment, and I know instinctively that that's not the way it should be.

HK: How would you do it?

PR: The various levels of terracing should lead down to the river, not to the East River Drive. Walking along the river is very important, and I see people go through great contortions just to get to the river's edge.

HK: It seems that Americans have never cared much for the river fronts, but now they are being rediscovered.

PR: That's true. Someone is always mumbling about Manhattan and the circumferential highway around it. I don't know how you could have ever done it otherwise, but that was the first step toward the building of a megastructure. It's too bad that building over it wasn't anticipated from the beginning.

JC: But it now happens haphazardly.

PR: One of the most compelling sequences of space in Manhattan is what happens along the East River Drive. It's really an architectural sequence of spaces in the scale of the motor car. You drive in, out, under, and get a kaleidoscopic, broken view in motion going underneath horrible buildings; you turn at a slight bend, and the U.N. bursts into view. There are elements shooting off, up and over. It's all very exciting.

HK: A very good description. But when you are driving along there, you can never stop. There is no place to stop to look at it. You have to keep moving, moving, moving. And you can't get out of the car. The moving automobile determines the perspective, and you have no other choice.

PR: You see, the federal government is paying the bill as long as the traffic keeps moving. As long as you're going, going, going, the American taxpayer will spend any amount of money. But once the car is parked, you find that the sources of money have disappeared. The parked car deserves greater attention because it demands accommodations. It is a very exciting thing, which can be a great asset, not a debit.

JC: You don't necessarily consider the highway the enemy of the city, and you don't necessarily want to put the parking garage on the edge of the city?

PR: It depends on the size of the city and location. It's very difficult to generalize about it.

HK: What do you think about the separation of passenger traffic from pedestrian traffic? There is a strong tendency now in the U.S.A. to separate the car city from the pedestrian city, for instance Philadelphia, Hartford, and Baltimore. But shouldn't there be some other solution? As far as we have understood you, you don't intend to eliminate the car from the urban center.

PR: I don't see that you can eliminate the car from the city in the foreseeable future. There is an imminent crisis, where finally we will understand that, in order to have any kind of efficiency of movement, certain areas have to be designated as carless. The resulting twentieth-century pedestrian plaza will be very different from the European plazas that all of us admire so much. The Renaissance rules of the relationship of height of enclosures to width between buildings is a very human thing, but our buildings today are much, much larger. The multistory building and its rules are very, very different, and we are just beginning to understand them. The harshness of our climate and the advent of air conditioning modify our thinking with regard to pedestrian open spaces.

HK: I have noticed that there are many new projects which cover up the pedestrian plaza with glass roofs so you get the nineteenth-century "galleria" again within the multilevel city.

PR: There are many architects who would not agree with me that the multilevel vehicular-pedestrian route is very meaningful.

HK: Philip Johnson, for instance, intends to cram the streets full of people in his Welfare Island Project. He doesn't like the multilevel city.

PR: Yes, there he is dealing with a very constricted piece of land, with a definite boundary, which is being planned all at once, like a new town. The single-level city has great meaning when it is small enough that cars can be parked at the perimeter.

HK: The multilevel solution doesn't work too well. The pedestrian level is put above the world and becomes very artificial. Very few people walk up there. One is lifted up and put on another level of experience which is not the real experience of the city any more. It is an artificial arrangement of "temples," piazza, fountains, and shrubs.

PR: It's all a question of how it is arranged. New York City is already a multilevel city. Rockefeller Center and Grand Central Station are prime examples. The underground routes of Rockefeller Center, and through much of Manhattan, are very important, economically viable, but quite often architecturally ridiculous. Two levels do not work until there are many functions to be accommodated, and even then the connections between the two must be adroitly handled.

JC: You would not be opposed to the Peter and Alison Smithson solutions in British redevelopment, when they put a pedestrian traffic way outside the building at the fourth floor, or even connect the buildings in the air?

PR: It depends on the need and how it is accomplished.

JC: They have published a book entitled *Urban Structure,* and it turns out to be a discussion about sidewalks. They hardly talk about buildings any more. They want to renew the life of the city merely by connecting buildings to each other by pedestrian bridges. Pedestrian traffic is their primary concern.

HK: This seems to be an overreaction to the early 1950's, when the primary concern was to adapt the city to the car. Books appeared like *Die autogerechte Stadt* [the self-sustaining city], the car's rules are the city's rules. Other concerns were omitted. Rostow, the author, built a very artificial city in Germany, the Sennestadt, near Bielefeld. There is no cohesion of a city because it is opened up for the automobile communication. There is pedestrian space, but it is boring, and the buildings are boring. Building simply for traffic needs eliminates other essentials. It is important to create exciting images which make the city interesting visually, as well.

PR: Of course, in discussing the city one can never leave out anything. No single notion will solve all problems.

JC: How does one begin to reach a responsible solution?

PR: No *single* thing works. I am personally fascinated with the fact that Americans are in love with automobiles.

HK: The rest of the world, too.

PR: Okay. And the planners and architects who say, "Let's get the car out of the city," are welcome to their own ideas but do not call the tune. People feel that the car gives them an unmatched freedom and convenience.

HK: You take up the existing problems of society and try to find a way out.

PR: Yes, exactly. I support programs for change.

HK: Utopia? The architect as the creator of Utopian structures asks for a change of life for the people who live in them.

PR: That's important. Architects should work on many levels: one which can be built tomorrow morning, and another which would be meaningful but must wait for the adjustment of conditions before it can be accomplished. Each is equally important.

HK: So you wouldn't object to proposals like those of the British Archigram group, or those of the Japanese who want to build cities out into the ocean?

PR: Certainly not, certainly not.

HK: The normal attitude of the architect is to affirm the existing society and to build merely what the society requests. Of course, that is too shortsighted. You want to be a step ahead of society?

PR: Architects, by implication, suggest the past as well as the future and make connections between the demands of society and Utopia. An example of this is the demand of society to build throughways which cut up our cities but which also are the first step toward building megastructures, which I see as a great unifying element in the cityscape. When I look out of this window, I see the beginning of a megastructure. You say, "Where do you begin?" I say, "It's already begun."

JC: To start with megastructure, do you begin alone as an individual or with a team of consultants?

PR: Of course, I would pay due homage to teamwork. You can't turn around without asking the mechanical engineer what the weather is like, the structural engineer whether it will hold up, the acoustical engineer, the lighting engineer, the soils engineer, the—oh, it goes on and on. The fact remains that everybody seems to cancel out everybody else. Sometimes it's easier if the project is very large, because there are so many people pulling and tugging that you quite often can fill a vacuum if you have the meagerest idea which is valid. That is fascinating. Finally, it is up to an architect to make up his mind how he feels the thing should be.

JC: Who are the specialists for humanity in building? Do you count on them as an architect?

PR: Specialist in humanity? Oh, I don't think there are any.

JC: The sociologist says he's a specialist in humanity.

PR: Okay, all right, then the sociologist. I'm all for their making their studies. Shouldn't we go have lunch now?

* * *

JC: Can a city planner determine what has been called the "anatomy of ambience"? Can that mean anything to you?

PR: I've never heard the phrase before. I assume it has something to do with the psychological implications of a given environment.

JC: I suspect that it means an attempt to include psychological and sociological considerations in urban design. It implies that it may be possible to program all aspects of environment.

PR: I would disagree with that completely. First of all, the intentions of even very skilled people having to do with three dimensions, especially on a large scale, quite often are not what was anticipated. What comes out finally is often not what people describe. As a former teacher, I can assure you that what students, and I would also say many architects, describe about a given project often has little or nothing to do with its actuality. Some planners and many bureaucrats are incapable of putting on paper, either in drawing or words, what result will be achieved. This takes a special imagination. The *intentions* in architecture and the results are two entirely different things.

HK: When we were discussing your Lower Manhattan project, we concentrated primarily on the traffic. There are certainly other components which have priority.

PR: Yes. The preservation of Broome Street is a primary concern. The scale of Broome Street, the Williamsburg Bridge, the commercial areas of the Italian neighborhood, the various institutional buildings, the small parks, the existing pedestrian ways and the streets at grade vary tremendously. Each scale must be respected and integrated into the megastructure. The symbolism of the bridges as an entrance to Manhattan could be celebrated by enlarging the megastructure at this point, giving a sense of "place."

HK: In the twentieth century, there hasn't been extensive city planning. Now, environment is the new concept, not building "the temple in the park." Contributing to the ambience became a primary concern. How is your work related to this new consciousness?

PR: I'm not altogether sure of this. In the nineteenth century, this country was built basically on the École des Beaux Arts principles, if there was any large-scale organization at all.

HK: Just a grid plan that was given for an entire city.

PR: It was not much more than that. Grand avenues reached out from a central square, but the squares were seldom realized in a three-dimensional way. These concepts were thrown over principally because of the automobile and its demands and the stylistic popularity of the so-called International Style. Zoning was introduced, but it has probably done as much harm as good. Wright proposed Broad Acre cities, but it had little relevance since Wright was anticity and really felt he should design everything in sight. Le Corbusier proposed tearing down much of Paris and placing great buildings in parks, all of which is fundamentally antiurban. However, when he did build in Paris, it was always with great sensitivity to the immediate environment. Gropius tried to reduce everything to a more scientific basis, formulating charts about distances between buildings dependent only on the amount of sun and air that they needed, but the result was usually boring. Mies was much more humble about city planning, taking the American businessman's site and putting the largest possible beautifully designed package

3–15. Model for Graphic Arts Center. New York. 1967. Paul Rudolph. Photo: Ezra Stoller © ESTO.

on that site, regardless of what was around it. When I was in school, it was generally thought that since everything was eclectic anyhow it should be torn down, and one of the "masters' " ideas could be utilized as generally interpreted by somebody called the planner. Architects willingly abdicated much of their heritage to the planner, and consideration of the existing environment was not really necessary. By and large, the automobile was considered to be ridiculous —to be kept out of the city.

JC: What is the dominant tendency in architecture since Mies?

PR: After Mies, the megastructure.

JC: Are there any models for understanding the megastructure visually? Or does it remain in the realm of ideas?

HK: One reason Le Corbusier became so influential was that he knew how to present his ideas visually. His Utopia was shaped through his drawings long before any building was built. Nowadays, megastructure exists mainly as a statistical abstraction. Your Graphic Arts Center for New York is one of the few exceptions [*Fig. 3–15*]. That may be the reason that the model was reproduced in so many magazines.

PR: Unfortunately, architects have been very timid recently about making idealized statements or sketches of what might be. They've been frightened somewhat by the complexities of the issues and by the planners and by the continuing cry that they are ivory-tower types. Action has now outstripped theory. In the Lower Manhattan Expressway study, the intent is to suggest what will eventually be feasible. *Prototypical suggestions addressed to existing problems should be made.*

HK: In your Lower Manhattan proposal, you combine many different entities of a city within one structure. You don't want to divide up the life of a city: for every area of function, a different area of buildings. You want to combine it all within the regions of the streets. Today, the only free space left within a city like New York is the streets. Now you are using the street as a building site and multiplying the levels.

PR: Relocation problems for housing have reached astronomical proportions, and we are removing many housing facilities without replacing them. In certain cases, new housing could be built utilizing air rights without relocating anyone. Once the new facilities are in place, the derelict buildings on either side of the megastructure could be removed, creating new open spaces.

JC: The density of the functions in your proposal raises new problems. Sound insulation surely will be difficult. Congestion of people and cars in one megastructure will intensify the air pollution problem. The car will always be present.

PR: Cars would be sometimes over and sometimes under people. The fumes and noise from rapid transit systems have often been made acceptable. Why can't they be for the car, especially if it is placed on tracks in intensively developed urban areas? The automobile will undoubtedly eventually be capable of being run mechanically on tracks, as well as by the individual driver on a throughway.

JC: This is difficult to imagine, living as we are in a Miesian world.

PR: Mies usually thought of the freestanding, complete-within-itself, beautifully proportioned, beautifully detailed building, unconnected to any means of transportation or to other buildings. Indeed, it is an element placed in space, pure, free, a temple. It may be 80 stories high, but, nevertheless, conceptually a temple.

HK: But, when you take the bold step from the temple to the megastructure, how can you possibly pay attention to every detail? Aren't you trapped by the major problem in dealing with such an enormous structure? It is to be 1½ miles long. Don't you lose quality in dealing with such quantity? Large projects always have a tendency toward monotony. The need for variety in human experience is easily forgotten. Megastructure may be opposed to variety because it grows out of a technology which is based on repetition of units.

PR: It depends on the qualities of the architect involved. I regard Le Corbusier's Chandigarh as a project having fantastic variety, being built over a considerable number of years, a large project, not at all monotonous, full of light and vitality. It's basically done by one architect.

HK: First, I don't consider Chandigarh a megastructure. The new city is composed of independent buildings. Le Corbusier assembled his buildings as huge pieces of sculpture, every one a work of art. At the same time, I feel a lack of planning for human needs. There are huge avenues connecting the buildings, but no place for a pedestrian, nothing to protect him from the sun. This might work well in Paris, but not in India.

PR: But the fact is that in Chandigarh the light and function are very much contained within each one of the major buildings, and there is little need for judges to go to the legislative building or the secretariat to the high court building.

HK: Therefore, he connects the different buildings by car; it's a car town.

PR: It's a car town. That's right. I might add that the only way that he could bring Chandigarh into scale with the magnificent mountain range beyond was to leave those great spaces between the buildings. Many people ask why the buildings are so far apart. If one has seen that project, one understands *immediately* why they're so far apart. You approach it and see only the upper parts of the buildings beyond the man-made foothills which he placed in the foreground. Then the mountains are in the background.

HK: Of course, the siting is ideal. One can do anything on virgin land. Le Corbusier's buildings are also temples in a park, great temples. Now you are dealing with New York. You are dealing with long, stretched streets, continuous lines throughout the city.

PR: Oh no, no, no. Its basic organization is the flowing automobile. It becomes a series of curved lines, and then connected from that at right angles come any number of different forms related to what is already there.

JC: Then it is not a unit for a grid plan?

PR: Not at all. It is like a human being, where there's a spine, and off the spine there are arms and legs and hair and all sorts of things [*Fig. 3–16*].

JC: Did you have any examples to work from for this idea?

PR: Oh, gosh, a lot of people have worked on megastructures. The best model I have found is the bridge in Florence.

JC: Ponte Vecchio.

PR: The Ponte Vecchio—the shops along the vehicular way, and over it marvelous housing. The scale of supports is in keeping with the vehicular way, and then there is a working down the scale. There is nothing new. That is a megastructure, and probably the purest example in traditional architecture.

JC: At present, your major model for a megastructure is the Graphic Arts Center.

PR: That is the first time I have put the idea down on paper and made a model.

JC: Looking at your model again, the complex clustering of units is organized around huge supporting trusses.

PR: Right.

JC: And how do the individual units relate to these trusses? How does it work?

PR: The individual units are *lifted* up beside the vertical core, which contains stairs and elevators, and the prefabricated trailer, mobile house, is transported to the site on wheels. The wheels are dismounted, and the unit is lifted up and attached to the tension members. Then the next one is lifted up, then the next, etc., etc.

JC: Now, these horizontal trusses . . .

PR: They are structural. They are literally sky hooks, if you will. The space in between them we have utilized as a playground in the air.

JC: You have a playground on every level?

PR: No, every tenth level.

JC: That means that the horizontal trusses are a structural necessity; but then you turn them into playgrounds as well.

PR: Yes, because you have that space. At every tenth floor, there is a horizontal truss. The individual units are suspended from those horizontal trusses. They literally hang; it's a hanging city. From a structural viewpoint, it wouldn't make much sense to carry all the loads up to the top just to be brought down again. Statically, it would not be an efficient way of doing it.

JC: The whole structure allows you the possibility to arrange the different units freely in between the trusses. You have great freedom to compose shapes within the given rigid skeleton.

PR: This is the great play. This is what makes it worth doing.

JC: It appears at the first glance to be a very arbitrary arrangement.

PR: It's not arbitrary, ultimately. The vertical is utilized for transportation, elevators, and stairs. It is basically a hollow tube, a very strong column, and it is in scale with the new cityscape. The actual *structural* columns become so small that they do not read from a distance. But the mechanical cores *are* large enough to read from a great distance. It has to do with scale. The whole idea of suspension is also efficient if you divide it into relatively small segments. We have determined with engineers that roughly ten floors between each horizontal truss is most efficient. It also happens that ten floors allows a relatively small grouping of people who can focus on playgrounds or restaurants or other facilities. Then one has to crossbrace against the winds. You will notice in the plan that the Graphic Arts Center is staggered. So the basic backbone could not be more logical or rational. Now, within that framework, there is great freedom of placement of the elements, almost playful.

JC: That freedom allows you to achieve an interesting and dramatic visual image.

PR: Variety. Visual excitement. Better orientation. A terrace for everybody.

3–16. Spine plan for Lower Manhattan. New York. 1967.

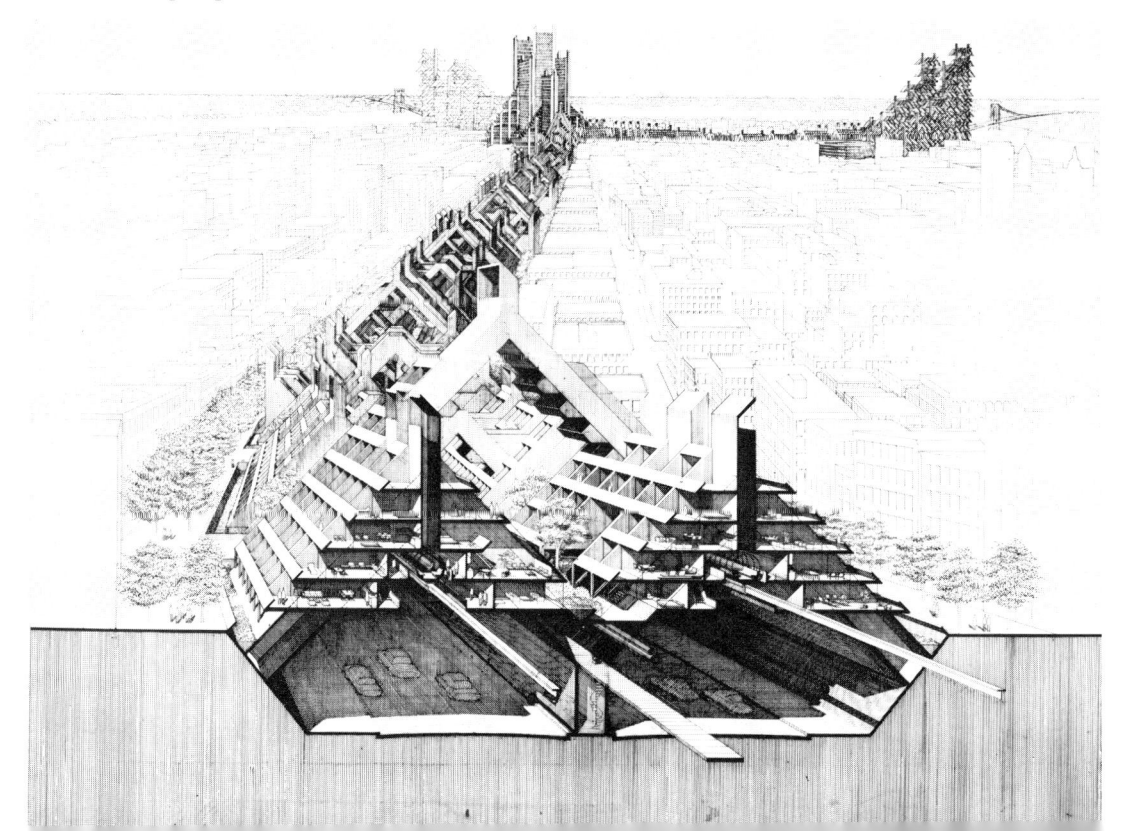

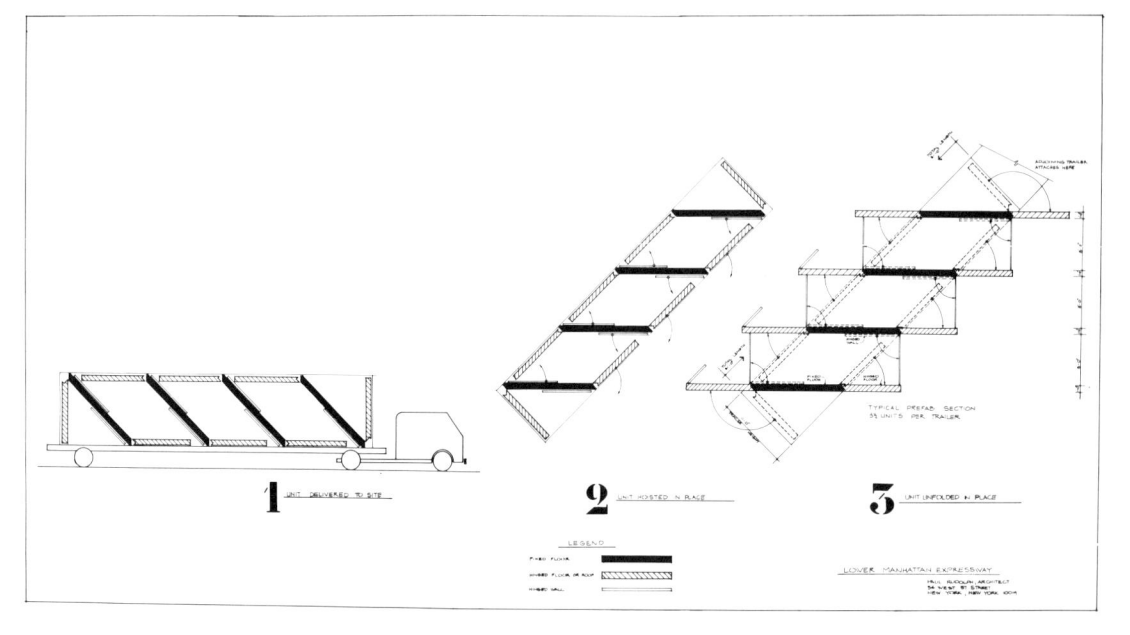

3–17. Graphic Arts Center. Module design with fold-out walls. 1967.

JC: Why wasn't it ever built?

PR: The labor unions killed it. You see, the use of prefabrication, large-scale three-dimensional prefabrication, was contrary to their interests.

HK: Considering the European scene, it is very surprising to see such a progressive project defeated by the labor unions. In the U.S.A., the labor unions want to preserve the traditional construction method, which insures higher wages and local production. This is one of the dark corners of the capitalist system in the U.S.A.

PR: For a hundred years now, prefabrication has been considered all over the world. Today it is not very far advanced, mainly because of the built-in interests of the individual labor unions. That is currently being broken down, partially because of the policies of the federal government, partially because of the ever-increasing inflation, and partially because there is so much need for additional housing. Now, the concept of prefabrication can take many different forms. But, in my opinion, the important thing is that it be large-scale three-dimensional elements which have heating, plumbing, ventilating, electricity, all in one package. The structure is only about 20 per cent of the total, whereas the mechanical systems become easily 40 to 45 per cent of the total. With earlier systems, the single wall panel entailed a great amount of on-site work and a great amount of mechanical assistance, not really a great step beyond bricklaying. There needs to be much more *pre*fabrication.

HK: There seem to be some similarities between your proposal and the British "plug-in" city idea.

PR: Yes.

HK: However, yours is closer to reality.

PR: This is based on the existing mobile house industry in the United States. Roughly a third of the new housing in recent years has been the mobile house: the trailer. That is a fact. The large-scale three-dimensional prefabricated structure is here. Architects and engineers have tended to ignore it, because they regard it as not having any possibilities, but out of the mobile housing movement will grow a "module" movement which already has profound meaning. You see, Habitat in Montreal is marvelous, but no one can afford it, really. Eventually, its equivalent will be constructed of lightweight modules, the offspring of the mobile house.

HK: The "plug-in" city also uses prefabricated box units, plugged into an existing core. To me, it seems to be rather naïve to think that people will want to live in a little module, in a space capsule. The "house" becomes a consumer item which can be discarded like an old car.

PR: There is one misconception in this comparison. The prefabricated units in the Graphic Arts Center are not mobile once they are hung on. It is too expensive to remove them. The mechanical systems are far too elaborate. I don't understand the argument about a family being dissatisfied with modules, because the modules can be interconnected, the ceiling height changed, and spatial variety achieved that is limited only by the human imagination.

One has to get around possible social stigma of the module. Someone should build *the* most expensive apartment house in America with modules. It's like the small car. It wasn't until very expensive small cars were made for the rich that everyone else felt all right about driving a small car.

HK: You may be able to have many bedrooms, but you cannot have one large space.

PR: No. In the Graphic Arts Center, you start out with a 12-foot width. That is the maximum you can ship down the road. But, if you will note that the walls fold out [*Fig. 3–17*], you can get a 24-foot width, which is considerably wider than most spaces in current apartment buildings. Also, if you can fold out the walls, you can fold up the ceiling, and fold down the floor, thereby gaining a fantastic variety of ceiling heights. This will lead eventually to an "unfolding" architecture.

HK: That's very fascinating. The first realization of that idea will probably be the Oriental Masonic Gardens in New Haven where you use similar units [*Fig. 3–18*].

PR: Unfortunately, they do not fold. We are stuck with the 12-foot module there.

HK: They do not fold?

PR: No.

HK: That means you are pinned down to . . .

PR: Twelve feet, which is something of a limitation.

HK: So the width is fixed but not the length.

PR: Sixty feet is the maximum length allowed in most states.

HK: So it's a tunnel!

JC: In low-cost public housing, you seem to have sacrificed your desire to create exciting interior spaces. On the one hand you have the restricted space of modular housing, and on the other hand in some of your campus buildings, you have those marvelous vertical and spiraling spaces. These seem to be opposing ideas.

PR: I've never thought there should

3–18. Oriental Masonic Gardens Apartments. New Haven, Conn. 1968. Paul Rudolph.

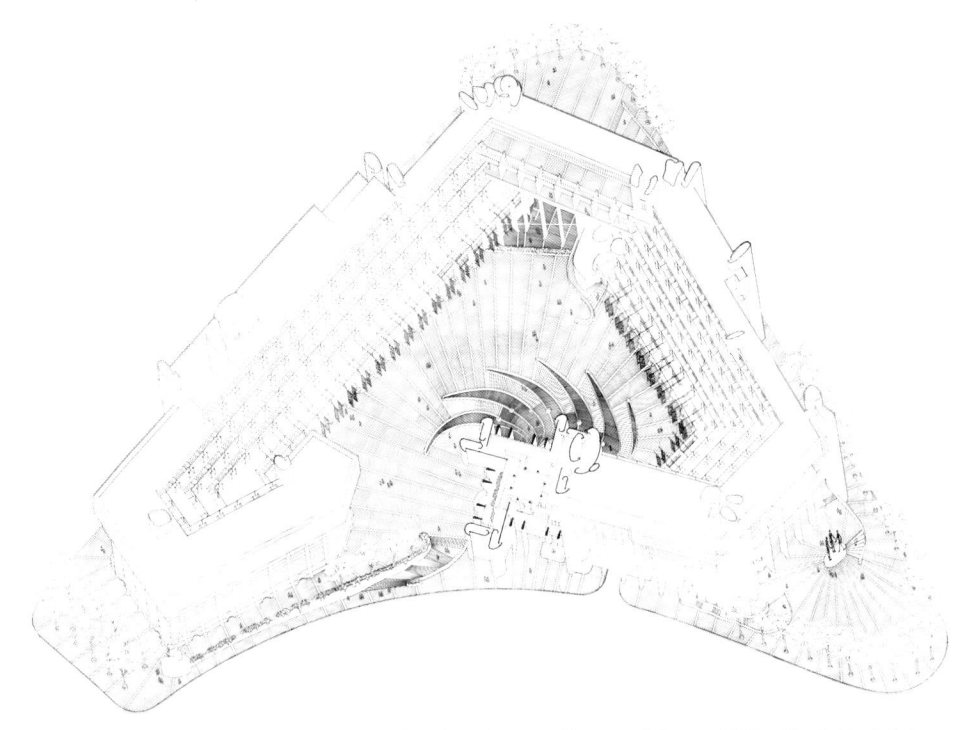

3–19. Model for Boston Government Service Center. Boston, Mass. 1962. Paul Rudolph, co-ordinating architect.

only be two ideas with regard to architecture. I would like to think that I had more than two. The point is that there needs to be a hierarchy of building types. For centuries, the building types at the head of the hierarchy were religious buildings and governmental buildings, gateways to the city, and institutional buildings. In terms of sheer volume, religious building is no longer at the top of the heap. Commercial buildings of all kinds, and housing, are much vaster than religious buildings. This has upset the hierarchy of building types. To make dominant a small building whose social function is high on the hierarchy of building types is an architectural problem of the first magnitude.

JC: For instance, the church wouldn't get lost within the Graphic Arts Center.

PR: From a distance, it would be difficult to find it, but, for its particular community, it would be prominent. The cohesion of the whole and the relationships of building types to each other remain endlessly fascinating. In public buildings, obviously, there is a difference of scale and different environmental demands. Psychologically, it's another ball game. Misplaced monumentality is often confused with scale. If one is interested in the cohesion of various building types, to make clear the environment, then the most important tool of the architects is the manipulation of scale, which has little to do with size. Of course, I'm anti-Mies. For him, an office building can look like an apartment building. A chapel could be the reception room for a factory. I am completely against that. The flexibility needed in an office building must be manifest, as opposed to the need for a series of relatively small, isolated, and private facilities for housing. The free-flowing space doesn't work for housing, for acoustical reasons, not to mention privacy. The difference between housing and office building should be absolutely clear inside and outside. I'm against the notion that loft-type buildings provide universal space, good for almost anything. The proportion of small rooms versus large rooms cannot be resolved in such buildings.

HK: Would you consider it important to make a visual difference between two kinds of office buildings, like an insurance company on the one hand, a government building on the other?

PR: Oh, yes. The Boston Government Center [*Fig. 3–19*] shows that very clearly. It is basically a series of offices and a mental health hospital. The Boston Government Center deals with a heightening of the scale around the perimeter and a diminishing of the scale at the courtyard. The perimeter at the street is large: The pedestrian interior courtyard terraces are scaled down. The use determines the scale as well as its place in the cityscape.

HK: But it goes beyond that. Not only the *use* determines the scale, but the fact that it is a governmental institution. *Architecture parlant!*

PR: What does that mean?

HK: It means to attribute to a building a symbolic language. It is the attempt to make a building "speak out" not only its function but also its meaning.

PR: I'm all for that.

JC: You think a church should look like a church?

PR: Oh, yes.

HK: But a church *could* look like a bunker. There is no established language of architectural meanings. But the problem is that when an architect today attempts to use architectural language, he merely goes back to the clichés of the past. The result is most often a traditional expression. "Government Center"—we immediately associate power and authority with it. The architectural result is quite frequently an impressive temple in the cityscape. Isn't it necessary nowadays to rethink what government is, before we illustrate it architecturally? Remember, for instance, the newly constructed police station in Boston near your Center [*Fig. 3–20*]. It has dark brown rusticated stone walls with very small windows high up. It has a fortresslike entrance. In short, it almost looks like a castle. The building creates an inappropriate and frightening image. Is that what society and the police need?

PR: I agree that new meanings in the cityscape must be found for the twentieth century, but associations of the past do not immediately fade away. In a sense, meanings are given to architecture after

3–20. Boston Police Station, Precinct 1, Boston, Mass. 1966. Shepley, Bulfinch, Richardson, and Abbott, architects.

the fact. Thus, the Washington Monument is associated with the "Father of our Country" after it was built, not before. Religious buildings are probably the most difficult of all, because religion itself is being thought of in so many different ways. In any event, one cannot make everything bland. The richness and variety of life must be celebrated.

HK: How would *you* build a police station? What value would you emphasize in their building?

PR: I would hide the police within my megastructure.

HK: Like the post office?

PR: The post office is still a social entity where people often go. My real point is that blandness and uniformity are creeping in on all sides, and there's no character left.

JC: But when you try to establish character or symbolism, you must call forth some standards. Do you look back into history for models of how the church, how the post office, should look? What vocabulary do you use?

PR: The principles of architecture don't change. It's only the means of carrying them out which change. The idea of scale and emphasis hasn't really changed. The human eye hasn't really changed. The reaction of the human being does change because of connotations. You cannot get away from the fact that we are born with images in our minds.

HK: But attitudes change. Around 1900, Mr. Vanderbilt and Mr. Frick wanted to have palaces in the middle of New York. Today, a millionaire hides himself in an apartment building. He doesn't want to be identified. In the same way, the attitude toward the government might change.

PR: It's true. One agrees with that, and my own feeling that differences should be emphasized and made more apparent is perhaps an overreaction to the uniformity which is around us. However, the idea of flexibility and anticipation of the future leads to blandness. One cannot escape one's time, but if a building has true vitality varying uses can often be accommodated. The result is a rich juxtaposition of the new and the once-new building. This "double reading" of an environment is very clear in great European cities.

HK: Your primary concern is to get character and variety back into the city.

PR: That is right. This may be so counter to the times that it ends up being merely picturesqueness.

HK: In this respect, Philip Johnson is one of the best examples. He was the closest disciple of Mies, but then he discarded the uniformity of the Miesian box, seeking a new variety and expressiveness. The result is an eclectic traditionalism. Take, for instance, the colonnade of the Kline Biology Tower [*see Fig. 1–4*] or the temple front of the New York State Theater [*see Fig. 1–23*]. He uses an architectural vocabulary of past times, which is worn out.

The architect, nowadays, is in a very new situation, where the identity between meaning and form must be reexamined. Do you know what happened in New Haven when the atomic alarm went off accidentally? People rushed into Kevin Roche's high school building, recognizing it as a shelter. Today, we are in a situation where architectural language is ambiguous and garbled.

JC: When you talk about giving the city back its character, doesn't that really mean that you want to dominate the city with your buildings? You said you want your buildings to dominate.

PR: Did I say I wanted to dominate?

JC: Yes.

PR: Dominate what?

JC: You mentioned that you want to relate your buildings to others, and yet you intend for yours to be dominant.

PR: Well, I didn't say quite what I meant then, because there should be background buildings.

HK: Yes, you did differentiate between

background and foreground buildings. However, you would rather build a foreground building.

PR: Yes. It's easier.

HK: Do you mean that building background buildings, that is, to remain modest, is difficult?

PR: Yes, it really is. No doubt about it. But I'm sorry if I conveyed the notion that I always want to dominate the situation. It's been said of the parking garage in New Haven [*Fig. 3–21*] that it should be very far down in the hierarchy of building types. After all, "it's just a parking garage." My response to that is, "Yes, it does dominate what is there." I would admit that. But if they would let me build on the other side of the street, I could very quickly and easily dominate that parking garage, I assure you. It's a question of which key one chooses to play in.

HK: You mean that, instead of that parking garage, you could have built just another boring building, and it wouldn't dominate. It could have been entirely overlooked.

PR: When the New Haven parking garage was being constructed, the remainder of the buildings in the adjacent blocks was not determined. They should have been designed to dominate the parking garage, but I don't see that they were.

JC: Your parking garage is certainly not an anonymous service building, which normally destroys the character of cities. Yours adds to the character of the city and plays an important role within the organization of the urban center. You have achieved that vitality by giving it plasticity, unusual proportions, stretched segmental arches, and dramatic balustrades. A rhythmic relief of alternating panels catches the eye.

PR: The parking garage is a peculiar twentieth-century phenomenon. The one in New Haven comes from the design of throughways. Most parking garages are merely skeletal structures which didn't get any walls. They are just office building structures with the glass left out. I wanted to make a building which said it dealt with cars and movement. I wanted there to be no doubt that this is a parking garage.

HK: Giving character to a building means more than meeting the functional demands. The treatment of your balustrades becomes "ornamental." One could call that a kind of aesthetic formalism.

PR: Well, let's face it. There's always a formal aesthetic involved.

HK: That's what I want to hear. Why

3–21. Temple Street Parking Garage. New Haven, Conn. 1962. Paul Rudolph.

do architects always deny it? They are still under the influence of the Bauhaus tradition. Everyone claims to do the "appropriate," just as you did earlier in this interview. In modern architecture, being "appropriate" means being "functional." However, how do you achieve "character"? You achieve character through the treatment of the façade. For instance, those balustrades serve a need, but they are arranged in such an interesting way that they become an ornament at the same time.

PR: I would use the word "ornament" differently. For me, the word "formalism" probably is a better one. There are certain formal characteristics in every project I work on. It is the intuitive at work. I would never say that it was sheer functionalism. It is nonsense to say that architecture is all based on engineering or program. It is also an art. Now, how do you arrive at the formalism involved? I'm not sure I can answer

3–22. Crawford Manor, Housing for the Elderly. New Haven, Conn. 1962–66. Paul Rudolph.

that. There are worlds which must be explored; one can never know.

JC: When one steps beyond sheer functionalism, he is in another realm of decision-making. At this level, results may appear arbitrary. It becomes a question of "designing." Your balustrades, for instance, could have been entirely different. Why did you design them this particular way?

PR: I could tell you that the design of the balustrades has to do with the nature of materials which, in this case, is poured-in-place concrete which, of course, is very plastic and can take any form. One of the fascinating things about poured-in-place concrete is the fact that its characteristics are modified by the material in which it is formed, in this case wood. The juxtaposition of these materials, where only one is shown and the other implied, has a peculiar fascination for me. For instance, wood can easily be used to form two-dimensional curves, but concrete will easily fill three-dimensional curves. In this case, the wood was the determinant. In other words, the balustrade design had to do with the nature of materials, but this is a simplistic answer.

JC: Then the question arises, the poured-in-place concrete balustrade could have been one long, unbroken, shooting wall, the full length of the structure.

PR: Yes, that is true. First of all, the reason for the offsets is that the expansion and contraction of the structure necessitated many joints. Secondly, the doubling of the columns allows them to read as a single column from a great distance, thereby "jumping the scale." The extension of the balustrades at the double columns emphasizes the vertical definition of space, so that, when looking diagonally down the street, as one is forced to do because of the narrowness of the street, one doesn't just see the horizontal, sweeping down the street, but the eye is caught at every double column. In this way, the relationship of the horizontal to the vertical is emphasized. Is that arbitrary? The buildings on the other

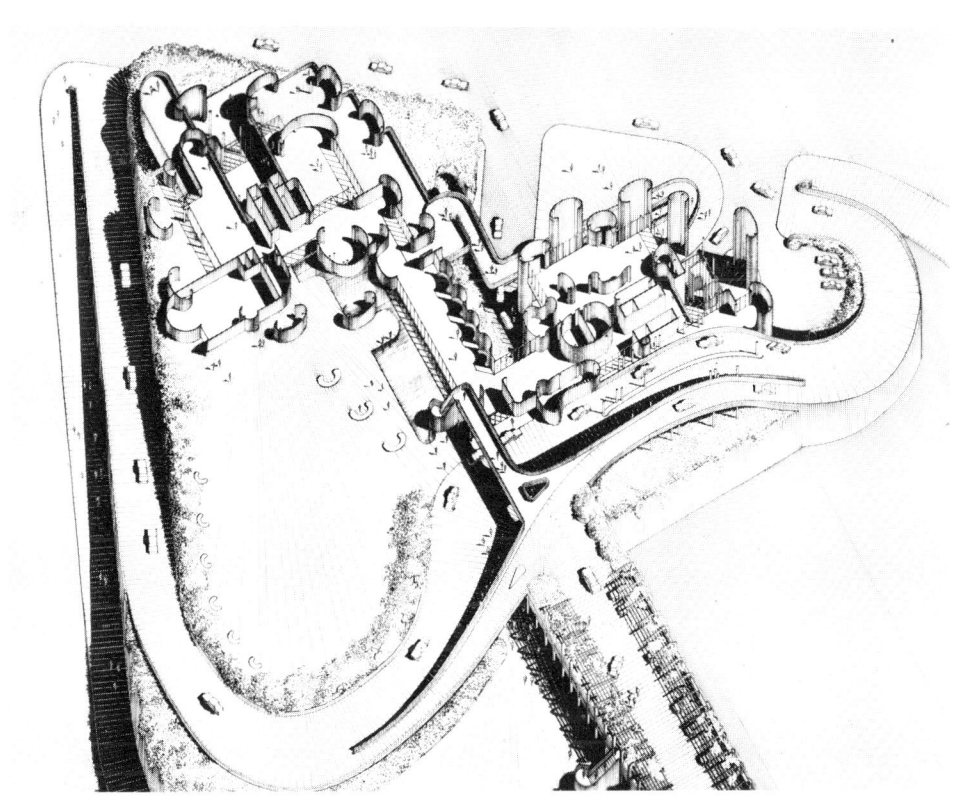

3-23. Tracey Towers. Bronx, New York. 1967. Paul Rudolph. Plan.

side of the street are valid in function and scale. For my building to react in any way with them, I had to punctuate vertically the 800-foot-long balustrades. I could go on and on and give an explanation of why each element is as it is, but one could never, finally, arrive at the real truth, because that is on deeply subconscious multilevels, many of which I am not aware of myself. It is simply that which makes each man different.

JC: You take the technical requirements and achieve visual excitement.

PR: It is neither a purely engineering solution nor an arbitrary one.

JC: A similar question arises in respect to your Crawford Manor [*Fig. 3–22*] in New Haven, especially in relation to the balconies. They certainly are not purely functional; they create a lively sculptural silhouette.

PR: Those balconies in the Crawford Manor are an alternation of thrusts, one out from the building and one parallel to it, in order to emphasize the essential organization of the building. If all of the balconies thrust forward, then the result from a distant view would be a kind of shaft. But, by making the thrusts of the balconies oppose each other, one senses the cubicle nature of the interior.

HK: This raises the question about structure. The ground plan of Crawford Manor is very loosely organized, a grouping of shaft units. It reflects the organization of the A and A Building, but tightened up and stretched into the vertical. A similar planning method is carried on in the tower of the Boston Government Center [*Fig. 3–19*] and in your Tracey Towers [*Fig. 3–23*]. These three towers have a strong relationship to each other, referring back to some of the design principles in the Art and Architecture Building. This, by the way, indicates the importance of the A and A Building in the whole development of your architectural language. In that process, the Crawford Manor still has those rectangular hard-edged shafts, although into that plan you introduce the rounded corners of the elevator and stairway cores. Finally, the Tracey Towers seem to consist entirely of curved walls. Looking at the ground plan, one gets the impression that they are self-bearing vertical shells. However, this result seems to have grown more out of formalistic concerns than any other.

PR: In Tracey Towers, the exterior walls are not curved for structural reasons at all, but because the site plan and traffic movement dictated an easing of the corners. They are also curved in order to lead the eye around the towers, thereby emphasizing their three-dimensionality. They are also curved because they give a heightened sense of security to the occupants of a very high building, and one looks out and sees these walls, which seem like huge columns, closely rising from the ground. However, they are not columns, but walls, but they are read as columns, which is as intended for psychological reasons.

The geometry of the car is curvilinear and is, in this case, related to the rectilinear organization of the building itself. It is the result of two dissimilar elements coming together.

JC: The movement of the car directly influences the shape of the walls.

PR: That's right.

JC: Mendelsohn's idea!

PR: Yes, I know. Nothing new. The tension between the automobile access and the building is fascinating. I am not terribly sympathetic with free-standing towers, which these, of course, are, but, to a large degree, the economics of the situation prevented us from building on the 1000-foot-long deck which covers the railroad tracks. These towers are placed at the end of the tracks in order to avoid them.

The owner wanted two round towers, but I felt that the resultant pie-shaped rooms were unlivable and, therefore, joined the geometry of rectilinear rooms inside with the feeling of two round towers.

HK: And he wanted to have pie-shaped rooms?

PR: Well, that wasn't of primary interest to him, but he loved the idea of the round towers. One should not be defeated by such notions, so I said to myself, "It's ridiculous to have pie-shaped rooms. Who can live in them?"

HK: Why not?

PR: Because the human being wants to live in easily definable, safe forms and shapes.

HK: He needs the four corners?

PR: Well, too much irregularity would be unsettling in day-to-day living. One cannot comprehend the pie-shape so readily. I can't quite put my finger on it. You could say something like, "Well, new rugs don't come pie-shaped." Have them cut! It is somehow alien to an appropriate sense of space.

HK: Isn't it just that we are not used to them?

PR: That isn't it. That's part of it. It's not the whole thing. The only thing I can tell you is that instinctively I don't want to have pie-shaped rooms. Now I must think more about why.

HK: But you yourself don't build plain square rooms.

PR: I am very much interested in the free plan, of course.

HK: Well, when it comes to housing, how can you keep the free plan?

PR: The free plan is very difficult in housing because of the need for private space. It is easier to achieve free-flowing space vertically than horizontally.

HK: Here again, you emphasize the visual experience.

PR: Well, always. It can never be *just* the visual experience, but there are at least fifteen others. In this case, the formal organization is such that the solids always read as curved elements and the voids of glass read as flat elements. Thus, the play of light between the round and the flat, and the different way the two materials catch the light, is brought together.

HK: The curved shell wall potentially could be a self-supporting structural element, as in Bertrand Goldberg's Hilliard Center [see Fig. 4–14].

PR: The curved shell concept would necessitate a poured-in-place concrete structural system which would have been much more expensive than the column with masonry infilling walls (in this case a special concrete block) which is, in fact, used.

HK: But aren't you wasting a possibility, a structural possibility?

PR: The central core takes all the wind loads, and the least expensive way to build apartment houses in the New York area is with a flat slab supported on relatively closely spaced columns.

HK: That means that the shape of the outer walls is independent from structural concerns.

PR: That is right.

HK: So you don't need the outer walls for the supporting of the building?

PR: You do not need the outer walls for supporting the building, but you need them vitally for psychological reasons of the inhabitants.

HK: Now, you are very different from Bertrand Goldberg. The Round Towers of the Hilliard Center at Chicago consist of curved shell walls which are self-bearing. They are not only outer façades, but they are at the same time the structure. So there is no distinction any more between an inner core and outside supported walls. It is all one.

PR: I do not believe that is the way those Towers are built.

HK: Yes, they are "deformed" shells, which provide enormous strength. It's a new structural idea, and it saves a lot of money.

PR: The economics of what can be done in one area are different from what can be done in another. We would not be building Tracey Towers today if it were based on the shell principle.

HK: So, you keep that freedom for the outer wall in order to play with a façade. Is that too strong?

JC: Are you frank enough to admit that you play with the façade? That would be of major importance.

PR: (Laughs) Only time will tell.

JC: We would be beyond the moralistic condemnation of the façade.

PR: I know, I know. Let's see how I can express this. The actual structural members of this tower are so small that they would never read from a distance. It is, therefore, necessary to introduce a wall joining two structural members which, therefore, symbolically suggest security. If you should expose the actual structural members, you would not have the *apparent* sense of structure, but only two small columns, which would not be reassuring enough.

JC: That means you exaggerate the support. You overdo it in order to make it visible.

PR: Exactly. The architectural problems of a tall building are unique, and we don't really know very much about them. You see, Mies knew all about this.

JC: Sullivan even more so. He exaggerated the supports by covering the skeleton with enormous pilasters.

PR: Yes, Sullivan also. Mies knew perfectly well that his thin columns would not give the sense of security necessary in a tall building, so he introduced as a symbol for the column his famous H mullions, which allowed the curtain wall to be so continuous that it finally read as a monolith.

JC: That is true, but his beam stays a beam. Nothing is added to it but the H profile. Is that decoration?

PR: You know it is. You can talk about the purity of Mies's structure till the cows come home. It's not pure. It rises far above that. Well, in my own way, I try to do the same thing.

4 BERTRAND GOLDBERG

HK: Mr. Goldberg, after seeing Marina City and the Hilliard Center here in Chicago, we wonder why you are not among those who take a permanent place in the history books of twentieth-century architecture, like Philip Johnson and Louis Kahn.

BG: Well, I wonder if there aren't several others who are not included. Mostly, the books seem to be written about our coastline architects.

HK: It's surprising to us because of the famous tradition of the Chicago School; after all, Le Baron Jenney, Sullivan, Wright, and Mies worked here. To us, it seems this tradition has not been interrupted. In fact, we believe that your buildings are among the very few which offer new possibilities and solutions for high-rise building, not only structurally, but also socially.

BG: Chicago architecture has always revealed its new architectural forms by use of innovative engineering. Too often, Chicago is wrongly regarded as the home of the post and beam.

HK: How do you relate your work to the Chicago School tradition? The standard work on the history of Chicago architecture, by Carl W. Condit, gives you a voluptuous description. He says your work is "a stunning exhibition of the unparalleled and inexhaustible power in the city's great building tradition."*

BG: I have to wonder about being placed in the Chicago School, because my general relationship to it has been one of reaction against its present development. My apprenticeship was in the Chicago School, of course, and I studied with Mies at the German Bauhaus. But my architecture is certainly not a natural extension of the present ideas in the Chicago School or the Bauhaus.

HK: Would you agree to Condit's observation that your Marina City Towers are structurally similar to Wright's Johnson Wax Company Research Tower at Racine, Wisconsin? Condit also says, "its [the Johnson Tower's] astonishing possibilities have so far been most thoroughly exploited in Bertrand Goldberg's Marina City project."

BG: I would not agree. My work grows out of an entirely different rationale. There may be some similarities which one could observe *post festum*. It's the historian's game.

JC: But you knew Frank Lloyd Wright.

BG: Yes, I knew him. When Mies first came to this country, I had the opportunity to be the translator between Wright and Mies.

JC: How did Frank Lloyd Wright react when he met Mies van der Rohe the first time?

BG: Very well, because at that time Wright had tremendous respect for Mies, and Mies had tremendous respect for Wright's work. There has been a rather close relationship between German and Chicago architecture. Condit's book has a great deal to say about the German origins of the Chicago School and vice versa. There has always been this link, so both men had tremendous respect for each other. But there was no question as to which one regarded himself as the leader: Wright felt as if he were receiving his disciple.

JC: Did Mies accept that?

BG: Mies was very interested and tolerant and very well-mannered. But Mies didn't accept Wright's dominance, and Wright became furious with him and his New York show [Museum of Modern Art, 1950]. There was one remark about that show which I shall never forget, and which characterizes the profound difference between the two. Klaus Grabe, an old friend from the Bauhaus and a well-known furniture designer in New York, said, "When I look at a Mies plan I can imagine the building, I know what the building will look like. When I look at a Frank Lloyd Wright plan, I never know what the building will look like."

JC: In which of these positions are you?

BG: I think, really, that when one looks at my plans he should know what the building looks like. I think that, in a time of industrialization, a plan should carry this kind of communication. Much of the East Coast architecture today does not. I think to this extent it is a throwback to Beaux Arts architecture.

JC: What about the TWA Building by Saarinen [see Fig 5–10], which cannot be understood by looking at the plan, but has to be experienced as a kind of monumental sculpture?

BG: I cannot accept it as an industrial or a contemporary form.

JC: Don't you feel there is room for both? Must it be either exclusively?

BG: You are asking me to be an architectural critic. Actually, I'm an architect,

---

* Carl W. Condit, *The Chicago School of Architecture,* Chicago, 1964, p. 219.

and I have pledged my architectural statement in one direction. And all the work which I do lies in that direction.

HK: Your Marina City Towers appear to be extraordinarily monumental [*Fig. 4–1*].

BG: Not by primary intention, but if this is the kind of monument which you are willing to recognize, a monument of rationality, ecology, and industrialization, which goes through a creative process and ends up with new forms, then the forms themselves which result from this process create the monument. Self-conscious monumentality is what becomes archaic. When we have finished planning the space of a building in these newly emerging forms, we say that the building is now inevitable; we no longer have any control over the design. There's only one way to build it because we have run over all the alternatives. I think that these buildings include a new system of aesthetic judgment. And I am discouraged by the attitude which has been exhibited toward these buildings as their being a *tour de force*.

HK: An aesthetic *tour de force?*

BG: Yes. I am working with one client who is staffed by his own architects; house architects. They cannot understand that the forms which we bring to them, that are unfamiliar to them, are not just arbitrary and whimsical developments of spatial arrangements.

HK: Up till now, a skyscraper usually had to be square or rectangular. At first sight, your buildings seem to be a pure reaction against that. You make them round. And when I see this picture here on the wall of your office showing a cluster of round Babylonian towers, I imagine that you may have a whimsical attraction to these shapes. But after understanding the design of Marina City Towers, one can discern two major ideas in it: the first is a structural solution and the second is a psychosociological answer to human needs.

BG: Yes. I would rather restate this by saying environment is a primary part of the architectural design and eventuates its own structure. In the Marina City Towers, the environment is optimal for the family without children. I did not replicate it in the Hilliard Center apartments [*Fig. 4–2*] where it was much more important to establish the individual identity of each family with children. In other words, I definitely have tried *not* to reduce all solutions for family life down to one fundamental spatial method.

JC: The variety you achieve is not for the sake of exciting forms, but grows out of meeting sociological needs.

BG: Exactly. And what are the results? Compare Hilliard housing with conventional planning. You know the Robert Taylor Housing on South State Street? That is the most depressing social statement that this country has ever made! There are 7,000 dwelling units almost identical, which are simply storage places for people. Now, we are asked, because of the tre-

4–1. Marina City Towers. Chicago, Ill. 1960. Bertrand Goldberg.

4–2. Raymond Hilliard Center. Chicago, Ill. 1963. Bertrand Goldberg. Left: Housing units for the elderly. Right: Family housing units.

mendous opposition which had been growing to this kind of public housing, to design a public housing project for about 750 units which would combine a total society. So we said we'd have an elderly society combined with a younger family society.

JC: No separation of ages, but a combination.

BG: A combination, which we feel is infinitely more important as time goes on, simply because our definition of elderly is changing so rapidly. But the results have been that whereas the 7,000 Robert Taylor units are solidly black, our units have kept a 50-50 white-black occupancy in *exactly* the same neighborhood where many people are walking at the risk of their lives

JC: Does it happen to be that way or is the 50-50 relation planned?

BG: The balance has always been planned in every public housing project, but it has never been achieved: There was no reason for whites to live in this sort of housing when they could find the same public housing in a white neighborhood. The Robert Taylor Housing started out seeking to maintain a 50-50 ratio. Today, there are very few whites left. A white child is subject to murder and knifing and extortion—it's jungle warfare. It is extraordinary that in the Hilliard Center, where we began with the same social makeup in the same neighborhood, this did not happen. It certainly has something to do with the architecture.

But, before I go further into the sociological aspect, I first have to tell you more about the structure of the building. The two towers for the elderly [*Fig. 4–3*] are constructed entirely out of concrete shells instead of a structural central core which then braces a surrounding post and beam structure [the Marina City structure]. I developed a bearing shell structure for the Hilliard Center which does not need a central core [*Fig. 4–4*]. Let me simplify: If you bend a wall into a semicircle, it becomes stronger and will stand by itself; if you stand many semicircular walls together in a circle, the construction becomes very strong and it stands up by itself. This is the primary structural principle of the Hilliard Towers and, of course, it affects the spaces. I was trying to achieve optimal structure and living space within one shell form. To illustrate this, I could give you many examples from nature, one of the best of which is the clam shell; it gains

4–3. Raymond Hilliard Center. Tower. Housing units for the elderly.

strength and gives space by being cup-shaped or deformed. We deform material to achieve strength and space—which is, of course, quite common in modern industrialization: think of the body of a Volkswagen.

We start design in our projects with what might be called a Detroit approach to industrialization rather than a turn-of-the-century approach. What I am saying here is that industrialization in the nineteenth century meant straight-line production. A machine was used for a single operation, repeated it endlessly, and resulted in what we call straight-line production: This is no longer modern industrialization.

The nineteenth-century industrialization mechanically duplicated the leverage methods of the human body, but contemporary industrialization *transforms* the nature of material through the machine. In contemporary industrial design, through deformation of the molecular structure of steel we are able to build lighter automobiles. Or we take cast material and we spin it and we make it denser; or we take an ingot of steel and we explode it into shapes that have heretofore been impossible. So we literally transform the *nature* of material by industrialization.

Now, this is *not* part of the post and beam tradition. The post and beam structure of the present Chicago School is still the old Victorian process of straight-line production. Much of architecture today continues to ignore the possibilities of transforming the use of the materials like reinforced concrete—architects continue to use concrete as if it were wooden logs. The transformation of material by change of shape has never been applied to architecture until now.

Our shell structure of the Hilliard Center can be built in slip-form concrete; this is made by a moving form which builds concrete at the rate of about 1 foot an hour. The movements of construction never change the form, never change its position related to an axis. The building simply moves vertically on a machine, and steel reinforcing is inserted as the form slips along. This method changes the whole industrial organization of concrete forming. The circular shell structure of the Hilliard Towers was designed for slip-form concrete and produces petal-shaped rooms [*Fig. 4–4*].

Because of the strict government regulations, the apartment plan for the elderly was limited to two rooms only. In the plan, you will notice two small petals next to larger petals. Or seen another way, we have two bedroom petals between two living room petals; then one apartment is made from combining one large with one small petal.

These spaces come together in a functional relationship which is able to develop freely, because there's no restrictive structural center. There is no core any more. The core as we had it in Marina City is no longer essential [*Fig. 4–5*]. Here, I have moved my structure to the exterior wall, where I can get much more rigidity for much less investment in material. Now I have a spatial core; now the center is space —not structure. In that space, you find what is usual in a service core, a stairway, an elevator, utilities, and a garbage chute. But there is still enough space left for community space, which the elderly people especially need. They have a much greater sense of communication, and I felt that they should have a space for meetings, for coffee klatches, and sewing circles.

JC: So almost every story has its own community room?

BG: Yes, and, if possible, you would furnish it with some simple furniture, television sets—have a library where everybody would pool his books. We tried to get all that and couldn't. We were lucky enough just to get the buildings. It took me *two years* of fighting with our federal government in Washington to permit me to build this. First of all, they said it would be too expensive. I said we would take the risk. If it is too expensive, don't pay me for my architecture. Then they said, "It's too good for these people."

JC: Literally?

BG: *Literally*. They told me that I was designing things that were too good for the poor. That is very Anglo-Saxon Protestant. That is punishing the poor because they have not been thrifty.

JC: Did they think they were too good because of the budget or because of the actual physical result?

BG: The physical result.

JC: You mean you could spend less money, but if the result were better, then it was bad?

BG: It was bad because such housing would make the people satisfied with being poor, you see. If you have pleasant surroundings, then there is no longer the need to move up in the economic hierarchy.

JC: Even for the elderly?

BG: *Even* for the elderly poor, but *particularly* for the family poor, because I did something greater for the family poor which I'll tell you about later. When I started the design, I discovered that since this project is federal housing, there were strict room area limits for both types of poor. So, when I made the design for the elderly, I said, "Let's start with where they are going to sleep and draw the bed." Then I reasoned further that the only place these people can find or afford living privacy is also in their bedrooms. So I made privacy possible with the same 120 square feet

4-4. Hilliard Center. Tower ground plan.

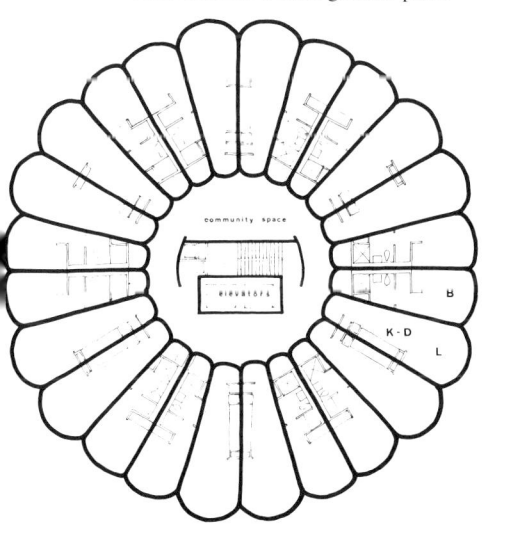

4-5. Marina City Towers. Tower ground plan.

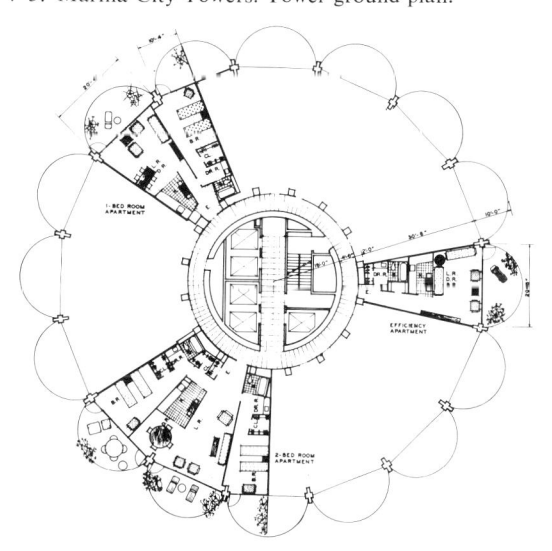

which we're allowed for a bedroom by the federal government: I made it possible by changing the shape of the bedroom from the conventional rectangle to another form, to have room for a desk and a chair, as well as a bed. And then I designed a larger petal-shaped room as the living room and combined it with the kitchen and closet designed as items of furniture.

HK: Mr. Goldberg, before we go into further detail, let's stay awhile with the structural problems you have solved. A young architect made the ironic statement recently that what twentieth-century architecture really does is decorate elevator shafts. What he was describing, of course, is the present-day high-rise building. The elevator shaft has become the module around which the whole building is constructed. But what you have done is a contradiction to this statement.

BG: Yes. What I have shown you is a structural pattern of enclosing walls. Our design has no columns, it has no beams, it has nothing in it other than space for people. The support structure is just the spatial envelope.

HK: And it carries everything. By forming walls in a certain way, they get a new static rigidity.

BG: Yes.

HK: Biologically, what you have done is reject the vertebrate system in favor of the invertebrate.

BG: Yes, but I hesitate to compare the post and beam structure with any total biological system. You might say that the post and beam structure is a skeleton without a biology, whereas we are using a most efficient biological system: We use the protective skin of the organism as the structure.

HK: When you designed the shell of the Hilliard Towers, was the structure determined solely by this new functionality, or did you also have in mind how the spaces would work?

BG: I know precisely what you mean, and I would be a damn fool if I said that this structural form was not affected by preconceived awareness of spatial forms.

JC: Having studied with Mies for so long, it would seem that spatial definition would be secondary to you.

BG: Well, but you see, this is a new realm of spatial forms producing structure. This is the antithesis of structural forms producing space. Within the post and beam system, the only architectural concern for space is a limited and secure vocabulary for the refinement of the right angles within the modular design of the framing members.

JC: So the complexity of life has been forced into the rectangle of the post and beam.

BG: That's it. But, remember, Mies as an individual consistently made great and noble spaces. His capacities as a creative man, as an artist, were never limited by the inhumanity of his system. Mies repeatedly said to me, "I will teach people how they should live." When I took him to see Frank Lloyd Wright it was horrible for me because I could not stomach Wright's lack of apparent system and the apparently whimsical way I found him handling space: I had no understanding of his spaces at that time.

HK: After you finished your architectural training, you did not confine your work exclusively to architecture?

BG: No, I got involved in other things. I worked for industry in Detroit. One thing I did was to design a bathroom unit which could be moved into any room as an appliance. With four connections, hot and cold water, a drain, and a vent, you installed a bathroom. We felt we could produce it for about $250. I went through the whole process, designing the tools and the dies and production; we used deformed sheet metal, and here I first learned a great deal about the transformation of materials. This was an important part of my experience in industrialization.

At that time, I also developed a railroad freight car. It was made from plastic. I had to develop the machinery for making a sheet of plastic 60 feet long. About 500 of these cars were built and used. The Association of American Railroads, the AAR, approved 5,000, but the executive committee on which the *steel* industry sits turned back that approval because they said they had no facilities for repairing them.

After World War II, I thought that the architecture for the individual was absolutely wrong, socially wrong, and that the only way in which architecture could develop would be through industrialization of components. It was my aim to build a system from the single largest component that I could possibly practically design. On the basis of what we learned when we did the freight cars, we developed and built several thousand of a modular unit called "Unishelter." This, since Habitat in Montreal, is currently being proposed by others for housing. We did it twenty years ago. I took the freight car tube and developed it into two types of tubes which had all the elements essential for living: the living room, kitchen, bathroom, and bedroom.

JC: When was that?

BG: From 1948 to 1950.

JC: Was it the first prefabricated housing in the United States?

BG: No. Thomas Edison probably was the first, with a concrete house early in the 1900's. I did prefabricated housing as far back as 1937, but then I used a panel system. I determined that the panel system was wrong because it required too much field labor.

JC: How large were the panels?

BG: Four by eight feet, as they are today. I learned back in those days that industrialization *must* come in large units. So I thought of a space unit as an enormous brick; in 1948, what I designed was the biggest brick which man had ever made, up to that time.

JC: Was there a market for these?

BG: Pressed Steel Car Company made about 2,000 of these for the Army.

JC: But it did not get into civil architecture?

BG: No, there was a certain resistance to prefabrication, which is still the problem we have with it today. Once, I talked to Laurance Rockefeller about it because he was having problems with a concrete prefabrication company. I said to him that the only thing which prefabrication had to offer was a mechanism whereby you could economically and rapidly plan for social need. And it still is. In other words, you can build a city or a community with prefabricated methods with just a little more effort than it takes you to build one house. I also told him that concrete was the worst material that he could get for prefabrication. I still believe it to be. It's a contradiction of the material as we now use it.

JC: The repetition of the same unit over and over again in a housing area offers little opportunity for variety.

BG: But there were different possibilities of *combining* the units.

Well, all this is very interesting in retrospect, but what is more interesting is what I learned from my experiences during this time. I learned that industrialization in architecture means almost limitless possibilities, peculiarly in architecture because our quantities are so fantastic. The amount of money that goes into one John Hancock Building* could start a whole new industry. The cost of the Hancock Building would pay for about the first ten years of production losses, as well as capitalize gigantic production facilities. Large companies would have to manage this, but even larger companies would result.

At the Marina City office building, we invented a lighting system which is at the same time a heating system. You are sitting underneath it right here [the office building of Marina City]; it is a lighted ceiling, which also heats the building in the winter time. We have no heating system. General Electric was interested in produc-

---

* The skyscraper in Chicago built by Skidmore, Owings, and Merrill.

ing not only this, but also many other firsts in this building. We are living here with 250 footcandles which generate enough heat so that we just peel the heat off the lights and then use it. We take the air of the room, salvage the heat off the lights, mix it with the outside air. This system actually grew out of a consideration of the sociology of business. Urban business is not going to be a nine-to-five business much longer. It is going to be a business of thinkers, primarily. The office workers are going to disappear. We're going to replace them with automatic typewriters, computers, as well as forms of more highly personalized communication. I wanted to have a building which was susceptible to many varieties of use. In the John Hancock Building, as a typical example, if you work past five o'clock, or if you work on Saturday or Sunday, they will provide air conditioning, but they will charge you a very substantial amount for it, because you are causing an unscheduled individual load on the general system of the building. Whereas, in our building, every office unit of 1500 square feet can control its own individual environment at any time of the day or night without penalty.

We handle ventilation requirements in a similar way to temperature. Those vertical louvered spandrels on the façade of the building between floors are functional. There is no central air shaft in the building. Instead, we have the repetitive use of the spandrels, which, when properly separated, become the individual ventilating shafts for either exhaust or supply of filtered air. If I put a chemistry laboratory in here somewhere, I can exhaust the fumes directly through the spandrels rather than take long, expensive horizontal runs to a central air exhaust shaft. No matter where I move the laboratory within the building, it can find its own exhaust system. The spandrel air system has proved itself remarkably useful.

There are offices in this building operating on a 24-hour basis which have selected this building because of this flexibility.

HK: This system design breaks down the rigid unity of a modern office building and allows for a variety of needs in it.

BG: The office building is an expression of man's work: The changing pattern of office work is nothing other than the stripping of rigid patterns from all human work. The office building should reflect the variety of creative effort—not the monolith of uniform ideas.

Let me read for you a statement which I wrote:

> Our age has shifted from the domination of the least common denominator to that of the most common denominator. This shift has moved us from the concept of a single structured idea to the understanding of multiple simultaneous co-existent ideas forming an organic unity.
>
> Architecturally we have expressed this change by structural method from the post and beam to the concept of *space* as *structure*. Space includes the elements of people and time; space includes materials, form, and self-awareness. These combined elements also include another denominator which I can identify as a structural system. These combined elements I have called kinetic space.
>
> Marina City was for us the first major high rise space which we liberated from the elaborate right-angle formality of the post and beam. In this exploration we became aware of the effect of kinetic space both on the dynamic response from people and on the static response from structure.
>
> Based on our Marina City discoveries, we made further kinetic spatial explorations in the Hilliard Houses. The structural concept of the Marina City core was replaced by a more efficient shell whose shape is the definition of space and the reflection of

the human movements within the space. The concept of the structural focus at Marina City was eliminated in the elderly housing at Hilliard and replaced by a humanistic focus; a commune of relationships located in the geocenter of each floor. In the Hilliard family housing the focus was the single family unit clustered within a high rise shell structure developed by the identical structural principles of the elderly housing expressed in another form. The family shell was designed to promote the more independent pattern of human action which is the outcome of the organic growth of the family unit. The geometrical irregularity of the shells yielded a natural bracing of structural rigidity unobtainable in post and beam design except with special reinforcing at additional cost.

Yet the disciplines of the humanistic Hilliard forms are more extensive than the disciplines for a mere engineering module expressed in post and beam design. These two structural systems might be compared as the disciplines of the most common denominator of the shell and the least common denominator of the post and beam.

Post and beam proposes the abstract discipline required by a dimensional system of engineering. The Hilliard Houses propose the humanistic discipline required by family activities: space used as structure. Rather than the assignment of space to the requirements of an engineer's module, Hilliard Houses proposes we extend our concepts of beauty of structure to include the systems of human emotion, of thought and of social environment.

HK: Can these concepts become principles? Can they be applied on a scale beyond the domestic scale of housing?

BG: As space must change its form, all structure that *is* space should follow the change. To paraphrase: *Structure follows space*. And today, for the first time in the history of man, we can build whatever space we can think of.

HK: When you started this new way of construction, were you thinking in terms of how to get away from the rectangle?

BG: I once asked Mies, when I was a student of his, "If the great architecture is to be the continuation of your rectilinear forms, why should there be another architect? Will our future consist only of copies of your work?" Mies's reply was, "*Na, Goldberg, genügt das nicht?*" ["Well, Goldberg, doesn't that satisfy?"]

HK: When one walks through downtown Chicago, with all its rectilinear blocks and buildings, it is a surprise to come to the view from State Street toward the Chicago River. The Marina City Towers stand like two corn cobs in the midst of cigar boxes [*Fig. 4–6*]. They give the whole town a new atmosphere. It is exciting just to see them. Were you intentionally trying to counteract the given environment?

BG: If I ever had any wisdom in my life, really simple wisdom, it was to realize that I never would reach another statement by *trying* for it. Either it would come from a development of which I would more than likely be unconscious, or it would never come. And this was precisely what happened. In 1954, we got the *Progressive Architecture* award for the best apartment project. The realization from this design was not that we had eliminated the right angle, but that right-angled spaces could be grouped in certain relationships that create a secondary, new, and more important significance. In doing this design, I became aware of what I have later called the geocentric arrangement of space.

HK: You achieved that for the first time in the Marina City Towers?

BG: Yes. I was still working with modules, but my module was not the module of the engineers' bay, it was the module of human use of space. And then I devised a pattern to group those spaces, because logically each of those spaces needed a similar service from a centrum. I arranged them equidistant from that centrum and started the design.

JC: You said before that this was not only a formal concept, but a social one as well.

BG: The core contained what might be called the "communal spaces" as we imagine them in a very simple fashion: the laundry and storage rooms, little meeting rooms, play spaces. Now, the evolution from there to the circular form was a very natural one, because each living space required equal participation in the center services. And the optimal locus of the living space was therefore equidistant from the center.

JC: Thereby avoiding long gangways and corridors.

BG: Yes, but this economy became less important than other results: The speculation on this became quite exciting when I realized that the problems that we always found in the corner support of rectilinear buildings are quite different from the internal and continuous points of support in our buildings. The problems of the corner disappeared quite by themselves. There were no corners. We had a never-ending line, a never-ending series of points. Then we worried about whether the resulting round form was just simply a *tour de force*. Could our previous problems be solved in a new but quieter, more familiar rectilinear fashion that we were not familiar with? Then we went back and checked all of the statistical details very carefully—all of the engineering details, trying to reproduce an equivalent area in a rectilinear or even a square form. I found that in every instance, ranging from perhaps 7 to 10 per cent as a minimum, and up to 25 per cent, the circular form had a greater efficiency of performance. It needed less material and provided more area within the exterior perimeter. There was less wind resistance, better mechanical distribution, better fire safety, and it went on and on. We made these kinds of comparisons con-

4–6. Marina City Towers. River view.

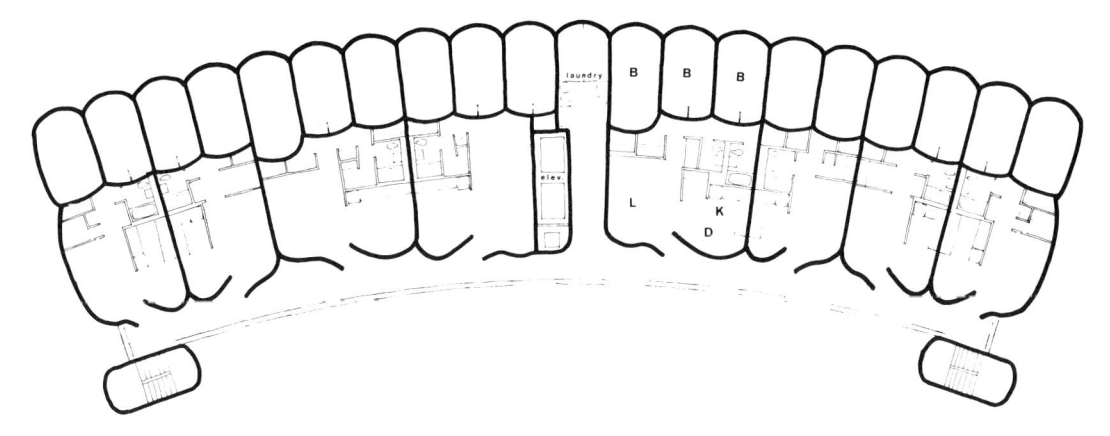

4–7. Hilliard Center. Family housing units. Ground plan.

stantly, rating them with other forms which are quite unusual, and we still continue to make such comparisons.

HK: That means you would even dispense with the circular plan if you found a more efficient one.

BG: Well, for example, in the Hilliard family housing, the circular plan is still there, but it is *unfolded*, you see, which is another very interesting form [*Fig. 4–7*]. We are currently doing hospitals which are plans of what might be called interrupted circles which form themselves into quadrants of space.

We then went further to explore the history of form. Had man constantly used the rectangle or the post and beam? Of course, the answer is no. There are many examples of irregular forms in the history of architecture.

HK: You're speaking of baroque architecture?

BG: Yes, or take the Nymphaeum of Hadrian's Villa.

HK: Or even simpler, the *tholos* of Greek and Roman architecture, the round temple.

BG: Yes. Also, the form exists in the architecture of many primitive peoples. Here in the Southwest United States, for example, in the Canyon de Chelly in New Mexico, the ancient Indian settlements have rectilinear spaces for secular functions and circular spaces for religious functions.

HK: That means that the round building is of a higher order than the rectangular building used for everyday life.

BG: For them, yes. I would say more than that. I would say that the building which has a continuing tradition and a permanent place in society is a round building.

HK: There are modern examples of round towers which come surprisingly close to your solution. I am thinking specifically of the 1959 design of Kiyonori

4–8. Tower City. Tokyo, Japan. 1959. Section drawing. Kiyonori Kikutake.

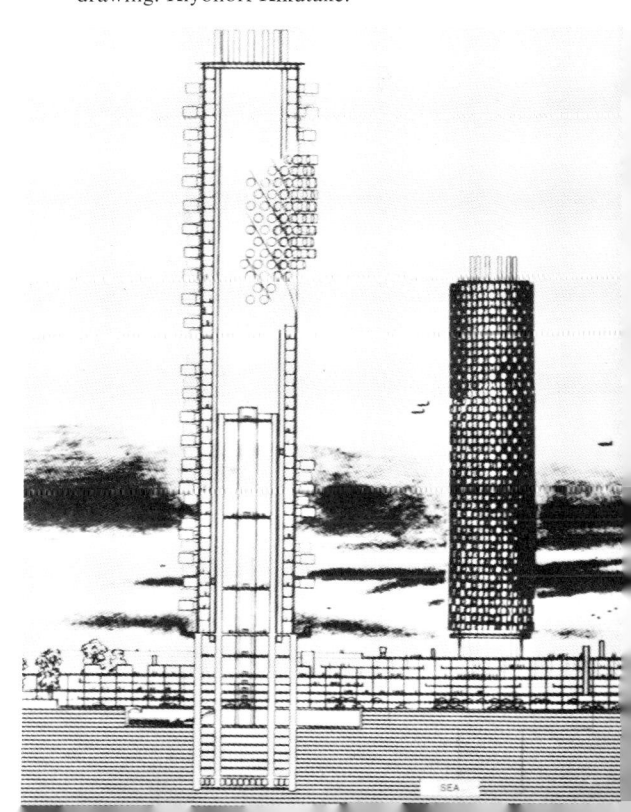

Kikutake, the famous Japanese architect, whose tower city appears to be a predecessor of Marina City [*Fig. 4–8*]. The round tower sits on a multideck substructure next to the water, just like yours.

BG: I am sure many others must be aware of this geometry. I have in my office a photo of a painting proposing an urban center of circular towers by Erastus Salisbury Field, dated 1876. We first explored the circular form, actually, in 1956 with Astor Tower, not the Marina City. We discarded this at that time because we regarded it as being uncivilized in this crowded environment. In 1954, I also explored a circular form, a spiral form for a parking facility for Shell.

HK: In that respect, another example comes to mind. Warren Chalk [British architect], who did a futuristic design for a "Plug-in Living Unit Circular Tower" in 1964, could have been inspired by your Marina City Towers [*Fig. 4–9*]. The lower part is a spiral parking ramp, and above it are the living units.

BG: Yes, that is very interesting.

4–9. Plug-in Living Unit Circular Tower. London Living City exposition. 1964. Warren Chalk.

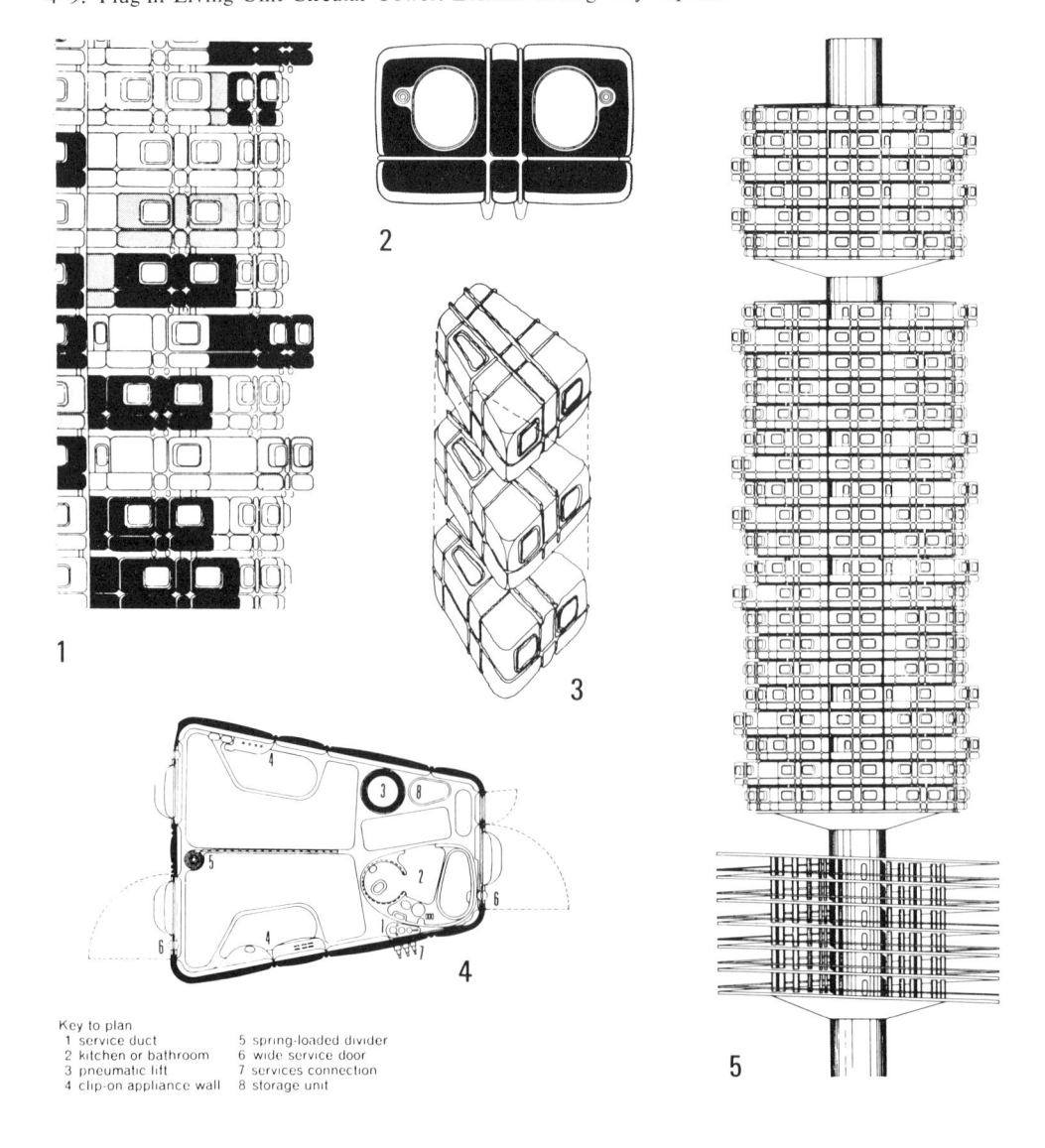

Key to plan
1 service duct
2 kitchen or bathroom
3 pneumatic lift
4 clip-on appliance wall
5 spring-loaded divider
6 wide service door
7 services connection
8 storage unit

JC: The basic difference, of course, is that yours is a reality and Chalk's is a Utopian dream.

BG: Possibly, because of economic factors. The Marina City opportunity then confronted me with what I had learned in my exploration of Astor Tower, namely the *efficiency* of the circle. And I realized in Marina City that, economically, we had to produce something that had never been produced before; in other words, we were required to construct a gigantic quantity of space in high-rise form at a price comparable to low-rise buildings. This could not be done using conventional methods.

HK: You mean that a high-rise building on the same site with the same volume, but built in a traditional method, would have been more expensive?

BG: Twice as much. The residential towers at Marina City were built for $10 per square foot.

HK: Extraordinary.

BG: Of course, you have to remember that this was in 1961.

JC: But when one looks at these towers, one gets the impression that they are high-priced, elegant apartments for the beautiful people. The strong image these buildings create is not achieved by dressing them up, but by employing the most efficient structure which was known at that time.

BG: We did not create an image self-consciously. You have to understand that had we not kept the cost down, we would not have been able to create the rent structure which was essential at that time to get Federal Housing Authority approval, and therefore make the whole project possible. You see, the FHA had prohibited the construction of the type of thing we were attempting to undertake, and our own zoning codes were set up against it. Under these restrictions, you could not combine those numerous activities which we thought were essential. We had to get the zoning changed. We assumed we could get it changed because the city was anxious to have new construction.

JC: What activities did you combine?

BG: Recreation, theater, marina, parking, residential, office structure.

JC: All of that on such a narrow plot?

BG: Yes, it's only a 3½-acre site. It wasn't the relationship of the activities to the limited space which caused the problem, but the relationship of the activities to each other. This is a typical problem of zoning laws and it still exists: A downtown business zone doesn't necessarily permit the construction of an apartment building. In Boston, for example, we had an opportunity to build a city on a perfectly beautiful site located near the water. It was a property of 13 acres which had been zoned for heavy industry. We could not build apartment buildings there because of zoning for a lesser use. We went to the city to get them to approve a change of the zoning. They misunderstood totally what we were trying to do. They turned us down. In place of families, they got warehouses, along with oil tank farms. It ruined the waterfront area, a perfectly natural area for the development of Greater Boston, and foreclosed its use for the present residents of Quincy, as well as the needs for the future, forever.

JC: How did you push your plan through here in Chicago?

BG: Well, I won't say that it was without some kind of political assistance which allowed us to be *heard*. Our message at that time was that the character of the American family was changing. The definition of a family was not necessarily a sandbox family, such as had been promoted by the FHA since its inception in 1930. The new concept of an urban family had to include the family in which children might be of college age, and in which the interests of the family were that of being in an urban environment. A family without young children is still a family; the FHA had not thought of that. As a result, the FHA changed the wording of Title 207 regulations from an intent to build for families with children to the concept to build for family living.

There are other families than the "sandbox type." You can even have a family life between an unwed man and woman. Other countries have understood this, and of course our sexual revolution has made this apparent in many instances. But, at that time, I had some rather brutal responses from the *regional* FHA in Chicago, and was compelled to take our case to Washington, where it was ultimately heard with favor.

JC: When you went to Washington, did you have the final plans in hand, or did you just give them your ideas?

BG: I am ashamed to tell you that, at that time, I was so worried and concerned about the concept of circular towers that I showed our towers as square.

JC: In order to convince them?

BG: Not necessarily, but in order not to bring up the issue of the design. I didn't want the idea to be as radical as the shape of the space. You must realize that there was no FHA approval available for downtown housing. The FHA conceived of itself as a ruralization force in our economy, a force which tried to get people out of the city and into the country. There was where a livable life could be lived. The city in our American ethic is regarded as the place of evil, the place where a good life cannot be, is not, possible.

JC: Frank Lloyd Wright?

BG: Thomas Jefferson, Lewis Mumford, it's a long list. There is a book title which says it all: *The Intellectual vs. the City*.*

Therefore, I had to do two things. One was to change the FHA concept of the family, and the second was to change their concept of where it could be desirable to live. They finally agreed that there might be a desirable living area in the downtown area *providing* the rents were low enough.

* Morton and Lucia White.

So, if Marina City had cost more than is usually budgeted for social housing, it wouldn't have been built. There was no private efficiency apartment available anywhere in the downtown or in the near-downtown area for less than $150 a month. Perhaps the FHA felt that if they could limit us to a figure lower than this (like $125 per month), we would fail by not being able to achieve it.

JC: What they asked for could not have been achieved normally.

BG: That's true, but they also figured that, if I could achieve this in some magic way, it would further insure the success of the project. Most people do not realize that Marina City is really a very, very low cost project.

HK: The planners and defenders of Co-op City in New York should have paid attention to this. In fact, all the typical urban renewal projects to me look rather ridiculous in comparison to this.

BG: In spite of the fact that everything looked as if we could achieve this great efficiency, and as if we could attain the prices we were seeking, and as if we could get the loan, and as if we could put all these things together, we nevertheless felt a tremendous possibility of some kind of hidden flaw. We really didn't believe ourselves to be so completely right. And so I urged our clients to build a full-sized mock-up of two apartments: a one-bedroom apartment and the efficiency apartment. We built them in a loft building in Chicago and surrounded them with a photographic cyclorama 80 feet long, a blowup of a series of photographs taken from a helicopter from a height equivalent to the 40th story of our projected building. And we achieved such realism that people were literally afraid to walk out on the balcony of these apartments, built in the interior of an office building. We gave this over to Marshall Field to furnish out of their stock.

HK: Normal everyday furnishings?

BG: Yes. I did not furnish it as an interior designer, but I wanted it to be similar to what the average person could afford. By doing this, I made my first discovery, really. While the existence of a very pleasant environment which I had guessed came to pass, *this* I did not guess: The space seemed larger to everybody than it actually was.

JC: And yet it was the same amount of space allotted in normal public housing?

BG: It was FHA minimum space, which in our judgment would probably not have been acceptable as a rectilinear space to a normal middle income family as a housing project under FHA Title 207. I tried, of course, to test reactions to these mock-up apartments. As people came in, they would usually say. "My, these are large apartments." This started me thinking: Why were these spaces, which were absolute minimum spaces, creating this impression? No one knew how much square footage was in each apartment, so the impression was absolutely a subjective one. I started to investigate this, and the best conclusion I could come to was that the so-called kinetic space created by nonparallel walls gave the illusion of expanding dimension.

HK: The ground plan of each room looks like a petal. Is that the "kinetic" space?

BG: Well, no, I call any space that has motion kinetic space.

HK: That means a baroque space like the interior of "Vierzehnheiligen" is kinetic space, space in motion.

BG: Yes, yes. Where the relationship of the individual to his spatial environment changes constantly as he moves through a room, you have a kinetic space. This doesn't necessarily mean that all circular spaces are kinetic. A perfectly circular space like the Pantheon certainly is not.

HK: This is the antithesis of classicism, where you are confronted with a space which is pinned down to the four corners or to the regular circle.

BG: The single statement of space that becomes apparent the very moment you enter is the classical static (nonkinetic) space. The statement never changes in response to any change of the human position within.

JC: Did you also build mock-ups for the Hilliard Houses?

BG: Yes, for both the family units and the elderly towers. The Public Housing Authority as clients had become as afraid of the new spaces as I originally had been at Marina City. They wanted to test them out in terms of people's reactions, particularly people of an unknown, unsampled sophistication in certain kinds of changing environment. We got enthusiastic receptions from the people who would live there.

JC: You mean you asked the prospective renters for their opinion?

BG: Yes, the poor people living currently in the Robert Taylor homes or other public housing.

JC: How many did you ask?

BG: It literally went into the thousands.

HK: What percentage approved?

BG: They not only did not object to it, they were unaware of it as a radical change. For them, it was simply a very pleasant new sensation. They loved the unusual windows. They loved all the things that were unfamiliar and possibly would have become fear objects to the middle income groups. The waiting list for applicants for these houses was quite marvelous. But, when we brought Mayor Daley in to see them, we were worried because he is known for his inflexibility in many situations. I was standing there when he came into the mock-up and his face lighted up and he said, "This is the way people ought to live." He had seen enough public housing to recognize what we had achieved. That made me feel very fine. So we have had these several major experiences with space, and we continue to move on with these spaces in other ways.

We are now planning about five health

care centers, including universities and hospitals: one at Harvard, and one at Stony Brook, Long Island; and we have received enthusiastic approval from the Catholic order in Tacoma, Washington, where we have broken ground for a very new design. We have received enthusiastic receptions from the dean of Stanford. At Northwestern University, while they are very apprehensive, we are proceeding with their approval.

JC: Of course, your unusual structures and spaces would naturally cause some skepticism among laymen. However, one would not expect it among architects. Have you discussed this with colleagues?

BG: Yes, but not with any great success.

HK: I had a very interesting experience when I visited the office of Mies van der Rohe. When I talked with his successor, Dirk Lohan, and asked him about Marina City, he just made a derogatory gesture. He told me that they are going to build the IBM building right opposite Marina City, and cover up half of it. The two most antagonistic statements of high-rise building in the Loop will face each other. It will be interesting to see which of the two will succeed.

JC: Do you run into a lot of derogatory response to your work?

BG: Oh, yes, considerable. I think that the discipline of Marina City has been totally overlooked by most of my colleagues.

JC: Do they think it is a fancy show?

BG: Yes. They take it as a *tour de force* to create some kind of novelty. I found with great interest that my buildings were more readily recognized by the European architects who came here than by the American architects.

JC: Do you see any reason for that?

BG: Yes. I think that particularly the German tradition has a happy ability to penetrate the principles of the forms, the structural principles, and the spatial principles without prejudice.

HK: I have noticed that, in America, the Bauhaus is not appreciated any longer. Of course, the functionalists who made dogmas out of the Bauhaus ideas are largely responsible for the boring cityscapes of today. However, you have been able to demonstrate how out of the investigation of clean structural principles a lively architectural form can emerge. It does not seem that the functional aspect has to be ignored in order to achieve a meaningful image.

BG: Of course not. I would like to emphasize that we have made a very extensive exploration of functional space and its effect on man. This, of course, has led us most directly into the problem of density, into urban density. It's perfectly true that it would have been extremely difficult in any other form than the Marina City form to have achieved the density of 500 families an acre which we achieved. I *think* that this is the highest density in *any* project in the world. Yet, we have left two-thirds of the area free and open without buildings. We have never been accused of overcrowding, quite the contrary. We have even made plans showing that we could house the entire city of Chicago on the North Bank of the Chicago River in a strip four blocks wide running from the Merchandise Mart to the Lake—by using the Marina City pattern. Think of the schools we could spend our taxes for. Think of how much cheaper our living, and electricity, and telephone would be.

HK: When you built the Hilliard Center, you also had a very loose setup, a lot of space in between [*Fig. 4–2*].

BG: Yes.

JC: Of course, much of modern town planning goes back to Le Corbusier's idea of grouping high-rise apartment buildings very loosely, mitigating the character of the city. Marina City and the Hilliard Center never break away from the density of the city, however. Even though there is space around the buildings, they never lose their relationship with it.

BG: I think my ideas of city planning are quite independent of Le Corbusier, and all I can say is that, if these men have had any effect on me, it has been *ex post facto*, both in the case of Wright and of Le Corbusier. My ideas on urbanization are not ideas that Le Corbusier would even have approved of. I think that he had some of the same ideas which Mies reflected; there is the same appreciation of the machine for living. If you go back to Le Corbusier's writings, you find that he said that the right angle is the most perfect of all forms because it was the only form which had measurements. This, of course, I cannot accept.

I started to say something else about certain qualities of space. There is an effect which we call "spatial anonymity," for example.

HK: What does that mean?

BG: It would mean anonymous space which has no relationship to the human being. It is space where he feels displaced.

HK: Would you consider the large spaces of a Miesian loft building as anonymous space?

BG: You don't have to have a gigantic space to be anonymous. I think that the average FHA apartment is this kind of anonymous space. The space does not reflect the human being. However, I think what the space does in the Hilliard Houses is to reaffirm the hope that these individuals have for themselves in society. And this is what I meant in my statement about the most common denominator. This is a new engineering of aesthetics.

We do this in our new design for the University at Stony Brook, Long Island. There, we are doubling the size of the university in the health-science campus, and we will be building 2 million square feet, more or less, in a single venture. To build 2 million more square feet is in itself a task, but to relate 2 million square feet to the individuals within this rather than produce rooms with numbers on them is really our task. We have to create what I call "villages of space," for lack of a better term. In a village, a man can associate himself with his neighbors, he has a focal point, he has a point of reference for himself. This point of reference in human activity I think is the all-important experience.

My Palladian tour, which I made in Italy in the early 1950's, was very revealing to me. Palladio understood space completely. He understood how to throw away space. He also understood how to pull it together so that it could relate to the individual. And herein lies his greatness as far as I'm concerned. I think it is necessary to create focal points, points of reference, for the individual in our megastructured society. I'm not sure we've learned to deal with it in terms of 2 million square feet, but we're trying like hell.

HK: The Towers of Marina City and Hilliard Houses are apartment buildings. Each room directly connects with the geocenter. Can you still stick to the circular shell structure when the program calls for more and larger spaces, for office spaces, say?

BG: Yes. Look at the model and ground plan for a skyscraper we designed for the American Broadcasting Company in New York [*Figs. 4–10 and 4–11*]. In this case, we no longer have a sequence of shells linked at broken joints as in the Hilliard

4–10. Proposal for American Broadcasting Company Building. New York. 1969. Bertrand Goldberg. Ground plan.

Towers, but a continuing undulating shell wall [*Fig. 4–11*]. That part of the ground plan which resembles a flower is the structure. The undulations produce (by design) two types of space: within the petals and between the petals. We produce by design two different kinds of space: The enclosed spaces are the introspective spaces, management spaces, and the glazed spaces in between are service spaces: waiting rooms, meeting rooms, and secretarial offices.

JC: So, again, you don't need a core. The undulating wall which creates these special spaces is the self-bearing structure of the whole building. The floors in between the petals are the exploitation of the negative space generated by the structure. The wide windows between the projecting shell become a curtain wall?

BG: Not quite.

JC: They are not free-hanging.

BG: No. I intended to use a single sheet of glass because I wanted the light. But I wanted no structure, and I was able to accomplish this by a single sheet of ¾-inch plate glass, which is available in the dimension which I needed. The reason I dislike your description of this as a curtain wall is that a curtain wall for me has always been a curtain of glass in front of a post and beam structure, whereas here the "wall," whether of glass or some other material, simply encloses a negative space. It is the enclosure of a space formed by the undulations.

The only statement I want to make further about the ABC structure is that the moment we have broken the structure loose from a structural core then the form of the undulations becomes a question of logic within a new freedom.

JC: Could you describe the distribution of the spaces?

BG: Our primary concept was that we had some three or four classes of introverted shell spaces. The major executive office would take a single space of that sort.

JC: One petal?

4–11. Model for American Broadcasting Company Building.

BG: Yes. Well, this is not precisely a petal, because the petal has to be connected to a core like in the Marina Towers, but now we're beyond the core. We have no core.

We then continued to divide the different structural spaces according to different functions. We also had to provide space which could be changed from a managerial space to a service space or vice versa. The space had to be flexible.

HK: What Mies tried to solve with the multiuse loft space.

BG: Right.

HK: Yet, unlike Mies, you are defining the spaces again and still providing for flexibility.

BG: Yes, but while we realize that every function may not be optimal under every spatial condition, we find every space in our design is, nevertheless, always useful. For example, one discipline which comes into being in an office environment is the discipline of communication. We had gone through the American Broadcasting Company and done something which they had never done before: We found out how their 1,500 employees were organized. Instead of its concept as one big corporation, we found upon analysis they were organized into small clusters of management or service. There were only two exceptions: the accounting department and the legal department. In those instances, we had up to eighty-five employees in one department, but all of the other departments throughout the entire business organization consisted of little managerial or service clusters of not more than eight to ten people.

HK: Typically, they would have all been together in one huge space.

BG: Yes. But in our proposed design, we tried to give each cluster a feeling of integrity and even more than this: We began to consider how much communication they had with one another. We found, for example, that there were patterned systems of communication. A man who was interested in producing a television film might talk to the legal department, or he might have to talk to the graphics department or the advance publicity department. Communications and accessibility of people became a great factor in our consideration of space. We created spaces where points of transportation were never more than 50 feet away; with our design we could achieve a systematized vertical transportation, either elevator or escalator, and minimize the number of steps that it took to get from one area to another. On that basis we were able to take the 1,500 employees and unite them into a much closer unit than any extensive rectilinear form would have done.

JC: How do you know that?

BG: After having designed this building, we had it examined by an office management group. We used as a basis of comparison a series of buildings that were already constructed. For instance, comparing it with the CBS Building [*see Fig. 1–5*], which Saarinen had laid out on a 5-foot module, we determined relative efficiencies. In spite of the seeming irregularity of our space, we had 10 per cent more useful space on each floor than Saarinen.

JC: Saarinen's offices are loft spaces around a central core.

BG: Yes. On a 5-foot grid. When I say 10 per cent more I mean 10 per cent of the *gross* building areas were occupiable. In other words, Saarinen's space was 68 per cent efficient, ours was 78 per cent efficient.

JC: Is Saarinen's building considered to be very efficient?

BG: I doubt that it's very efficient. For example, the most efficient building that we found was a Sinclair Oil Company building which has 200,000 square feet on a floor.

JC: Would that be more efficient than yours?

BG: I doubt it when you consider all of the subdistribution areas for traffic. By the time they built up public corridors and horizontal transportation spaces, I would guess that we would come out equally well.

JC: Do you know any American architect right now who thinks in structural terms as you do?

BG: No. I find architects who are working with space, but the spatial explorations that they are undertaking are frequently what I call "whimsical"; they are either without philosophy or technical understanding.

HK: There seems to be either very "cheap" space or a kind of artistic space. For instance, going into Saarinen's TWA Building is like walking into a big sculpture [see Fig. 5–9].

BG: Nervi [Pier Luigi] said so easily about that building, "This is an awful lot of labor to construct a space."

What I am after, the creation of an art within an industrial vocabulary to develop a humanized space, I find in no other architectural effort.

HK: What about Nervi?

BG: I don't think that many of Nervi's things, which I admire so very greatly, would be possible in our kind of industrial civilization. Nervi's structures are possible only where the relationship between hand labor and materials exists because of the maladjustments of our world. What I am trying to foresee is a one-world concept of a relationship between labor and material, where we will not be able to exploit the human condition in any country any more. To say that we can continue to design certain handmade things, because some countries pay their laborers a dollar a day, to me is repulsive. There can be antihumanism in art and architecture.

I think that there are some anomalies that exist because we are in a rapidly changing society, and here my architectural spaces may be more advanced than the society. We have to build buildings for present needs and nevertheless try to anticipate what the future demands will be. Ideally speaking, I should not have to provide the kind of flexibility I have sought in the ABC Building. The architecture makes a very simple statement: We have designed managerial spaces and service spaces. But the future use of these two spaces will become more and more similar as the service methods become more and more mechanized, and people are removed from industrial tasks. One has to look at automation and business administration. Administration has become simply a system of information retrieval. By automation, this process becomes more and more miniaturized as time goes on and businessmen have time to be more creative. You need service spaces less and less as the system becomes smaller and smaller. This I regard as being the change in the future of the urban business space: Business is no longer the byproduct of systems engineering, but of very highly developed idea structures personalized by highly individualized managerial relationships, and only buttressed by the information retrieval system. The statement that I made for managerial spaces is intended to provide the environment which would create a pathway to personalization of business conduct.

HK: Out of these considerations, you are revolting against the multiuse spaces which were an answer to the debacle of not knowing how the spaces should be used.

BG: But multiuse spaces are also restricted because they are too general. That sounds like a paradox. There is still a lot of Victorian thinking behind the multiuse solution in the single form. We were seeking, as Victorians, a single truth for all human environment, and we were thinking a single science to explain the single truth and give it structure. And every human endeavor was to be created out of modules of this truth, multiplied by some x factor. This was the Victorian concept, whether it came from Freud or Marx or Mies.

Now, I think, we have really developed the concept of confusion of individual ideas and concepts of probability, if you will, but a productive confusion; we call it pluralism. The *new* thought style in De-

4–12. Raymond Hilliard Center. Detail of towers, striated surface.

troit, for example, has to do with splitting and individualizing the top management of the greatest industry in the world.

JC: Your design for the ABC Building was turned down; could that mean that they haven't gotten that far?

BG: It may be.

JC: We have discussed the functions of structure and space. It's difficult to identify the aesthetic sources in your work. Can you separate aesthetic considerations from the functional? Obviously, the total form, in its siting, makes an impact which actually *is* the aesthetic experience.

HK: It seems to me that there are some details about which purely aesthetic decisions had to be made. The surfacing of the Hilliard Towers is a good example [*Fig. 4–12*]. The striation of every single shell matches the one above it, so that the vertical pattern created by the wooden forms on the concrete is carried all the way to the top. This striation did not have to match, but could have been haphazard from one floor to the other.

BG: Yes. We even had to ask ourselves whether we wanted *any* texture at all. At Marina City, we used plastic forms, not boards, thereby avoiding any surfacing. The exploitation of the industrial process eliminated any texturing of concrete. Board striation, which Le Corbusier introduced out of necessity, now appears as decoration. It's no longer essential. We can build a far better concrete by having the smoothest forms we can achieve. So which shall we do?

It finally is a matter of finding a vocabulary which will please us. At the moment, we use the outside texture because we don't have any other forms which please us. We did not need a striation at the Marina Towers because of the lively pattern of the balconies, whereas the solid walls of the Hilliard Towers called for some texture.

4–13. Raymond Hilliard Center. Family housing units.

4–14. Raymond Hilliard Center. Convex façade of family housing units.

4–15. Raymond Hilliard Center. Undulating walls of entrances to family housing units.

4–16. Raymond Hilliard Center. Fire stair shafts.

HK: Now the old question of ornamentation comes in, the question of pleasing the eye.

BG: Oh, yes. Ornamentation and dirt. Survival of the form.

HK: I want to ask here about the shape of the windows as well. It reminds us of a streamline airplane or train window, a rather modernistic shape which reoccurs in house trailers and Pop Art pictures. In this case, I suppose it has to do with the structures of the deformed shell.

BG: Yes, it is a structural necessity. In monolithic concrete walls, the stresses invariably follow the distribution of material, and if you change the direction of stress radically you get into trouble, you get build-ups of stress. This happens in aircraft and in automobiles. And it has the same rationale in monolithic concrete. We originally had an ellipse in the design, but in order to put a frame window into it, which was cheaper, we had to make it ellipsoid. The ABC Building model had windows truly elliptical.

JC: Is the ellipse structurally more efficient?

BG: Efficient, yes. Because it permits a transfer of the stress in a more flowing pattern.

JC: We have talked more about the Hilliard Towers for the elderly than about the family units [*Fig. 4–2*]. We have discussed the three types of the centralized group plan, the petal system (Marina City), the shell system (Hilliard Towers), and the indeterminate undulating wall (ABC). But what is just as interesting, though less dramatic, are the family apartments of Hilliard Center [*Fig. 4–13*]. You once mentioned that, in this case, the circle had unfolded itself.

JC: Upon seeing these, one has two first impressions, so to speak: One has to do with the structure, and the other with the siting. Each block is curved to increase structural stability, but, at the same time, the curves stand as reflectors in relation to the towers. This double effect is typical of your work, and one wonders which came first, the chicken or the egg.

BG: The chicken and the egg. These circular family blocks do "contain the elderly towers," as well as make a reflective statement back to the Robert Taylor homes; so they have a double reflectivity.

HK: But as to the structure. The convex side consists of the shells as they are in the towers; they give strength [*Fig. 4–14*]. The concave side consists of undulating walls which turn the entrances to the apartments toward the direction of the exterior corridors [*Fig. 4–15*]. The visual interest of the moving façade seems at the same time to add structural strength.

BG: All the forms give the buildings a rigidity that they would not have with a continuous planar wall. But, additionally, the unusual movements of the walls are the byproduct of the use of interior spaces: More space was needed in the living area than in the kitchen area. And, therefore, the living room walls in almost every instance were moved outward beyond the kitchen walls. The overlapping of these has created individual entrances, the sense of the individual house. While the bedroom structure at the rear is a recognizable organic shell form, the undulating wall which forms the living area in front is a less familiar continuation of the organic structural space principle; it is a shell, but of another type.

JC: The exterior corridors provide play space for the children, link the elevator in the center of the building with the apartments, and, finally, lead to the fire stair shafts at the ends of the buildings [*Fig. 4–16*]. Those fire stairs are another structural surprise. The shaft consists of two shell walls facing each other, supporting the stairway between them. Doesn't the building help them to stand up at all?

BG: No, they stand up by themselves.

JC: Well, it's like walking up a smokestack sliced in half.

BG: Let us hope they don't become that.

5 MORRIS LAPIDUS
ALAN LAPIDUS

ML: I will never forget my first sight of Coney Island. I was brought to the United States in 1903 as an infant from Russia and raised in the ghettos of New York. To a child who had no idea what a merry-go-round was or what electric lights were, to see this thing unfold was not just another experience, it was a miracle. The fact that I ever got into practice was a minor miracle for me because of my fear as a child of going out into the world. What happens to the child affects what the man is to be. As a boy, I was hampered by timidity and fear; as a young man I was full of trepidation trying to outgrow deep-seated feelings of inferiority. Later in life, it was years before I dared go into practice, even though I knew I had had good architectural training.

HK: What was your early training?

ML: My background from Columbia University School of Architecture was completely classical. As I was completing my architectural studies in 1927, when I graduated, we had at Columbia a sort of insulated academic background—so much so that none of the instructors or professors would even talk about the International Style, the Bauhaus, and what was going on in Europe. That was 1923–1927. Of course, the International Style was well along by then, but Columbia University was quite reactionary, conservative. They just did not talk about it. It was only in one lecture that we were told about it; and I remember that lecture so well. We were almost taken in, as if we were going to be told some dirty stories. "We'll tell you about it, but forget it," and then we learned all about Gropius, Le Corbusier, Mies van der Rohe, and some of the De Stijl group in Holland. It was Professor Boring, dean of the school, a man in his late sixties, who delivered the lecture.

Most of our professors were of that vintage, and they were fighting for what they felt was their professional life. They were seeing everything being destroyed and they were holding on, saying, "Look at it but forget it."

We did have one man, Professor Hirons, who was a great classicist, and he was doing what he thought was contemporary architecture uninfluenced by anything that was taking place in the International Style. He, too, was fighting for his very architectural existence. Instead of a Corinthian capital, he would use foliage, influenced partly by Art Nouveau, partly by De Stijl, and partly by his own innovative approach. His buildings indicate a nice classical simplicity. That's about as far as he went. We were using classic proportions and stripping them of their columns, caps,

5–1. Fontainebleau Hotel. Miami Beach, Florida. 1952. Morris Lapidus.

5–2. Summit Hotel. New York. 1959. Morris Lapidus.

5-3. Parisian Bootery. New York. 1928. Morris Lapidus.

and bases, but it was far from the International Style because you could still see the perfect proportioning which we learned in our classic studies: the orders, etc. Another instructor who came in at that time, but wielded very little influence, was Wallace Harrison. He was my last design critic, and I was his shining light, so to speak, in school. Because he hardly gave me any crits, I became his unofficial assistant. But even a man like Harrison was still not ready to take the plunge.

My first indication of anything that was happening was the Paris Exhibit of 1925, but there was very little of the International Style there. It was simply a wild approach, to tear everything apart and see where we were going.

Another influence at that time was the Tribune Tower competition in Chicago in 1922, which was won by Raymond Hood with his Gothic architecture. For the first time, at Columbia, we saw the work of Eliel Saarinen, and we began to see a new style. Another critic at Columbia was Harvey Wiley Corbet. Corbet's philosophy was interesting, because when we questioned him about Saarinen's design, in comparison with the Woolworth Building [1913], we said, "How can you reconcile Gothic architecture with this fine example of a modern skyscraper?" His answer was that the structure was contemporary but the dress was unimportant. "If you took a Chinese man and dressed him in Caucasian clothing, he would still be Chinese. So the Woolworth Building is a modern building; the Gothic dress doesn't change it." That's as far as the philosophy of design at that time went, and that's what I was exposed to.

At that time, there was one man who influenced me more than anyone else, but whose work I think the least of, and that is Mies van der Rohe. He did one thing in the Barcelona Pavilion Exhibit [1928–29], namely, the destruction of closed rectangular spaces. That has probably been the most important influence in my career. When I saw it, I said, "This is great, this sense of space." He used the rectangle, but I ignored that. Why do we think in terms of rectangles? We can build in any form, and basically that's been my philosophy. Just because real estate is sold in rectangles, why must a building be rectangular? I eliminated the rectangle in my later work, the Fontainebleau Hotel [*Fig. 5–1*] and the Summit Hotel [*Fig. 5–2*].

My early work was all stores and shops—from 1927 until 1945—a long stretch. Actually, I was not an architect as I thought of the term at that time. To begin with, my early exposure in the field of architecture was working for other architects. There was the firm of Warren and Whetmore, the great classicists. I worked on the ornamentation of the New York Central Building because I could draw acanthus leaves with my eyes closed. I was drawing all the canopies and other things because my training was classical. All they had to do was give me a surface and I would cover it with acanthus leaves, volutes, egg and darts, and dentiles. Just call it out; I had my alphabet, and there it was. So the few years that I spent in architects' offices I was going nowhere.

Since then, I have been a maverick.

I went with a building firm where I was an employee, and I remained with them for roughly fifteen years. All they did was build stores and showrooms, and I was their captive architect. But I didn't consider myself an architect. I didn't become a member of the AIA [American Institute of Architects]. I felt that I had sold my birthright for a mess of pottage. I didn't meet architects; I didn't talk to architects. I had sort of exiled myself from the field of architecture. There was a sense of guilt that, although I had studied architecture, I was no longer an architect. I felt that what I was doing was not architecture because I wasn't building buildings, I was designing stores.

And yet, strangely enough, *Architectural Forum* wanted to publish (but never did) one of my first shops. From that time on, I was a well-published architect who felt he wasn't an architect. It was the Parisian Bootery [1928, *Fig. 5–3*], influenced by the Parisian architecture of that time. An insurance office interior was published, however. In that project I was doing what I thought was contemporary design, but it was far from it. In any case, I was designing a desk that didn't look like any desk that had every been built before. I designed a chair that was a very poor copy of the metal chairs that were being designed in Europe; that was 1928 or 1929. I had more publications on nonarchitecture than many other architects, because during the entire period I was a captive architect. My work was published again and again, but it was all store work. I was published, I imagine, because they were looking for directions. I could experiment with a shop and it might be torn down five years later, but no architect would experiment with a building.

The editor of *Interiors* [magazine] called me the master of three things: "the bean pole," "the cheese hole," and "the woggle." "The bean pole" because I was using a lot of stemmed things in the interiors, "the cheese hole" because I designed decks with holes in them, and the "woggle" because I refused to stick to the rectangle. In shops, I didn't have to stick to the rectangle. When I laid out an interior, I would start making woggles. I felt that people did not live—or shouldn't—in rectangular cubicles. They should live in free-flowing spaces because the average person doesn't walk in a rectilinear pattern. The basic idea I got from Mies van der Rohe. One curved wall in an early design, the Tugendhat House, set me thinking, and kept me thinking in curves to this very day.

Through the years, I have developed certain theories, which I write about now and then. One theory is that people don't walk in straight lines except when they are going somewhere in a hurry. If you watch a stroller you'll see him meander. Watch someone walking around a room or going through a museum. He will walk away and turn around. People don't walk or move in rectangular patterns. In my storefront days, I developed a theory that led to my bent-glass period. People can be led very easily. They're walking down the street and they're looking at a shop window, and, if I turn the corner sharp, they keep going. Unknowingly, I'd start moving them in. They'd move right into the store.

Another theory I developed is that people are like moths; you make a bright light, and they're going to head for the light, not knowing why. We go toward brilliant light; whether we like it or not, we're drawn to it. So the line and the light together pull people in. Then I began to evolve the open storefront. Whether this was my invention or not I can't say, but I was trying to destroy separations between the storefront and the interior. I felt that the barrier should be torn down. In the old stores, there were real barriers: "This is a show window! Look at it! Then come in!" Well, that's silly. I tried to destroy any demarcations. I think, in many ways, I was influenced by Richardson, who moved in curves. He picked a style in which he could do it, the Romanesque style, everything is turning again and again. Of course, I didn't know it then, but after reading [Sigfried Giedion's] *Space, Time, and Architecture,* I realized that the baroque does that also. I wasn't too familiar with baroque. I didn't realize that the baroque style was doing what I was trying to do, and that is to destroy the hard line planes.

When I got to design my first building, I was doing exactly the same thing. The very first building I ever designed was the Fontainebleau Hotel in Miami Beach [*Fig. 5–1*]. Here's an architect who never designed a building from 1927 to 1945. I had been a consultant on other buildings, but my first commission to design all by myself was the Fontainebleau [1952]. I started by squiggling lines. About six years earlier, by accident, I had gotten involved in hotel work as an interior designer and design consultant.

5–4. A. S. Beck Shoe Store. New York. 1949. Morris Lapidus.

It came about in a rather interesting way. If anyone had come to me and said, "Design a hotel," I would have said, "No. I'm sorry, I'm an interior designer and store architect." I was designing some stores for A. S. Beck. I think one of them still exists on Fifth Avenue [*Fig. 5–4*]. While I was working on the Fifth Avenue store, the Beck architect called me and said that a friend of his was building a hotel in Florida. He wasn't satisfied with the work, which was being carried out by his local architect. The hotel was going up, and the architect said, "Would you like to have dinner with us? This man would like to meet you." My answer was, "I'll have dinner, but why?" He said, "Well, come and talk to the man." And I did. He showed me his plans for the hotel, which is the Sans Souci Hotel in Miami Beach. He asked me what I thought about it, and I said, "It's a hotel, but there isn't anything very exciting about it." He had heard that I had a way of creating flair and drama, and a sense of ex-

LAPIDUS 151

citement, in anything that I did. The sort of thing that people stop and look at. The man from Beck thought perhaps I could give this man some ideas to create a sense of excitement in the hotel. I said, "Well, I don't know anything about hotels, but if you want my thoughts, I'll give them to you." I started with the interior. "You've got to get rid of this rectangular interior. This is ridiculous. Why don't you work some curves and terraces, a few decks, something like that?" He said, "What would you do to the outside?" I said, "Break it up. You have got the beginnings of a tower. Make it feel like a tower. Your canopy, get a little curve to it, a little sweep to it. As you come into the hotel, start terracing, sweeping, curving." I always work with the sweep and the curve because I feel this is what appeals to people. I made sketches. He asked my fee and I gave him a ridiculously low fee, $15,000—consulting architect and doing all the interiors. He said, "You're too high." This, by the way, happened to be the man for whom I finally designed the Fontainebleau, Ben Novak [the Miami builder]. So I said, "Here are all the sketches, Mr. Novak, accept them as a present. Give them to your architect." I got a call a few days later. "Come on down to Florida. You've got your fee." So I became the associate architect and interior designer. That led to a half dozen other hotel clients. They had heard about me and what I had done for the Sans Souci. In a way, the Sans Souci is the beginning of the contemporary hotel, in contrast to the classic hotel.

JC: Was it immediately accepted?

ML: Accepted? More than accepted. People started talking about it. As a rule, people would walk into a hotel and say, "Well, it's a hotel. This is the desk. This is the lobby. I go up to my room. This is a hotel." A classic example of the hotel, to my mind, is the Waldorf, which is the last great classic hotel. But it followed the usual procedure: the lobby, the check-in area, etc. Everything proceeded on a straight rectangular pattern. It is beautiful, but there was no sense of excitement. You didn't wander off into a corner and say, "I wonder what's happening there." I taught the guests to walk upstairs, downstairs—I forced them to walk around curves and created a sense of interest. I would place brilliantly lighted things around, which meant nothing. And as people came into a hotel for the first time, they were exposed to a show. You couldn't take it in and say, "Here it is. Fine. Now I'll go to my room." They had to come in and walk around. They had to talk about it. They had to keep moving around. I wanted them to keep coming back and discovering. It was casual, and yet it had a sense of heightened excitement. You couldn't see it all with one walk through.

JC: Did you want the guest to feel important?

ML: Most of the people coming to the hotel were looking for something flamboyant. Most of the people coming to the hotel were not especially literate. These weren't college professors. These weren't essentially cultured people. Some of them may have been, but they'd forgotten their culture. They weren't coming to Miami Beach for culture, they were coming for a vacation.

HK: But the critics have torn you apart for this "sense of excitement."

ML: People have damned the hell out of me—not people, architects. They say, "Why in hell do you do these things?" Tom Creighton, who was a great critic, a real admirer of mine, would say again and again, "Morris, why in hell do you do these things, you know better." I said, "For one reason, Tom. I don't want anybody to pass one of my buildings without noticing it, especially hotels. I want them to stop. I don't give a damn if they say, 'My God, who the hell did this thing?'" I've stopped the man on the street. Otherwise, people walk down the street and they don't even look at the damn buildings. This may be exhibitionism or showmanship or ego, I may have designed some of the most criticized buildings in the world, but with only one thing in mind: "By God, don't walk by me, I'm an architect. I'm trying to show you something. Look at it." And that may have led me into all kinds of errors, architectural errors. But I've rarely designed a building which doesn't sometimes stop somebody who'll say, "What the hell is this?" Philip Johnson said, "I like it. It's crazy, but I like it." There's one thing he said on the radio: "Lapidus used twenty-eight colors. I don't even know that I want to fight him about that. It's great. It's amusing."

JC: Are you understood by your architectural colleagues?

ML: Perhaps—they are usually strongly for or against my work. The usual label that is put on me in biographies is "controversial": "Morris Lapidus is a controversial architect," which simply means that as a rule part of the profession doesn't agree with me. In the meantime, I'm having a ball.

If I am going to do anything serious, it will end up as a good job. I designed a temple [*Fig. 5–5*] opposite the University of Miami. It's taken seriously. I've got a triform shape at the entrance. People feel it has a Biblical significance. Well, if it has, I don't know what the hell it is because I just said, "This would be sort of nice." The people at the university have admired this little temple. It's not a major piece of work. It's clean. I did something which was almost meaningless, a form. I don't know where I got it from. It's accepted as a Biblical form. I have no idea what the Biblical implication is.

JC: Aren't you serious in "A Quest for Emotion in Architecture"?*

ML: There, I'm being deadly serious.

JC: But, at the same time, you say, "Don't take these Miami Beach hotels seriously; they're built for fun."

ML: That's a serious business. People want something. They're willing to pay for it. My client is spending millions to give them what I or he thinks they want. But it's fun business, even if it is serious. My hotels are always serious financial adventures, but they are not serious pieces of architecture. When the AIA met at the Americana–Bal Harbour [*Fig. 5–6*], there was quite a to-do. They had a seminar called "A Quest for Quality in Architec-

* *American Institute of Architects Journal*, November, 1961.

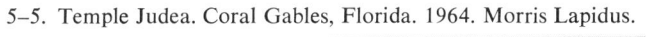

5–5. Temple Judea. Coral Gables, Florida. 1964. Morris Lapidus.

ture." This amused me because I had already written three quest articles, two published, one still hanging around. I was there at the general discussion. One of the panelists was the designer of Coventry Cathedral, Sir Basil Spence, also Wally Harrison, Roy Allen, and Nikolaus Pevsner, and each of them, in talking about a quest for quality, would begin by saying, "Now, let's take this building, this hotel, as a horrible example." Sir Basil Spence said, "When I approached this building, if you could call it that, I thought the thing would rear up and bite me." Pevsner said, "A building like this is not to be taken seriously. It's not quality in architecture." Allen ripped it to pieces as a cheap, tawdry thing, and there I was sitting through all this and by now half the people there, a couple of thousand architects, were all looking at me. I was on the hot seat. A question and answer period came up and I was faced with the decision whether to sneak out, crawl into the woodwork, or get up and say something. So I raised my hand and said, "I'd like to ask a question." And the question was, "Gentlemen, you are talking about the quest for quality in architecture, but my question to you is, 'Do you want that kind of quality here?' You people came here for a convention, and you selected this area because at the same time you wanted to enjoy yourselves; you wanted to have fun, but that's part of a convention. What I'd like to know is, are you enjoying your stay here? Are you enjoying the nonsense I've created? And if you are, forget the architecture." Whereupon, each one took the occasion to apologize, and said, "It is a wonderful place to be." Pevsner said, "It's a delight to walk around here. I enjoy it." Sir Basil Spence said, "Well, taken in that context, yes, it's delightful. The lobby, I've walked around, I've enjoyed it. So let's not look at it as architecture." Well, that's exactly what I wanted. I'm not trying to create monuments. My hotels are not primarily designed to impress architects as fine pieces of architecture.

I'd like to tell you a little incident I'm

5–6. Americana Hotel. Bal Harbour, Florida. 1955. Morris Lapidus. Photo: Ezra Stoller © ESTO.

rather proud of. When Frank Lloyd Wright was at Miami Beach for a talk, he was taken around and, of course, the outstanding beach hotel at that time was the Fontainebleau. They passed by it and they asked the master, "What do you think of it?" He looked up and said, "An anthill." That's all he had to say. The Florida and Miami papers took that up and said, "The sage has spoken. It's an anthill." And they asked me what I'd like to say. What could I say? I said, "I'm very flattered. I think the ants have created some fine structures which man hasn't yet achieved." It was just a cute way of getting out of it. But about a year later, he was given a reception at the Metropolitan Museum of Art and I was there. Somebody said, "Would you like to meet Frank Lloyd Wright?" I said, "I'd like to meet him. I'd like to know that I'd once said hello to the man." There was quite a crush of people around him, everyone wanting to meet this man. One of my architectural friends, who knew Mr. Wright fairly well, came up and said, "Mr. Wright, I'd like you to meet Morris Lapidus, an architect who has done a lot of work in Miami Beach, where you have been." He turned to me and said, "Miami Beach? You've done some work down there?" I said, "Yes, sir." "Well," he said, "if I were you, I wouldn't talk about it." Whereupon, I tried to get out of the crush but I couldn't get away. There I was, just pushed up right alongside Frank Lloyd Wright. He had just hacked me and there was a lull and I was stuck. I couldn't get away. He turned to me and said, "Young man, do I know any of your work?" I said, "Yes, Mr. Wright, you commented on it, the Fontainebleau." He actually put his arm around my shoulders and said, "Young man, you can talk about that one." This, of course, was a great accolade. So, you see the usual approach. Most architects might damn it right away, but given a chance to rethink it, they might come back and say, "Well, it does serve its purpose."

AL [Alan Lapidus, son of Morris]: The function of a hotel is two-sided: to make people enjoy themselves, and to be financially viable for the people who own them. The two are very heavily linked together, and I think the results of that are in the hotels my father has designed. They are probably the most successful hotels operating. None of them has ever lost money.

ML: They're all successful. One of the hotels I have been criticized for more than any other is the Summit [*Fig. 5–2*] in New York. We designed a nice contemporary hotel building with 500 rooms. My clients wanted more rooms. So I started playing with sweeps and curves. The line got longer, and more rooms kept coming in, and we added 300 rooms by distorting the building. As far as the financial function, it is very successful, an S curve on a small piece of land. The fact that Peter Blake, an editor, said, "Let's not have any snake dances on Lexington Avenue," didn't upset me. So he's against snake dances. But, on the other hand, he would say, "That S-shaped building housing project on Chatham Square is a fine building." Now, you see, the difference is this. The person who designed that housing project can do no wrong. Lapidus has never done anything right, according to some critics. So the snake dance on Lexington Avenue is not satisfactory, while the one on Chatham Square is all right. Frankly, these barbs hurt from time to time. I do have sensitivity and I'm trying to create good architecture. I feel that I have done my utmost to design a fine building. That's it.

IC: Mr. Lapidus, you combine incongruous elements. For example, at the Fontainebleau you put a French formal garden right next to a sleek sweeping modern pool deck [*Fig. 5–7*].

ML: I was forced into it. My client said, "I want it." The name is "The Fontainebleau." I thought it was ridiculous. I told him so. He still wanted it. I said, "All right. So I'll put in the Versailles parterre there." I still think it's silly. On the other hand, you talk about style. Let me sum it all up,

5–7. Fontainebleau Hotel. French garden and pool deck.

and this is like letting my hair down and telling a psychiatrist how this all happened. When I started the Fontainebleau, it was going to be contemporary. Once and for all, I was going to design a beautiful contemporary interior. I drew the first sketches, and the owner said, "You must be crazy. I don't want this. I want French Provincial." When I heard that, I felt sick. So I took out some pictures of French Provincial, and I said, "Is this what you want?" He said, "Oh, my God, not that old-fashioned French Provincial. I want that nice modern French Provincial." Now, try and solve that. I figured I had to produce what he thought was French Provincial or French something. My client was just as illiterate and uncultured as many of his guests. I was faced with a problem: "What do I do with this problem from an interior point of view?" So I thought, "I'm appealing to popular taste. I'm trying to create a sense of opulence and excitement and 'French Provincial.' What kind of chop suey is this?"

You see, I try to understand people; my whole architecture is based on people. Who are they? What's their background; their training? They're going to come to Miami. They've heard that on the former Firestone Estate the fabulous Fontainebleau is going to be built. To begin with, it had to be *fabulous*. It had to live up to this dream picture, the dream drawn by the advertising people. Where do these people get their culture? I finally came to the conclusion that most of them get their culture not from school, not from their travels, but from the movies, the cinema. If that's so, what was I to do? Suppose a director came to me with a script that called for a fabulous, luxurious tropical hotel setting. "Give it to me. Knock their eyes out with it. It has got to be fabulous." I'd say, "All right, I'll design a fabulous movie set." And that's what I did. Now, some movie sets are just plain nonsense—but this was wonderful nonsense. I gave him his French, which is not French. I gave him fluted columns which are not contemporary. They are not French. I showed him a picture and I said, "Now, look at this. It's a

French column, this old-fashioned column. Do you want it?" "Oh no, no, no." I showed him my fluted columns. "Now you're catching the spirit," he said. In other words, I was selling him. All through the interior I created is a potpourri of anything I could put my hands on. It's no more radical than a pop artist who says, "I don't have to follow any rules." Now I'm using a palette. My palette has materials and stylistic things left over from the past. I use them any way I want. They have no interrelationship. There is no attempt at establishing a style. The Eden Roc Hotel [*Fig. 5–8*] carried some of that feeling, a wonderful nonsense in the classical manner. My original "Americana" interior in Florida is again wonderful nonsense of no style. Oh, a little Mayan architecture thrown in; a little feeling of Colonial, nothing too much of anything. And yet, I created no special style. No one will imitate it. I've simply done something as a pop artist might do it. I want to do it. You can't tell me I'm wrong.

JC: Your comment about movie sets speaks to the fact that man likes to act a role.

ML: I'll go a little further than that. At the Fontainebleau, for instance, the entrance to the restaurant, a very lavish, elaborate restaurant, is on the same level as the lobby. You really should walk right in. But what I did was walk people up three steps, bring them out on a platform, shine some floodlights down on the platform, and then walk them down three steps. Now, you've got to be out of your mind to do something like that. Why walk up, walk across, and walk down? And yet no one has ever realized that there was absolutely no reason for it at all, except as a dramatic entrance to a restaurant. You walk out. You see everybody. Everybody sees you. You are dressed in your best bib and tucker. Your neighbor is there. He sees that you are at the Fontainebleau. It's straight showmanship. I put those people on stage and they love it. And to this day I'm waiting for someone to ask me, "What the hell kind of crazy idea is this?" But, if anything, that entrance sums up my whole theory that people love the drama and excitement of being a part of the scene. Of course, this happens in some fine buildings. The same drama. In Lincoln Center, the

5–8. Eden Roc Hotel. Miami Beach, Florida. Morris Lapidus. Photo: Ezra Stoller © ESTO.

5-9. TWA Terminal at Kennedy International Airport. Long Island, New York. 1956–62. Eero Saarinen and Associates.

5-10. TWA Terminal.

drama is there [*see Fig. 1–22*]. The stairs in Harrison's opera house—which is about the best thing he's got—are great. Of course, he's got an example in the Paris Opera House. Being on the stairs, walking the stairs, being a part of the show. It's been done through the years. I'm simply doing it again in my own way.

HK: The TWA Terminal Building [*Fig. 5–9*] by Saarinen has stairs like that.

ML: Yes, that's one of the best spaces ever created, but it's a clumsy-looking building on the exterior. It looks like a dead grasshopper [*Fig. 5–10*]. But the inside is just fantastic. It's wonderful, this feeling of going into large space, then into a small space, and coming into large spaces, interesting, moving. He did in the grand manner what I've been trying to do for years.

HK: Such as that sweeping staircase in the lobby of the Fontainebleau [*Fig. 5–11*]?

ML: That staircase doesn't actually go anyplace. When you get up there, there's a little space where they have a television set and a card room, nothing else. Here, I have this grand stairway and there's nothing up there, really.

AL: As my father said, the Fontainebleau was designed as a movie set. When Hollywood wanted to make the ultimate romantic movie about Miami Beach, "Goldfinger," the James Bond movie, the ultimate escapist picture, they needed a gorgeous setting for spies and girls. They had the set already made for them, the Fontainebleau.

ML: Mankiewicz [Joseph L.], the movie director, came to the opening of the hotel, and I was introduced to him. He said, "You know something, Lapidus? You've created a setting here. I could shoot a picture in this thing. I wouldn't have to move anything, a perfect movie setting."

HK: By creating movie-set hotels, don't you pander to a mediocre taste, a kitsch taste?

ML: Yes, I am doing that. I've been accused of it many times. I've been asked,

5–11. Fontainebleau Hotel. Stairs with Piranesi print.

"Why don't you raise the level of people's taste?" The answer is that I don't think I have the special talent to pull them up. I go halfway and realize that I'm over their heads, already. And, although Mies van der Rohe says it is the architect's function to educate, I have talked to people who lived in Miesian apartment houses, and all I hear is, "This is the worst apartment house; this is a ridiculous place to live. There are too many windows. We hate it." And so, I say let Mies do the educating. And in the short span that I have, I will have fun by saying, "At least people liked what I did."

You see, in my background I have a tremendous indoctrination in merchandising. I spent fifteen or twenty years studying what makes people want to buy something. It's a training you don't disregard. I learned that I could make people do things, make them walk into a store and buy. I did a shoe store which was 200 feet long, and the owner wondered how he was ever going to get people to the back of it. So I put an extravagant bit of nonsense at the back of it [*Fig. 5–12*], which was nothing but a luminous display, showing nothing, by the way. I would sit in the store and watch a woman come in and be offered a seat, and she would refuse it and walk back 200 feet for a chair. If you'd ask her why she did it, she wouldn't know that I had preconditioned her to walk back there. It worked. Now, when you get somebody who has spent so many years studying human response, he will be influenced by the human element that he has worked with for so many years. Given a project, I unconsciously know I'm trying to sell them something, because I am still selling. I'm still a merchandiser. What am I trying to sell them? I'm trying to sell them what they're looking for. That's what I mean by having people like what I do—I plan it so they will.

Even though I've been criticized for it, I seem to be getting a sort of late recognition. The Architectural League, and some of the architects who are influential in the League, are concluding that apparently what I did in my early years was rather exciting, and perhaps trend-setting. They have given a one-man show of my interiors at the League. They are more interested in the interiors as setting a mood. Also, a writer of architectural subjects is doing an article with six pages of my interiors; mainly, he's talking about why they were right and why many of the things that have happened since were wrong, and why we're heading back in the same direction.

We're living in an uncertain world, the kind of world, at the moment, where we've lost goals and we've lost the sense of what the true realities are. There are two things happening that seem completely unrelated, and yet in my mind are strongly related. On the one hand, you have the hippies and the psychedelic happenings and all the wild things going mod, mod. On the other hand, you have the general public, which ignores contemporary architecture, so-called modern architecture, especially interiors, and *hurl* themselves back into the past. They want traditional homes, they want traditional furnishings. There are the squares of "Squaresville" and there are the hippies. Yet both of them, I think, are motivated by the same thing. They are both a reaction to the dissatisfaction of the times we are living in, the background we're surrounded by, the backgrounds against which we live our lives. They are going in opposite directions, but each is apparently looking for that from the very beginning: for a human touch, for something which touches man more than the superficial modernism of contemporary architecture.

HK: But you were trained in a classicist language and suddenly decided to throw it all away. How did this come about?

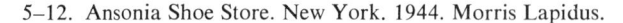

5–12. Ansonia Shoe Store. New York. 1944. Morris Lapidus.

ML: The first firm that I went to work for for any length of time was a storefront outfit. I realized that none of my classic training fitted into stores.

JC: Why?

ML: Because, in the first place, that's what the stores were like already. There was no challenge.

JC: You didn't want to copy the old tradition.

ML: No point in it. The first job I got was a florist shop that had been designed by an architect who'd made sketches—a classicist. It was all done in a lovely Georgian style, and probably that's why these people were anxious for me to go to work for them. I had taken the man's sketches and developed them and detailed them. The architect thought it was great, and my moonlighting client, who eventually became my boss, thought that I could detail this stuff beautifully, and could therefore fit into their picture quite well. That was in 1927. But I wanted to see a challenge. I could not see a relationship between selling dresses, for instance, and Georgian pilasters.

JC: Was the style of the dress contradictory to the style of the architecture?

ML: I remember when I designed something that I thought was contemporary architecture in the store, the client said to me, "What's that got to do with dresses?" And I said, "What are you selling? Crinolines or modern dresses? Why do you want these Georgian cases?" "Because we always sold them that way." "But you're not selling Georgian dresses." "Well, maybe you've got something. Let's see what happens." So I had an opportunity that very few young architects have, the chance to experiment. It wasn't a building about which the owner would say, "Look, mister, you can't do that to me; it's going to cost me hundreds of thousands or millions and I'm not going to let you experiment." I was fortunate that I was able to experiment in these inexpensive shops.

I think I began to realize that fluidity was the thing I was looking for—like Mendelsohn's sweeping lines—without knowing why. My enemy all through my career has been the rectangle. Cities are laid out in rectangular patterns, we live in rectangular rooms, buildings are built in rectangles. That's been my hang-up.

HK: Do you have any memories from your childhood in respect to living in a rectangular environment like New York?

ML: Not exactly, not anything that I can pin down. One does not respond intensively to the everyday environment, but to the exceptional, such as my first exposure to an open sweeping field of wild flowers. This was my first experience of what I could call "beauty"; otherwise, for a child, that word meant nothing.

HK: You hadn't seen anything like that before?

ML: No. And I suppose living in the city with streets and little boxlike rooms was perhaps why I developed this peculiar aversion to rectilinear architecture. But, strangely enough, it was two or three examples of Mies van der Rohe's early designs which made me aware of the curving line in architecture. And there are only two examples in his entire work, two early skyscraper designs.

He later dropped it and never again used a curve. Those designs were experiments which he must have felt were wrong. Later, everything had to be modular, and a sweeping curve cannot be moduled out, so he dropped it.

JC: When you were doing storefronts, were you borrowing from sources other than architecture?

ML: Yes, there was another very strong influence. There was and still may be a German magazine called *Gebrauchsgrafik*. In the 1920's, they were doing marvelous things in Germany, France, and Holland. I liked the freedom with which they attacked their problems—the use of free forms and the use of color were probably two of the greatest influences. The *Gebrauchsgrafik* was a sort of Bible with me. I still have them bound up. For years I kept binding them, referring back to them, and actually I think it's still an excellent source material to go back and learn from.

JC: Why did poster art advertising techniques and display ideas which you found in *Gebrauchsgrafik* interest you as architectural sources?

ML: How does one attract the attention of people? What are the media? One, strangely enough, is the circus barker. He stands in front of the sideshow: "Come on inside, we've got this and we've got that and you'll see the greatest wonders in the world." Then, one performer walks out and spends a minute or two and goes back in just to titillate you. So, here's this man shouting at the top of his lungs. If he whispered, if he spoke in a gentle way, no one would stop. This man had to be raucous and loud and at the same time not be objectionable; these barkers had the wonderful talent of catching you and holding you and not letting you go. That is what a poster does. I introduced this idea into my storefronts.

I had to make it loud enough, colorful enough, and yet not too gross for people to stop and look, even though it might not be beautiful or aesthetic. But it had to stop short of being vulgar. Perhaps, if you want to describe my work all through the years, it is exactly that: exciting enough, titillating enough, loud enough, but still short of being vulgar.

HK: A circus barker made promises which were not kept once you got inside.

ML: Very true. Perhaps that's what my architecture has been accused of, that it's exciting but rather empty. Empty of full meaning. Lacking true direction. If my work has been an influence, it is only to say, "Try to do something, try to be exciting," but I can't say that my kind of work will ever establish a school like Mies van der Rohe's. There's nothing to follow except an idea. In other words, the barker was giving you the idea. It may not have been fulfilled inside, but it was enough to draw you in. The rest is up to you. There can never be a Lapidus school of architecture.

JC: But your work obviously influenced motels and hotels everywhere. Their interiors show that they have learned your design vocabulary of carefree elegance. But what is less obvious, though equally important, is the influence of your early storefront work. It not only introduced a new type of shop, but with it, elements of the International Style from Europe. With your experimental attitudes as a shop designer, you did what nobody else was doing on the East Coast.

HK: On the East Coast, you were among the very first to transform elements of De Stijl and the Bauhaus to the American Main Street. You put it right in the people's faces. Those small houses of William Lescaze and Morris Sanders in 1934 and 1935 in New York were among the first American town houses of the International Style. Morris Sanders was one of your best friends. Those shops actually made the new style digestible because you were including them in an eclectic way into your personal design language, which drew from many sources, both traditional and modern. Perhaps architectural historians assumed they could omit your early contributions because they found so little to praise in your flamboyant hotels. This is how history works, but, on the other hand, as far as we have understood you, you don't take your early works seriously, either.

ML: This conversation is almost like being on the psychiatrist's couch. There's a sense of guilt about it. I felt that my shops were not architecture. My friend Morris Sanders said to me, "You gave up architecture to go into this field of store design in order to make money. That's not for architects."

HK: But because of that you had the freedom to do things no other architect had.

ML: I could do anything I pleased,

mainly because the stores were successful, and so the commissioner would tell me to go ahead and do some of my "crazy things."

HK: The funny thing is that all the other architects we have talked to are very much aware of the importance of their standing in the world of architecture. But we have the impression that you disregard those aspects of your work which may give you some historical importance. Your desire to be an accepted architect dismisses your early achievements as a designer.

ML: Again, the old complex. I suppose I was trained to do one thing and I was doing another. I never spoke to architects, I stayed away from them. I was embarrassed to be known as an architect. In the late 1930's, I began to realize that I was doing worthwhile things. That was when other architects began to come into the field of store design and their work began to be published. I said, "My God, is 'Morris Lapidus' catching?"

JC: Do you know who claims to be the first modern American storefront designer?

5–13. Herbert's Home of the Blue White Diamonds. New York. 1930. Morris Lapidus.

5–14. Swank Jewelers. New York. 1931. Morris Lapidus.

ML: Morris Ketchum is now being credited with it. But he got into the field in the late 1930's. I was there in the late 1920's. I was doing the rough spadework. It was showmanship. It was the old circus barker doing his bit.

JC: The works of Ketchum and Fernandez [shop designer José A.] were published early, and claims were made about them which should have been made about your work. In fact, they borrowed many of your ideas. A careful study of all the architectural journals in the United States between 1925 and 1935 indicates clearly that no one else was ahead of you. The spadework which you did in shops like the Parisian Bootery [*Fig. 5-3*], Herbert's Blue White Diamonds [*Fig 5-13*], and Swank Jewelers [*Fig. 5-14*] introduced all the new elements which made the shop a showpiece, an environment which linked graphic art with good business. Your storefronts became eye-catching billboards which relate to present-day movements in architecture.

ML: I'm being told about it and I accept it reluctantly.

I may have been the first on the American scene, but I depended upon other people's ideas. The magazine *Gebrauchsgrafik* was one source, as I mentioned earlier. Another one was the *Ladenbau,* a magazine about shop building in Germany. The French were still tied to their classicism. The German stores appealed to me because they were experimental.

My storefronts were billboards [*Figs. 5-15* and *5-16*]. When I began a design, I would figure what part of it had to be display, just like the picture in the poster. Part of it had to tell what you were selling, the sign and the lettering. Boldly display the name and use some graphics. (I don't even think the term "graphics" had been invented yet.) So I built the picture, and found the kind of lettering I was looking for.

HK: How did you get away from the traditional ornament?

ML: I was very much in search of what I called "an alphabet of ornament." We had an alphabet of Greek ornament, or of Romanesque ornament, or of Gothic, or of Egyptian, etc. Of course, I finally came to the conclusion that our era does not need ornament.

My quest for a new alphabet of ornament started back in the 1920's, when I took a typical pilaster, which had a Georgian capital, and began to work it into a skyscraper motif. It became a sort of wedding-cake capital. Then, around 1929, I became disillusioned with our skyscraper architecture and I asked myself what else there could be. In my next job, I went to the human form. It was a pilaster with a human figure in it. I still had the pilaster and cornice. Then I tried fan-shaped things growing out of pilasters, like on an Egyptian capital. You see, tradition is hard to break. Of course, a few years later I got rid of the pilaster and cornice altogether. Instead of looking for new ornament, I became interested in poster art. I was really hung up on lettering. I think that is something which architects today are neglecting. I was really practicing graphics.

At this stage, I had to stop and ask myself where I was going. I'd tried a lot of kooky things. I began to think seriously of what I was trying to do. To eliminate does not mean to negate man's love for adornment. I really believe that the point at which man became truly a human being rather than an animal was the moment at which he started to adorn his abode. There was a primitive desire to adorn himself and to adorn his cave. This is so basic to human nature that I don't think it can ever be eradicated. I also believe that the human being would be much happier if he lived in flowing spaces. People didn't live or shouldn't live in boxes. Then my ceilings grew out of that. In other words, I'd take a ceiling opening, sweep it around, and punch it full of cheese holes.

HK: Are the cheese holes for the light fixtures?

5–15. Doubleday Doran Book Shop. Detroit, Michigan. 1934. Morris Lapidus.

5–16. Schwobilt Clothing Store. Tampa, Florida. 1936. Morris Lapidus.

ML: Not especially. I put lights everywhere. I was disenchanted with lighting fixtures: A fixture is really an outgrowth of the torch, the kerosene lamp with electricity. But now we have a source of light without a flame. So why show the fixture? My first attempt, years ago, was a disaster. In one store, I decided—no light fixtures. I put the lamps high up in the ceiling, a lot of them. But I got a call from the owner who said, "My light bills are terrible and my store is absolutely dark." I said, "It can't be. It's the most modern way to light a store." "You better get down here." So I took the train to a city in the South to see the shop. As I approached, I said, "Why in the hell don't they turn on the lights?" It looked black because the light was pouring straight down onto nothing. And I learned my first lesson in lighting, that light itself can't be seen. You've got to light up a surface. Luminosity of surface. Lighting has played a very strong part in everything I've done.

So, instead of ornament, I depended on sweeping walls, graphics, and lighting. Color also plays a very important part in my work. Mies van der Rohe's credo of black, white, and gray never became mine, and I became a great believer in exuberance of color, of light, and sweeping walls. People like light, they like color, and they like forms which require investigation and study so that you don't walk into a room and say, "I've seen it," but rather, "What's going on there?" and "What's in behind there?" Curiosity.

JC: Your Seagram Bar [*Fig. 5–17*], in the Chrysler Building, already has all these characteristics in it.

ML: Yes. I designed that in 1933.

JC: That whole interior you designed for the Seagram people is surprising in every aspect. The Chrysler building in itself was a symbol of modernity. You entered the grand lobby, got on the elevator, and went up to the Seagram's floor; doors opened and suddenly you were in the past, in Elizabethan paneled rooms. That was the first surprise. Then you entered the supermodern bar with its sweeping curves and luminous surfaces, cheese holes and

5–17. Seagram's Private Bar in the Chrysler Building. New York. 1934. Morris Lapidus.

woggles and curving sofas, etc., much like you later did in your hotels. That was the second surprise.

ML: There was a rationale behind it. None of these things just happened. I never did anything without a reason, although I never explained it to anybody. Prohibition was over. I was still working for the store builders Ross-Frankel. Frankel had brought in a new client, Seagram's, who asked, "What would you do—we're coming into the United States; we're a Canadian outfit." Liquor was the horrible monster, and we were allowing this horrible monster into our lives again, and they put it to us: "What kind of interiors should we have?" I went through some mental gymnastics, which I never explained to them. I handed them the result and said this is what I think you should have, and they really liked it. My thinking was this. Drinking and liquor had been outlawed. We were going to try it again, but it was the destroyer of human lives, and all the other nonsense the prohibitionists used. It was not respectable. Drinking was something you did in speak-easies. The bootlegger produced liquor. I could just feel that these people were saying, "Make us respectable; make us come back in as honored and respectable people." Secondly, "Give us an image of dignity. We're an old company, and there'll be a lot of new companies coming in, but give us a feeling of belonging, of having been there for a long time." So, in my own mind, I had it figured that what these people wanted was a period stage setting, a setting which is so historically respectable that no one could very well say, "Here we go again with this whole thing of intoxicating liquor." So I went looking for a style. First, I knew it had to be a setting. I considered that we were in an ultramodern building. If I created a modern lobby for Seagram's, I wasn't accomplishing anything. I wanted the people to walk in and say, "This is different." I wanted them to have a sense of awe, something you can't quarrel with. I went through the styles: Georgian?—people have it in their homes. Colonial? American? They have it in their homes—too familiar. What is a style which would have enough tradition so that people would be afraid to say there's something wrong with this thing? I wanted something you couldn't argue with. So I hit on Elizabethan, going far enough back so that the average person coming in would feel that this was history. I put them on stage in a historical setting. I put in a huge, beautifully carved wood fireplace. The two horses at the secretary's entrance had crowns on their heads, Seagram's crowns. The paneled offices had this great dignity. As far as I was concerned this was done entirely with tongue in cheek, purely as a stage setting.

I put on a serious face, and told them that this was refined elegance, but I know what it is. I'm not deceiving or kidding myself. When I designed the Fontainebleau, for instance, even my client and my client's client suggested that it was beautiful, traditional. "It's what?" I said. "It's French Renaissance." Now, I know what it was. It was nonsense—wonderful, joyous nonsense—an elegant setting for a vacation.

JC: The Church, and others, might accuse you of being cynical.

ML: I'm glad you used that—the Church. They're the greatest cynics! They produce the most marvelous stage settings so the worshiper will *accept*. The clergy says, "We have to prepare you for worship," in other words, "We are preparing a setting in which you are ready to receive your God." The great cathedrals are nothing but stages for the acting out of the drama of religious ceremony. It takes a strong drive to find God in a little cottage or hut, but it's easy to find him in a beautifully staged interior.

HK: Couldn't your designs for the Seagram offices have emphasized the new times, the postprohibition era, new forms as a complete break with the past?

ML: It was too new. I didn't trust myself. The only place I could cut loose was

5–18. Alan Lapidus with model for Olympic Building. New York. 1970.

in the bar, where I was expressing my feelings of what contemporary good living with liquor might be. I took the chance in the bar, and I went as far as I knew how to go using my own idiom. Had I used the 1933 idiom of contemporary, I would have had white walls with black bar stools, the great big green plant in the corner, and the mirrored bar. I would have been back in the speak-easy again. I didn't dare do that. I went as far as I could go in this bar in expressing the contemporary and good life today. Not tomorrow. I didn't know tomorrow.

JC: In those offices, were you attempting to be authentically Elizabethan, or were you doing the same thing as in the lobby of the Fontainebleau: suggesting a certain respectable atmosphere merely by alluding to values with symbols?

ML: I used it very literally, but had my own little jokes. I knew I wasn't creating a true Elizabethan interior. Here was an executive, not a duke, sitting at a desk. Here was the entrance to the chairman of the board's office. I asked him what was characteristic of Seagram's that I could pick up. He told me that Seagram's ran a marvelous stable of horses, so I used the horse's head and put the Seagram's crown on it, which is the symbol of Seagram's today. This concoction guarded the entrance to the chairman of the board. This was my own little fun. The desk of the chairman was a very dignified version of an Elizabethan desk. It had the combination of Elizabethan and contemporary. It wasn't too whimsical, but now and then the whimsy would show through. Basically, it was a stage setting.

JC: Did they enjoy this for what it was? Did they take it seriously, or did they see the humor in it?

ML: No, no. Most business people have no sense of humor about *their* business. They're earnest. That was Seagram's.

JC: [to Alan Lapidus] In your office we have seen an astonishing model [*Fig. 5–18*]. It seems to be your intention to build a skyscraper on Fifth Avenue which will smother Saint Patrick's Cathedral, and quite a few other buildings under it. How did it all start?

AL: We first learned about it two years ago. We had been trying to convince the client to let us take a try at it, but he didn't really think we were capable of it. Finally, after he went to several architects, he told us we could try it.*

The building will be the first "air rights" structure, though that is a misnomer. Very simply, it is a building which is allowed to fill up a zoning envelope. If one building doesn't fill up a particular zoning envelope, you have the right to fill it by building on top of it or adding on to the building. You cannot specifically buy air rights, but you can use your unused floor-area ratio, or FAR. So a consortium of people got together which consisted of Arlen Properties, the owners of Best and Company, and Aristotle Onassis, on whose property the main supporting shaft of the building will be built.

HK: So, on this narrow strip of land on Fifth Avenue, where the Olympic Airlines office now stands, one of the supporting shafts of an enormous skyscraper will rest?

AL: Yes, and the other shaft is on 52d Street.

JC: What about Cartier's on the corner?

AL: Cartier's is controlled by the members of the group. Between the three of them, Best, Arlen, and Onassis, they own all these buildings.

JC: So you actually could have torn down the whole corner of the block?

AL: We could have, but that would have created enormous problems. With certain buildings, it didn't pay to tear them down. Some people had leases that ran for twenty-five years, and Cartier's, which is a landmark, should not be torn down; it is a world-famous institution. The trick is not to interrupt their operation in any way while our building is going up.

At face value, this ended up being a box sitting on two legs; it tended to look ridiculous. Even though, structurally, it could be built—and we saw some of the other schemes—it just looked somewhere between silly and unsafe; two thin legs with a huge box on top. They were willing to spend more money on engineering and design than they ordinarily would because they were getting this without buying any land. They're still coming out ahead in the game. So we figured out how this could happen and the idea was very, very frightening: putting a building this size above other buildings, and making it float there [*Fig. 5–19*].

HK: Above Saint Patrick's Cathedral?

AL: Right, but not over Saint Patrick's Cathedral, next to it, totally breaking scale with the rest of the avenue. We realized that, no matter what we put there, we were going to be in for severe attack and tremendous criticism. But the issue is how to do it right.

5–19. Model for Olympic Building. Morris Lapidus.

---

* The project has since been canceled. Skidmore, Owings, and Merrill has been hired. Existing buildings have been demolished, and construction is under way.

5–20. Early sketch for Olympic Building. 1970. Morris Lapidus.

The first premise is that "air rights" buildings will be coming in. It's the only way for the city to function. These buildings *must* happen. One was designed to be put over Grand Central Station, but it was legislated against and killed.

HK: Do you know any of the other designs which were submitted by other architects for this Fifth Avenue project?

AL: One of the solutions was like the rejected Grand Central design. They were going to fill in every bit of space above here [the space above the lot on 52d Street] and come up.

HK: And simply go higher.

AL: Right. We disagreed. This was a totally different species of building. It was as different from all the other buildings as the skyscraper was from the 5-story building that had been there previously. This is a whole new departure in building and it should look like it. Since it was enormous, it would be seen from very far away. If it were a conventional glass box, you would expect it to come straight down to the street, so, when you approached it and found that it didn't, it would look wrong to you. Therefore, we felt we had somehow to signify that it was not a normal building.

HK: That's what Kevin Roche is doing right now in his design for the Federal Reserve Bank [*Fig. 2–21*]. It is a huge glass box sitting on four enormous concrete legs.

AL: We felt that was a wrong solution because, in relation to these other buildings around here, it would be too much of a surprise. The problem is scale, treating a building as enormous as this as a backdrop for Saint Patrick's, without making Saint Patrick's look small. This problem was unsolved in the Pan Am Building in front of Grand Central Station. Grand Central starts to look like a toy because it's thrown out of scale. It either disappears or looks silly. So, we felt that a feeling of overwhelming verticality should be accomplished. This was my father's first idea: Bring that shaft all the way to the top of the building, don't cut it off. Don't stop it at the platform.

JC: Your father has shown us one of his first drawings introducing a general scheme [*Fig. 5–20*].

AL: Yes. When I called him in Miami and told him we were going to do it, he said, "Let me sketch out some ideas and send them up to you." So he did and said, "I've gone as far as I can go. You take it from there." But the idea of continuing the shaft upward, without a break, we could not do for various practical reasons.

We can bring the shaft from street level up to a certain point. But then we had to transfer elevators. The upper elevator shafts had to go either in front or in back. Therefore, we couldn't bring one solid shaft right down to the street. So we started getting various elements, and realized that the most important thing was to differentiate rugged elements from smooth elements, solids from voids. We started playing with these forms as sculpture, and bringing them out of the glass box, and breaking the glass box.

HK: And you have an enormous clamp shape completely around the box.

AL: Right.

JC: So you put the elevator shafts in the vertical claws of the clamp?

AL: That's one area I feel very guilty about, but I decided not to feel guilty about it. The clamp is not structure, but it's solid, and we made it read as strong as structure. We have the shaft, which spreads out down below, coming up on the truss level. We have the clamp coming around to give it a feeling of containment and solidity, so that it doesn't look as if it were going to topple. And then, for the glass box itself, the most important thing to do is to treat the scale in such a way that it doesn't impose itself heavily upon the existing cityscape. The original rationalization for having glass buildings was the beauty of having the sky reflected in them. This very rarely works. But with the advent of reflective glass, it does work. We felt that, because of the angle of vision from the street, we should make this a full reflective façade. Looking up at this building, you will get a perfect reflection of the sky, which will be incredibly dramatic. The glass box wouldn't disappear, because the clamp brings you back by defining the borders, more or less like a picture frame. Inside the frame, you would see a shifting pattern of clouds and sky. It would be there. It would make no excuses for being up there. It wouldn't be frightening with those buildings down below.

Our first idea was to integrate it with those buildings, finish it with stone, have a deep relief façade. But that was absurd. It would be like making a skyscraper look like a 5-story building.

JC: This will certainly be the most expensive building per square foot in New York City.

AL: Yes, but they didn't have to spend the staggering amount of money it would take to buy land for a building this size on Fifth Avenue. The thing that I'm girding myself for is the attack that's going to come against this building for several reasons. One is the sanctity of Fifth Avenue, which I intend to refute simply on the grounds that the new Tishman Building has already violated the virgin. I know that two wrongs don't make a right, but I think ours is an architecturally positive building. Another ground for criticism will be simply that Morris Lapidus designed it.

JC: You expect Ada Louise Huxtable to dislike it?

AL: She'll have a fit. I was very interested in the criticism that Marcel Breuer got for the Grand Central design. Everyone was agreed it should not be done, but it was criticized in the gentle tone of, "It's the right building for the wrong place; it's a very fine building in itself, but it really shouldn't be put there." I don't think they're going to have those kid gloves on when they come after us. And I think that any criticism we have had before is going to be child's play, compared to what this is going to do.

HK: But it is so much different from what your father has done before. If we compare it with his earlier hotel architecture, it's a new world. Your father always took into consideration the attitudes and desires of Mr. and Mrs. America. You certainly cannot count on that for this building. It doesn't fit into their world.

AL: But it does fit in if you're talking about the tourists coming into New York. This will become one of the major tourist attractions, especially since the public can go up and visit the gallery on the platform. They will definitely want to see this thing; they expect the unusual in New York.

JC: Like the Empire State Building.

AL: Yes. My fantasies are in this design, too. Whereas my father's visions of the future came from Busby Berkeley musicals of the 1930's, mine came from Buck Rogers comic strips of the 1940's. I always remember those glistening silver buildings. The genealogy of this building is that the black stone is my father and the mirror is me.

HK: The black stone refers to the facing of the clamp?

AL: Yes. The facing will be of black granite. I was very conscious that we were designing a building that would be the building of the future, a whole new type of building that would be coming up here and probably in Europe. I felt that we could not use the same vernacular used in building skyscrapers. The building *had* to look like this, nothing is forced about it.

HK: Why is the building lopsided?

AL: The building is asymmetrical because of the zoning law. We have a strict line to adhere to on one side of the street. But in order to get the economics of the building, we have to cantilever one side further than the other—which doesn't bother me.

HK: You cantilever on the side where the zoning law of 51st Street does not affect you. So you start where the zoning law stops.

AL: Right. And that slanting line of the support on 52d Street is a tension member to keep the building from overturning.

HK: What kind of office space will this building provide?

AL: Very expensive office space. It will probably be the most expensive office space in New York. The building doesn't exist yet, but they have informed me that it is all rented. One of our clients, the one who owned Best, has a fantastic private collection of art, modern art. He intends to have a public gallery in this building.

HK: That means there will be a large public space in the horizontal truss underneath the glass box, and a private art collection will be exhibited in this panoramic gallery.

AL: A public park, in effect.

JC: A public park 25 stories in the air.

AL: Right.

JC: In order to make the public accept the building?

AL: Right. But we're not really asking for anything. In other buildings, particularly downtown, they ask for street closings, and they bargain in return for a park. We ask for nothing. This is all strictly legal. It will be quite a startling building for the city, but we are not asking for anything from the city.

HK: You mentioned you'd face criticism, but you might even face the problem that the city could change the zoning laws because of just such a building.

AL: That's a possibility.

HK: The people who make the zoning laws could not anticipate your solution here because they think in traditional constructural terms. Normally, the traditional zoning laws prevent inventiveness. In this case, they encourage it.

AL: I would like to hope so, but I've been too conditioned by the publicity we've gotten in the past; in anything we do that's large I expect a battle. I bear the same scars my father does. Everyone hates us but the public.

I have had more apprehension about this building than with anything I've done. I keep feeling like a kid with a toy—they're going to take it away at some point and not let us do it! And at another point I think, "Oh my God, they *are* going to do it!"

HK: Is there a real chance that it will be built?

AL: Yes, definitely. They are already heading for construction.

JC: How much will it cost per square foot?

AL: I would think somewhere around $50 per square foot, the most expensive building. But it will get the most expensive rents in New York City. There will be no doubt what building it is when it is talked about. To some extent, this is achieved in the Lever House and the Seagram Building, depending on which level it percolates down to, but certainly everybody knows the Empire State Building and the Chrysler Building. I believe everyone will know the Olympic Building.

HK: So you create an image people want.

AL: Right. It gives the building enormous prestige.

JC: Are the commissioners interested in the prestige the building will give?

AL: Most definitely. They're all on what is known as ego trips at this point. Apparently, there was a hell of a battle over what name the building would get, who would have the honor of having the name. So it was bartered off. The one who didn't get the name got the top floor.

HK: And Onassis got the name, Olympic.

AL: Yes, Onassis's airlines!

HK: Did he see the plans?

AL: Yes. His first opinion, given laughingly, was that it looked sort of funny. But he was very pleased with it and gave it his blessing.

JC: Won't it be difficult for Onassis to adjust to the modernity of this eighth world wonder, or do you give him a Corinthian column behind his desk?

AL: He hates classical columns, so we gave him a Minoan one.

HK: Then you aren't really so different from your father after all. You want to give Onassis what he wants. Both of you want to let people identify themselves with fake imagery. People come to believe in these symbols. They become proud of their pseudoaristocratic setting.

ML: Very much so.

JC: So they establish a certain image of themselves, which is not real any more. Of course, this is much more true of your hotels than of the Olympic Building. As long as the circus barker barks and promises something, he has to live up to . . .

ML: A good show?

JC: Yes. But, very often, he promises more than he can fulfill, in fact, it misleads. A rather modest man can walk into your lobby and be made to think, "My God, am I important!" He can yell at the servants and pretend he is a plantation owner for two weeks. There is a whole kaleidoscope of emotions which you encourage. They may be fun, but they are often tasteless.

ML: If you were saying that about someone's home, I would say it would be the wrong thing to do. Some people demand the stage setting. They want background. They want status, just as the people in Seagram's achieved status because they sat against this impeccable historic background which no one could question; they had instant status.

Let me digress for a moment about this status. I visited the same chairman of the Seagram board many years later [now deceased], sitting in his huge office in the Seagram Building of Mies van der Rohe. And here is this little man, only about five foot five or six. In the Chrysler Building, he was seated behind my very modest but beautifully carved desk and he felt he had arrived. Now, I see him sitting behind a huge desk in a huge room with probably a half million dollars' worth of art upon the walls, the finest woods and the richest carpets, a little man in this huge office. In this conversation, he said to me, "Morris, you remember my first office which you designed?" and I said, "Yes." He said, "I enjoyed that." Then he said, "What do you think of this one?" and there was such a feeling of uncertainty in his voice. He said, "I look around me and I say, 'What does all of this mean?'" He had reached maturity. He had been given this huge, wonderful background, but he didn't relate to it any more. He felt that something had passed him by. He had reached the point where the setting was no longer for him. He had acted his part, but he was on the wrong stage. He couldn't go for this role.

Now, going back to hotels, I dare say that there are people who would come to the Fontainebleau and say, "This is not for us. This is ridiculous." A very small minority of people would think, "This is gauche, this is flamboyant, this is stagey." But Mr. and Mrs. America have made up their minds that they are going to the most expensive hotel in Miami Beach. In their own minds, they have already conjured up a picture of living the life of a millionaire. So I designed what I did for *them;* the immensity of a meaningless lobby, the overabundance of beautiful antiques, the feeling of great opulence. When they walk in, they *do* feel. "This is what we've dreamed of, this is what we saw in the movies, this is what we imagined it might be." But I've never left my characters in this charade alone. When they come to the registration desk, there is a coat of arms for the Fontainebleau, a baronial coat of arms. They're signing in on the beautiful marble top. The receptionist is signing them in behind a wicket of wrought bronze. The setting, the mood, is maintained. They step into the elevator (and, incidentally, I designed all the costumes for all the people in the hotel), and there is an elevator girl dressed like a little mannequin bellhop. The elevator has frills and things on it. They get off at their floor and there is a beautiful antique mirror, an antique clock, and a couple of antique chairs. Antiques. Wealth. Tradition. It's all there. The wallpaper shows the Fontainebleau palace with the coat of arms I designed for them. Fontainebleau, France, luxury, royalty. They step into their room, for which I designed oversized pieces of furniture which look ridiculous anyplace else. But here it is right, because it's what they've dreamed of. It's their great fulfillment. The whole design attitude is summed up in my entrance to the restaurant, which we've talked about already. That platform, that parade, is the most idiotic thing anyone can do. It isn't functional, it isn't necessary, but it satisfies that emotional ego.

JC: What happens if Joe and Jane from Shreveport go to the Fontainebleau for their two-week vacation? In a sense, you tease them into believing they are in a musical comedy, they are heroes for two weeks. Don't they become dissatisfied with reality when they return home?

ML: No. It's a treasured memory! It's something they can talk about with their friends. Just to come home from the vacation without something to talk about, pictures of what it was like, is not a vacation. I always go back to the human element, the idiosyncrasies of human nature. As someone has said on more than one occasion, "That's the trouble with you, Morris. You *pander* to people. Why don't you upgrade their taste?" My answer to that is, "I don't feel that's my function." Let Mies try to do it. In fact, the more I heard Mies, the more I said, "Well, I'm glad he's doing it, because I don't want to do it."

HK: Your idea of beauty stands in relationship to the subjective human experience. You do not object to kitsch.

ML: Kitsch is the word. I never felt that I was a status architect. I resolved early in my career that, since I probably would not leave my mark, I might as well enjoy what I'm doing, and have the people who use my architecture enjoy it as well. And so, I was accused of catering to their tastes. But Alan, my son, has said to me, "You know what you did, Dad? You created architecture for people. In all previous epochs, architecture was something that people could understand. A theater looked like a theater, a church like a church, and when a building was built, they became involved. They could talk about it." I feel that architecture in the 1950's left that out, seeming to say to people, "If you don't understand it, you're stupid." I felt my role was to please the people, allow them to get involved. They loved it or they hated it, but nobody just walked by my buildings. Maybe a few stood in front of the Summit and said, "My God, who the hell did that?" Maybe that was my way of trying to find status for myself.

JC: As far as your hotels are concerned, don't you think you have a colleague in this kind of architecture in Oscar Niemeyer?

ML: Didn't I mention him? He had a great influence. I went to Brazil in 1949, and, of course, the one man I had to see was Oscar Niemeyer, because he was a man who was doing things the way I thought they should be done.

HK: He had the wavy lines, undulating walls.

ML: Yes. All of that. But you must

remember that, in 1949, I was still very unsure of myself, didn't think of myself as an architect doing anything worthwhile; only stores and offices. But I had watched Niemeyer and, actually, in 1949, he wasn't firmly established yet. He had designed Pampulha [*Fig. 5–21*]. I spent more than half a day with him in his office, and then we spent an evening together at his home. We talked and talked a great deal, and I'm sure that his influence must be there pretty strongly. However, I found his influence only in the architectural shell. His interiors were quite barren. He had no feeling for interiors. They meant nothing to him. He wanted sculptural architecture like Le Corbusier, his great teacher.

HK: The early 1950's was the time of the kidney table. Suddenly, everyone wanted a kidney table, wanted a moving, flowing line. It became a fashion all over the world. That is the context into which your hotels fit. But you were sensing these possibilities at a time when few others were aware of them. The same is true for your sense of decoration. The Fontainebleau was an ornament in itself.

ML: In the broad sense, yes. I was adorning the area, dressing it up, giving it background, but all influenced by the desire to avoid the attitude of, "Once you've seen it, you've seen it all." If you look at the Fontainebleau closely, you'll find a major curve and an opposing curve and another circle. It's not something like a Seagram Building, for which one look suffices. You don't have to wander around in it, there's nothing further to see, and if you did wander through it, you wouldn't find anything else. My kind of architecture has to be something that must be seen, must be lived in, must be moved around in, experienced.

JC: But it is difficult to experience your larger spaces. When one enters some of the larger ballrooms in your hotels, he is absolutely lost. He is swallowed by the space. And something happens to the scale. The flair and excitement and intimacy of what you do in smaller spaces does not find a corresponding quality of scale in your larger spaces. There are enormous designs on the walls, and the furniture seems to be clumped together just because you have to take care of great crowds.

AL: That's not the problem; that's the solution. My father remarked at one point that people feel better in formal clothes at one of his hotels. In a ballroom, you are in formal clothes, you are at a great gala, you're at an affair. You want to impress and be impressed, so this is the place for gigantic designs. You don't want to feel particularly intimate. When you're going to a grand ball, you want to feel as if you're walking into Versailles.

ML: Yes, I would say that I intention-

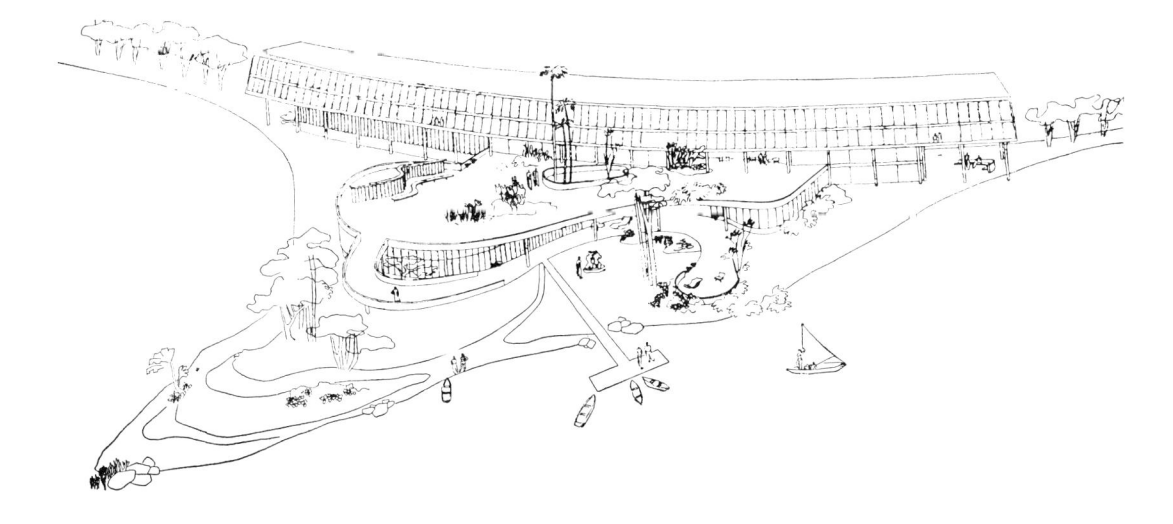

5–21. Pampulha Casino. Brazil. 1942. Oscar Niemeyer.

ally overscaled ballrooms. I used every chance I could to make it seem even larger. I wanted everything to move away from the human scale. For instance, the great Winter Palace in Leningrad, which I visited, was done just to be grandiose. That same feeling is what I've put into the ballroom again.

JC: What I mean is something different. The classical ballrooms of the past, like the Plaza or the Pierre, achieve grand space which nevertheless avoid the empty airplane hangar feeling. There are transitional details which grade the scale from human to grandiose.

ML: What you criticize, I did intentionally. Those ballrooms you're referring to, the Plaza, for example, actually took their cue from the grand salons in Europe. A salon was a place where you walked around and greeted your friends; you sat around and talked to them. When the music started, you went out and danced. It's a whole way of life, salon living, but a way of life of the nineteenth century; we don't have it any more. A ball today is a mass event, and a ballroom has to contain it. Today, people feel they are having a better time when they are herded together in great numbers.

HK: In other words, as the distinctions within society faded away, the differentiations of scale were lost.

ML: Again, I'm pandering to people.

HK: But the question is, are you *creating* desires, or are you affirming existing desires? Newspapers print sensational stuff because they have a certain audience for it. But, at the same time, that audience is influenced by the newspapers. It's a vicious circle. In other words, you support this mentality.

ML: Yes.

JC: What do you do if you have to build a church or a synagogue?

ML: I think that religion is separate and apart from everyday life, as opposed to religion as it was in the Middle Ages. It has to be. Today's religion has to compete with so many other institutions. I try to fit the syn-

5–22. Hebrew Academy. Miami Beach, Florida. 1960. Morris Lapidus.

agogue into the cityscape, but I try to separate it so that you could recognize it as a place for religious worship.

When we go to worship, we demand that it be something separate and quiet. To me, in my faith, the synagogue isn't a place to visit every day; I go during the high holidays. You've got to be able to walk by and say, "That's my church, that's my synagogue." You shouldn't feel that you *have* to go in or feel conscience-stricken as you walk by, as a Roman Catholic might if he walked by Saint Patrick's. It's there, and, since you're a Catholic, you'd better go in. Churches aren't built that way any more. They tell us, "When you're ready to come in, we're ready for you." So that's the way to design them. As you approach it, the building should start setting the mood for worship. If I can achieve that on the outside, and yet be a part of the city, then I think I've achieved something.

JC: When you get a commission to build a school, is there a certain environment you try to create which is different from a hotel or a synagogue?

ML: Yes. It's a place to learn, but a pleasant place to learn, where learning is fun. I've only done one school, that's a Hebrew Academy in Florida [*Fig. 5–22*], and I tried to break away from a formal school background. There are patios, walkways, bridges, open stairways. There's a sense of movement, a sense of fun. Learning should be fun; it should be pleasurable.

HK: When you pander to society, if that is what you do, do you pander to that part of society which revolts?

ML: I don't think architecture has reached that point, nor will it ever reach that point. Revolution wants to tear down not only institutions, but established ways of doing things. I take established ways of doing things and dramatize them, sensitize my people to them. What another building might do in a restrained manner, I will do in a flamboyant manner. I won't be discreet, nor will I be . . .

JC: Conservative?

ML: No, not conservative. I want it to be as obvious as all hell. Damn it, you're entering a synagogue, this is a synagogue. You're coming into a hotel, this is a wild place, you're going to have a ball here. You're coming into a hospital, you're going to be cured here because everything seems so beautifully attuned to you as the patient, and you'll get well. The reception room, the corridor, the bedrooms, all have a warmth and color. I try to relate it to the human scale, not to the clinical scale. And, in each case, I will not be subtle. I'm bold as all hell, as obvious as all hell. But that isn't revolution! Let's just say you like ice cream. Why have one scoop of ice cream? Have three scoops.

JC: In the 1950's, Auntie Mame said, "Life is a banquet and too many bastards are starving to death." Would that describe that special 1950's quality in your work?

ML: Yes. Why not? It's absolutely so. Our buildings should be pleasant places. Life is tough enough; don't teach, don't preach. If you're going to preach, do just as in the Catholic Church. When the priest gets up for his sermon he doesn't have to preach to them as hard as a black preacher in a cabin. Because in the church they've already accepted it! You've set the stage. You've accepted it, you've become a part of the drama. The poor black preacher in the cabin has to hammer away, but you've *got* religion. When you enter Saint Patrick's, you can't help it. You've got it just by walking into the church and being overwhelmed by it. I try to overwhelm people like that. You want to have fun? Don't try. You are in my hotel. You're having fun, you're having a ball; this is the greatest experience of your life. Poor fellow doesn't know if he's enjoying himself or not. But I've set it for him. He *is* enjoying it.

6 LOUIS KAHN

JC: You have just returned from Dacca, where you are building the Second Capital of Pakistan [now Bangladesh], begun in 1962 [*Fig. 6–1*]. Are you satisfied with those buildings now being built?

LK: I saw the buildings recently. I think they are wonderful, and now I recognize that my idea of landscaping is completely different from what I first thought. I want nothing but grass as a setting, a great carpet in front of a strong geometry.

JC: You've just decided that?

LK: Yes, now. Before, I thought I needed everything. But I don't need the picturesque.

JC: But the people who will live there might want some trees.

LK: If they want trees, then that's their concern. *I* must make it so strong that they *don't* want them.

HK: Your famous Yale Art Gallery comes to mind at this point. Specifically, the enormous bare brick wall on Chapel Street [*Fig. 6–2*] which comes down straight next to the sidewalk—no trees, just a narrow strip of grass. The architecture students have fiercely objected to this wall because it is so alien to the pedestrian standing there waiting for a bus. No bench, no shade, no space, just a wall. It may be a wonderful wall, but it's hostile and too monumental. How would you answer this criticism?

LK: Personally, I must answer, "Nonsense." Yet I must give another answer, because I always respect the other man's opinion. If it's the collective opinion of *more* than one person, I have no regard for it whatsoever. If it's the opinion of one person, I have a great regard for it.

I don't think it's monumental; I don't think it's anywhere near monumental. A wall is a wall. I considered rain as important to the wall, so I introduced those ledges to wash the wall at intervals. I could have left the wall bare—just for monumentality.

HK: Mr. Kahn, this is a picture of your design for a high-rise building for the Universal Atlas Cement Company done in 1957 [*Fig. 6–3*]. Would you explain it to us?

LK: It's a building which personifies, in a way, how a structural order must have the power to make itself, not as a willful design but as a characteristic. And it's a kind of belief in the potentiality of man willing an order, a psychological order asking for a physical order. At the same time, it recognizes that the characteristics of a physical order are the measure of it. It is desire calling on nature, the maker of all presences. In this case, it was allowing a physical phenomenon to evolve without interference; but knowing that the spaces which evolve are useful for man.

HK: It is not a Utopian design?

LK: It is not, in any sense, Utopian. Before design, there is existence as form with its undeniable elements; there is, as yet, no presence. Design is to *give* presence. It calls on the physical orders for approval so that the nature of the spaces and their making are one. The height of a ceiling in a room was chosen basically as 11 feet, which became the module of the tetrahedron.

HK: So you didn't need a central core?

LK: I had no need for an ordained central core. The vertical spaces needed for elevators were inherent in the course of the spiraling of the structure upward. Nothing was broken in order to accommodate. The acceptance of the tetrahedron also reveals spatial opportunities. The structure teaches. This is the natural shape which a tetrahedral system will make without interference.

HK: So it does not need to be held up by a backbone?

LK: No. The building makes itself strong by reason of its triangulation. The spiral form is natural to the tetrahedron, so the shape is not mine at all.

JC: You are well-known for having a very personal way of explaining what you do. You said earlier, "The designer gives presence by calling on nature to satisfy the requirements of man." Would you expand on your conception of the role of the architect?

LK: To sense the spaces that the desires of man present . . . to find the inseparable parts, or the form of the "society" of spaces, good for the activities of man. When he designs he has always the inseparable parts in mind. He calls on nature to find a means to make.

JC: Is this nature, for you, something constant or is it a set of historical circumstances?

LK: What is has always been. A validity true to man presents itself to a man in circumstances. A man can be a catalyst to a validity. Yet it has to await its realization, it has to be given presence.

JC: "To be given"? *Somebody* has to *give* presence.

LK: Presence against existence! Yes.

6–1. Government Center of Bangladesh. Dacca. 1962–. Louis Kahn.

Somebody has to. But validity is always there as though it were in the air. But, circumstantially, it could only grow to the realization when one says, "I realize it is so." The artist is only a vehicle for what always has been. Nothing can really be given presence unless it already exists potentially.

JC: Does the artist provide the realization in any individual way or is he simply the agent who taps what is there?

LK: The artist senses human validity. Validity transcends time. What *is* has always been. What *was* has always been. What *will be* has always been.

JC: In this sense the artist is a philosopher. Where is he as a maker?

LK: I agree. The artist works by motivation, which is the drive to his work, but the artist by his work does not satisfy motivation. He is always greater than his work, therefore he seeks more opportunity for his expression.

JC: Can science lead the artist to more decisive answers and expressions?

LK: The wish in the fairy tale is the beginning of science. Man knows quite well that he's not going to fly just by wishing it, but he must still satisfy that wish. Man's first sense must have been Beauty, a sense of total harmony. Next to it Wonder, then the realization of the opening of the doors of the treasury of form which inspires design, the process of shaping into presence. Presence emerges from a wish and Rule. Rule guides the maker to seek Order. Order is nature, nonconscious. Rule is man's order.

Man lives to express. What motivates expression serves Art. A work of art is an offering to Art. Everything turns into itself, you know. There is no sort of ending.

HK: I have the impression that you no longer distinguish between subject and object, you do not acknowledge the difference between human subject and the objective world. I am reminded of Heidegger's ontology.

LK: Yes.

HK: In another sense, it reminds me of Mies van der Rohe's credo. He might say, "What I did was actually nothing individualistically important. I only did what time and my presence have given me. And I just expressed what had to be expressed." The artist, when you interpret him that way, is humble, and presents his work as an offering.

LK: Yes, yes. He is tremendously grateful. Grateful is not the word, but he feels *serving*. What you're saying is exactly right, and your analogy with Mies makes me feel terribly good, because I know that the kind of humility and sense of joy that he is expressing is the very essence of my thought. You cannot make a work of art except in joy. Mies is expressing a joy of being. He was in a certain position where a certain realization came about. That source of realization is a truth which is man's fact. Anything that happens is a truth.

HK: Did you want to do anything else, before you became an architect?

LK: I would say that it happened quite circumstantially. There is no denying that I would have been either a painter, sculptor, musician, or architect, because of my love for that which yet is not. If I had to describe the very core of the decision, it would have to do most basically with that which is in question, that which is yet not. You see, it refutes need. It only deals with desires.

HK: By "needs," do you mean everyday desires for money, shelter, bread, and all these other . . .

LK: Need stands for what is already present, and it becomes a kind of measurement of the already present. Desire becomes a sense of the yet not made. That is the main difference between need and desire. And you can go so far as to say that need is just so many bananas. The architectural program that comes to you then becomes transformed, because you see the needs in it, *and* you see that which has not been expressed in the inspirations you feel. The society of spaces talking to each other in a plan is what reveals itself as an archi-

6–2. Yale University Art Gallery. New Haven, Conn. (left) 1951–53. Louis Kahn.

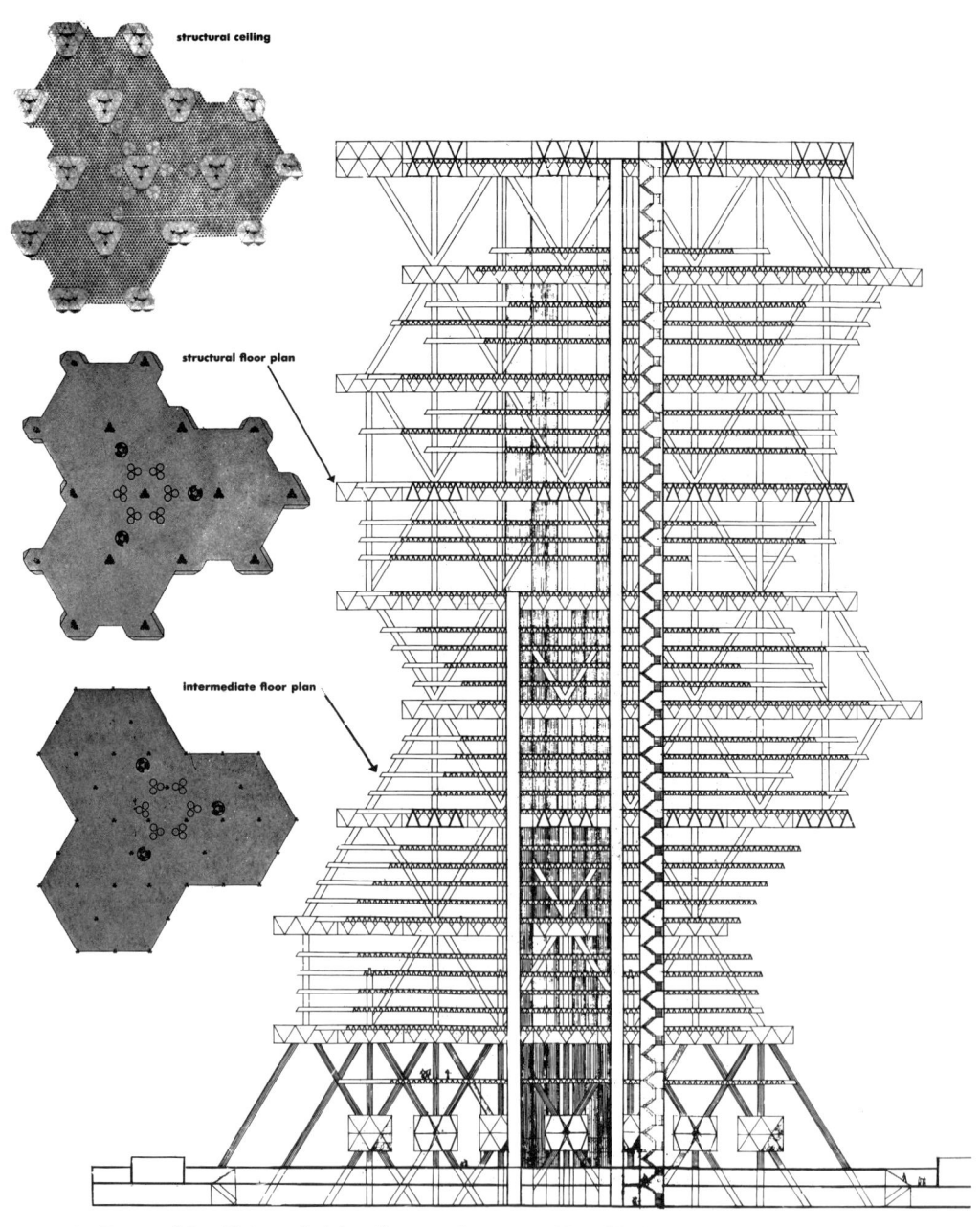

6–3. Proposal for Universal Atlas Cement Company. New York, N.Y. 1957. Louis Kahn. Structural section through building.

tectural validity, a harmony discovered out of the mere areas in a program. From area to space is the transformation.

JC: You mean that the program refers to needs, and the architect expresses desires.

LK: Precisely. It also occurs to me what I thought of the astronauts and their view of the earth: a marble, blue and green and rose. Looking at it, somehow Paris disappeared, Rome disappeared, and the dear places made by the play of circumstances.

But somehow The Fifth Symphony by Beethoven could not disappear. It simply brought out the very essence of spirit. The unmeasurable was indestructible because it was so close to the spirit.

HK: Does that mean that *your* desire to express goes more in the direction of music than in the direction of building architecture? Isn't the problem really that architecture is too close to the reality of mundane needs to be "pure art"? It is so close to the needs that architects during the last half-century wanted architecture to be nothing but a service to those needs and functions, thus abandoning art. They wanted an architecture which was purely technical, not aesthetic, not an art any more. But *you* want architecture as an art, without ever questioning it.

LK: The only language of man is Art.

HK: Doesn't the architect ever build just for needs?

LK: No. Never build for needs! Remember what I said about bananas. As an art a space is made a touch of eternity. I think a space evokes its use. It transcends need. If it doesn't do that, then it has failed. One might say that architecture is directed by function more than painting is. A painting is made to be sensed for its motivation beyond seeing, just as space is made to inspire use. It's psychological. There is something about a building which is different from a painting: When a building is being built, there is an impatience to bring it into being. Not a blade of grass can grow near this activity. Look at the building after it is built. Each part that was built with so much anxiety and joy and willingness to proceed tries to say when you're using the building, "Let me tell you about how I was made." Nobody is listening because the building is now satisfying need. The desire in its making is not evident. As time passes, when it is a ruin, the spirit of its making comes back. It welcomes the foliage that entwines and conceals. Everyone who passes can hear the story it wants to tell about its making. It is no longer in servitude; the spirit is back.

HK: What do you do with a client who wants to have a building that's nothing but utilitarian, a pure instrument of everyday needs?

LK: You build what he thinks he's getting. There's no problem there. I also get what I want.

HK: In other words, you are not talking about art when you are dealing with a client.

LK: No, no.

HK: You're talking about his needs.

LK: The art, then, is the art of trying to find the words in common, the words which get you away from your code, in order to reach him. That's very important, to you and to him.

JC: We have been talking about individual buildings. How would you build a city? Or let me put it in your own words: What is the nature of a city?

LK: The city is the assembly of the institutions of man. In other words, the city is the place where the institution occurs to man. The gathering of men and legislation establishes the institution of what is wanted commonly. I believe "availability" is a more meaningful term today than institution. The measure of a city is the character of its availabilities; how sensitive it is to man's pursuit of well being. The traffic system and other needs are only the servants of availability.

JC: Where is the sociologist in this scheme?

LK: He is an observer and advisor but not the planner. A social plan is an arrogant plan. One has to make a distinction between a way of life and a way of living. One is general, the other is personal.

HK: By making such a distinction, do you mean that you achieve a variety of architectural forms inspired by the urges of what you call availability? If so, one would not have to invent...

LK: Yes! You don't invent. You don't force invention without motivation coming from a sense of commonality. You don't invent circumstances, but when they happen, they reveal human nature.

JC: Let's take your Philadelphia City Plan of 1952–53 [*Fig. 6–4*] as a specific example.

LK: First, I love my city and I want it to be good. This means to me that its acts in the process of development are true to its particular character, sensitive to its scale in relation to its people. For example, it is a place where one can serve the validity of an open field without limiting it in size because land is expensive, regardless of how much you know about the cost of real estate, or whether it's sensible or not to put a playing field in a city. If you know that a child who lives in the city loves to play as much as one in the country, you cannot make that playground big enough. It's a powerful right.

I have no questions about the existence of the city, not only because it is there, but also because the city is inevitable. It answers a prime inspiration: to meet.

HK: Would you tear down Philadelphia in order to build a new one, if you had the power to do it?

LK: No, because you wouldn't know where to begin. The city itself becomes a point of departure. There is so much left in the city already which determines its paths of happenings. The results cannot be anticipated. The circumstantial things which

6–4. Philadelphia City Plan. 1952–53. Louis Kahn. Above: Proposed movement pattern. Below: Perspective of movement pattern looking west.

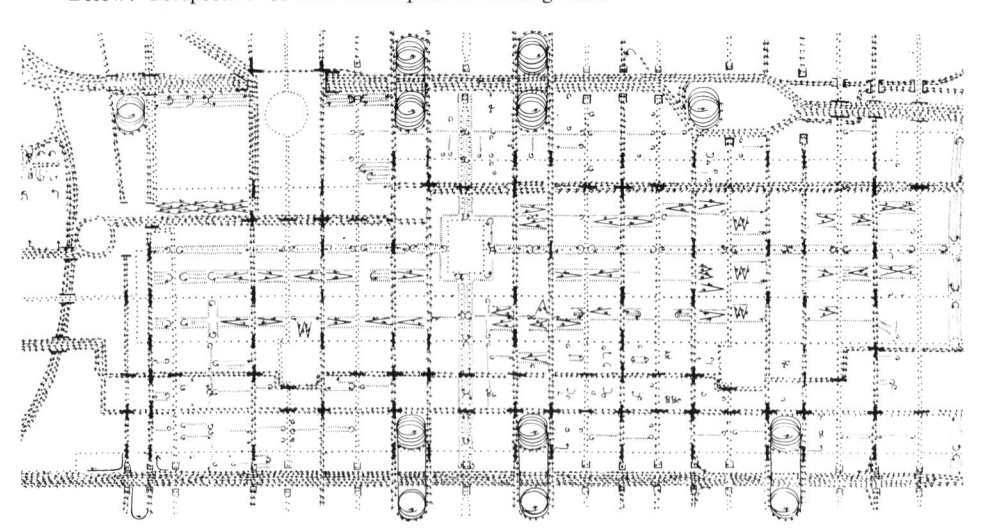

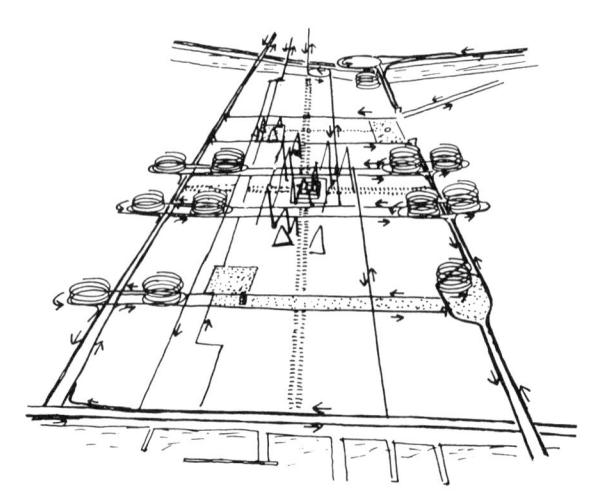

6–5. Philadelphia City Plan. Sketch of buildings for stopping.

happen cannot be anticipated. This is the difference between a plan and what happens because you cannot plan circumstances.

HK: These considerations which you mention now are not evident in the plan as it has been published. When I look at this plan I have the impression that the city means the traffic in it and how the traffic flows.

LK: I have one remark to make, right from the start, which has to do with a broader view of the 1952 plan. I believe that a city is measured by its availabilities. This plan does not touch on this question. It doesn't give anything but a sense of land disposition in the order of movement. So, therefore, I try to find a physical validity to movement. I distinguish certain streets from others by the sense of their movement value. Now, in this plan, the importance of stopping was emphasized. It's getting somewhere, then stopping. And the design of stopping is what I was really concerned about.

HK: That's the new aspect about it. When you drive around Manhattan, for instance, you are forced to go on moving because everybody else moves.

LK: Yes. You have a hard time stopping. When you want to stop, you've got to keep moving. You see, the whole thing is not very smart.

When you think about the meaning of moving, in relation to stopping, you get a much bolder solution. Any building, even an important one, would be torn down if it obstructed the order of movement, which includes stopping.

HK: What does stopping mean in your sense?

LK: Stopping means that there is a strategic station where the car can be parked in relation to a sector of the city.

HK: Then, that could mean a parking garage?

LK: It could mean that in the system of movement, the intersection of a street could become a building. That building would be a station for stopping. If you say it is a "garage," you would hate it. But if it is a building for stopping, in a city of movement, then it's something else. It could be just as important as the most important place in the city.

I would say that, in 1951, I sorted out the idea that the streets are rivers, in a sense, and these rivers need docks and wharfs, need station points [*Fig. 6–5*]. Out of this grew the sense that there were strategic areas where the docks were larger than at other places. At that point, I conceived that the station point could also be in the form of a stadium surrounded by parking; the center, with little capacity for parking, was the stadium. In a sense the shape of the stopping place provides the space for the stadium for nothing.

HK: There were those enormous round towers.

LK: Yes. They weren't just parking garages. There was obviously no sense in wasting natural light on a parked car, so I planned to use the outside edge of the round towers for hotels, motels, or even offices. In the inner core were to be the services for the car, and on the outside were to be the living and working spaces.

JC: Returning to the traffic pattern for a moment, don't you think that an uninterrupted flow through the city is important?

LK: No, I think the uninterrupted flow should be outside the city. Inside a city, there should be a very organized flow to places of stopping.

HK: As vehicular traffic increases, won't our cities finally be stuffed with cars? We may eventually have to ban all cars from the inner city. This is certainly the case in Europe.

LK: The closer you get to the heart of the city, the more the contours of the land must change. This part of the city could have its spaces which personify the country —maybe on the third, fourth, or fifth level. The contours below, which are now the first, second, or third levels, must surrender a broad area in order to make the services to it possible, no matter what the transportation system may be.

HK: Does this eliminate the pedestrians?

LK: No. It's a city for pedestrians. But on new levels.

HK: This means that you would have to change the city to quite an extent. It could mean that the houses we see out of this window would have to be destroyed for such a new traffic system.

LK: In the impetuous acts of building in cities you would hurt buildings very little if you modified the first levels and established new entrances on the levels above, leaving the vehicular traffic below. The top level would have no cars at all and would be truly a *street,* not a road; it would be purely pedestrian. I think it important to consider streets as something which can be used to bring about great changes. The intersection is a piece of city-owned real estate: By acquiring the four corners, the city can add property to the making of a new street-building for the needs of movement.

HK: Then the new levels you speak of also become a building.

LK: Yes. The street will become a building, certainly. I see that the city doesn't realize how wealthy it is. It should consider the land above the streets as its property. What is the real estate value of one-third of the city?

HK: But if the street becomes a building, where is the open sky, the fresh air?

LK: Wait a minute. The mere fact that the real estate is there as real estate and that it can be built over is not realized. It's only considered as a street, sky over it, very beautiful, and please don't change it, you see. The streets themselves have not been used, even though they are worth billions of dollars. Fresh air and sky would be above the vehicular level.

JC: One approach to city planning is to determine what has been called "the anatomy of ambience."

LK: It doesn't ring true to me, "anatomy of ambience." Ambience is something that must be felt, and it is not a physical characteristic that can have an anatomy. If you would say "spirit of ambience," I would like it better. I don't believe in sociology as judge. No sympathy for this whatsoever. I wouldn't like somebody to say there should be a certain social pattern or even to anticipate a social pattern. I don't think you can do it.

JC: You can't plan a city sociologically?

LK: Only if you're a fascist. It's the only way you can do it. You have no idea about one individual meeting another individual. This is completely unpredictable.

JC: One denies spontaneity when the sociologist plans the city?

LK: You deny it. Absolutely, you deny every part of it. And nobody can ever make a pattern, except a completely rigid and inhuman pattern. As long as the city planners try to make a science out of it, and not make science work for that which is human, I have no use for it. City planners who make a walk in the sky, say, a linear walk, are not really thinking humanly. People do not walk in straight lines, except when they meet a train, but they're not *"enjoying"* at this moment. City planners imagine that there's a great enjoyment in being up in the air. It's the same thing when New Haven builds towers for old people. Planners think of this from the sociological viewpoint, distinguishing old people from young people, and so forth.

HK: Let's say New York asked you to build the 5-mile renewal strip on the East Side. How would you proceed?

LK: I would first proceed by being elated.

JC: Do you really think that an architect can be a *homo universale?* Is he able to know everything he has to know in order to build such a city? Is an architect able to know it without asking sociologists, psychologists, city planners, traffic engineers, and statisticians?

LK: When you build a house, you are able to talk to the family. When you build a church, you are able to talk to a committee. But, when you build a city, you are probably unable to talk to the inhabitants, let's say 50,000 people. That means you have to abstract the whole problem. Suddenly, you're all by yourself. But in a way, a house is not different from a city. I know that I will not have many people here, and there's a certain limit which you say is "house." In the form house, I also think of commonness. I think of every person who can live in this house, not just a particular person. In the same way, every person should be able to live in the city.

HK: When you build a city for 50,000 people, you have to think about what kind of facilities these people will need: shops, services, streets, etc. Simple, straightforward things. Some architects now start to employ sociologists for basic information. A huge block like Le Corbusier's Unité at Marseilles includes a lot of shops which are not used. He thought that all those people would need those shops on the center floor, but they are hardly used. That means he probably reached a statistical solution only. So many people, so many shops. He didn't consider that people want to *leave* the building in order to shop—the desire to go outside. The statistics forgot the psychology. Maybe Le Corbusier should have consulted a psychologist, as some architects do today.

LK: It's a pity, though. I don't think you should. I would never have that problem, because I know the difference between shopping and buying. Maybe Le Corbusier was misunderstood. Shopping isn't necessarily where you buy. It's the very nature of shopping, the very nature of commercialism, that it cannot be isolated. You don't go to the baker next door just because he's there, you go to the best baker. It doesn't work mathematically. It works until you sense the realization: what is its nature!

If it's unsuccessful, it's not in the nature. The crocodile must want to be a crocodile for reasons of the crocodile. It has nothing to do with man's reasons for the crocodile. It's most remarkable that order can be the same for everyone and design can be so different. What the crocodile wanted to *be* meant that his predilections, his urges for wanting to be, were somehow different from yours. There must be nothing but a state of wonder in you. You must be so full of wonder that you wouldn't want to touch a crocodile. You wouldn't destroy one. You can almost say it's a condemnation of humanity when it destroys animals which are really so innocent.

HK: You're not a hunter?

LK: I'm not a hunter, but I understand the cul-de-sac. I would be the one to defend the hunter because I know that man can be this way. He is not inhuman, he is very human, only his predilections run in this way, and he cannot avoid being himself.

HK: It's a kind of fate?

LK: It's not fate, it's a kind of nature which expresses itself.. I believe in schools of talent. I don't believe in education because it implies method. You cannot *force* a man to know what is not part of his predilection. People say you have to try to develop your mind. That does not ring true. A man cannot be changed, as far as his predilections are concerned. He can exercise what he has a natural talent for. He develops by being able to express it. He will pick up a book and read it. But you can make him hate this for the rest of his life if he has to read something not a part of his predilections. It's not a matter of training, but if a man is jealous of those around him, of their singularities, he will pick the book up; otherwise, he won't bother with it.

I would never enjoy being a lawyer, for example. Some people would die for the law. I never felt the least jealousy of the doctor. But I felt terribly jealous of one who could write. This kind of beauty got me to the point where I couldn't see straight. Why was it so difficult to know where to put me? I had to be put with my own little private war going on with myself, with others, and that made me strong. So, if you show me a few tricks, like picking up a pencil right, I'm operating. That means I'm happy.

I must overcome my shyness near a tape recorder; it bothers me. Therefore, I wrote something for you. Let me read it. "Man's spirit created architecture. Its wonder crystallized in the great styles. The styles of architecture in the future are unpredictable. The inspirations which will give presence to the yet not thought of, yet not made, will depend on the visions of our leaders. An inspiring leader will be the natural collaborator for an inspired architect who by his works will reveal the spirit of architecture in a new way."

JC: Sorry to interrupt you, but what do you mean by "a leader"?

LK: By "leader" I mean a person with vision. The great leaders all had vision. Even the most despotic.

HK: Of course, we might think immediately of Hitler and of his architecture, a complete failure.

LK: Yes, but he felt he did not need an inspired architect. That was his trouble. If he were really a great leader, he would have realized the greatness of another leader.

JC: In the twentieth century, we have had many great leaders who didn't inspire good architecture. Roosevelt didn't, Pius XII certainly didn't, Mussolini and Franco didn't, and Stalin may have been the worst.

LK: Maybe it's not as direct as I put it there. By a leader I don't necessarily mean a *national* leader. I mean a leader like Jonas Salk. He's a leader in a true sense of the word because he was really not a person who thought of himself first. A leader isn't just a man who wants something; it's usually a man who wants to *give* something. Don't think of Hitler and Stalin, think of Oppenheimer and Salk, Beethoven and Newton. Then you have what truly are leaders.

JC: Well, you are talking about great men.

LK: We're always talking of the great man. Hitler was bound to be a failure. What he wanted to attain would not answer the immediate comprehensions of commonality. He proposed a "giant race," for instance. People are not giants. It's an assumption which you cannot apply to man.

HK: Hitler's architecture needed to symbolize in a very artificial way a self-serving sense of power. Although Hitler's architecture is monumental, it is purely the function of politics. It remains in the realm of "needs."

LK: Just think of it, you must build beyond what you need! You build a room which tends to inspire when you enter it. There's plenty to say about a room. The room can be said to be the beginning of Architecture.

Think of a home, for example. When you're doing a house, you're serving the institution of home. As you build, you keep thinking, "Can this be a home?" Sure, but it depends on those who occupy it. A house,

6–6. First Unitarian Church. Rochester, New York. 1963–64. Louis Kahn.

you see, meets a need, but a home fulfills a desire.

HK: Let us be specific about the distinction you make between needs and desires. Your Unitarian Church at Rochester, New York [Fig. 6–6], consists of one great inner assembly room surrounded by an outer shell of small rooms used for church school, kindergarten, and social functions. The outer wall of these rooms is broken up with alcoves projecting the window line. By doing this, you achieved a very special interior space and, at the same time, that famous cubistic exterior.

At first, these alcoves seemed superfluous to the people. In talking with them, I learned that they didn't know what to do with them. They were totally consumed with the attitude that every room and every part of a room has to have a function. They were somehow frustrated, wondering how to use them, until they learned that they had no specific purpose. But the children in the kindergarten like to sit in these little alcoves, they like to hide and play in them. They were drawn to spaces which were apparently superfluous. Then the adults began to appreciate them by experiencing these spaces. The whole room would have been without character, as rooms can be, if these "superfluous" alcoves had not added spatial interest, evoking the unexpected in their light.

LK: I worked on the Unitarian Church in two stages. The first stage was just the entrance and the main building. Then I added another piece to it, which was done later. In both cases, the amount of money budgeted was very small. But in both cases, the people who administrated the spending of the funds and the planning of each little portion were very exacting about their needs. In my first designs, I had much bigger spaces, more wonderfully conceived, I think, richer in environment, and capable of delighting so many more people, but I had to give them up because of the frugal means. If I have to get more frugal, I look to the Shakers* to help me out. Previously, it would have been richer, with many more facets to which one could respond.

* An early American religious group which built very plain but impressive buildings.

But I knew I couldn't give up those alcoves. What you say about them is true, I think. Their use—and their appreciation—can come from desire and not just *merely* from the need. If you didn't have these alcoves, the rooms themselves wouldn't have been able to transcend need at all, in any way. They were essential in my plan all along.

I wasn't dealing with a personal place for somebody, but with a place for many. Even when serving the dictates of individuals, you still have no client in my sense of the word. The client is human nature. It makes no difference if you are serving one person or many. This church building is a little world within a world, just as a house is *its* little world within a world, but, nevertheless, they are very different. The one makes a home. The other makes a place away from home, where home is also. So you never lose sight of the home, because a person coming from his home to a place away from his home must feel he is in a place where home is not *away* from him.

JC: The one who gives you the commission . . .

LK: Instead of saying "the one who," let's say "the way of life that gives you the commission." Forget about who it is, whether it's a king or a simple man. You don't take a commission from a person. You take it from the way of life. That means that when you are designing a house you are designing it for the *person,* but you are designing it also for the person who will take it *after* this person. Otherwise, you don't serve architecture at all.

You can't make terrific castles which no one can afford, because the way of life won't let you; it tells you that you can't do it. There are no kings any more. Today, an ordinary person, a schoolteacher, for instance, can tell the architect what he wants. Now, this is the way of life telling the architect this. So it really isn't the schoolteacher, nor the shopkeeper, nor the banker, but the way of life which commissions you. The expression of an era can come only from architecture, which has the way of life as its commissioner.

JC: There are clients who behave like kings, and might not even reflect the era in their wants, who have extravagant and fanciful ideas. How would you talk them out of their fanciful ideas which would ruin the building?

LK: To order "extravagance" is unmotivating. It is not the issue. The issue is truth, is it true to the era?

JC: Or let's say you have a client who wants separate facilities for blacks and whites in a bus station or a doctor's office.

LK: I would tell him absolutely, "That is not true. I couldn't do it for the world."

JC: Or you have a client who wants to build a Miami Beach Hotel with a French Provincial lobby.

LK: If he thinks it's the way of life, he's wrong, because somebody is telling you, "print this," and you say, "I can't print it." To me, that is something which is not going to distinguish our era from another era. No sir. It won't do anything of the sort. The same thing is true in the theater. When you copulate on the stage as an expression of the freedom of expression, theater is no more; symbols are defiled. The act becomes incidental and circumstantial, a whorehouse in the wrong place. Theater does not depend on the literal. In fact, the very essence of theater is analogous to my understanding of the essence of light: It is infinitely more brilliant than it would be if I had to *illustrate* it.

JC: We would like to know more about the process you go through from the primary stage of intuition to the final result, or, in your own words, from desire to realization. How do you go from the wish to the building?

Let's take the specific examples of your two skyscrapers, the one with the tetrahedral design [*Fig. 6–3*] which was never built, and the Kansas City tower [*Fig. 6–7*]. The first is a fantasy, the realization of a wish. The second has gone through all the stages of the demand for practical needs. It will be built. These two buildings turn out to be very different. The Kansas City tower is more familiar to a city block. Why are they so different?

LK: That's a wonderful question. *Why are they so different?* This is wonderful. You might say that the tetrahedral skyscraper was something which had truly to do with the fairy tale: You wanted a skyscraper to come about and not have to learn anything about skyscrapers. Just wave your wand and have it. It is the employment of freeing nature, the way nature makes things —with a very inaccessible answer to what dictates its making. Its dictates are tremendously irrefutable. It's very far away from history. I knew that one had to take care of the wind when a skyscraper is built, but I didn't know anything about the formulas for wind. I didn't want to graft on a wind idea but find an order which takes care of the wind. I knew a triangle was nondeformable, and I trusted that this would do it. It was really waving a wand. I never deviated from the natural spiral growth of the tetrahedrons.

HK: Could it actually have been built?

LK: Yes. But, you see, it's out of range with the society of leadership—which is really what I mean when I say "leader." The society of leadership is not there. You see, I am always dependent on someone else for the carrying out of a project; that someone is a man with his own predilections.

What I wanted in my tetrahedron design was freedom to discover. There are drawings which one makes having no client. They are marvelous drawings, manifestations of sheer heart. Think of Boullée or Ledoux, who did drawings which haven't the demand for serving anything other than the spirit of architecture. What is very big in the mind simply must come out.

HK: There are weaknesses in Utopian architecture which one has to recognize. There are architects who want to force their Utopian ideas, and architecture which wants to resemble the greatness of architecture rather than the realness of life. Even Boullée's gigantic exaggerations tend to create an unreal world of pure fantasy.

LK: He's still a man, that means the wonder of a singularity revealed can touch another. It's the judgment which is bad. Just now, you were judging, too ready to classify. That is very much the habit of historians. They make up their minds about what they want to kill and what they want to save.

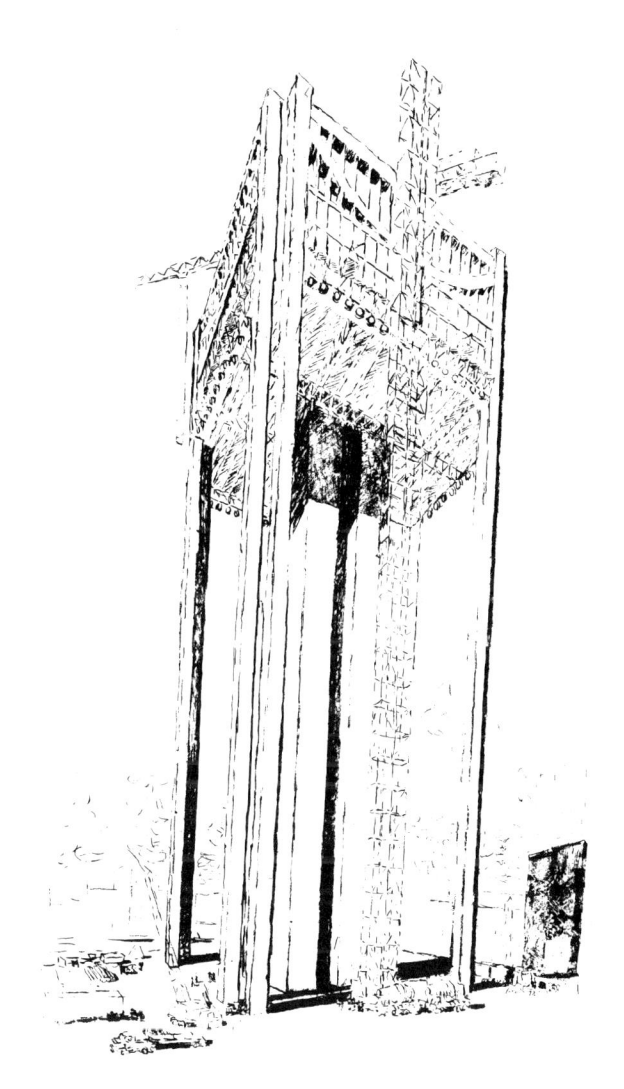

6–7. Kansas City Office Building. Missouri. Louis Kahn. Sketch of tower under construction.

6–8. Kansas City Office Building. Drawing.

JC: But there is one kind of Utopian architecture which grows out of reality, and another kind which is imposed upon it.

LK: If you eliminate the fairy tale from reality, I'm against you. It's the most sparkling reality there is. Utopia somehow is a reality, it's in reality. That's the point: Utopia is real.

JC: Is there any Utopian architecture today?

LK: No. I would say that Utopia inspires. But Utopia itself?—no, there's no Utopia. But if something were really Utopian, I would excuse everything about it. It would be, in a sense, an expression of youth, it would be like Boullée and Ledoux.

HK: Today, there is a misunderstanding of Utopia, taking its clues from a hypothesized vision of life in the future, a vision determined purely by expected needs. It is conceived as a mechanical megastructure of functions—like Warren Chalk's Plug-in Living Unit [see Fig. 4–9]. It is more futuristic than Utopian.

LK: That's another thing which you cannot say. Because you can only build for the present. It isn't a question of the present conceived as though it were a formula, and, in the other case, the future comprehended in a formula. There is futurism in Beethoven, but he's not a futurist in any sense. He knows the sense of something, he knows his realm so beautifully that he can transcend the present. That's all. Whoever builds *never* builds for the future.

JC: Let's say you are given a commission, a specific project. Do you begin as if you had no client—with dream drawings fresh out of desire?

LK: *It must* begin there.

JC: Must *every* project begin with that kind of . . .

LK: Absolutely. It must begin without a client, because the client must not order. If the client orders something, it will just add up to an assembly of given elements, and he hires you only because you can choose materials and make it look handsome. You've accomplished nothing, absolutely nothing. You're not in any sense an architect. You're an exterior decorator, maybe.

JC: Did you conceive of the Kansas City tower in terms of its environment [*Fig. 6–8*]? How does it relate to the street and to the other buildings? Did you worry about that?

LK: No, not really. I didn't worry about it because there has to be a society of inter-respect which the buildings themselves give you. If around you there are buildings which you do not honor, then it's a natural tendency to establish yourself clear and simple as being the one which you hope is honored. But when you work in the presence of something else you honor, then be very deferring, as though buildings themselves were people, as though they were living things.

JC: Was there nothing around you to which you could refer positively?

LK: No, there wasn't.

JC: Mr. Kahn, in looking through one of your sketchbooks, I noticed some drawings of Roman work—especially of Hadrian's Villa at Tivoli. I wondered if these Roman ruins exert a special influence on your work, particularly on the buildings at Dacca and Ahmedabad.

LK: No. I would say "influence" is another one of those words which can be misinterpreted by everyone. It could mean that you sat down and copied it. I'm not constructed in this way. I'm not one who takes things verbatim from some place. I think things out for myself. Even if I read a scientific statement, I would draw out of it what's me about the scientific statement. I wouldn't take it merely as a matter of fact or use it as a source from which to work.

JC: I have seen a comparison of Dacca and Hadrian's Villa; they were printed side by side as a kind of explanation . . .

LK: Ridiculous!

JC: You think that's ridiculous?

6 9. Government Center of Bangladesh. Arches of porticos in the hospital.

6–10. Indian Institute of Management. Ahmedabad, India. 1964–66. Louis Kahn. Masonry detail.

6–11. Government Center of Bangladesh. Detail of arches.

6–12. Erdmann Dormitory complex. Bryn Mawr College. Bryn Mawr, Pa. 1964–65. Louis Kahn. Door handle design.

LK: Absolutely!

JC: That's an easy way out. Why?

LK: Maybe some external features, or some fragment, maybe. The circle, for instance [Fig. 6–9]; I would never think of using a circle I saw somewhere else unless it conformed to a sense of order in which I am looking for something that answers it. The difference is very great. If you look at it very carefully, some of the circles are really not a circle. They're even broken in the center, and I chose them for earthquake reasons. In Hadrian's Villa, you see the use of some circular forms, which I know very well. But who owns the circle? It's ridiculous.

JC: But you can't deny that your brick arches remind one immediately of Roman masonry work.

LK: It's the nature of masonry work. When you use brick you come to certain solutions which sometimes look like Roman brickwork, because brick is brickwork. I don't hesitate to do it, even if it does look Roman, because it's the order of brick. Where in Roman brickwork would you see the segmental arch used like this [Fig. 6–10], without having much buttressing of masonry? That restraining member made a composite order, brick and concrete. The use of concrete stems from knowing brick for what it is. I would never be able to do this, nor come to this realization, unless I respected brickwork in general, Roman or otherwise. Nobody possesses it. This is not a shape of any kind. It's not a motif. It's in the order of brick.

HK: The large openings in the screen walls at Ahmedabad and Dacca seem to have a predecessor in an ornamental motif at Bryn Mawr [Figs. 6–11 and 6–12]. In your dormitories, there are door handles made out of flat plates into which circles and semicircles are cut.

LK: I know. That is true. I have a tendency, even in my drawings, to make a round opening, to make an opening somehow, or an arch.

HK: This is a combination of shapes, which appears for the first time in the door handles at Bryn Mawr. Isn't that door handle somehow a screen, a miniature of your great walls in India and Dacca?

LK: No, that's going too far. It isn't that way.

HK: But regardless of size and function,

can't one have a certain liking for a particular form?

LK: Oh, certainly, but I have an entirely different interpretation of that. Even if the shape may be the same, it has more to do with structure and the sense of forces within the plane. If I had a door with a rectangular panel system in it, where the panels are already square or rectangular, I would readily make an opening conforming to the given shape. But, if I have a flat surface, and have to punch a hole through it, I want to ease the opening, I want to arch it as though it needs no frame. It's the sense of forces that I see in the door; these forces are playing and resisting my making an opening—as if I were making an incision in the door. The door is apprehensive about how much it will be destroyed. I make it the most benevolent opening I can, and that means this shape.

It isn't a liking in it so much as a belief in it. It comes from belief in it. I would never play around with new shapes just to avoid being stereotyped. As a means of forced variety, I could never do it.

JC: In the wall of the house at Ahmedabad, there is the suspended horizontal concrete member [*Fig. 6–13*] . . .

LK: The restraining member which keeps the arch from pushing out. It brings it back into the wall. I call it a composite order. I recognize in which way concrete is helping brick to be used again. Brick has within it its own death, because it is not resourceful enough. If I had not found the composite order, the whole project would have been concrete.

JC: Why was it necessary to have that long segmental arch at the roof line?

LK: On top of each house is a terrace. They sleep on the roofs and, therefore, I needed a balustrade, and I needed that opening created by the segmental arch so that the air doesn't get blocked. If it were a railing, there would be no privacy. If I put a curtain on the railing, there would be no air. Somebody might use rails, but I didn't want another material. I wanted to extend the order of brick and not have many, many materials enter the scene—like a man who is very rich and has too many dishes to eat from. No. I wanted to eat frugally, so I extended the order as far as I could. That, to me, is symphonic. It's the same thing as writing a waltz, and you don't try to write a symphony into it. You are dealing with a single kind of composition of materials, brick and concrete.

The concrete helped me avoid great heavy walls and achieve as much air as possible. The concrete was like the strappings

6–13. Indian Institute of Management. Housing units.

on a trunk. You make it out of wood, but you use metal to reinforce the wood. That's also a composite order.

JC: In the tripartite composition of the façade, if I may call it that, the concrete restraining member of the central section seems to be unnecessary; the flanking concrete members are enough to hold it up.

LK: Yes, I could have done it that way, because the two restraining members, one on each side, are all you need; it has enough muscle. But it really does need it for another reason. I need the opening for the air in the center section as well.

HK: Do you sometimes think back to your early training, the time when you were drawing Corinthian capitals and Beaux Arts plans?

LK: Just in the sense of appreciation of the meaning of order. That training made *me* understand order, that is, an aesthetic order.

HK: Decorative order?

LK: No, no, because it wasn't really decoration, it was ornament. It was ornamentation of the joint, of the event; that's what it really was. I recognized that a capital had to hold its volutes out to invite the span. It had to reach out, receive it, and the receiving of it had to be bigger than what the column was. This was a tremendous realization, and it's no different now in concrete from what it was a long time ago in columns.

HK: You wouldn't use a column any more?

LK: You can't. If you use a column today, it's never really a stone column or a brick column, because it doesn't have enough force, enough power. If you were to make a big building today using brick columns, your spans would be short and your construction would be very heavy.

HK: Could we say that the clarity of the joint, your celebration of the joint in your architecture, today refers to the meaning of a capital?

LK: Yes. To make it more understandable, it is really the celebration of the meeting of material.

HK: What is the function of those huge walls with circular openings [*Fig. 6–14*]?

LK: In those hot countries, you need a porch which protects the building and the people from the sun. At Ahmedabad [*Fig. 6–15*], I did not plan for air conditioning because no money was available for it. Here, the worth of air conditioning is almost nil because the orientation of the buildings is right. The fact that you're always thinking in terms of never allowing the sun to come in makes the maintenance

6–14. Government Center of Bangladesh. Dining complex.

6–15. Indian Institute of Management. Dormitories.

of the air conditioning much less. These walls are sun screens, and they give you a wall of reflected light, which cuts the glare that comes from the openings.

HK: That defines the function. Yet, they became incredibly impressive images.

LK: I know. But if I had been looking only from the functional standpoint I would have made a *brise-soleil*. But, since I was thinking in terms of architecture, it had to become a porch. And the porch is a room. Out of it came something which was more than just taking care of the function. You can take care of it with screens or some adjunct means, which is not in any sense a kind of architectural identity. But I created buildings within buildings. The sun screen became the exterior wall of the porch which protects the interior building from the sun. In a sense, the porch is an offering to the sun.

Of course, there are other ways of shielding a building; Ed Stone's American Embassy building at New Delhi is a good example. He built a beautiful interior court. I mean it's beautiful if you don't stay too long. It's beautiful because there's constant water play for quite a large area. There's a very large pool and from it comes a very diffuse spray, and above the pool is a *brise-soleil* through which the sun shines. You do not see the sun, you see only the spray, and there's a glow of light in there that's really quite mysterious. But when you get close and you see the *brise-soleil,* you hate it because the sky is broken up into little diamonds and looks very, very ugly. He could have gotten something extremely beautiful by letting the water make the porch.

I made porches out of brick. Concrete was very expensive. I used it only for floors. I used no concrete columns anywhere. Brick was used for the walls and supports. And since there is no beam because there is no column, the arch became the opener, the making of opening.

HK: From the beginning, you had to deal with a rather conservative construction method.

LK: Yes. It's an ancient construction method.

HK: Therefore, you have arches which remind one of the Roman arch.

LK: Right. The word "conservative" is not the word to use. What might be called a conservative or traditional construction answers the demand of today for a larger opening; this might have been demanded in ancient days as well, but they didn't know how to answer it. Now, concrete becomes the reviver of the potentiality of brick. The concrete member holds the thrust of the arch in and allows it to extend almost to the end walls without sending a thrust against them.

HK: So you were able to keep the walls thin and save material.

LK: Well, I was able to make large openings. That meant you could open your mouth bigger because that brought in more air. I found a partner in concrete for the brick.

JC: Could you tell us something about the concept of Ahmedabad?

LK: It is a national institute of business management established to bring together men of various castes who have talent in the field of management. It is patterned after the school at Harvard. They had professors from Harvard help initiate and demonstrate methods of teaching.

I had the whole campus to design myself. It was somewhere in the neighborhood of 65 acres of land, on which there were to be a school, dormitories, houses for teachers and servants . . .

JC: All around a natural lake?

LK: No, it's a lake I made. I made a lake. The dormitories are right next to the school, as if they and the school were one [*Fig. 6–16*]. In the total plan, the dormitories and classrooms are held together as a unit distinguishable from the rest of the campus, which is composed of faculty, administrative, and servants' housing.

JC: And you respected the caste system when you made this plan?

LK: I simply took the country as it is. I want to create an atmosphere in which the students will not feel that living and learning are separate. That is what the dormitory-classroom complex achieves. Even the porches serve as classrooms. The porch of each dormitory house becomes a transitional space where living and learning meet. The porch not only protects you from the sun, but also can be a community room. Next to the porch there is a tea room; tea is the national drink, you might say. It is served very often. Each student's room opens directly onto the porch, thereby avoiding the need for corridors.

But let me describe the whole dormitory plan [*Fig. 6–17*]. The dormitories are made up of a series of complete houses. They are an assembly of houses turning toward the breeze. Everything is closely knit, because the closer the buildings, the better they protect from the sun.

JC: The plan of each house consists of rectangular rooms opening onto a triangular porch facing a square.

LK: Yes, and in that square are the toilets and other facilities. The entrance stairway is in the triangular porch. You enter the porch and you are indoors.

JC: Is the unusual juxtaposition of these two shapes, square and triangle, demanded by the sun and the wind?

LK: Oh, yes, the orientation is correct in relation to the wind and sun.

JC: Are those deep setbacks, those sharp angles, which actually cut into the body of the building, made to catch the breeze?

LK: Yes, they serve as vents to draw the air, and also as shade.

HK: Could you just describe the classroom building plan?

LK: Yes. The building combines classrooms [A], library [B], administration [C], dining hall [D], kitchen [E], and center court [F]. The major entrance is a ramp which leads from the parking lot into the center court [between B and C]. [*Fig. 6–16*]

I didn't want a bare court because they can be devastatingly hot. I put an amphitheater in the court itself, and this amphitheater is nothing more than an awning-protected place where everything can happen. It's really a place within the court which is protected from the sun. I did not want an amphitheater staring at you, not being used.

HK: Also, within the court in front of the library there is a surprising arrangement of arches which turn away from the axial pattern of the ground plan.

LK: Again, it is a porch which protects

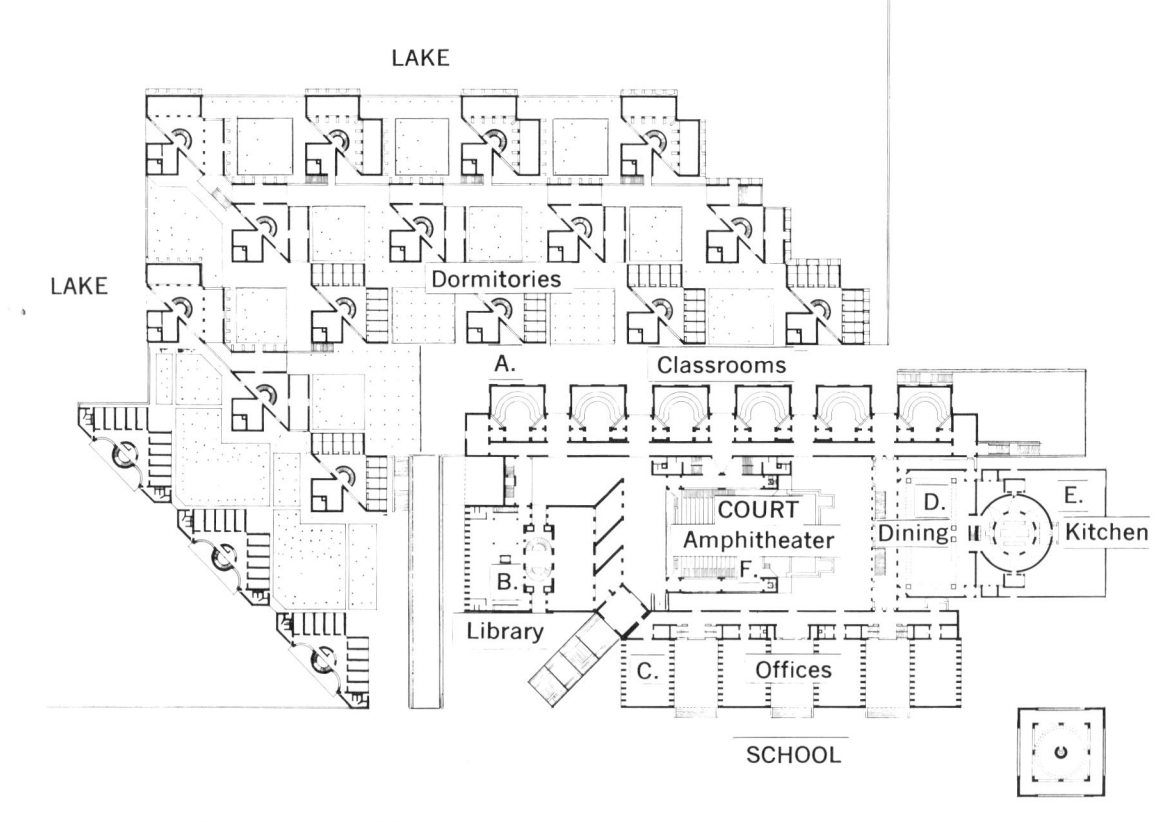

6–16. Indian Institute of Management. Ground plan of school and dormitories.

from the sun and turns toward the breeze. The arches refer to the oblique axis of the dormitory plan.

JC: There is another surprising shape in the ground plan, the round kitchen attached to the square dining hall.

LK: The kitchen is made like a big ventilator because they make so many foods that are highly spiced and so smelly that the kitchen is made as though it were a big fan. It's really a kitchen inside a vent.

JC: It's a great exhaust.

LK: The client said that the kitchen should be a mile away! I told him that I could make it close and still have it a mile away! I then invented this idea, which he accepted. The kitchen is still sited away from the center of the campus, and the breeze carries the odor away. At the end of the plan, where the kitchen is, I have placed a cooling tower [G] for the air conditioning of the dormitories and the administration areas. It is also made like a giant vent in which the air comes in at a certain point and aerates the warm water of the air conditioning plant. The water is pumped up to the top of the vent, then it flows down across multiple glass surfaces upon which the air can play and cool the water. Then I pipe the water to the air handling units, which regulate the temperature and give cool air to the interior.

HK: You put all the service buildings at the same end of the campus.

LK: Yes, you want to keep the exhaust air away from the buildings. The cooling tower is also the water tower, by the way. It's a tank for the water supply; they have their own wells. So I integrated all those things.

I used a similar idea for a city in India, where these towers punctuated the entire area. It is a beautiful idea. It was to be a town on a large river, which is dry in the

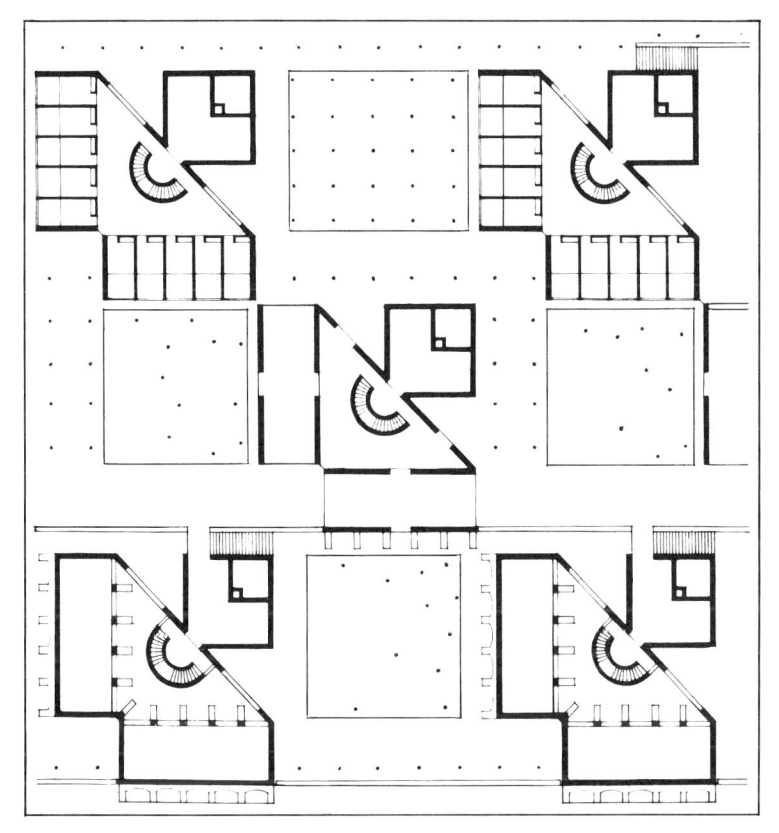

6–17. Indian Institute of Management. Detail of dormitory ground plan.

summertime. This city is known as Ghandinaga, which means city of Ghandi. This river becomes flooded in the time of rain. The water comes from the Himalayas. It's a beautiful sight to see, because it comes, as they say, like "galloping horses." Suddenly, you see this big gallop of horses coming down the dry river bed.

My idea was to capture this water at intersections, with structures over the water —kinds of bridges—and bring the water to the city, and hold it in tower reservoirs; this way, the city would never be dry in the summertime. I began the city with these important stations, the water towers, which would also be utility stations. Water is a gift to a city in India. Water does not always come in pipes. Here, it is a river source, and it can be dramatized here, whereas in other cities it cannot be dramatized.

Another primary consideration was the mango trees. There is a law in India which prevents taking down a mango tree. Consequently, I made the sections of living depend on where these trees were. The sectors were also determined by the connections between these towers and the mango trees. The government buildings were to be built along the river. The monsoon rains, as they fell from the land to the high banks of the river, form very picturesque and sculptural erosions. My thought was to make a park out of these washaways, firming up the ground with brick construction, following the contours as they are, just making them firm so they wouldn't continue to wash away. They could have become the most magnificent nature-inspired playground you can possibly imagine. Those shapes! Of course, this didn't pan out. Now the army engineers are doing something there. They are starting to ruin this area, really ruin it. It's horrible. I had even planned for the industry which would make the bricks to

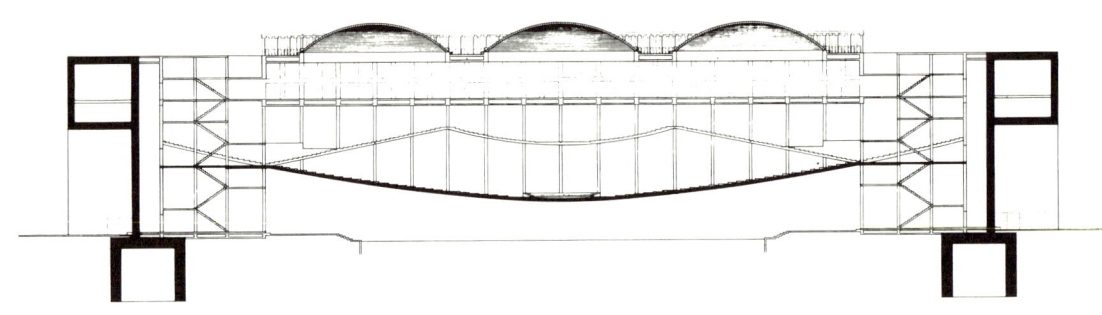

6–18. Congress Hall. Venice, Italy. 1969–. Louis Kahn. Section drawing of three auditoriums over Hall.

build the town, and the rejects would have been used to firm up the river banks. It was to be a city of 500,000 people.

HK: What are they doing instead?

LK: They are building a boring grid-plan town.

HK: Mr. Kahn, in a recent lecture, you discussed your project for the Congress Hall in Venice [*Fig. 6–18*]. Your first point was that you had to assemble a large crowd of people, and you went to the blackboard and drew a circle. The circle was somehow a symbol for you of the assembled crowd.

LK: Yes.

HK: Then you went on to say that the building had to be on a long, narrow lot. So you cut off the upper and lower parts of the circle.

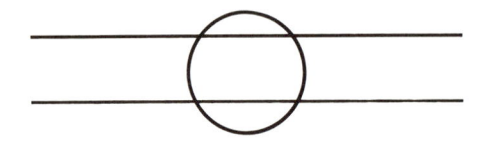

The remaining center part you kept as the basic concept of the ground plan [*Fig. 6–19*]. This seems to be an illustration of your way of thinking. Your conceiving, your thoughts about the needs of a building, somehow materialize and merge as primary forms.

LK: That's very well put. I don't know how one identifies the first idea, but for me it is usually the sense of the building in its core, its full meaning, its nature, *not* its shape. Its nature was that of involvement, of participation. A simple shape which only emphasizes a direction doesn't have the nature of participation in it. It is, on the contrary, analogous to watching or hearing, not participation. The circle, to me, was participation. The fact that I could adjust to a site which was narrow has to require that one side looked to the other. But the shape should not be adjusted to that narrow site in such a way that it becomes purely directional, because there would be no participation.

HK: Isn't it rather arbitrary to see an assembled crowd as a circle?

LK: Participation may not mean that every person speaks up. If you are in a theater, you have no participation, you are observing. It may be true that you are involved because you feel the person next to you, but it's really pretty much centered around yourself, there's actually no participation. It is just a performance.

The Congress Hall, which was started with a sense of form, which was a pit or a bull ring, had to adjust itself to a narrow area. In the center of this is the organiza-

6–19. Congress Hall. Ground plan.

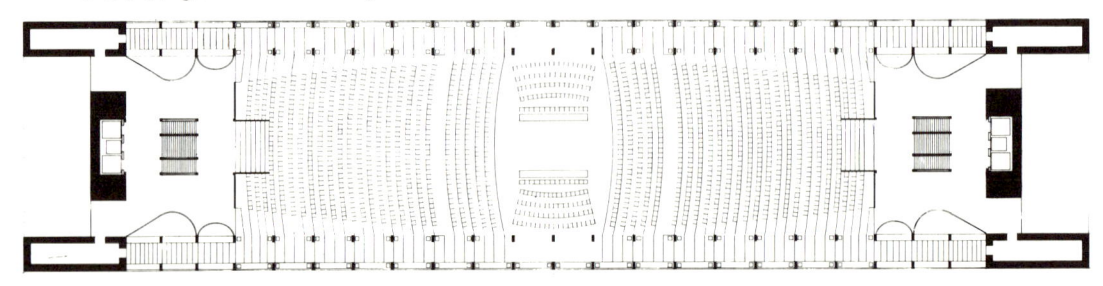

6–20. Philharmonic Hall. Berlin, Germany. 1960–63. Hans Scharoun and Werner Weber. Interior.

tional position, and this center was the dimension I had to include to make sure that people saw people. It was a confrontation of people with people.

HK: It is an arena, a bull ring, as you say. Isn't a circle a bit too simple as an image for a crowd? Isn't it too rigid, this forcing people into a bull ring? Couldn't it be as it is in Hans Scharoun's Philharmonic Hall in Berlin [*Fig. 6–20*]? Although a large crowd of people assembles around a center, the crowd is broken up into smaller units. The primary emphasis is not on the simplicity of the whole, but on the complexity of many parts achieving assembly and participation.

LK: I wouldn't do what Scharoun did, but I appreciate immensely what he tried to do. I could show you early sketches of what I myself had in mind for Venice. It was the same kind of thing, in which you did not hold rigidly to the geometric shape, but felt as though there were separate areas of people rather than a geometric disc plan. But, you see, my sense is different. I don't see in a painterly way. I don't see it even as a sculptural thing. If I were to place one group here, one group there, one group here, I would be forcing them more into an area than I am in placing them in a very general frame, where their minds can make their groups. Their minds make their groups, not the architecture.

HK: You don't like a casual arrangement?

LK: No. I don't like it nailed down. If you could move it and change it every day without making a *nature* out of it, fine.

HK: On the other hand, Mr. Kahn, it could be that an architecture of casual shapes would reflect on the minds of the people, and make them casual. Maybe the audience in Berlin needs to be loosened up?

LK: I think maybe what you say could have a big influence on me. I'm just telling you this. It could have a big influence on me, and I can with easy readiness employ a value which gives more casual arrangements than I do. But there's another thing, which constantly pushes me in other directions. I see a building in an anthropomorphic way, as a body. I don't want to be conscious of how my body functions. I always just expect it to be tremendously resourceful. I have need for things which my body can always handle: to run, to jump, to move quickly, to move slowly. I want to take *any* position, not just certain selective positions. Therefore, my tendency is to make a room without any willfulness, except that which the inspiration of the room itself can offer.

In an assembly, people choose to get either close to or far away from the speaker. If the people grouped themselves into groups in the midst of multiple choices, which the arrangement at Venice gives you in an orderly way, then I would say that what they are doing is truer to the nature of men gathering than a structured arrangement of seats. I don't like to freeze them, because not as much happens as when it is laid out as a field in which anything can happen.

It is best not to be conscious of limits, no matter how glorious these limits are.

HK: When Mies van der Rohe and Hugo Häring were together in Berlin during the early days of modern architecture, a constant question was, "Should architecture create specific spaces which tell people how they are to be used, or very general spaces which allow people to decide for themselves." Häring made very complicated, irregular, but highly interesting ground plans. Mies, of course, created the "Vielzweckraum."

LK: Yes, the all-purpose room.

HK: Mies ended up with huge spaces defined only by the outer wall; the inhabitant defines its use. Your Venice proposal relates to this idea, yet you and Mies are quite different.

LK: Very different. I am much more conscious that the space must have the evidence of how it was made. If a Mies space is undivided, and has this relationship, I would agree with him. If he subdivides his general space, I would not. I make a space as an offering, and do not designate what it is to be used for. The use should be inspired, that is to say, I would like to make a house in which the living room is discovered as the living room. I will not say that it is a living room and you must use it as such. Also, the bedroom, which, in a sense, must also be a living room, never has the specific characteristics of a bedroom.

HK: I've noticed in the way you describe your buildings that the functions everybody else focuses on are secondary to you. For example, when you build a library, you have to have spaces for bookshelves, catalogues, desks, and so forth, but the sum total of all these spaces doesn't make it a library for you. Incidental things that are in it, such as a little space where you can drink a cup of tea, make the life real.

LK: Yes.

JC: When we were discussing the proposed Mellon Center at Yale [*Fig. 6–21*], you said, "As long as I have considered only the functions of the building, I still cannot build the building." A building which simply functions wouldn't be a building in your sense.

LK: No. Nor would it have a lasting quality. It would not have the quality of being in a life, of being in a living thing. When you make a building, you make a life. It comes out of life, and you really make a life. It talks to you. When you have *only* the comprehension of the function of a building, it would not become an environment of a life.

JC: In the Mellon Center, you said it is essential to emerge beyond the solution. The building begins *after* you have solved the problem.

LK: Oh, yes. That's certainly what one means about the character of the spaces. One thing is the need of the space, and another is the character of the space [*Fig. 6–22*].

6–21. Paul Mellon Center for British Art and British Studies. Yale University. New Haven, Conn. Louis Kahn. View of corner at Chapel and High streets. In design 1970. Now under construction.

6–22. Paul Mellon Center. Drawing.

JC: And the need of the space is not always identical with the character of the space?

LK: No. The need of the space is definable. The character of the space is not definable. The building can be high in character, or low in character, and still function.

JC: When you have met all of the problems that you are supposed to solve at the Mellon Center, how far along is the architecture?

LK: After you've solved the problem, you can begin to be concerned about the architecture. That's where it starts. It is that assembly of spaces where it is good to be, where the function is almost not discernible.

HK: You would not agree that form follows function.

LK: No. You could say that form follows function if you think of form being a nature, that the answerable part to the nature is that which is intended to function a certain way. If you can consider how the building will affect the individual, that is not a question of function.

I just believe that the word "function" applies to mechanics. But you cannot say that it should also satisfy "psychological *function*" because psychology is not a function. The function aspect is that which gives you the instrumentation upon which psychological reaction can take place. You might say it's the difference between the mind and the brain. So the function aspect is the brain aspect; but the mind is not something that you can regulate with any kind of requirement. The beginning of architecture is after the function is thoroughly comprehended. At that point, the mind opens to the nature of the spaces themselves, which are released only in the mind after the functions are understood, and the spaces emerge in their psychological satisfaction.

JC: That means, in your words, "the building has a mind."

LK: The building has no mind, but it has the quality to respond to the mind.

JC: Could we have an example? Let's take the Bryn Mawr dormitories [*Fig. 6–23*]. What was the process by which the result became more than function?

LK: This is a very good and pointed question, and I need more than one try at answering it. But let me attempt it. First of all, for the function of this building, the rooms were for one person only, so that

6–23. Erdmann Dormitory complex.

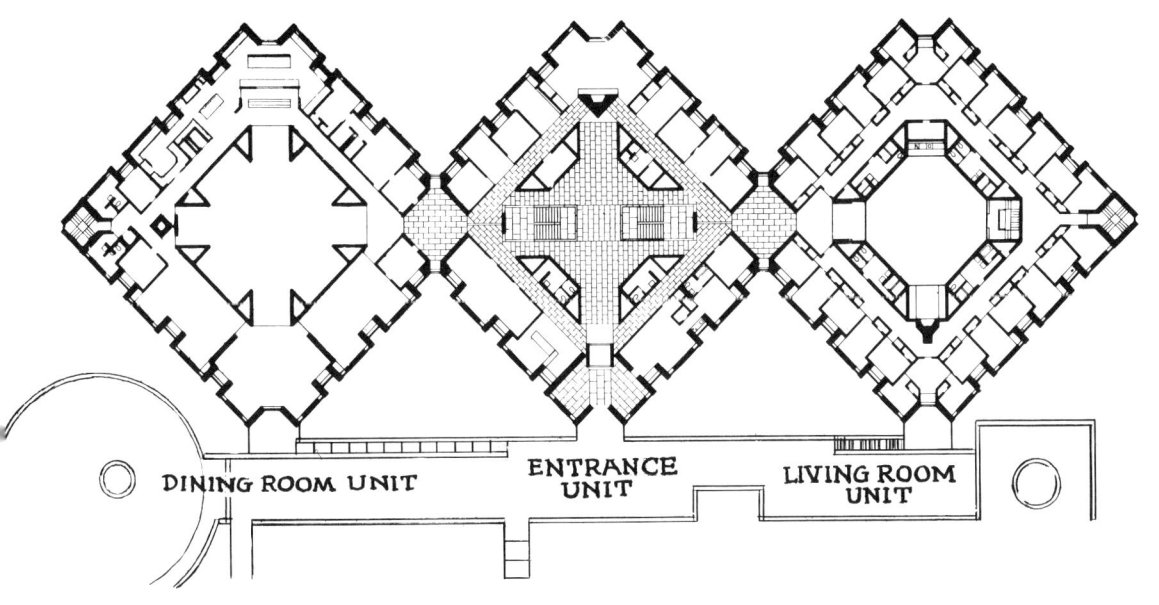

6–24. Erdmann Dormitory complex. Ground plan.

any strife that might come about between one person and another is eliminated. With this situation, a person may seek out whomever he or she wishes for companions.

JC: Was that the primary fact for the program?

LK: This is not purely a physical, but already a psychological, consideration. I don't exclude it. These are humans, not machines. There should be a dining room, a living room, and a place to come in.

JC: Again, as in Venice, these elemental requirements of the program find immediate expression in the ground plan; the dormitory has a tripartite layout based on three squares [*Fig. 6–24*].

6–25. Erdmann Dormitory complex. Entrance.

LK: Yes. The functions are simple in this building. Now, for the requirement of an entrance, I have made not simply an entrance, but a meeting place [*Fig. 6–25*]. I considered it not a dimensional problem, but an environmental one. What I did was to make an entrance room equally as important as a room-dining room, a room-living room; that central entity in the ground plan became the entrance-meeting place.

I insisted on the presence of fireplaces, because I said that a fireplace was a man in the room. That's what is required in terms of function . . .

JC: For a girls' dormitory?

LK: I insisted on the fireplaces, so that the sense of invitation is felt. I counted on the receptivity of the girls to these rooms, because there are fireplaces which are sort of man-things—a man usually makes the fire. My clients needled me about keeping these fireplaces. They succumbed to the psychological importance of the fireplaces. They were costly and the building was very strictly budgeted. They felt that I was right, that they were a part of the *life* of the building, the character of it.

I mean to say that a dormitory is not, after all, an apartment building. There is a sense of communal living in not placing the dining room away from things. Therefore, I surrounded the dining room with students' rooms, as if each area of combined living has its own environment of responsibility. So those who live around the dining room or the living room felt as though they could identify themselves, as though they belonged somewhere. If you belong in a block where all the girls are away from the facilities, you would not have the sense of belonging which a house should give you.

The entrance hall was always common. Therefore, it was the place where you entered, and it was answerable to nothing except entrance. One is led to divide the house into two parts, one around which there is an environment of pure neighborhood, the neighborhood of the living room, the neighborhood of the dining room, and the other, which centers around the entrance, around which there is a sense of the street. The geometry is good, because there is a sense of division in the places.

JC: You actually joined three houses, three separate units.

LK: Yes. Now, the central rooms have nothing to do with function. I could equally make it function if I had designed a block of dormitories with corridors; you could walk from your room to the corridor to the dining room. But I rejected that for very basic reasons. Here, there is more a sense of pulse. It is, in a sense, a house, because around you are always the things you associate with; they aren't made into separate elements you have to go to. They are in the center of living.

The reaction which came back to me from the students implied this very sense of feeling at home, not really in their *own* home, but they felt the sense of home, the dormitory sense of home. Nobody was fooling anybody that it was home, but the fact that you're associated with a common facility, that you have a sense of invitation, that you have your section to live in, and you can go to another section to enjoy common spaces—all these add up to something much better than living in a block of rooms separated from all other facilities. It *does* function, of course, but the distinction of the Bryn Mawr building is that it has this sense of invitation. I am around the courtyard; I am around the dining room. There is something communal about this, which is missing in others.

Another important aspect of the design is that I did not try to make connections with unknown places. Somehow, you're not going from place to place, really. It sort of blends together. It becomes one house, instead of three divisions. The linking space between the units is a delicate point. I go through it not feeling that I'm going through an odd space. The transition has value in itself.

JC: It's possible to have three main community areas with rooms around them and still not have the sense of "mind" or sense of joy which you have achieved there. There must be other things that go into making the character.

LK: Yes. What it really is is the *mood* in these places, and it is gotten by the character of the natural light reflecting in through the concrete shell [*Fig. 6–26*]. You'll see it especially at the close of the day, when the lights come on inside and the light outside is still in fullness. Then you feel like "living" there. And that is what really makes the "mind."

JC: You seem very far away from your former student Robert Venturi, who is seeking "ordinariness," a refreshing alternative to the "heroic idiom."

LK: If he could only use the word "commonness" and express it in the simplest of terms, I would agree.

JC: But I'm afraid that's not what . . .

LK: But "ordinary" for the sake of being ordinary is not in the nature of man, at all. He doesn't *know* it's ordinary. Unconscious ordinariness can be the most beautiful; but it's never given because it's ordinary as a virtue. No. I don't agree with that. There is such a thing as a need to begin all over again, which I think is great, rather than simply accepting what is already given. Certainly, that quality of beginning over again, making something which is not special, but something which is a new beginning, which can also have the starkest simplicity without the slightest sense of conscious exaltation, can be very, very great. What, after all, is ordinariness derived from? It is the sum total of all the solved and unsolved practical problems. It is an interpretation of man which says, "We have problems, economic problems, site problems, technical problems, etc., and we have to work so hard just to make a building stand up." And then it is known to be ordinary because of this. And, because there is a repetition of similar problems everywhere, almost everything is ordinary.

I still believe that all buildings belong to architecture. Ordinariness could inspire

6–26. Erdmann Dormitory complex. Community room interior.

beauty, but not if it's meant to be ordinary for ordinary's sake. I can see how a building could become beautifully ordinary. Then it has a tremendous validity in the ordinariness.

HK: That's actually what Venturi tries to do.

LK: Now, if he's looking for the beauty of this ordinariness, then I'm definitely for it.

HK: He is reacting strongly against the present-day trend of creating dominating heroic architecture.

LK: How could anybody not agree to this? But I'm afraid the word "ordinary" is what I'm not sure I want to include, except passing through the hands of a poet.

HK: Ordinariness that passes through the hands of a poet isn't ordinary any more.

LK: No, wait a minute. There must be a beautiful way of saying this, because it has to do greatly with what is called simplicity, in the true sense of the word. I have made statements about the Richards Laboratories towers [*Fig. 6–27*]. I have said, "These shafts are independent exhausts." Now they are being taken as show pieces. I wouldn't think of that. They are not worthy. These ducts are generalized units for certain services, without knowing what they are. I wasn't making jewelry out of exhaust ducts They are simple, but they are not ordinary. I sense the differences in instruments in the broadest way, but I don't know every mechanical detail. First of all, I don't know the instruments that well. I cannot distinguish one thing from another. So I put them all in one great big wastebasket, and that's the exhaust duct. But to pull it out and make a submarine out of it, that's ridiculous!

Let me put it a different way. The space you live in can be beautiful, especially if it is unfettered by all these other things. I don't believe in pipes in living rooms. I hate them. I believe they should be in their place like children. I want to remain ignorant of how the mechanics really work. I'm impatient with the restrictions of mechanical and construction engineers and with details about how every little thing works. But its *place* I think I know. I want to express that which is worth expressing, that which has grown to be a distinct characteristic. When one is characteristically different from another, I don't want to make a homogeneous mixture of the two. I want to bring out the difference. But I care very little if one pipe goes east and the other goes west. I don't want to make a special characteristic out of pipes, because I know that mechanical things are the first things that are going to be changed or altered; but the space you live in must be alive for a very long time. The space is a new landscape, which is to last as long as the material lasts. But the spaces which are serving it are made to change. Their position must be very general and they must be big enough for change and addition to take place. That is truly the nature of architecture. It is not giving service an individual shape.

A room has a nature, just as a certain part of the world has a nature. When you go into this harbor, you know you're there. You go into this room and you know you're there.

HK: When you separate service shafts from the spaces, you actually create shapes that have an impressive image. They are not ordinary wastebaskets.

LK: I think this is very important. I think this is the beginning of the modern plan, as far as the distinction between service and space goes.

HK: The first time this separation was done in an explicit way was in the Richards Laboratories. But the idea seems to be at work already in the Yale Art Gallery in the ceilings [*Fig. 6–28*].

LK: Yes, the ceiling was the beginning of such a realization. There's no question about that. I simply made a service space out of the ceiling, and it can be read as such. In my first sketches, the ceiling was a series of vaults; the space for the pipes was above the vaults. This scheme was unsatisfactory because the vault intervals de-

6–27. Alfred Newton Richards Medical Research Laboratories. University of Pennsylvania. Philadelphia, Pa. 1958–60. Louis Kahn.

6–28. Yale University Art Gallery. Interior.

termined where the room divisions had to be. So I had to discover a multidirectional construction, which was open and had the characteristic of having space already in it. That was what the tetrahedral ceiling gave me, what I'd like to call a "space slab." It was as though it were a single slab, only it was an exposed articulation of this slab. A ceiling of 40 feet in one span would require a thickness of 12 inches of concrete. This was my guide. I thought of this idea, which would give space for air and light at frequent intervals, as well as provide for multidirectional partitioning. The partitioning could not be fixed because of its being a gallery, so I made multipurpose spaces, which are rather like Miesian spaces. At that point, the consciousness of releasing the serving spaces from the spaces served had not yet come, but the essentials for doing it were certainly there. The ceiling is really a place where the many needs are accessible. The solution derives from the feeling that the way a place is made must be visible and not concealed. It was the revolt against the hung ceiling which caused all this to be made. It was the first ceiling of that type.

HK: Were you inspired by Buckminster Fuller?

LK: No. Because Buckminster Fuller's work was structurally much more advanced. It does not apply to a flat ceiling. I understood very well what he was trying to do, but I never had a desire to make what Fuller was making, nor would I want to make a building such as Le Corbusier makes, even though he was my teacher, but didn't know it.

JC: The Yale Art Gallery has, as you said, rather Miesian spaces, but your concept of space is entirely different from his.

LK: I always think that the client presents you with the need of certain areas, rather than with certain spaces or certain rooms. He presents you with area requirements, and the architect has to translate these into spaces. Spaces have to be entities.

JC: Isn't a space less defined than a room?

LK: No. Space is not a space unless you can see the evidence of how it was made. Then I like to call that a room. What I would call an area, Mies would call a space, because he thought nothing of dividing a space. That's where I say no. Let me draw a diagram. Here is a large area:

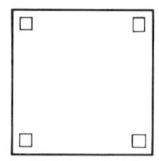

You can divide it into four parts:

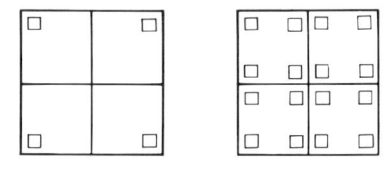

No matter how many partitions are in it, Mies would always call the whole area a space. I would call any one of the four divisions a space, but, after you divide it, the whole thing is not a space any more. I would call this a space, provided it is never divided. What you see in the third diagram are four spaces. I consider these four rooms. Mies would consider this a space within which divisions could be made. In the Miesian spaces he allows division, but for me there's no entity when it is divided.

HK: Why do you insist so much on showing the supports in your rooms?

LK: Because I think that the room likes it. That's why. The room feels its entity, its completeness, it has a right to have a name. It can be called the "east room," for instance.

JC: But in the Miesian plan there can be no "east room."

LK: It cannot be given a name.

HK: Can't it be given a name without showing the supports?

LK: No, because it's not yet worthy of

its name. Ask that kind of room how it is made, and it will have to say, "If you go next door, you can see the columns of me in that room." And this is what stops me from naming it. But going back to the third diagram, each of these four rooms has its own character because of the light. One has north and west light, one has south and east light, and so on. Each room has its own character. And, if I were being delicate about this, the window of one would not be designed the same as the window of another. Now, each room has its own light, and if I go to the east room at a certain time of day, my memory tells me to *expect* something there. The structure is the maker of the light. The structure can make an opening, just as a column and a beam can. This is an opportunity for light. And that means if I hide the structure I've lost the opportunity. I go through an immense amount of trouble. If I didn't assume that I needed to do this, my plans would be vastly different. I regard natural light as that which makes a room have its nature, its characteristic, its mood.

6–29. Jewish Community Center. Trenton, N.J. 1956. Louis Kahn. Plans and section.

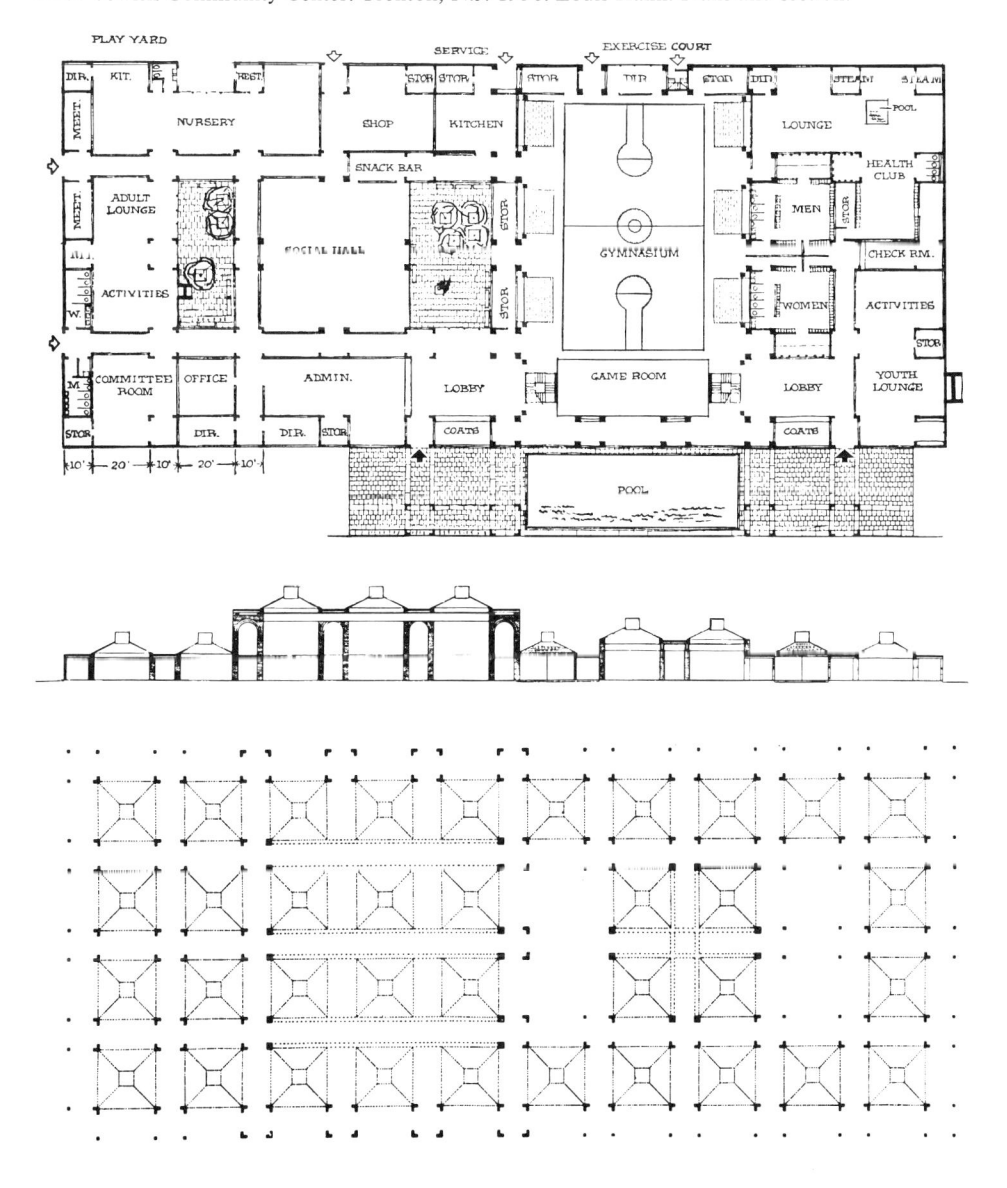

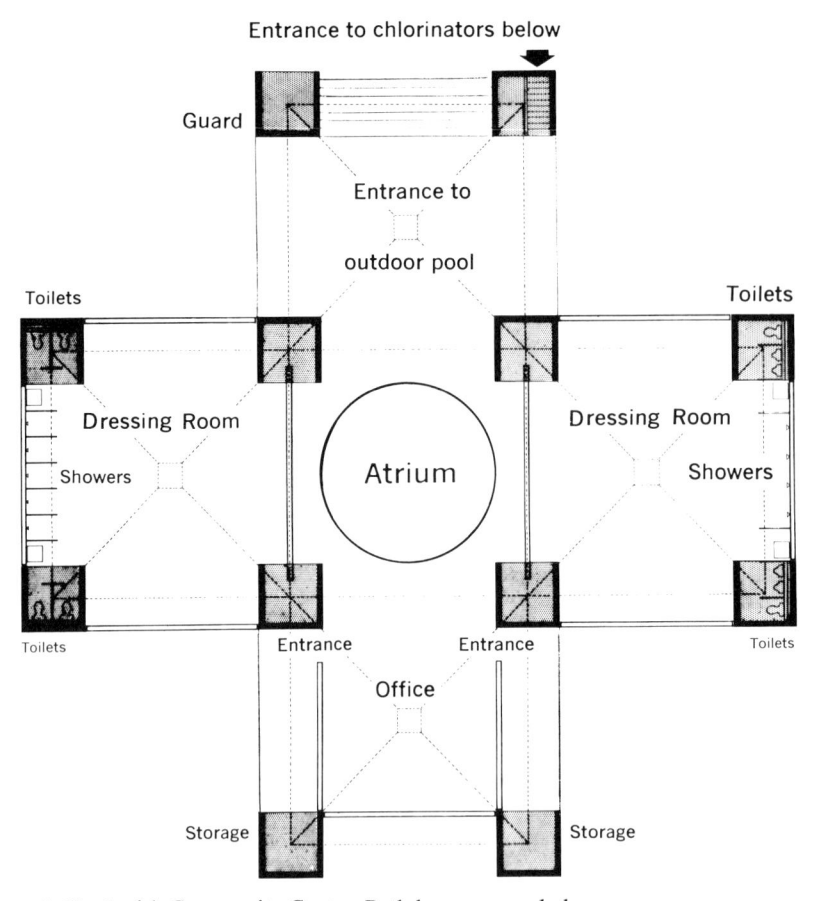

6–30. Jewish Community Center. Bath house ground plan.

HK: You would always deny artificial light?

LK: I do not believe that any room is worthy to be called a room itself in artificial light. That means that any interior room would have to break through the ceiling to get the natural light, as is the case in the dormitories at Bryn Mawr.

HK: In other words, there are two major elements which individualize a room: structure and light.

LK: Structure, which *gives* the light.

HK: Then, actually, this square you drew with divisions is alien at the outset to your concept. You should take it apart, as you actually did in the main building design for the Trenton Jewish Community Center [*Fig. 6–29*]. There, every single entity of space is separate but related to the others. You start out with a given area, define the spatial entities, and then combine them again as an entity.

LK: Yes, combining again. But, you see, I did all that in order to teach myself. It was a matter of teaching myself its meaning. The Community Center has this feeling of defining space so that each facet is clear in itself, and also gave room for those areas which would serve the larger areas. It had to be reasonable that the passages and the areas that serve, which are between the actual rooms, could be useful, and make the spaces themselves be more useful.

JC: So you could use the space in between the units as a service area, as a corridor, for instance, or it could be incorporated into a room.

LK: Exactly. That was a very exciting period. The Trenton Bath House [*Fig. 6–30*] gave me the first opportunity to work out the separation between the serving and the served spaces. It was a very clear and simple problem. It was solved with absolute purity. Every space is accounted for, there is no redundancy. I used hollow columns as entrances to the rooms [*Fig. 6–31*]; I used them as a maze, a baffle, and I used the hollow column itself as a storage area. I used it for toilets, which must be enclosed. And I found, during the expression of this very simple building, the concept of the serving and the served spaces. The desire to employ this with greater extension came with the order for the community building, which I never built because it proved in *their* eyes too expensive. It was really a very inexpensive building. But there were some spaces which they felt were not necessary; strictly speaking, according to their own program, I would say that maybe 7 per cent were not. I invented certain uses for these extra spaces. Where they wanted four rooms, I may have had five, all of which did not prove to be necessary.

JC: Just as you define the service shafts of the Richards Laboratories as separate units, you define service units in the supports of the Trenton Bath House.

LK: Yes. I thought of a support as being a hollow column which can be used. That's the only place where I could put the services. So the source of support, the column, became the place which *harbored* the services of the building. The columns of yesterday, which were solid, could be made hollow and contain something. But even the

6–31. Jewish Community Center. Bath house interior.

old columns (pillars) sometimes contained something, too. They knew that the mass wasn't altogether necessary because it was only the edges of the mass that supported the building, not the mass itself.

HK: Like the pillars of the nave of Saint Peter's in Rome.

LK: Yes, like those niches and passageways which open the pillar. Actually, this idea comes for me from the real reverence I have for "pocket." You know what "pocket" is? Each one of the supports of the Trenton Bath House is made out of four walls enclosing space, and this stems from buildings of old, which have tremendous areas of "pocket," which are the spaces within the structural supports. My hollow columns, which contain rooms, are similar to those piers in Saint Peter's, which contain a space which is a passageway. The sense of the hollow column is really what inspired me.

The opportunity to introduce the hollow support idea came as a lucky circumstance, which made each element in the Bath House accountable: the maze, the toilets, the kiosk, the chlorinating plant, the storage spaces. They were all useful in the hollow columns somewhere.

HK: Mr. Kahn, let's assume that we have come to you as clients. We want to build a house for a family of families, not an apartment building, but a house where families would share certain facilities in common, and yet maintain some privacy. Let's say that we want a common playroom for the children, a common kitchen, and some sort of central meeting place for all the families. The rest of the rooms would emphasize privacy. The goal would be to provide community and the sharing of responsibilities, as well as the possibility for retreat. The present one-family unit today, with all its problems, may be too isolated.

LK: What you say is tremendously attractive. My thinking regarding the meaning of the street comes to mind immediately. The street, which is a room, is the unspecified position of common space. But you are looking for something which becomes consciously more specified than the street, which is a very general room. But, when I think of something that is a generator of conception, the street becomes the starting point. No matter what is built, it must be good for another reason as well. So the street still stands there, without being specific, as the first answer to your problem. In a sense, the community room of early American architecture, where people met on the village green, was this kind of home, except you met not for family interengagement, but for general meetings.

A family of families has similar connotations. You surrender certain rooms commonly, but what you keep as strictly yours, as I see it, must have in it the living room and the kitchen. I am talking about a way of *life,* and you are talking about a way of *living.* I feel there's a difference between the two. The way of life asks for a common acceptance, no matter how humble. The way of living asks for the right of privacy. A conception of the way of life surrenders freedom to a way of living.

What you want, in this house, can only be successful if the scheme has within it the connotations of the way of life itself, so that the house, when it changes hands, automatically adjusts to the way of someone else's living. I can't help but say that within your idea lies a great beauty, ultimate beauty. But is it a way of life? I say no. Is it a way of living? I say yes.

HK: Would you build a house just for the way of living?

LK: No, I wouldn't. I should reject it. However, if this is sincerely thought about, it might be a new realization of what is really valuable and what is not valuable. If this is designed in a way which respects the way of life, I think it would be a great advance in the building of places to live. Really good.

HK: We are living in a time when "the way of life" is changed by the way of living. What appears to be merely arbitrary and momentary may eventually become part of the essence of a new way of life. The distinction between ontology and history is not so apparent as you indicate.

LK: I sense that what you say is a thing of great beauty. It could lead to a new sense of planning and a kind of truer economy.

HK: Not only economy. I think it gives a new sense of family, too. In a three-family house, children will grow up in a very different way. They will not focus upon their mothers and fathers alone, but on other families as well. The distinction between "us" and "the others" would not be so rigid.

LK: I agree. But, you see, people, according to their various ages, change their attitudes toward life, and then living is altered.

HK: You mean that a certain time will come when we shall realize that we have outgrown this house?

LK: That's right.

HK: And then we have to tear it down.

LK: Yes. But, more important, the rooms which are common must not take something away from that part which you consider your own, the place where you are not answerable to any rules or regulations which are implied in the common rooms. There must be a place where you can make your own cup of tea. Such a plan is almost a revelation of how little you fear other people. It's almost as if you learned not to respect as much fear as you did before. But, I'm afraid that man has established a completeness for himself too firmly to live in such a house. You cannot break out of that very quickly.

HK: It might be enough to have one big common room and a common kitchen.

LK: No. You cannot take away that which is the memory of a house, of *your* home. You can forget maybe your bedroom, you could even forget sometimes your living room, but you can't forget your kitchen. The memory aspect is tremendously important. Also, there is the aspect of invitation, which is lost if your kitchen is lost.

HK: Well, Mr. Kahn, do you think it would be better to build three separate houses on this lot?

LK: No, but I would like you to think about the religious place of each family. I think one of the most religious of rooms is the kitchen. If you build around the kitchen, it would be a tremendous lesson in interresponsibility. But I really think the kitchen must be your own kitchen. Otherwise, you would always feel as though you couldn't invite anybody. The way you make a cake is very important, because you want very much for the other fellow to like the way you make a cake. And don't forget that the kitchen is the woman's domain and can cause any amount of jealousy.

The young people don't have such a violent sense of ownership. However, I could readily live in a social area such as this. The thought of immediately having this kind of family is very wonderful. I feel much better when I know the other person is there, but I don't have to see him. If I had a room next to another person, I would feel even better. Then, even the closed door is communication, yes? The *next* thing that would make me feel better would be having a garden between his room and mine. It tells me that more can be done with the architecture of connection. It tells me we must meet again.

7 CHARLES MOORE

CM: Our office is especially interested in solving problems that are normally not considered elegant. Our biggest interest, right now, is housing. We've grown very interested in trailers—well, industry doesn't like to call it that—*modular* housing.

JC: You're talking about architecture as the purchase of a package deal.

CM: Well, it isn't exactly a package deal, it is a process. The module manufacturers have production lines which turn out their awful products. They could revise their production lines to turn out what they regard as *our* awful product; I found myself insisting on more windows than they had because I wanted to avoid the cramped spaces that are characteristic of that sort of modular housing. I am not interested in making an issue of the baseboards, or the trim, or the wall.

JC: Traditionally, an architect likes to design down to the ash trays.

CM: I care more, in this instance, about the plan configuration.

JC: Must an architect be an artist?

CM: I think he must. I lectured about this recently in a course called Advanced Fenestration. It was based on a T. S. Eliot quote about art and artists. He was talking about playwrights, and making the point that the artist's function is to give the listener or looker a look at order in reality, in order that he might have the chance to develop for himself some perception of the order of reality. That seems to me an interesting place to start, because it talks about *order* the way architects are endlessly doing, but it also talks about *reality*, which architects almost never mention. My claim is that simply to make order, the way architects did in the first half of the century, is to run the danger of being as irrelevant as a playwright who deals in drawing room comedies at a time of social crisis. The order is not very interesting by itself, unless it has to do with the order of some kind of reality that seems important. I extrapolate from that to note that buildings are like plays, narrative objects which can have the same variety of roles that plays have. Buildings, that is, can make comments about the situation, about their site, about the problem of holding the outside out and the inside in, about the problem of getting themselves built, about the people who use them or the people who made them—all sorts of things that can be funny, or sad, or stupid, or silent, or dumb. I maintain that all those things are legitimate things for buildings to do, and that architects who have tried to make everything sublime, however stupid its purpose, have done the same thing as the drawing-room-comedy playwright, and, by doing it, have lost the attention of the public.

HK: For instance, in the International Style, the building lost its character, became neutral. Man's desire to live in a varied environment was ignored.

CM: That's very accurate. The things our buildings have spoken of have often been folksy, or crude, or dumb, or irreverent, which is all right with me. I think that's the right way to do them, when that is what's indicated. Our commissions, so far, have not been the kind which have given us the opportunity to make a "keynote speech." Our most controversial job at this point, for instance, is the Church Street South housing project in New Haven, Connecticut [*Fig. 7–1*].

JC: How did that come about?

CM: Where's the best place to start? Mies van der Rohe had been the architect. He didn't even bother to quit, he just went away. There was left a model, which I responded to in a very negative way—a sort of green field rendered in phlox, with little buildings standing far apart and a few towers. He had done a school in the middle of the site—kindergarten through fourth grade—for which bids had come in something like 100 per cent over the budget, and he had thrown up his hands and said it was hopeless. The Redevelopment Agency changed their signals, and we got into the act with an opposite set of attitudes about it. The former mayor, Dick Lee, was broken-hearted about this project more than once. He was sad about losing Mies, but he was also sad when we got under way, because of what it looked like, because it wasn't elegant, it wasn't a beautiful monument to anything. We wanted to weave it into the fabric of New Haven, but here the "fabric" was a set of giant monuments by Kevin Roche, an expressway, and wide boulevards. Vincent Scully had been pushing very hard for respecting the street. That's pretty hard to do in this instance, which we discovered as we tried. I thought that we ought to be thinking about tying into the city, and since, for fabric, at this place in the city, all we have is streets, we ought to be responding directly to the streets. The apartment blocks flank the streets, and at one end there is an 8-story elderly housing building. The city

7–1. Model for Church Street South. New Haven, Conn. 1968. Moore, Lyndon, Turnbull, and Whitaker.

planners hate it. They say it looks like the worst architecture in Bridgeport.

HK: How much per square foot will the project cost?

CM: About $18.

JC: Including the towers?

CM: No, the towers are approximately $22. We were able to allocate some of the land for city parks. There are meant to be a whole series of things that couldn't have been afforded on a housing budget: walks, lights, pine trees, stairs up and a bridge over the connecting street, concrete walls with holes that give a controlled view [*Fig. 7–2*], fountains, and fancy paving. We managed to persuade the FHA to build up the commercial area from something like 1,000 square feet to 8,000.

JC: The commercial area doesn't flank the street, but actually fits into the complex.

CM: Yes. The commercial area is visible from the street, but it's really pulled into the complex. We have used billboards as big, colorful decoration. I hope to have art students paint them. The large, decorated walls will go in a little bit later than the completion of the apartments. In the meantime, I'm awfully afraid of the negative image. Originally, the apartment blocks were to be made of precast concrete, in bigger scale than is normally used in the United States. There were, and still are, 4-foot-wide, 31-foot-long concrete planks, spanning from front to back wall. Originally, in our design, we were using one-story-high, 9-foot by 31-foot-long precast concrete panels for the outside walls. In Massachusetts, they had been used transversely in the buildings as partitions by the same builders, who were then able to do fancier architecture along the façades. We had the great idea of reversing the use—turning the system inside out so that the ordinary dumb piece, the unchangeable panel, was the architecture. We had devised two basic panels to be used throughout the project, one with four windows, and one with two doors and two windows. It turned out very late in the design stage that concrete precast panels in Connecticut are controlled by a single company and cost too much money, so we had to go to concrete block. The change was very sudden. We got as much pleasure as we could out of contrasting ordinary concrete block with one designed with a very rough texture, but the buildings have come out to look much more barrack-like so far than we hope they will when we're finished; this, I think, is because of the wide, fast boulevards around; as you drive by, you're more aware of the project as a lump than you are of it as something that is helping make a series of spaces. We think these spaces, properly landscaped, will have a positive, memorable identity. We've been very interested in establishing the identity of places, and in establishing a chain of events that hook them together. One is supposed to think of where he lives as being at such-and-such a place. Hopefully, he will think of the way to get there, and the place itself as memorable. This, obviously, is bought at the expense of the identity of the single unit. We had to say that it was the green court or park rather than the single unit that was memorable, though we're furnishing one apartment in as wild a manner as we can manage.

It was, for me, a new and very interesting act, to submerge the individual identity of the unit in order to strengthen the identity of this as a project. We would have been erasing its identity at all the edges, and concretizing the memorable or the imageable place where one lived. Now, that's where I think we went at least partially wrong. There is a sameness about all the buildings there, which started out for good structural reasons that don't exist any more. What I wanted was to have no project identity and no single home identity, but to have a sort of street identity.

JC: When you changed to concrete block, could you have avoided the awful sameness of the buildings?

CM: Yes, if we'd *begun* with the concrete block instead of the precast panels. By hindsight, it now seems to me that we should have linked some of the buildings together. We should not have separated the building blocks, so that one would not have the chance he now has to keep an image of the blocks in mind as he drives around, like so many sausages.

HK: But, on the other hand, by separating the blocks, and facing them as they are, there are always views opening up.

CM: There are lots of interesting little vistas [*Fig. 7–3*].

JC. The emphasis in the whole area is placed upon those things which are normally considered superfluous. The addition of ornament makes the place more human. If you didn't have it, it would remain bleak.

CM: If you didn't have it, it would be

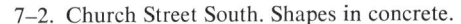

7–2. Church Street South. Shapes in concrete.

7–3. Church Street South. Small vista.

7–4. Church Street South. In the distance, the Knights of Columbus Building by Kevin Roche, John Dinkeloo, and Associates.

just awful. That is worth noting. It is central to our philosophy that there should be this applied ornament—that we depend on it to make the identity. We're not depending on the integral beauty of the buildings.

HK: You kept most of the buildings more or less on the same level. In Europe, there's a very strong tendency to vary the height of the different buildings to get a more lively . . .

CM: We tried to do that once, for the mayor especially, who came by and said it looked like Fort Dix. We couldn't find the money. Three and four stories is the highest we can get. We couldn't go lower than that because of the density we needed, and we couldn't go higher than that because we would have needed elevators.

HK: Even with all the "pretty" ornaments, you still have the horrible sound insulation problem. You have cardboard walls. You can hear every . . .

CM: You're supposed to call them gypsum board, not cardboard.

HK: You can stick a knife into the wall.

CM: We have just the FHA requirement of 51 decibel sound reduction.

HK: It's again minimal . . .

CM: Well, as is usual with the FHA, the minimum equals the maximum. You can't afford to do any more than that, and you're not allowed to do any less. You should not hear a neighbor dropping a shoe or a mattress squeaking. What tempted me to take the job, 51 decibels and all, was the possibility to do something with nothing. It depends on a lot of old-fashioned artistic things.

HK: Like placing two boring blocks in a perspective foreshortening, in order to have the Knights of Columbus Building right in the center of a view [*Fig. 7–4*].

CM: The whole sequence has alternate views of our towers and of the Knights of Columbus. These are considerations which our revolutionary students would regard as flat bullshit. They don't see any relevance to that outmoded idea.

HK: Visual composition doesn't count?

CM: Apparently not. I think they are wrong. As someone involved in their concerns, I feel very much the villain, and often hopelessly trapped. In some lectures in Denmark last year, I tried to put it in terms of order and reality from the Eliot quote I mentioned. It seems to me that our predecessors and the elegant people—the establishment architects practicing now, like Philip Johnson—are interested in order. People like me are interested in order and reality. The students are really interested in the middle—going to the values of one side and then the values of the other, back and forth.

The students are against shapes and say that people who make shapes are bad. I still don't see how you can make something that doesn't have any shape. It has to have shape, even if it's dull and stupid. However, I do agree with the students that most of the shape-making by architects has been irrelevant and unreal. I think I would agree with the students that to spend a lot of money to make shapes when other needs are not being met is folly and criminal and piggish, and maybe people who do it should be considered criminal.

JC: The whole concept in Church Street South might collapse without shape-making, and the addition of ornament.

CM: Yes. Now, that's very different from Mies's attitude, say, for he wouldn't have been able to do this within the limits which were set, because the requirements were so hopelessly impure and full of cheapness.

HK: As soon as you accept the FHA program, you become a member of the establishment.

CM: Right. That's what I damn well am —I'm a dean of an establishment, East Coast, Ivy League school, I am an architect in the AIA, and have been for quite a while, and I have spent a lot of time at Ivy League establishments like Princeton, learning how to manipulate shapes, in order to achieve effects that are considered desirable by somebody, and I damn well mean to ply my trade. I choose to put the emphases in different places from where Philip Johnson puts them, but I am being an architect in the full, establishment pig sense of being an architect. It takes the energy of other people; what you're doing is making a scheme for directing the energies of other people, so that they build something instead of something else. And, just how that's done in an altogether communal and non-hierarchical way, I can't imagine.

JC: Wouldn't it help to try to change the program of the Federal Housing Administration?

CM: Yes, it would help to change it. It comes down to gathering experience about how far one can go, the same way a naughty child (or any bright child) does. This was my first big housing; I didn't know how far I could go. I went as far as I dared without losing the job, because once I started, I couldn't afford to lose the job. That was another part of my inexperience. I didn't have the kind of contract that left me ready to back out at any moment, without going to jail. I was trapped in several ways. I pushed the commercial area from 1,000 to 8,000 square feet. We probably should have pushed to 30,000, but 8,000 was as far as we got. Next time, I'd know enough to have a better contract, and could push harder.

JC: The better you are established, the more you can try for changes.

CM: Yes. Another trap, of course, was that the whole thing was designed for one level of technology, and then was built on another. We thought our principles in the project were good, despite the traps. The principles included the regarding of the making of place as the important thing we were doing, and the use of reality, which in our terms meant commonplace things that people were used to, as a kind of hook onto the ideas we would be at any time trying to develop.

JC: In other words, architecture belongs to existing reality. That means not just building your buildings and ignoring others.

CM: Yes—it means it should adjust itself to existing reality—which includes the kind of imponderables in the souls of clients and users, as well as the more obvious environmental realities.

HK: I think we can illustrate with one of your earlier projects, the Citizen's Federal Savings Bank [*Fig. 7–5*] in San Francisco. You had an existing late nineteenth-century, classicizing, Beaux Arts building, and built an extension. I think this can illustrate how you use an existing physical reality.

CM: Yes. I was an associate in the office of Clark and Beuttler in San Francisco, in charge of the design. We all had to fight hard to get that to happen, because the bankers were interested in tearing the building down, or facing it over to make it look modern. It was one of the few buildings left from the 1906 fire—as they call the earthquake there. It wasn't a great building, but it was a legitimate piece of 1904.

HK: What was your argument?

CM: It was a fine building, it was old, part of San Francisco; what could you gain by defacing it or tearing it down? We had the chance, because the clients had bought the corner as well, to do all the code stuff, elevators, stairs, toilets, in the new spaces, and to get . . .

HK: You cleaned it out.

CM: Cleaned out the inside of each floor. It was much more interesting to me to design the little corner piece that made it all happen than to design an ordinary office building. On the ground floor, we opened it to the corner. It was important to them to get a Kearney Street address in San Francisco, so we put a door over there. And, as far as I was concerned, that was as real a reality as anything else.

HK: It now turns out that your corner extension gives the existing building a new value. You didn't hesitate to use forms which were not fashionable.

CM: That's right. I'd been at Princeton in the years before that, an assistant to Enrico Peressutti, who would come every year from Milan. He and I would work out the previous year what the graduate class would do, and I would lay the groundwork. We had a series of problems in the three years I helped him, in which old things were looked at and new things were added to them. Each time it was, in Peressutti's words, an exercise in learning to live with old things, and to complement them and to make them exciting. Like being a friend of somebody's, he kept saying, making the thing that was there more special than it had been before. So this was a quite simple outgrowth of those attempts in graduate classes at Princeton.

HK: All the old centers of Europe are really in danger of being torn down. You are much more aware, apparently, of the few old things you have. We Europeans take the tradition for granted. We think we have so much, it doesn't matter if we tear down one more building; finally, there's nothing left. You Americans have also made some horrendous mistakes in the area of preservation, but some good attempts are being made.

CM: In this part of the country, the eighteenth century is beloved, and the nineteenth is ill-regarded. Great buildings in Philadelphia were torn down in the name of restoration—a Furness bank, for instance. Some wonderful buildings were laid low to make greensward around some stupid little eighteenth-century shanties. Gradually, though, the prejudice against great gutsy stuff is being overcome. My problem as a practicing architect is that I don't get enough of those restoration jobs.

JC: Your new Jewish Community Center tower in New Haven is built directly across the connector from the Knights of Columbus Building. How do you relate to it? Do you compete with it?

CM: Inevitably, we compete with it. We thought a great deal about our building's re-

7–5. Citizen's Federal Savings Bank. San Francisco. 1962. Moore, Lyndon, Turnbull, and Whitaker.

lation to the Knights of Columbus. There are differences which are very strong. Roche's cost $11 million, ours cost about $2½ million. His has about the same number of square feet, but they are far more elegant square feet than ours, and therefore more expensive. Our floor-to-floor height is less than his, so our building is going to be much lower—only 60 per cent as high.

And we're down in a slight hole anyway—his is on higher ground. I'm worried about how ours will look in relation to his, just because it's a lot smaller, so that it may look like some baby brother tagging along behind. It is, like his, a square, and it's self-consciously turned back on the New Haven grid, instead of 45° from, like his is, although that makes ours 45° from the new grid in our part of town. We wanted to face our flat corners with the same tile he was using on his round corners, but we couldn't afford it.

There are a number of curious optical things that happen. His is remarkably transparent in the middle, and I think it will stay that way, because I don't think they're going to program any partitions. Because of the towers, it looks very wide, whereas ours, with the corners chopped off, is going to be, from almost any angle, quite slender. They'll come off, in perceptual terms, quite opposite.

JC: Are there commissions you would not accept for sociological, political, or moral reasons?

CM: Yes, we turned down one, not long ago, to design housing on the People's Park in Berkeley, California. We were asked by the University of California if we would be interested in being on a panel of three architects to look at the job; they didn't say in what capacity. I went very carefully, because the people who offered it were friends of mine from the old days, and I looked at the history of that whole scene, with tear gas and helicopters, and concluded that anything that was done was not going to be socially acceptable. It was to have been a $5.5 million . . .

JC: How much money would you have lost?

CM: The fee would have been about $300,000. We wouldn't have made much, however. It was an exciting chance to do something, and our office in San Francisco needed work. But I couldn't accept it because I didn't believe in the good will of the Regents and the Governor. It's not much of a park; it never was. But the fact that people had been pushed out of it by troopers and tear gas was the major issue.

JC: Let me put the question a little differently. Would you build a private house for the Governor?

CM: Yes, then I could put lead paint in the walls.

JC: Does political preference have much to do with architecture?

CM: Yes. One of the reasons I didn't pursue the California housing was that my picture of myself as a liberal would have been at least partly destroyed. It would have been destructive of my vision of myself to take on some hireling job for what I think are forces of repression. It isn't because I'm moral, it's because I have some vision of what I am in favor of, and that wouldn't have fit it.

JC: Would you take the advice of sociologists and psychiatrists as consultants for housing?

CM: Sure.

JC: What would you get out of it?

CM: There's the rub. I've been to numerous conferences and confrontations. I remember one where the architects and builders sat on one side of the big table, and the sociologists and parapsychologists sat on the other side. The architects and builders were supposed to look for answers from the academics. Of course, nothing happened. The architects didn't know what questions to ask, and the academics certainly didn't know what answers to make up for the questions that hadn't been asked. There's a much bigger gap than people in the architectural schools are willing to admit between the attitudes of the practitioner and the attitudes of the academics.

HK: Sociology as an independent science discusses problems that stay scholarly. It's up to the architect to take out of the scholarly context some practical suggestions.

CM: It doesn't really want practical suggestions. The architect is one of a set of people whose ideas mean nothing, unless he gets the stuff built. He's in it to cause something to happen, and that something is normally a kind of physical structure. The sociologist is in the opposite position, where the purer the theory the better, and the more muddled the theory with reality, the worse. It's hard for the sociologist to understand the architect's impatience with inaction.

JC: Did any sociological theory influence your work at Church Street South?

CM: Very little. One of the things of importance to us is that our solutions should be specific. Even those few great buildings that there are in the world which rise above the specific into some eternal realm had to start from a need to respond to a particular program, place, time, climate, and set of people. A good deal of what makes modern architecture terrible is that it is so often an attempt to get the universal solution to what isn't the universal problem. I found it very difficult when we started on Church Street South, because we had no real specifics about who was to live there. That was sort of numbing for us. We decided that, since it was the late 1960's, most of the people who were going to live there would be black. We needed someone who was knowledgeable about lower and lower-middle class black life-styles in order to get some specific insights. We went to the New Haven Redevelopment Agency, and they climbed right up on the desk, because it's a political issue that more black people are coming into a city which has a long tradition of Italian rule. That is, the sort of people who think Italians are better than anybody else seem to be in the slight majority in New Haven. The people in the agency didn't much like the idea that we, as knowledgeable WASP architects, would try to find out what black life-styles were and thereby admit that a sizable number of black people would live in this project.

JC: They didn't want to admit this?

CM: No, sir! Everything must be as "American" as mom's apple pie, and everybody's alike. We would have welcomed any specific input we could have gotten about anyone's life-style, but the official vision doesn't allow for any differences. None of my designs for anything, from one-family houses to the Community Center, could be said to have been consciously influenced by sociology. The influences have been consciously specific and individual, and never consciously general and normative—except, of course, where normative documents like the FHA Minimum Property Standards have touched us.

HK: The one-family house is still a standard building type in America. It is usually the first commission an architect gets; this is true in your case.

CM: Yes, I still have strong feelings in favor of one-family houses as legitimate architecture, even in the late twentieth century. I've taken a lot of gas from students about still doing one-family houses, because they are considered to be antiurban and, therefore, antiblack and antipoor.

HK: You spread the suburbs. Greater Los Angeles, for example, is nearly as large as Denmark.

CM: It's true, but we still have a long way to spread. There's Nevada, hardly even touched yet. That could be suburbanized. Still, it has to be said that the single-family house, or semidetached house, the dwelling on the ground made out of wood, and made simply, is still, for almost everybody in the United States, the only really economic thing to build, the only thing that people can actually afford with their own money.

HK: It may be the only hope to get privacy.

CM: The amount of money it costs to build high rise, and to build with fireproof materials, and to make stairs and elevators in the inner city, is simply far more than almost anybody can afford. Just to pay for what it costs to cart the junk around, and get the wrong things out of the way, and assemble the materials, and pay the wages, and build it in New York City, brings the cost to a ridiculous amount of money for a public housing unit that still doesn't have

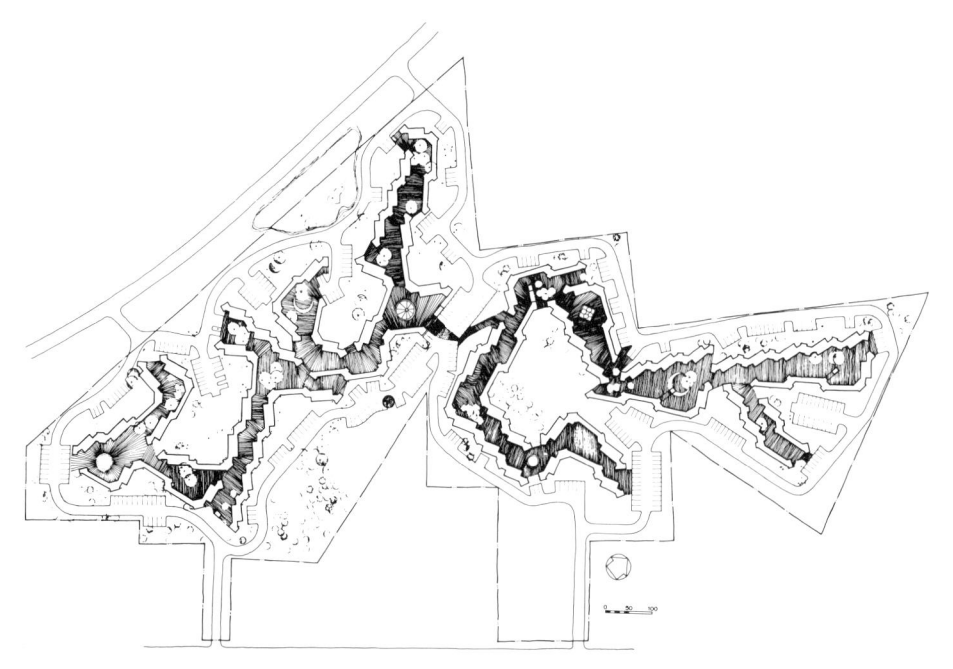

7–6. Housing project. Orono, Maine. 1970. Moore, Lyndon, Turnbull, and Whitaker. Site plan.

any privacy, and doesn't have any outdoor space attached, and doesn't have any of the standardly presumed amenities. For half that, you can build a pleasant house in the suburbs, with a backyard, and a frontyard, and a place for the bicycle, and sunshine. Although granted that a unit in the suburbs takes up more space, at this point it seems to me to be the only possible way of getting decent housing. Let me show you what I am working on. This is about a 17-acre site in Orono, Maine [*Fig. 7–6*], next to the University of Maine. It is divided into two areas. One has 40 units on it and the other has 160 units. The site for the 160 is really quite beautiful, with big old trees and a young pine forest, so there's a chance to wiggle the buildings in among the trees and have something like the simpler Finnish housing projects, whose pleasures come from simple, well-considered buildings on a handsome site. I've been working harder on this than on anything else lately. The units are very simple and inexpensive [*Fig. 7–7*]. They are modular pieces that are made by a trailer company and trucked to the site; they can be delivered for $9.50 per square foot, which is cheap, and they will be put on regular foundations, which will be built on the site. The funny little vestibules we mean to paint up like guard houses or candy boxes. With a few special pieces for the laundry building, with the painted vestibules and some fences, with a couple of sort of triumphal archways—things that can be painted fancily—with a landscaping scheme, and the trees already there, and, finally, with some luck, we can get this to look good, and to be a very pleasant place. There is a local art council which is talking about making a set of pieces of sculpture and play yards, or maybe painting some crazy designs on the asphalt, by which people can orient themselves.

Though it looks very picturesque, the whole village is composed of standard units. The limit to these units is that they can only be eleven feet eight inches wide in order to be transported on the highway. They can be up to 60 feet long. In order to make them feel like something other than trailers, we have to have big windows. Each apartment opens directly to the outdoors, and everybody has a garden. Three trailers, or modules, make one four-bedroom apartment. The idea is to avoid the standard trailer appearance, and also to avoid having a lot of rooms lined up along a hallway; we put them together so that a shorter hallway gives access to more spaces. The units will probably have a plastic roof and masonite with a plastic coat on the outside. Our scheme is to have the walls white and roofs white and the snow white and then . . .

JC: The White Charger!

CM: Yes—and very New England. These vestibules will be painted brightly in curious shapes, except in the section for the elderly people, where we thought they could be dark green, in the manner traditional to New England. The vestibules, where the swinging "Now" type students will live, we felt should have huge purple and orange diagonal stripes, and other appropriate signs.

HK: Most of the interest is focused on the porches. They provide variety, not only because they are painted, but also because they shoot up beyond the roof line.

CM: We leave them up high for no good reason, except a visual one.

JC: Is there uniform fenestration?

CM: Yes, of two types. I think in the kind of jumbled complexity of these things there's a considerable advantage in having some things sort of stupidly simple. Church Street South, for instance, has only one size window, and it bugs some people, but I think it's a discipline which saves us from pure chaos.

JC: The interesting thing about this, more than the single unit, is the total layout of the project. The site is strangely shaped.

CM: Yes. They bought up different pieces—which happened to turn out that shape. I wasn't sorry it was strange. There were times when I was a little depressed with its complexity. Our notion was to have a pedestrian street: simple, cheap houses, with their own outdoor spaces and their own gardens, that could be linked together with other houses and put along a pedestrian-scaled, highly imageable, picturesque circulation spine. Old people, especially, and students, as well, would not be isolated in a parking lot, but were somewhere where they could get to other people and still have privacy. In the site plan, the pedestrian street is the shaded area. It is to be graveled. At points along the way, there will be art, or something brightly colored, or a place to sit, or something else special. The rest of the idea of the plan is simply that there should be a driveway that rings the whole thing and lets you park your car in your own place, near your back door. Every unit faces onto the pedestrian street on one side, and the parking area at its back door.

HK: There is a strong differentiation between the interior pedestrian area and the exterior driveway.

CM: Yes, and I've worked very hard at it. You can imagine the FHA and others not being too excited about that. Somebody at the FHA wants to run a 50-foot street down the middle of the pedestrian walkway. We have had some turmoil about it. Part of the problem is to keep the pedes-

7–7. Housing project. Orono, Maine.

trian walkway strong enough, useful enough, so that it really matters.

HK: It's not just a passageway. It links a sequence of little places, then stretches out, and opens up again. It's very lively.

CM: I think so, though I'm sure that people like Venturi, with his antipiazza, prostreet attitude, would regard it as screamingly picturesque and dubious. We expect to push the natural forest cover back with a bulldozer while the units are being built and then slip it back into place, so that it is as undisturbed as possible. Everything is going to be homemade; even these pieces of so-called art in the pedestrian area are not going to be somebody's Frank Stella thrown on the ground, but are probably going to be mounds of asphalt with stripes and arrows painted on them.

JC: Can the children play on them?

CM: Yes, that's the way we planned it.

JC: It integrates the playground.

CM: I'd like to have some fountains, too. Not basins, with all the troubles that a basin has, but something like four giant showers with a tile floor, so that kids in the summertime can play in it. A play fountain.

JC: Is your plan for Orono, Maine, only a local solution, or does it have a more general significance?

CM: I think it's worth making a set of distinctions: One of the things which I find myself railing against is the standard picturesque site planning of a suburban nature that keeps being applied, no matter what the site: resorts in Colorado, for instance, that look like pages from an Alpine tour guide.

JC: Vail, Colorado.

CM: Vail is a most beautiful example of this. And, it seems to me, dead wrong. I'm urging some students of mine, who are doing a thesis on Copper Mountain, Colorado, to make their little valley have a main street straight with a grid crossing it. I wish they would make a false-front façade on both sides of the street to create a piece of man-made order in the great jumble of the mountains. It's much more useful, I think, than the picturesque, phony attempts at an Alpine village.

It is always a matter of balancing and making some tension between the pieces and the whole. In this project in Maine, the pieces are just dead simple. The only thing we can play with is the space between the units. So we have a highly disciplined beginning [the module], which we had to break out of. I can imagine, in other circumstances, with a more interesting unit, that it would seem to me perfectly legitimate to have a simple, rigid site plan. Now, this is a small place. It's very limited in its narrative scope and power. It's playing the same note over and over again in ways that try to sound different, but it's not a diagram of a way of life. It's a very low key, small thing, that tries very simply to make decent housing look pleasant. This scheme certainly is not susceptible of infinite expansion. Even though we are using identical units, we attempt to let somebody know when he is home, to make his own place special without its screaming at all the others.

7–8. Model for Coronado Island Condominium project. Coronado, California. 1962. Charles Moore.

It is interesting to compare it, I think, with Albertslund in Denmark, a very recent housing project in the suburbs of Copenhagen, a new town, really. There are some very nice patio apartments there at fairly low cost, and some garden apartments. But it has an absolutely rigid site plan, straight out of the 1920's, with every street the same, and every street straight, bam, bam, bam, across the flat fields of Denmark. The units are lovely, really very pretty, but the project has the standard bugaboo: How do you know when you are home? There's a Kafkaesque atmosphere, desperately oppressive.

HK: Your description sounds like someplace in New Jersey.

CM: Right. Which is what makes me think people should abandon New Jersey. I suspect it will be the first American state to be asphalted over from border to border.

HK: The Coronado project in California was your first large housing project [*Fig. 7–8*].

CM: Don Lyndon and I worked on this in 1961. The problem was an interesting one. Coronado is an island that separates San Diego Bay from the Pacific Ocean. It is flat, and completely settled with a lot of retired Navy people. The whole island is laid out on a grid. There's a magnificent hotel, the Del Coronado; it was built in 1888, a huge wooden structure—very high, very picturesque, glorious, and goofy. Then the rest of the town is 1-, 2-, and 3-story houses. So, the whole visual atmosphere here made us attempt to take the scale of 3-story buildings and pile it up, to get a high building that was still not a monolith, or of such a scale that it was hostile to the surroundings. The various city boards liked it and gave it zoning approval. But it never happened, for a long series of reasons. It was a condominium that came too soon.

HK: This project is very interesting historically. These years around 1960, of course, are very important because of the big change that came about when architects began to break away from the box shape of the International Style. There are three different designs for that project. The second one interests me especially because you suddenly introduce a rather unusual movement into the whole body of the building. That was not common at that time.

CM: It's more exciting than the first one, which did revel in great tensions among its more or less simple spaces; but the latter shows a great deal of pushing and pulling among the elements, and that, I think, makes it more interesting.

HK: In the first plan, you stick to the traditional Bauhaus concept of arranging geometric blocks irregularly. In the second, there is a significant change. You now have blocks which incorporate the play of elements in the body of the building; a flat rear wall and a concave sweep in the front façade. By reinterpreting your project, you reflect at the same time the change in the history of modern architecture.

CM: I was talking to Don Lyndon recently about what we were both doing then. I think that what we did together there had quite different effects on both of us, and I think it's accurate, for both of us, to say that what was true then would not be true now—the kind of naughtiness of that scheme. We were doing very dangerous things. On the one hand, we had to make something that appealed to a fairly conservative town; on the other hand, we wanted to make a statement against things we felt were wrong, a revolutionary statement.

HK: You considered that as a revolutionary statement?

CM: Yes, but a kind of *sub rosa* revolutionary statement, since it couldn't be so revolutionary that the retired admirals would tell us to get lost, so that's why I use the word "naughty" to describe it.

HK: The façade has an irregular broken sweep, and, within that, many things happen.

CM: It would have been awful to have a flat façade. Within something which kept us pretty heavily constrained, we found ourselves pushing and pulling and trying to make something that was varied and special and did the other things. The reason that it is any good is probably that it was very hard to do. We had to press hard just to get a fairly taut curve. That is why it is as disciplined as it is.

JC: Yet, you introduce variety and original shapes.

CM: We didn't *have* to have the elevator equipment dangling out in space at great expense, but it seemed important to us for that sort of thing to be there. Today, many architects automatically do it. I just couldn't do it now, but it seemed important to do it then.

JC: Did you know the work of Aalto at that time?

CM: From the books and magazines.

JC: Aalto had achieved similar qualities earlier, for different reasons. His concern for acoustics in large spaces led him to curving walls which break in angles, specifically in his famous church in Finland in 1956.

CM: Of course, we knew of Aalto, but I'd never seen Aalto's work until this last summer.

HK: At that time, there were just a few mavericks, notably the late Hugo Häring, Scharoun, and Aalto, who didn't fit into the general International Style concept. It was much later, around 1960, that their ideas became more and more accepted as a reaction against the rectangular box.

CM: I have a different background. I graduated from the University of Michigan and got my first job in 1947 in San Francisco. There, the wildest and most wonderful work belonged to the past. Bernard Maybeck and other splendidly crazy people were still very much alive in 1947. The Greene brothers [Charles and Henry] were among us, and the work of Willis Polk. There were a lot of shingle fantasies, very Beaux Arts. In northern California, there was still a sort of more or less controlled goofiness in the Bay region. The ones who followed after William Wurster, for instance, had brought it to a sensible, carpenter level. But the previous generation had been altogether crazy in a wonderful way.

7–9. First Church of Christ Scientist. Berkeley, California. 1910. Bernard Maybeck.

7–10. Faculty Club. University of California, Santa Barbara. 1966. Moore, Lyndon, Turnbull, and Whitaker.

HK: Maybeck generation?

CM: Yes. The Christian Science Church [*Fig. 7–9*] in Berkeley is a wonderful building across from the People's Park. I think it is an infinitely better building than Wright's Unity Temple of the same time, much more rich and exciting, with a lot of just nutty details, like Gothic tracery upside down. Maybeck was really a kind of declaration of independence. He said that the rules which might obtain elsewhere didn't really obtain in California, and he wanted to do what *he* felt was right. In our Coronado project, there was a good deal of conscious revolt against what was thought to be right. By 1960, there was a sort of John Carl Warnecke successful-practitioner syndrome which pretty much dominated things in San Francisco, as well as everywhere else, and it was no longer nice to do things that weren't altogether straight and square. Right now, Don Lyndon and I are having

7–11. Reverdy Johnson House. Sea Ranch, Gualala, Calif. 1966. Moore, Lyndon, Turnbull, and Whitaker.

a great controversy about the Pembroke dormitories [at Brown University], because he has an eye for differentiating and specializing—he has pages and pages of window details, which seem of great importance to him. But I managed to persuade the people who are making the working drawings to put all those pages at the end of the set, so we can lose them when we have to.

JC: Yet, you are very interested in fenestration, yourself. You simply play with the window shapes and use them as an ornament.

CM: That is a major difference between Lyndon and me. I think the most interesting way of doing fenestration is to do it with very simple, ordinary units, to use one size window next to another size standard window. I normally use a minimum amount of effort on each of the windows by using the kind you can order by the numbers. It seems to me a very important part of concentrating effort in those places which really matter.

HK: You achieve variety with standard units.

CM: Yes. Don is much more anxious to make each window special.

7-12. Faculty Club. University of California, Santa Barbara.

JC: He tends to overwork?

CM: In my terms, yes. In his terms, I tend to underwork.

JC: Of course, you don't limit yourself to standard windows. One of your special characteristics is shape-making, cutting interesting holes into thin walls, outside and inside.

CM: I think probably the first time we did that was in the Santa Barbara Faculty Club [*Fig. 7–10*], although there are some private houses that were finished earlier where we did the same thing. In the Johnson House [*Fig. 7–11*], these cutouts simply derived from the situation. The roof goes down and makes different-height walls, and you can either poke a wide window into it, or a high, narrow window into it. If you want something more complicated than just the windows you can order by telephone, you grab a saber saw and saw some holes, preferably inside, where you don't have to fit glass into the openings. In the Santa Barbara Faculty Club, the chance to play with those things became, for the first time, an exciting possibility for me. The front wall of the club, which faces the lagoon, is partially the result of a controversy with the campus architect, Charles Luckman. When he saw our building, he said it was unacceptable, looked terrible, didn't look like his stuff, and had to have a *brise-soleil*. He thought that would cause us to put a screen over it which would hide this awful building that we had done, and he wouldn't have to worry about it any more. It swept over me, in the middle of the night, that all we would have to do is have another wall in front of our opening, with other holes in it. Thanks to Charles Luckman, then came the first of our free-standing walls.

JC: Your free-standing walls are very thin. They never gain the massiveness of present-day "brutalism." But, by overlapping the screen walls, you gain a plasticity which the brutalists try to achieve with massiveness. It's a three-dimensional juxtaposition of shapes.

CM: To do this was especially effective in a place like Santa Barbara, where the light is very elusive and beautiful and comes shooting down in beams that make other patterns on the inner walls. It's easy to take a free-standing wall that doesn't have the problems of climate and cut holes in it, and do whatever you want [Fig. 7–12], let the rain come on in, if that's what it's going to do. I find it simpler and more pleasant to juxtapose fairly simple elements, in such a way that the relationships get complicated, instead of making one thing that is complicated within itself.

JC: Of course, one thinks right away of Louis Kahn's grand screen shields at Dacca [see Fig. 6–9], which are different, yet somewhat similar.

CM: Louis Kahn is right there from the beginning in the Santa Barbara Faculty Club walls, which are a dead steal from Kahn's Luanda consulate in Angola, which was very carefully worked out by him. There, he developed the idea of having white walls in front of the windows, screen shield walls, as you call them. They were bright, but not nearly so bright as the sky, so you could look out a window and see an intermediately bright surface which broke the glare. Ever since Kahn described that to me and others, in the late 1950's, we had been waiting to use it. It is of great importance to play with the light in such a way that it is possible to look out of a window without it being simply a glaring hole. In the Santa Barbara situation, it got to be interesting just in terms of the shapes. I thought it would be fun, too.

JC: At the same time, the critics admire you for building ordinary architecture. It seems to me a certain contradiction to admire you for your ordinariness as well as for your fancy fun, your shape-making popholes.

CM: The whole business is fraught with contradiction. It is not an act of ordinariness, but the building is meant to do what it does by very ordinary means, with a minimum of strain in the areas in which strain would be inappropriate. One does it with cheap materials or with standard forms or with minimum budget. I have some Scotch-Irish moral compunction about spending very much of a client's money when we don't have to, and it seems to me not particularly nice to engage in the kind of structural or shape-making gymnastics that require a great deal of huffing and puffing, and the spending of lots of money.

HK: You are often compared with Robert Venturi.

CM: Venturi says, and I guess he means it, that Main Street is almost all right. If he means that great revolutionary cataclysmic changes in the environment are not sensible, suitable things to seek, I agree. If he wants to maintain Main Street as it was, I don't agree. I think that the environment is lousy, and there is hardly any place in North America that the hand of man has touched that it hasn't ruined. Anything we do has to be a great deal different from anything we have done before, if it's going to begin to meet the human needs attached to it. I think that to be ordinary, in the sense of simply continuing what is already known to people, is wrong. I get very upset at the standard student approach now which supposes that, if you interview enough housewives in a housing project, and write down what they like best about where they live, you'll know what the solution ought to be. This can't be true. However, I think it would be a mistake to tear everything down in order to arrive at some new environment, even though what is there isn't any good. It is a mistake to throw away everything that's familiar. My particular interest is in using familiar pieces, mostly cheap pieces, putting them together in ways that they have never been before, so as to get something that's strange and revolutionary and mind-boggling and often uncomfortable, but only using the ordinary pieces. I think that's a better way of making a revolution than just inventing a whole new crazy set of shapes. That is, I'm not really, for instance, moved by Bruce Goff or Paolo Soleri. I'm astonished sometimes, but it doesn't help me.

HK: Mr. Moore, what you describe here is identical with what Mr. Venturi wants to do. There is no apparent antagonism between your theories and Venturi's. The results, though, the buildings, may be very different.

CM: I know that, and I know that Venturi is often misunderstood. We both put existing pieces in a new light, so that you notice them. The semipop musicians, like Dave Brubeck, do something very similar; they take ordinary themes and mess with them just enough, so that you can still recognize the themes, but you notice them for the first time, because something, maybe something awful, is happening to them, they're being kicked around in a way you didn't expect.

JC: Even though you use common elements, you aggressively deny anonymity. To the common materials, you are adding a certain pop-art vocabulary.

CM: I think the only way to do commonplace things so that people will look at them is to drive them right to the edge of disaster, without, hopefully, their falling off. My hope of their not falling off is based on the pleasantness, the cheerfulness that we mean to surround almost all of our stuff. We try to make it happy, which is different from Venturi. Vince Scully contends that Venturi is virtually the only American tragic architect since Louis Sullivan, and he says that I am not in his league because I am not tragic. So be it. I think that it is all right if Venturi is tragic, but the special importance of it is lost on me.

HK: Of course, there is always the danger of sliding away into *ordinary* ordinariness. Things become ordinary in your work even if you don't want it. Because it needs to be cheap, it stays cheap. Then all the theorizing about the values of ordinariness sounds like an excuse.

CM: Yes. That's certainly my main danger, and a very present trap. Church Street South is the most vivid example of the danger, it is the most dangerous piece of work we have done.

JC: If you don't get the money for the little pretties on which the whole environment depends, Church Street South is going to be a new boring zero. Are you afraid of being banal?

CM: We are on the edge of banality, whether we want to be or not. That's just the nature of our work. It has something to do with the tiny margin of leeway between just doing a really stupid job and doing something that has elements in it that make it all right, make it worth having done.

JC: Clients are still not used to adding on the jewelry, there's always a tendency to withhold that little bit of money you need to make it pretty.

CM: Right. If it's a house we have done, the client says, "To hell with you, Charles Moore, we've spent all our money, all $9,000 of it, and here's the house, and it's all ugly; go away." And I say I will not go away, I will come with a paint brush and I will do a picture, transform it, or reveal its worth.

We did a house once in Bedford, New York, a nice house, but very conservative, with a sloped, gabled roof to fit a "colonial" neighborhood. It was turned down by the developers because it wasn't colonial. Though I had thought it was colonial, in that it was congenial in colors and materials. They didn't mean that, they meant "colonial," Cape Cod. So we decided to do a double-scale Cape Cod cottage, in which the chimney in the middle of the building was 15 feet square, and actually had a fireplace at each corner and a skylight in the middle so the space went up, and it was all kind of like a Piranesi prison inside of a double-scale Cape Cod cottage. We figured these developers were stupid enough not to read the scale off the drawings, so they would only see the nice standard Cape Cod elevations. We lost the client somewhere along the line; it cost too much money.

HK: It is actually a Roy Lichtenstein idea to blow up comic strips, and thus make them suddenly frightening.

CM: Yes.

HK: Architects have the tendency to dress up their drawings in order to make them look full of life. They add a couple of nice little trees, a young lady with a child walking down the street, and all the other devices to make one overlook the architecture. To count on trees, to count on grass which finally will never grow, to count on nice stairs which sometimes don't get built, you know what I mean . . .

CM: I remember Ernie Kump came to school when I was at Michigan and told us to do that. He said, "Now, when you make a drawing, be vague about everything you are building, but draw in their dog."

HK: In one of your presentations, you have some people riding on horseback. It gives it the touch of New England aristocracy, of course. That's cheating.

CM: I confess to getting very scared of those pretty drawings. As a matter of presentation, I like much more the rough card-

7–13. Faculty Club. University of California, Santa Barbara. Dining room.

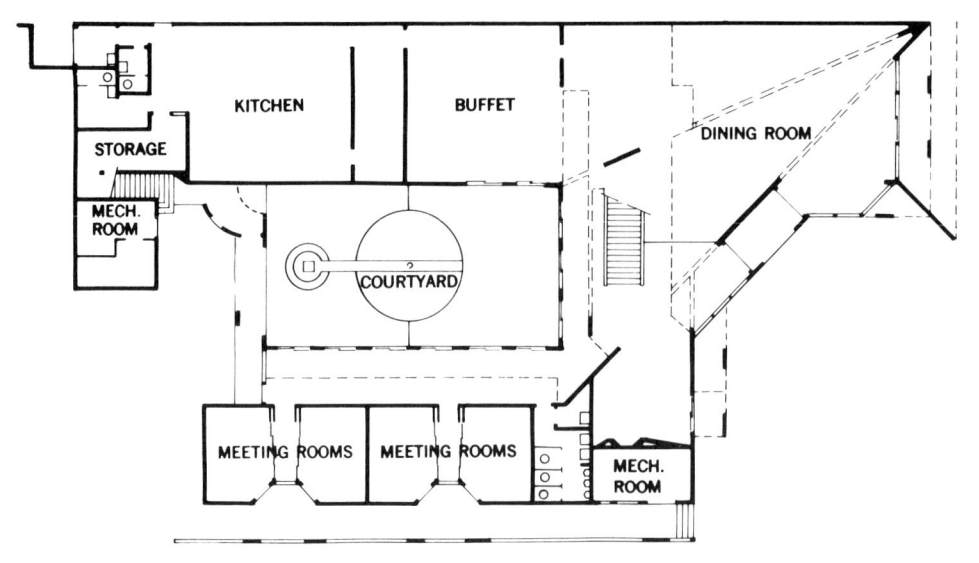

7–14. Faculty Club. University of California, Santa Barbara. Ground plan.

board model rather than scenery full of cheat. It's going to be the late twenty-first century before most of those trees are there.

JC: You accent the elements of irony in your architecture. Do you ever give in to a self-conscious seriousness?

CM: I think it's very important for people to take the work in the spirit in which it's offered, which is often one of some levity, but often quite straight. I confess that I'm made less uneasy by triviality than by portentousness.

HK: You don't want to overinflate the client's ego?

CM: I like them to feel as though they're undergoing an adventure. I think that the dining room in the Santa Barbara Faculty Club [Fig. 7–13] is perhaps our most successful space in this respect. It is an exciting, even breath-taking, place to be, but not ostentatious—it's too goofy to be ostentatious. It's damn strange in a way that is not unpleasant. It can be thought of as a medieval banquet room in the shape of a piece of pie [Fig. 7–14]. People in there may get a kind of vicarious enjoyment out of all the historical precedent, without supposing for a minute that they are living it. This kind of playing with reality is often taken with great seriousness by people as a personal attack on them. Their lives are so important that anybody who is screwing around with their environment in this fashion is suspect; they take it as laughing straight at them for being such pompous fools. I'm not laughing at them for being such pompous fools. They can laugh at themselves, if they want to, but I am interested in laughing at their environment. They may be pompous fools, but they have that right.

HK: What would you do if you had to build a bank?

CM: We are now remodeling a bank. We have invented a magnificent neon sign for a little bank in Westport. It is a recent, very handsome Davis Brody building which we're remodeling about two years after it was finished, because the bank had been enlarged and everything was wrong. We're doing the graphics, as well as the revised interiors and front. It is called "County Federal Savings," and we invented a sign that says "County" in elegant letters, with a star inside the "o" of County. "County" is blue, and the star is red, a sort of Texaco sign. The "o" is neon.

HK: And this is the sacrosanct place where people bring their dollars? Don't you need some big, impressive, heavy columns and walls?

CM: Davis Brody gave us all the heavy walls we need. We were going to have an enormous blown-up $5 bill over one of those heavy walls, but the bank president doesn't want it. In fact, he doesn't want anything we've suggested so far. He seems quite negative.

HK: He certainly wants to have a serious building that people can trust.

CM: He's got a serious building. It is a very trustworthy building, but needs one simple little neon sign to help it.

I find myself in the paradoxical role of at once designing and undesigning. I function as a designer, using the elements I have in hand very carefully, within my capacities. But I also have to speak as an undesigner, saying that what's wrong with us architects has been a narrow concern with composition that doesn't allow for the importance of people. On the one hand, there are still the designers, the Philip Johnsons and the Paul Rudolphs, who are actively composing. On the other hand, there are the students, announcing that the architect should devote his life to a service in which people are led to decide for themselves what they want to live in. I don't believe in either of these extremes. I find myself in the middle, like any liberal. I think there is still a role for the composer to compose something, if it is sufficiently uninsistent, so that people's lives can go on unencumbered by it. I also suspect that, when it comes to practice, much of the rhetoric of the students is going to turn into the same kind of solid arrogance that the Rudolph-Johnson way of doing things already includes.

JC: Do people want the superficial decorative treatment you give to the brutal basic elements [*Fig. 7–15*]?

CM: Let me throw in some pseudohistorical terms. We have been led to believe, by functionalists of the twentieth century, that the ridiculously expensive building and the pompous monumentality of the nineteenth century was all done with the outlay of needless amounts of money. If buildings were stripped down to their essentials, they would be pure and true and wonderful. It turned out that, when they were stripped down to their essentials and were hence so wonderful, they cost more than they ever had. It had not followed that it was the ornament that was making the building unavailable to the people. The ornament disappeared in favor of secret ornament. When Mies van der Rohe glued bronze mullions on the skeleton, it was as much ornament as some Greek-inspired anthemion of the generation previous.

The issue is that that generation built be-

7–15. Church Street South. Circle and light end wall.

yond its needs, and our problem is that we build beyond our means. Most apartments cost more than the people who live in them can afford. Many economists say it's just because people aren't prepared to commit enough resources to the place they live. But I think the whole method of building is too high-priced. In a healthy situation, people would have a wide choice within their economic range. They can have that in selecting their automobiles. The means of building houses is beyond people's control and imagination. You sort of take what you get.

HK: Take the cheap FHA units and look at the insulation problem, for example. The noise level is unbearably high. In fact, there is essentially no privacy. I was not even surprised that you accepted the 51 decibel minimum FHA standard at Church Street. I am now living in a 51 decibel cardboard apartment, not living in it, but controlled by it. I'm entirely dependent on the neighbors who live up above. They go to bed and get up at different times than I want to. Their schedule now determines when I wake up and when I go to sleep.

CM: That's really what I'm trying to get at. You, as an inhabitor of something that's given to you, live at the mercy of these forces. We're all wrapped up in an altogether artificial scene, in which people get what's built according to a set of standards that have all been codified. If you were a southern European peasant of some time ago who lived in a house that was too small, you would simply build another room on it, and you would build it with mud from your fields or the rocks from your fences. In our situation, hardly anybody has that kind of freedom. Even the middle-class suburban dweller discovers that to add a room is going to cost him $10,000 or so. In this situation, we as architects have to depend on something that *is* under control, something very superficial, like paint and trivia, in order to make this anonymous housing special.

JC: You count on the trivia as an essential part of the architecture.

CM: I do, really. Our contribution is in two parts. One, the functional point, is independent of art or understanding of society or anything, it's like solving a puzzle. And the second is to take a perfectly trivial margin of money and involvement in order to make at least a token claim on these places on behalf of the people who live in them. It is a simple response to an almost futile situation.

It seems to me that buildings ought to be narrative—not just pure serious play of forms and light, but things saying something. And, if anything is going to say something, it's got to have a certain amount of freedom of speech to say something shallow, or banal, or dumb, or already said.

JC: Or maybe also intelligent.

CM: Maybe also intelligent. But you have to have the options of saying all those other things in order to have the chance to say something intelligent. And, indeed, you wouldn't know if something was intelligent, unless it were somehow in doubt and jumping up out at you from the masses of stupidity that surround it. The basic freedom and lightheartedness of that opportunity is the critical point.

It seems to me that in Venturi's recent writings, for instance, the whole opportunity for expression is taken as a burden, and it becomes a dreary need to be profound and serious and meaningful—and all of that is to be done with the "ordinary." I am interested in getting the freedom from seriousness to mess around, so as to allow a chance to have something exciting and unexpected and wonderful happen. I'm really very heavily distressed by this sanctification of ordinary that begins to make *it* as difficult to kick as the elegances of the Johnsons and the Rudolphs. I attempt to deal with things that are not so ponderous that they can't be lifted, and to keep a certain silliness afloat so that results can also come out of circumstance and out of accident.

JC: When do you call a building "narrative"?

CM: The chief element of narration is

7–16. Grand's Restaurant. Philadelphia, Pa. Venturi and Rauch.

usually what is said about the trouble it's gotten into and is struggling to get out of. A building that is a pure cube is not saying anything you don't know already.

JC: Could the narrative element be a billboard?

CM: Yes. Tim Vreeland has a beautiful slide of a gas station near Albuquerque which is an old cinder block box building. Separate from it, and very high, at the scale of the desert, is a sign that tells you what it is.

JC: The sign is important, the architecture is not.

CM: It means that men put most of their energy into the sign, which becomes the architecture, really. The sign draws the business, not the building.

HK: I would like to know more about the background of the ideas which led into what we might call "Pop Architecture." I think it's important to give the right people the right credit.

CM: I don't know where it started. Venturi was the first one to do what has come to be called "supergraphics"—in his Grand's Restaurant in Philadelphia [Fig. 7–16]. As far as I know, the whole business of paintings and flat-footed messages on the exterior and interior walls started with that restaurant, destroyed seven or eight years ago. In the Santa Barbara Faculty Club, we have made comments, however abstract, about what was going on in the more permanent materials that lay under the paint. In the simplest case, on a water pipe, we might paint "water pipe." We all owe so much to Lou Kahn that he has to be taken as a source of it, too.

HK: Where is the connection? When we talked with him, he would not accept Venturi's or your ideas. He would not have anything to do with pure decoration, just painting on words.

CM: That's true.

HK: Were there any narrative elements in Louis Kahn's architecture which you picked up?

CM: I started to say that much of the narrative aspect of buildings comes from the building's trying to say what it wants to be, not from flat-footed separation of functions. For instance, one takes a difficult detail which has an awkward solution; the detail could have been thrown out, or covered up in favor of something slick. There, I say no; take it, show it, emphasize it. The dining room of the Santa Barbara Club [Fig. 7–13] has an absurd beam, a great big beam, which cuts the pie-shaped room. It goes whaling off to some other wall, where it finally comes to rest. I make a great deal of it and hang lots of lights on it.

HK: You emphasize the awkwardness.

CM: You emphasize the awkwardness and *then* try to solve the problem.

HK: You emphasize what other people hide.

CM: I emphasize the trouble, yes. If you're being eaten alive, you don't stand there pretending everything is all right. You dramatize your plight. Then solve your plight as neatly and completely and elegantly as you can.

HK: The functionalists also claim that they don't cover up—by showing the function, they show the truth.

CM: What they showed was the structure and the system. They showed the front organs, the things they wanted to show as being important in the hierarchy. And what they didn't show was the stuff which didn't fit, the oddball stuff, the functional misfits, the things which were unsymmetrical. I am interested in the sort of backdoor stuff that didn't fit in that earlier kind of formal statement of the truth.

HK: Why do you want to get away from the slickness of the International Style?

CM: Because I don't think it is a very useful, interesting, meaningful, worthwhile description of what's going on. It's like the prepared statement of a politician. It's very important to spend a lot of time preparing a statement, as the Bauhaus did preparing a building. But I'm also interested in what the politician really thinks. I want to know what lies behind the statement, or what incredibly sordid deals are made in the smoke-filled back rooms. The private asides are a legitimate part of the whole. Looking at the building, I would like to know all of this as well as the Bauhaus-approved face. I don't mean that the Bauhaus is putting on a false face. They were against that. I would be perfectly happy to accept a false face, if I could know that behind it was something else, also available. This puts me in absolute opposition to something like

the Paul Rudolph parking garage [*see Fig. 3-21*] in New Haven. The last thing in the world you need to do is make a sculptural statement out of a place where you put cars. Why not just put cars there? It is not appropriate to its use, which is storing cars. Cars don't need sculptural storage. If the sculpture gets in the way of the tops of the Volkswagen buses, then it's worse than useless. It seems to me out of control. It is not an interesting piece of narration because it is not talking about anything which has to do with anything. If it would just shut up and house cars, or talk about something interesting, then that would be much more to the point.

JC: What would be interesting about a garage? What if you had a large block in the center of town to build a garage on? Rudolph says that even a garage can give character to the town and can help organize the urban chaos. Therefore, he doesn't want to make an ordinary garage like millions of others.

CM: He and I would disagree about whether a soft, sculptural thing would do it. If you want to have a strong statement in town, you make a strong statement in terms of the *town,* you don't flossy it up. This is like having a police force in drag, it seems to me.

JC: The question is still what you would do.

CM: When you drive into a garage and park your car, the car is dead, and you become a pedestrian. The place where you get out of your car and start to walk should become a place of great importance, and a place where a good deal of environmental excitement could happen. In Rudolph's garage, no excitement comes from driving the car in, and no excitement comes from walking away from it. When you drive in, you are too concerned about whether your aerial will be ripped off. When you walk away from your car, your only excitement is whether you're going to survive. There are no sidewalks, you have to walk in the traffic. All of the excitement there is solely in that giant ash-tray shape, not in you as somebody using it. That, I believe, is the wrong way to get excitement. There's plenty of excitement potential in the whole set of actions one goes through, if one only looks at it from the viewpoint of the user. But there's not much potential excitement if you look at it as a statement of "parking-ness" or "urban automobileness."

To me, this narrative function that we have been talking about is all of these things together, the building being as descriptive as it can about what is interesting about it—either the way it's built or the way people use it; the message is either shouting, or being quiet, or hiding, or pretending to hide but letting you know what is going on. I think Louis Kahn would say that this is trivial in the extreme. But it certainly stems from his idea of having the building be what it wants to be.

JC: This seems to be the point where you see an obvious relation to Kahn, but you take a phrase of his and interpret it very differently.

CM: A building itself has the power, by having been built right or wrong or mute or noisy, to be what it wants to be, to say what it wants to *say,* which starts us looking at buildings for what they're saying, rather than just accepting their pure existence in the Corbusian manner.

HK: In the International Style, a church could look like a factory—like Oud's church at Rotterdam. The meaning was no longer important, because functionalist purity was all-important. When a Beaux Arts architect wanted to build a bank, he just took a marble colonnade with a pediment, and it was a temple, "The Bank." When you build a bank, it has a neon sign on it. The whole value context of estimating what a bank is is changing. A bank may not need to narrate security and stability any longer, the building doesn't need to look safe, but the alarm system has to function. Nowadays, a bank could even look like a gambling house.

CM: Yes, it depends on the value system of the society. Our bank looked, to some of the directors, perfect and wonderful, and they were very excited. To some of the others, it looked like a Texaco station, so they killed it. Now, we're doing it over so it doesn't look so much like a Texaco station.

HK: Don't you often run into the difficulty that the client wants the building to have a different message than you want to give it?

CM: Indeed, that is a problem which I shall probably face if I ever get large enough commissions. We just don't have very many institutional clients who have such an elevated notion of themselves. As soon as we get that kind of client, we will at least pretend to listen.

JC: Morris Lapidus is one who listens. He designed his Hollywood movie set hotels in order to give people what they want.

CM: I think a lot of Morris Lapidus. To me, what he and his son Alan are doing is even more correct than what Venturi is doing. It's a little more real. I think their illusions are not so extensive.

JC: Yet, is that architecture or merchandizing?

CM: I don't really know what is meant by architecture, I guess. If architecture consists of building pyramids, then clearly we don't need it. If you march through history and look at the central preoccupation of every civilization, one by one, in order to see what architecture is, I doubt if you'd come up with enough common denominators to let you know.

JC: Listening to you, it seems that everything that happens, from the foundation to the play mound in the piazza, is architecture.

CM: As far as I'm concerned, it's all architecture. I don't have any way of cutting off anywhere and saying that it's somebody else's province, or irrelevant to mine. I'm not concerned about refining a definition of architecture, but about the fact that architecture has remained too pure. My criticism of previous arrangements would mostly be based not on what architects *did* say, which is fine in almost every case, but on what their language left out. It is important to make architecture talkative again.

JC: When the narrative aspect takes over, and the jewelry, the billboards, and the asphalt mounds become essential, then architecture is the making of an environment.

CM: The environment has to become architecture, because if it doesn't nothing is going to be. You can say that there was a time when a certain aristocratic fringe of what was built was "architecture," and the rest was vernacular trash. If you say that fifteenth-century Florence consisted of some palaces and churches, and left out all the rest that didn't make it into the history books, then you haven't adequately described the nature of Florence.

JC: In other words, you care about the shacks, too.

CM: Yes. Florence looked the way it did because of the important edifices which had something special about them, as well as all the other buildings which made up the urban milieu that made palaces possible. It is just as useful to take them together as to separate them. We have standardly separated them for the purpose of identifying the important ones in the first category . . .

JC: In order to write a neat history of styles. Most of your architecture fits into the category of the vernacular. Would you have built a Boston City Hall?

CM: It seems to me that one of the neglected aspects of the American city is the public realm. There have to be buildings that are identifiable as belonging to a lot of people and used by everyone. A hospital, for instance, is not a very good public symbol because it belongs to the sick. But a city hall is still in a position of being a public symbol. It still has to say what it is in ways that are honest and appropriate.

HK: Would you use marble on a city hall?

CM: No, I probably wouldn't, it's too expensive. Even in a public building, I think I'd feel uneasy about spending money which might be better used for policemen's uniforms or something equally trivial. I just don't see any reason in our society to put on the dog in such an everlasting fashion.

HK: How would you make it stand out as a public monument?

CM: It probably should be a monument, it should be an identifiable place, a monument in the sense of a *marker*. It should not just be a building like a lot of others in a street.

HK: What if you had to build a city hall next to Paul Rudolph's Art and Architecture Building?

CM: The only thing I would do would be to withdraw from the competition, make a little park with the building underground. Power by contrast.

HK: Your little house in New Haven [*Fig. 7–17*] was in a rather ordinary neighborhood. What made you buy this place?

CM: It was very cheap, and I was sick of driving into the city. The house had been lived in by a little old lady who died, and the price was very low, so I bought it.

HK: When you bought it, did you already have in mind what you were going to do to it?

CM: No, I bought it because it was

7–17. Charles Moore's House. New Haven, Conn.

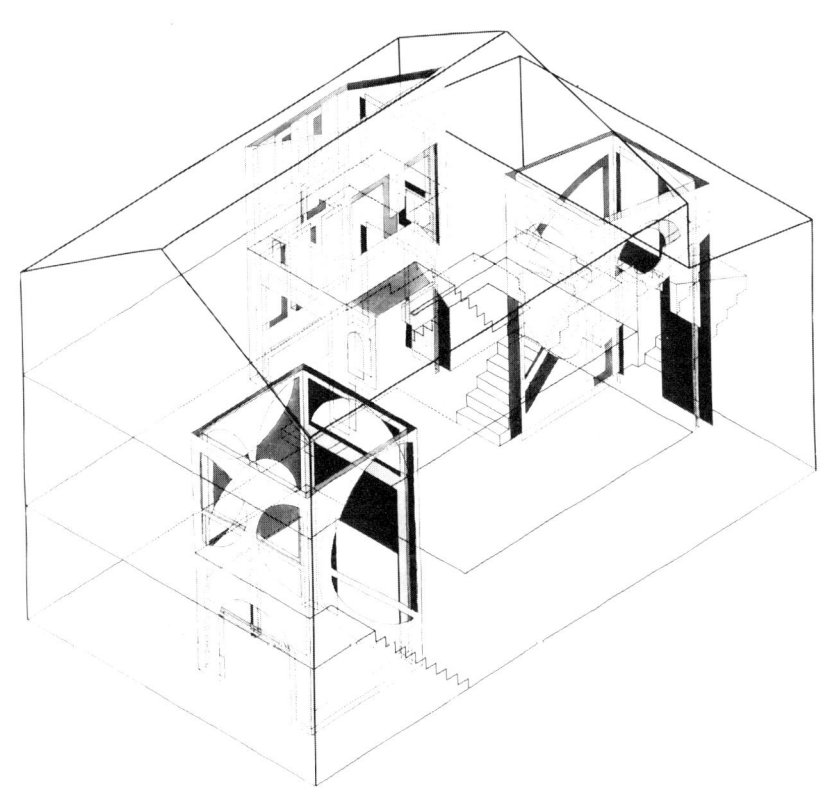

7–18. Charles Moore's House. 1966. Moore, Lyndon, Turnbull, and Whitaker. Isometric drawing.

pleasant the way it was. I wasn't at all sure that I would do very much to it. I didn't want to gut it and make a Mies van der Rohe out of it. I wanted to have that funny little old house and play with it. I bought it in December and didn't touch it until May. Just came over and sort of looked at it, wondered what to do with it. In May, I started tearing into it [Fig. 7–18]. When I did the first layer of remodeling—moving the bathroom and putting in the stairs and cutting the holes—I still didn't know what I was going to do with the plywood.

HK: Did many things come by accident?

CM: Yes, it was done piece by piece. When I started in the entrance hall, I had no idea what the rest would be like.

Bob Rosenblum came when it was first being finished and announced that it was a piece of contemporary sculpture and not architecture at all. I like to think of it as furniture design.

It is also important to my way of thinking that those plywood walls, with all kinds of shapes and colors [Fig. 7–19], are not very serious. They're made fairly cheaply and very quickly. We just opened them up with a saber saw. They are not travertine, they're not pigskin like Philip Johnson's bathroom, they don't represent any eternal investment. They are statements of pleasure and prejudice. It really becomes important just in terms of my style and pocketbook. They don't represent a big investment of concern, but are a response to fleeting things, light and air. And when they don't seem to be accurate responses any more, they can be torn down and replaced easily. I like to think that this house is, in the best sense, trivial.

These interior spaces have different names. The first one, at the entrance with silver-painted plywood surfaces, is named "Howard," after a dog in New Orleans. I thought it would be better not to try to put functional names on them, since they had no functions. You walk around in what was originally the very tiny living room of the house, which is now just a sort of foyer, a set of cutout sliding numbers in it for lack of anything else. And, from that, you come into what was originally the main dining room. When you walk into one end of that room, you're in a space that goes up all the way to the roof, where there's a skylight. That space is named "Berengaria," who was the wife of Richard the Lion-Hearted. It's a name I like, and I've had cats named that. And then you go downstairs and into the lower level of the house, that is, if you didn't take the stairs which go up to the bedrooms. Down there is the dining room and the kitchen. Indeed, it's sort of nowhere, not in an uncomfortable way, but you're just not on stage, whereas Howard is a more difficult place to be. The hammock is downstairs in Howard. I seldom use it; it looks very attractive, but I hardly ever find myself lying in it because it is "on stage."

HK: You actually apply forms used in modern sculpture, but you make an environment out of them that people can live in.

CM: I think that's true. I'm baffled by going into the Museum of Modern Art. I am baffled when I go into a dark room and have it called "art" for me, or when I go and confront a room that's painted white and has a fluorescent light leaning against one wall. I'm not affronted by it, or moved by it, or anything. I may think that's a nice thing to do, but I'm always astonished that it has taken a sizable part of the energy of somebody to have done it. If you wanted one, it would cost you a lot of money, which I also think is strange. I think that what lies behind all that ardent sculptural effort is very much worth messing with, but only in a very casual way. I would find it very hard, for instance, to do this house in travertine, or even stainless steel, because it would make it serious, like those rooms in the Museum of Modern Art. And that would really upset me. There are things that a sculptor does that an architect can't, of course. But many of them turn out things which are not in scale with the effort. For them, making that statement honestly becomes a principle as legitimate as the structural honesty of a generation or two ago. I have the opposite problem; I get lots of crank mail from people who announce that it's all a giant put-on.

HK: Architecture very rarely has been ironic. It is serious because it affirms the existing society.

CM: One of the great paradoxes is that art appears to be, by its very nature, revolutionary, but architecture, at the same time, is also establishmentarian art. And I find that very puzzling. Those architects who are most affirmatively doing the affirming of the *status quo* are the ones who will most loudly tell you that they are dealing with an art. I don't see how that can be.

7–19. Charles Moore's House.

8 ROBERT VENTURI
DENISE SCOTT BROWN

JC: Mr. Venturi, the very few buildings your firm has built have had a major impact on American avant-garde architecture. There has been a great deal of comment on their formal aspects. What would interest us is more information about the preliminary stages of planning and the process through which your buildings evolve.

RV: If you are referring to the theories of process that architects are talking about a lot now, that is, the methods for designing and then solving very complex program problems, we do not do much of that. We don't for two reasons: We have not been given very big jobs with very complex programs, and we have been more interested in content and image in architecture than in process in architecture. We have not been concentrating on the theories of process and program. We haven't had much incentive because of the rather small jobs we get. I have a reputation for being theoretical because I write and lecture. It's rather funny, because I'm not very good at talking or writing, and I don't like to do them. I've been in a situation where I've *had* to do a lot of thinking and theorizing because I haven't had much opportunity to work. My ideas have been my opportunities. That's the reason I have talked a lot. I don't really want to; I'm not by nature a theorist. I'm very much a pragmatist and a craftsman.

HK: Your book *Complexity and Contradiction* is possibly the book most discussed among American architects and critics, but, at the same time, you are one of those architects who doesn't have enough commissions. There is a contradiction in the situation itself. Commissioners apparently want something other than what you are interested in, but the language you developed to talk about architecture is imitated extensively. The architectural awards given by the magazine *Progressive Architecture* [January, 1970] directly reflect your value system by awarding architects whose projects take up your ideas, and yet you yourself are still sitting around waiting for commissions.

RV: I agree, generally, and I get a little bitter about it. We're asked to lecture all over the country, all over the world. We are now saying to the universities who invite us: "If you can get us a commission for a building at your university, we'll lecture for nothing; otherwise, please ask your campus architects to lecture to your students."

What happens is that, usually, the man who does a new thing the second time does it better, in a way. I mean he builds on it, he does it cleaner, he really sees the situation more clearly than the man who sweated and struggled to slug it out the first time. The other reason is that our architecture is, evidently, hard to take, especially for many other architects. I don't understand why, but we irritate architects very much.

JC: What would be a position of yours which irritates architects?

RV: For instance, we like to look at the existing landscape and go on from there, looking at it nonjudgmentally at first. This horrifies architects very much, because they've been saying all along that *everything* is all wrong. Their whole reformist attitude is . . .

JC: Paul Rudolph, for instance, has said that Venturi's architecture is already built, it's already there. If Venturi accepts the existing cityscape, then he doesn't need to build any more.

RV: Yes.

JC: If "everything is almost all right," using your famous phrase, then why continue?

RV: But, of course, I never said that. My statement was, "Main Street is almost all right," with a careful stress on the "almost." Besides, it is rhetorical. It is not to be taken too literally. We say our buildings are "ordinary"—other people have said they are ugly and ordinary. But, of course, our buildings in another sense are extraordinary, *extra*-ordinary. Although they look ordinary, they are not ordinary at all, but are, we hope, very sophisticated architecture designed very carefully, from each square inch to the total proportions of the building. Literary critics have known about this all along, that is, about the use of clichés, the use of common, everyday language which makes the literature of Eliot and Joyce, for instance, *extra*-ordinary. This is a widely-used method in all art, and it is well-known, except, apparently, to architects.

JC: Why use the term "ordinary" at all?

RV: It was partly a polemic, but also because on one level it *is* ordinary in the present context. It is a reaction to the heroic stance of architects like Paul Rudolph, for example.

JC: Would you prefer to use some other term now that there has been so much reaction to "ordinariness."

RV: The primary meaning of the word doesn't matter too much. Not to sound pretentious, "Gothic" and "baroque" were originally derogatory terms.

HK: You don't want to destroy the existing environment; you want to adjust yourself to the existing environment and still build a building which is not the same, not identical with the environment.

RV: Yes, but I don't think this is the answer for all time. We're people working in the context of now. The original source of our feelings about the ordinary, about starting with the existing landscape, looking at it without a chip-on-the-shoulder attitude, was an artistic, intuitive one. It did not develop out of a rational process. We just didn't *like* what architects were doing to the landscape when they engaged in total design. We don't like the megastructural, heroic, pseudoprogressive stance of establishment architecture now. We think it has neither validity nor vitality, and this was an emotional, artist's response.

And then we went and looked at architecture that's not *trying* so hard, architecture of the everyday landscape, and we felt there was a vitality and a viability there. Then, we rationalized our original reactions and tested them against a social and technical critique based on real needs and feasibilities in this country today. I think another point is that much of this attitude comes from our own experience as architects; we get commissions for very small jobs with very modest budgets, and it hurts to make a pseudoheroic building when you don't have a heroic situation. In a way, we're making a virtue of necessity. Okay, if society is giving us little jobs with crummy budgets, that is the state of architecture for us. (In fact, it is the true state, relatively, for almost everyone.) Let's not fight it. Let's joyfully make something out of it.

HK: What if you had gotten the commission for the Boston City Hall [*see Fig. 3–10*]?

RV: Boston City Hall is, to me, a very good example of what's wrong. It's bombastic, I think. Boston City Hall is trying to do something through architecture that architecture can no longer do. In the past, architecture *could* be monumental. It could denote civic monumentality in the city.

HK: Just by form?

RV: Just by form—by pure architecture. Siena could have a *palazzo publico*, but not Boston. Philadelphia could do it rather well in the nineteenth century with its lovely monstrosity of a City Hall. The urban renewal people, with their urban revival of traditional urban spaces, are trying to return to Italian monumental urbanism. Urban renewal has tried to bring the center city back via pure architecture, and it has not succeeded, because this is not the era for grand architecture. Every age has its medium. The medium for now is not pure architecture. The Boston City Hall employs the formal vocabulary of late Le Corbusier: These pure, heroic forms were great as the tense manifestation of late genius in a Burgundian field for monks. Not so for bureaucrats and citizens in a Bostonian piazza.

What the building should be is an ordinary loft building, or a shed that will shelter and accommodate the bureaucratic processes that go on in City Hall. Then you cover that shed with a great big sign that blinks "I am a Civic Monument," if that is what you want. In other words, for us the main impact must come from media other than architecture. What I have just described for the City Hall is what we have called the decorated shed. Modern architects have maintained essentially that the impact comes from the expression of the process of designing and building: The image of the building is a resultant of structure and space and program, and these all work harmoniously. We don't agree with that.

We think that these architectural elements can be contradictory to each other—that the outside might want to be different from the inside, for instance—and that the impact cannot come only from pure architecture. The history of architecture can tell us that architecture always incorporated iconographic and symbolic meanings. The Gothic cathedral is a decorated shed, to some extent, teeming with mixed-media messages. The image is not just architecture. In fact, there are contradictions resulting from the complex image: The façade of Amiens is not "organically" related to the building behind it. Or, rather, a disunity exists if you look at the building as pure architecture. But this is not only a building. It's also a billboard facing a *place* which broadcasts a message. The billboard functions more in front, the architecture more in back; up front, architecture alone wouldn't have had enough impact.

JC: What is the medium for today?

RV: Well, I'm not sure, but I think the medium is less abstract and more symbolic in nature, less architectural and more graphic in nature. We came around to this through the commercial strip. In our landscape, the architecture which makes a unique impact is the strip [*Fig. 8–1*]. The idea of the symbol in space over the form in space applies not only for the commercial strip in our landscape, but also for the residential suburbs, as our learning from the Levittown study at Yale showed: The iconography of housing developments is rich in symbolism. But, for civic architecture, the commercial strip applies very directly, because that is what makes an impact over big spaces at high speed. The car is here to stay for a while, and our buildings in the auto landscape of parking lots are relatively insignificant pimples on the surface of the land, and they cannot "read" without the reinforcement of signs and symbolism. Orthodox architecture, pure architecture, has to be savored as you *walk* through it: It cannot stand the distractions of our hostile environment. But, today, the real environment is where you can mix symbolism and architecture. And it is here where you get back to the symbolic architecture which history abounds in.

Everyone has his own methods of learning. I'm someone who refers to historical architecture; looking at past building can be stimulating as a method; it helps me see in new ways. And, now, I am enjoying looking at the iconography of historical architecture.

In the recent past, architects of my generation went to Europe to look at space and piazzas and spaces between buildings. What we saw was the equivalent of abstract expressionism. The buildings around the piazza, for us, were merely abstract forms making space with textures, patterns, and colors. The symbolism, we did not see. Only the art historians remembered the symbolism in that architecture.

HK: The idea of symbolism might not be clear for everybody.

RV: There are different kinds of symbol-

8–1. The Strip. Las Vegas, Nevada.

ism, and that can get you into the intricacies of semeiology. But I'm being very simple-minded here: I refer to the shape of the building itself, like a hamburger-shaped building where hamburgers are sold by the side of the highway, mixing the media of painting and sculpture and architecture. Or the symbolism might be *on* the building, in the form of a sign. Today's architectural iconography connects with advertising art, which is another stimulus. We like looking at ads. Suddenly, they are interesting.

HK: Most of your buildings are dwellings. There is little opportunity to introduce a kind of symbolism, because there is not much need for public messages.

RV: Actually, we have built only two houses. But one's thinking is always ahead of one's architecture, because architecture takes a while to materialize. You can get an idea in a fraction of a second, but it can take five years to become architecture. So our architecture is tame compared to what we are saying. Also, we try not to make our architecture a vehicle for our ideas, so there is purposely not too literal a correspondence between the two.

What we are trying to do is to make an impure architecture—bringing sculptural, graphic, pictorial, and other associational qualities to bear on architecture. As we have said, all this existed before in eclecticism and most other architecture. Our method, generally, is to do what roadside architecture does, which is to make architecture the sheltering aspect, separating the meaning—expressive—artistic aspect from the building aspect. This is antiarchitecture, if you will, and it is defining architecture, to some extent, as the decoration of structure: This is an admitted dichotomy. Even the Italian *palazzo* is essentially a decorated shed in this view. For three hundred years, the structural-spatial configuration did not change much. It was the outside which was given changing symbolic and ornamental surfaces.

HK: The problem, of course, is that the American society wants to have an architecture of strong images in a traditional way. There is still a predilection to build impressive public buildings which demonstrate power. This predilection leads architects in the direction opposite from yours. Architecture as pure architecture still seems to be the best vehicle for demonstrating power, as in Beaux Arts times. The value system of American society has not changed very much.

DSB: You find the same thing in advertising. Think of the many products which are sold "just like grandma used to make," or "finger-licking good," which are reminders of days back on the farm. Now, Madison Avenue can handle that need very well. Why shouldn't architects be able to?

HK: But you do just the opposite. You take the existing subculture of the strip and pull it up to the level which traditional architecture has considered to be *its* domain. Our environment is, as a matter of fact, strip architecture, but we haven't been able to accept it. There is an antagonism between the strip and Boston City Hall. What you are doing now, actually, is to bring the strip up to the level of Boston City Hall, but in doing so you are alienating the existing society by saying what it really is.

DSB: I would put it a little differently. I would say that we are taking a very broadly based thing, which is the popular culture—and I wouldn't exactly call it a subculture, because it is so broad—and we're trying to make it acceptable to an elitist subculture, namely, the architects and the corporate and governmental decision makers who hire architects.

RV: The thing gets very mixed. I agree with you that the current orthodox, establishment architecture is Beaux Arts, but, on the other hand, the image of modern architecture is avant-garde because originally modern architecture was revolutionary and progressive, or claimed to be.

JC: When you begin to translate the strip into architecture, it becomes a self-conscious strip.

DSB: Yes, it becomes high culture rather than low culture.

JC: In addition to the conscious use of

the strip vocabulary, you bring a sociological awareness into your architecture. We haven't found many architects who care for sociology.

HK: Most architects despise sociology.

JC: But, in your studio, there is an enormous amount of energy going into the sociological questions before the design stage. Does this mean that the architect needs to become a sociologist at this point? Can he afford the time it takes to evaluate a society before he starts building?

DSB: Most architects scorn the notion of sociology. You'll find that Louis Kahn says that sociologists deal with families with 2.5 members. He is criticizing the social *physics* side of sociology, the side which involves measure, and he calls it the whole of sociology. When I first came to America, I had a course with Herbert Gans at the University of Pennsylvania and thereafter worked with several social planners. I don't believe the architect becomes a sociologist, but he certainly has to look at the information of sociology from an architectural viewpoint. I like the fact that the influences upon us are the pop artist on one side and the sociologist on the other. There are very few good links between them, but we in the middle can learn from both. In a sense, on one side we're fighting the architects who say there's nothing we can learn from the sociologist, and on the other side the sociologists are telling us that we architects will have to extend our conceptual framework before we can learn from them. I say we will have to extend their framework as well, since they have neither the tools nor the outlook to take it into our field themselves.

JC: From what we have discussed so far, two of the major components of your architecture are the discovery of the strip and sociological awareness. What else?

RV: Also, the symbolic content of architecture which the strip shows us.

DSB: Also, interest in popular culture as it is able to influence and inspire high culture. I'm sure that there has to be a relationship. If we're to get another kind of architecture different from urban renewal architecture, which we believe is not really relevant, there must be an acceptance of this other kind of architecture at the decision-making level. Taking popular culture and interpreting it in the light of high culture is the only way you will get changes of attitudes in people who judge competitions, people who award contracts to architects. However, it's no use just criticizing urban renewal, and it's no use just reading sociology. You never move directly from a sociological idea to an architectural idea. There has to be an analysis of form, a change of formal vocabulary, and working with a new, more relevant grammar of form; and this we think we get from looking at the strip and urban sprawl.

HK: That makes the difference between the existing "ordinariness" and the conscious use of an "ordinary" vocabulary.

RV: Representational art in painting and sculpture has a long tradition of depicting ordinary things and scenes. Another aspect of this subject involves meaning and iconography, but the subtleties of these subjects I know little about; they were not part of our education. We studied space. Some English architects are now considering meaning and the whole subject of semeiology in a way relevant for architecture now. In my day, you studied imagery from a *Gestalt* standpoint of perception; it was a game in abstraction, without the elements of association and past experience and their effects on perception.

JC: Then it would not be fair to criticize your use of ordinariness as an invitation to blandness?

RV: Andy Warhol said, "I like boring things," and we consciously make our buildings boring. On the other hand, we want to make them tense. We work hard to give them tension, and architecture with tension is not boring. Again, "boring" is a rhetorical exaggeration, as a reaction against the building up the street which is theatrical.

JC: One thing we haven't mentioned is

humor and irony in your list of priorities.

RV: Right.

DSB: I was going to say that when everybody was posturing and being extraordinary, being quiet and ordinary was very unusual. It has shock value.

RV: Modern architecture has taken into its theory what is called indigenous architecture, architecture without architects. You know Le Corbusier went to the plastic architecture of the Mediterranean, and others went to huts in the Pacific. He went there and, like the others, appreciated it presumably for its structural honesty and its directness. But never for its symbolism. The anthropologists tell us that this architecture is extremely complex. It is not simple. It is teeming with symbolic and iconic values, as well as inherent structural values which appear straightforward, and maybe they are. But these other qualities are not. So when we are talking about "ordinary," we are talking about the symbolism of the ordinary as well as the substance of the ordinary.

DSB: Nevertheless, we get accused of being "slaves to the mediocre."

RV: We have also been called "Nixonites" and "Reaganites."

HK: That, of course, is because you affirm the existing landscape.

DSB: And people's right to have their own architectural values.

HK: The traditionalists look to the past in order to escape the present. The Utopians look into the future in order to overcome the present. You point at the reality of the present. As long as there is a desire to build a Boston City Hall, there is no desire to accept the strip, the present.

RV: But the strip is full of fancy—more than the theatrical pomposity of current architecture. I really think that our culture *is* supporting the strip.

HK: In other words, the Boston City Hall is already a dead monument.

JC: When you consider the strip, and those forces which produced the strip, then you have to be selective and decide which forms can be relevant. There are architects who have reflected the mentality of popular culture, yet have come out another way. For example, Morris Lapidus is an architect who consciously or unconsciously . . .

DSB: That's highly conscious in his case. He has a whole rationale.

JC: At any rate, he comes out with a very definite solution which, at the same time, is very different from yours.

DSB: We really haven't worked out what the difference is. We agree there's a difference. We perhaps were surprised to find how much his rationale and ours went together. He has his reasons for what he does. It was a very conscious decision to make a kind of 1930's movie Valhalla in Miami, based on his analysis of its users. I think his training as an actor helped him, as well as his old-fashioned architectural training, which developed his skillful ability to draw beautiful things.

JC: When Lapidus says, "I want to build what a man wants," something is imposed upon Lapidus. But your approach is to determine what man wants in order to help establish it for him. In a way, *society* defines Lapidus's architecture, but *you* define what is society's architecture. There is the contrast.

HK: Morris Lapidus is affirmative. He takes what exists and does what is wanted. You take what exists and change it, thereby actually negating it.

RV: Perhaps, on one level. That's what the pop artist has done. But I feel we both negate and affirm. And I'm not too happy with the thought that we define what society's architecture is. Isn't that what architects have been arrogantly doing for society all along?

DSB: We parody and use irony to some extent, as a way of expressing judgment. I think it's a loving irony, not a cruel one. The problem of judgment and permissiveness didn't start with architecture, by any means. Psychiatry was already concerned with it at the turn of the century. Being nonjudgmental has very respectable ante-

8–2. Mathematics Building. Yale University. New Haven, Conn. 1969. Venturi and Rauch.

cedents; the people who called us "Nixonites" should call Freud a "Nixonite" too. But we don't say we don't judge. We just say we *defer* judgment. In deferring it, we let more data into the judgment, we make the judgment more sensitive. Why do we accept certain aspects of the strip and not other aspects? The basis of that judgment is partly social, partly aesthetic.

JC: The Mathematics Building at Yale [*Fig. 8–2*] is a very different set of demands. It is interesting to us that what is perhaps your first major building will be built in a stronghold of contemporary "pure" architecture. Will you alienate the campus or affirm its existing values?

RV: We have tried to make the Yale Mathematics Building in the tradition of ordinary architecture. Ordinary in the way the eighteenth-century Connecticut Hall at Yale was ordinary—in its construction, program, and appearance: ordinary in the sense that it *is* conventional and it *looks* conventional.

HK: Then you relate it to the oldest architecture on that campus, rather than to the most modern.

RV: Modern architectural theory has acknowledged ordinary architecture—calling it anonymous architecture—but mainly for its "straightforward," traditional techniques of construction, indigenous to the place, and for its supposedly simple form as a background for more heroic architecture. Never for its symbolism of the ordinary or for its style, because symbolism and ornament are scorned in architecture now. Yet symbolism and explicit association are essential and unavoidable in architecture, in the creation of it and the perception of it.

JC: In relating to the old "ordinary," you introduce a new model as well. This is much the same way you use the architecture of the Las Vegas Strip.

DSB: Perhaps ordinary architecture with some decoration is a good model for university architecture. University buildings combine low budgets and high aspirations. Although they must provide down-to-earth, generous, kickable accommodations for some of society's toughest users, they must also express the values society places on education. Campus architecture of the turn of the century—not only the Sever Halls or Cope and Stewardson's

Washington University and Princeton complexes, but the early College Halls of many American state colleges—accomplished just this combination of tough generosity and rhetoric. They are loved for this quality and have become the image of the American college. Yale's Gothic buildings, although later, share this quality, and not only because of their Gothic styling.

RV: Modern architecture, too, has tried to express aspiration through poetic simplicity and adherence to the directives of function and structure. Yet, ironically, the modern architecture of Yale, the architecture of the 1950's and 1960's, did not stress the simple virtues, but sought instead "original" forms derived from "advanced" technology, resulting in heroic monuments. Here, as in the rest of modern architecture, symbolism is cast out in favor of expressionism: expression of function, structure, and mechanical equipment by complex articulation of elements of the building [Art and Architecture Building; *see Fig. 3–3*]; or expression of the "imperatives" of industrialized construction [Beinecke Library; *Fig. 8–3*]; or expression of heroic aspirations by reference to a heroic architectural "form giver" of the modern movement [Becton Center; *Fig. 8–4*]. But, somehow, instead of revolutionary architectural aspirations or scholarly academic aspirations, these buildings seem to express most clearly the munificence of their corporate donors.

HK: The intention in your proposal for the Mathematics Building does not affirm the heroic architecture of the 1950's and 1960's at Yale.

DSB: Perhaps this showplace architecture, and the new value system behind the student protests, caused the writers of the Mathematics Building program to call for "workable space" and "the integration of new buildings into the strong existing fabric."

RV: This is not the time, and ours is not the environment, for heroic communication via pure architecture. Every medium has its day, and the statements of our time

8–3. Beinecke Rare Book and Manuscript Library. Yale University. New Haven, Conn. 1963. Gordon Bunshaft.

8–4. Becton Engineering and Applied Science Center. Yale University. New Haven, Conn. 1969. Marcel Breuer.

—civic, commercial, institutional—will come, not from architecture alone, but from combinations of media: an impure, eclectic architecture of words, sculpture, and associations, more adaptable to the scale, tempo, and timbre of our cacophonic environments.

DSB: Ordinary architecture, with superficial, openly acknowledged, symbolic, and associative ornament, harking back to the traditional campus, seems particularly suited to the changing values of the campus. The students and faculty will admit of a little rhetoric if it is skin deep and witty (a kindly parody, really, of academic and corporate rhetoric), while their aspirations will, we hope, be suited by the tough-abundant quality of the rest of the building, which gracefully allows them to make it their own.

RV: Architecture for a time of questioning cannot be monumental. It cannot be a barracks, either. But it must be more than a loft. To the extent that it is successfully more, in the spirit of the protest, it will help express the aspirations of that protest.

JC: Your proposal carefully selects the associations you want to make. You contradict and affirm, while relating to the Neo-Gothic building next to the site [*Fig. 8–5*].

DSB: In designing the Yale Mathematics Building, we thought of institutional building of the recent past on one hand, and of Gothic decoration on the other hand: Explicit association with existing models was part of the design method. In looking at this building, we hope you think of these earlier examples.

HK: When Philip Johnson designed

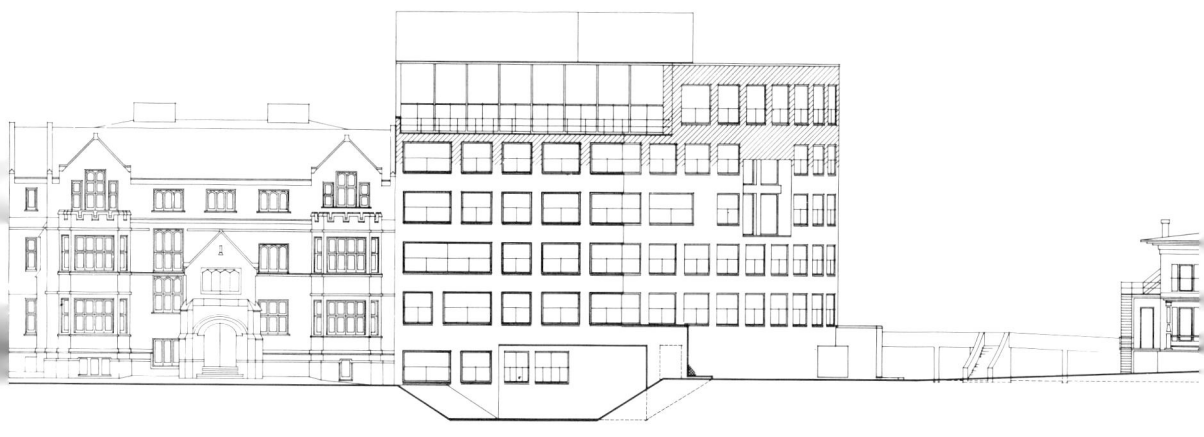

8–5. Mathematics Building at Yale University (right). 1969. Venturi and Rauch. East elevation. Leet Oliver Building (left). 1908. Charles Haight.

the Kline Biology Tower [see Fig. 1–1], he created a monumental symbol for science at Yale. Do you create an image for mathematics at Yale?

RV: The *image* is ordinary: a working building, enhancing rather than upstaging the buildings around it. The rhetoric lies in Leet Oliver Hall, which has enough for both, and in the relationship between the two. The Gothic porch [Fig. 8–6] in concrete and the quatrefoil paving pattern in back are small stylistic appliqués on the loftlike bulk, making explicit the relation to Leet Oliver through symbolism, as well as through compositional form and scale.

Not only the image, but the *substance* is ordinary: conventional windows and brick curtain walls on steel frame for economical

8–6. Mathematics Building. Yale University. Ground plan.

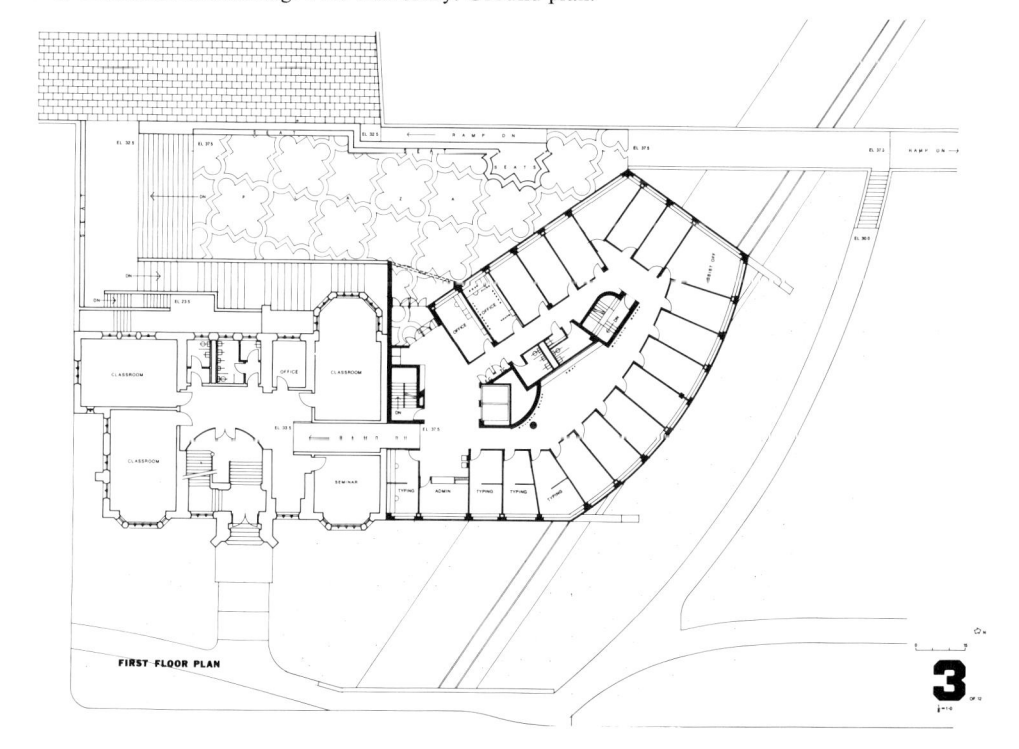

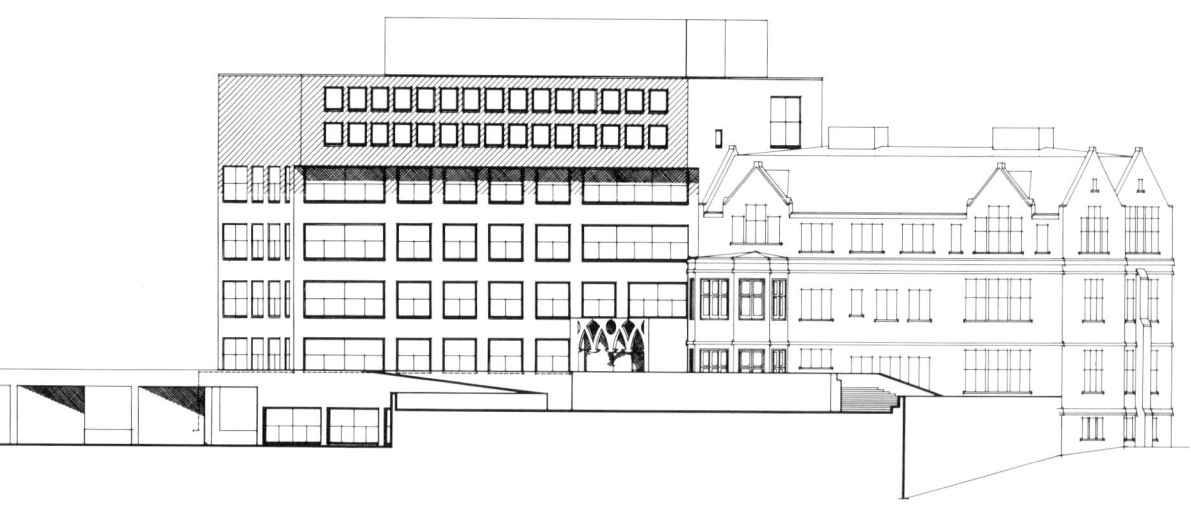

8–7. Mathematics Building. Yale University. Southwest elevation.

construction and maintenance. More rhetoric, but of a "second glance" order, will come, we hope, from the generosity and careful proportions and detailing of the conventional elements.

JC: It is a tall order to insist on the ordinary, in your terms, considering the site where it will stand and the prestigious and special architecture of Hillhouse Avenue.

DSB: The new building is an addition rather than a monument, but a big addition [Fig. 8–7], to be accommodated to the delicate architecture of Hillhouse Avenue.

JC: How do you manage to do that?

RV: We have tried to maintain a big scale, yet diminish the necessarily big bulk by shortening the façade on the street, setting back at the upper floor, changing the color value at the fourth floor, and—important in its relation to Leet Oliver—by inflecting the shape of the plan; the big, new building, because it is dependent on Leet Oliver: It could not stand alone, or without Leet Oliver.

HK: But the mansions at the north end of Hillhouse Avenue define a space and scale different from Leet Oliver.

DSB: The new building reinforces the space of the street by maintaining the building height and line of the street and the scale of the institutional buildings across the street and to the south. Yet, through its bowed side elevation [Fig. 8–8], it terminates the row of big buildings and, by inflecting toward the Dana House, and the march of distinguished houses up Hillhouse Avenue, it connects with the changed character of the street toward the north. By its diagonal shape in back, it suggests enclosure, terminating Becton Plaza, but without an added wing, thereby maintaining its generous scale.

RV: Harmony with Leet Oliver is sought through contrast, as well as analogy: The windows are different in type, yet similar in scale; the material is different in type and texture (glazed brick), yet similar in color to that of Leet Oliver (gray limestone). At the back, the paving pattern of the plaza and the tracery of the entrance are different in scale and material from the ornament of Leet Oliver, yet similar symbolically.

JC: What are the major "interior demands" in this building?

RV: Inside, heavy circulation is limited to the basement and part of the first floor. Ramped access for the handicapped is available from Trumbull Street and Becton Plaza. Since the building is an addition to Leet Oliver, the entrance from Hillhouse Avenue remains in Leet Oliver, and, since the two buildings are functionally integral [*Fig. 8–6*], the generous spaces of the old building can suffice for the new, and new public space is minimized in favor of amenable private spaces. However, portions of the new corridors are wider than is needed for circulation and are planned as gallery space for incidental meeting and communication, where seats and bulletin boards abound. The same idea carries into outdoor accessways to the large lecture halls and the rear plaza, which is planned to encourage informal meetings and groupings. The common rooms are central and face the view up Hillhouse Avenue. The reading space of the library [*Fig. 8–9*] also has this good view.

DSB: Interior furnishings, particularly of common spaces, library, and lecture rooms, will, we hope, avoid the cut-rate, Knoll-executive imitations which are available through most campus purchasing departments in favor of something tougher, more banal and "funky," and also more expansive and comfortable. The image of the club lounge translated into vinyl with "soft" armchairs and alcoves—spaces and furniture to be lounged in—seems one which is attractive to today's students and faculty.

HK: There are technological advances in architecture which allow low-cost construction as well as new formal characteristics, for instance, some of the concrete construction by Bertrand Goldberg. In your commitment to the "ordinary," you seem consciously to avoid such advances.

RV: We have rejected technology as a channel for architectural expressionism, but not the valid technical issues which arise and need solutions. In this particular project, for instance, we need to span a railroad. The supporting structure spanning the railroad cut is treated as a special incident requiring special construction [*Fig. 8–8*] a touch of frame piercing an otherwise consistent skin-clad building and mediating between the regular geometry of the steel framed building above and the protruding piers below. Architecturally, these spans are not too carefully related to the rest of the building and certainly not treated as a predominating "feature," but rather as one of the incidents of a complex building.

JC: How does one understand the architectural results of the Venturis? What role

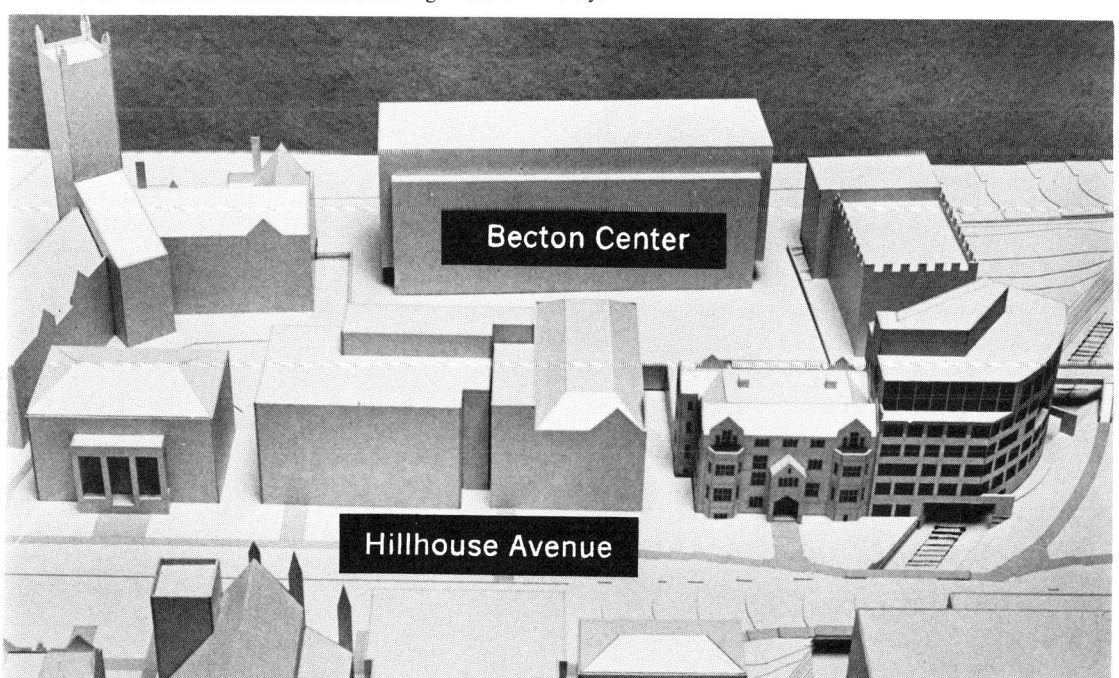

8–8. Model for Mathematics Building. Yale University.

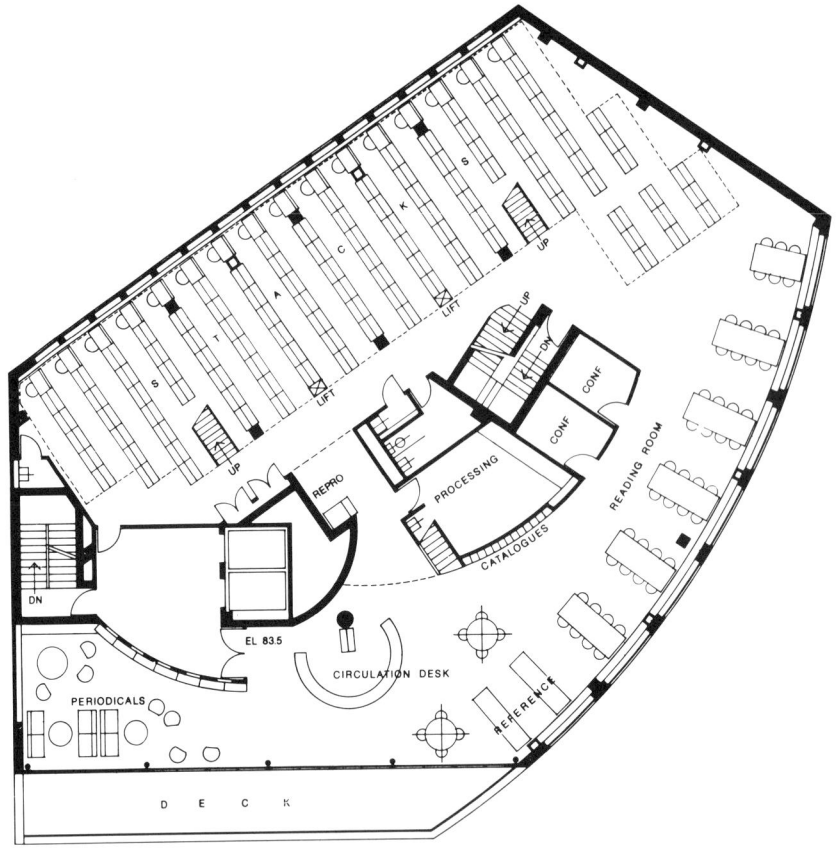

8–9. Mathematics Building. Yale University. Fifth-floor library plan.

does each of you play in planning and design?

RV: It's very complex. Certainly, there is a distinction. Denise's training is in architecture and planning. In teaching, she is very much the leader. In design, she is mostly the critic, but in the very creative sense; the critic that T. S. Eliot meant when he said creation is nine-tenths criticism. John Rauch is also very important in understanding the way we work. On one hand, he is the businessman and technical partner; on the other hand, he is a crucial critic, very at home in thinking abstractly; he is ten times more intellectual than I.

DSB: John Rauch started off as a painter. When it comes to questions of presentation in the office, John, Bob, and Gerold Clark are a very close-knit team. I remember one competition when Bob debated an overly long time about a small point—on what trees to put on a drawing—till John came and said, after a few minutes of experiment, "Here, Bob, do this."

RV: We call John our Rauch of Gibraltar. He knows what I'm doing more than I do. That could really be said of Denise, too.

DSB: Bob and I were faculty members at the University of Pennsylvania. We were sort of underground, in that most of our architectural colleagues were not interested in our ideas. In the office, I am the one who pushes functions of a social sort. I emphasize these early in the design stage, as we decide what the determining problems are in the project. In *making* the form, Bob is by far the most important person in our office.

Then there is Gerold Clark. He is probably the one with his ear most sensitively to the ground about pop art and other media. Bob will turn to him with great trust because of his sensitivity to new forms. In this aspect of our work, he is the expert. We depend on him for sophisticated aesthetic criticism.

JC: I think these answers are covering another very important aspect of your work. They mean that, in your office, you not only include these other areas which inform your architecture, but you do not have the kind of prima donna master who determines the design with a rigid hand. You are describing a team action.

RV: I don't like putting it that way because it sounds too much like a Walter Gropius architectural collaborative. But I like the fact that we work together.

JC: Would you accept being called "the Venturis"?

DSB: I use Scott Brown when I write, since that is the name by which I am known (and to perpetuate the name of my first husband, who died before he could make his own), and to maintain my own career identity against rather strong pressures for submergence. For example, Bob was accused of bringing the Nixon regime into architecture because of an article I wrote. It is always "Venturi's article" and "Venturi's architecture" (rather than the architecture of Venturi and Rauch), because architects are male chauvinists, and they go by the prima donna—or should we say primo uomo—system.

RV: Our major problem is that we haven't got much work and haven't built much. And I also, to repeat, don't like my reputation as a verbal type, a theorist for whom architecture is secondary.

JC: That is because you first wrote an architectural treatise.

RV: Yes, it's because I've written. I *am* a critical architect, because I think anybody who is an architect is a critic, and I subscribe to T. S. Eliot's emphasis on criticism as a part of creativity. I think some architects who talk build to prove what they are saying. I know our buildings are buildings first. We really don't think too much about our philosophy while designing. When we sit down to design, we really think of our buildings as solutions to the problems given. And then, almost later, I begin to realize that something I've thought about earlier has connected. That is why the

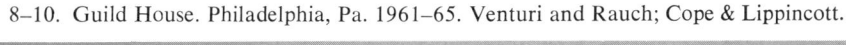

8–10. Guild House. Philadelphia, Pa. 1961–65. Venturi and Rauch; Cope & Lippincott.

Guild House [*Fig. 8–10*] does not have as much decoration, or as much explicit symbolism, as one might expect.

DSB: A building is not merely a physical explanation of a theory.

RV: It's not a vehicle.

JC: Sometimes, it works the other way around. You take the theory from the building.

RV: Certainly. I do that, too. I think that's all right, because you get to it intuitively, and then you realize what you've done.

HK: When we visited the Guild House in Philadelphia, the "famous" gilded television antenna had been removed.

RV: That was taken down because it was not a real television antenna, very cheap, not made to last, and it was falling apart. We could not afford a lasting sculptural one. The clients will not replace it, perhaps because they are Quakers. We had quite a battle, in the first place, convincing them to spend $600 on imagery.

HK: Could you explain the gilded antenna to us?

RV: The bulk of the building is conventional and ordinary, but the narrow front façade is monumental by contrast. That is why we have a curved window at the top which terminates the stack of balcony openings on this façade, so that this configuration becomes one whole—a kind of giant order in contrast to the 6-story scale of the rest of the building. We wanted the building to be ordinary and monumental at the same time. We like the idea of putting a piece of sculpture on top of a building in a Renaissance way (although they never placed a piece of sculpture in the *center* of the roof line). Ideally, we would have liked to have had a plaster madonna with her arms outstretched in the pop art manner, but that would have been inappropriate for a Quaker building, so we used a television antenna—a commonplace element, but enlarged and gilded, giving it a new meaning as well as the old common meaning. Then, there is also the symbolism of old people who look at television.

HK: Critics took it as a derogatory symbol for elderly people's way of life.

RV: We didn't mean it that way. It's not for us to tell people that television is bad, and they should read books. That horrifies us—the implication, that is, that art should be explicitly for the betterment of people. What a real bore.

JC: The antenna wasn't functional?

RV: Originally, it was going to be functional. Then, we found it wouldn't look good if it were a working device, so we made it not be.

DSB: When Andy Warhol looks at a Campbell's Soup can, I don't know whether he hates it or loves it, and I'm not sure that he knows, either. This ambivalence gives the tension. The same thing is true of our television antenna up there. Is it hate or love? It's a bit of both, which is a very real human emotion. Again, it's a question of judgment. The ambivalence, the mixture of both emotions, is not going to be resolved. That's our world. Why shouldn't we express that? We think we use parody not hatefully, but lovingly; with tears, maybe.

HK: Accepting what exists, in order to show what is meaningful, can make you end up affirming something like Co-op City [*see Fig. 2–1*], which, as a matter of fact, you have done. Co-op City is "almost all right." At what point do you become critical of that which exists?

DSB: There are certain things which we criticize very strongly. I don't think the expressway through the ghetto can ever be done well. I don't think water pollution can ever be done well. I don't think war in Vietnam, to put it mildly, can ever be done well. But we felt slight changes might make Co-op City good; that's where the "almost" comes in. We haven't said that we should be totally nonjudgmental about *all* aspects of life. We just want to suggest that changes for the better don't have to be catastrophic, and that when they are, they are sometimes for the worse; think of urban renewal, for example.

8–11. Proposal for Football Hall of Fame. New Brunswick, New Jersey. 1966. Model. Venturi and Rauch.

RV: If someone says everything is all wrong, he is usually copping out. Usually, the visionary is somebody who walks away in disgust, saying, "It's just impossible," and nothing happens. Many architects imply, "We want Utopia, and we are superior because we can envision it." Meanwhile, the world is going to pot and needs some good, expedient, immediate action. I think the artist is seldom an explicit visionary, and when he claims to be, I get suspicious.

DSB: "The artist is the dreamer who consents to dream about reality" [Santayana].

RV: I think the artist really wants to deal with reality, to get his fingers dirty in the "how." In the end, he may be a visionary as a byproduct, but he is not trying to be a visionary from the beginning. So, in a way, we pride ourselves on getting into the fray. I think that's really the artist's method.

HK: In distrusting the visionary, you might go too far in the other direction. Architecture like Co-op City doesn't need to be defended. It is taking over, anyway.

RV: You accept it only at the very beginning of the process of thinking about what to do next.

DSB: Co-op City is giving people just about the lowest-cost rentals in New York. We cannot ignore it, because we know there are 800,000 people living in substandard housing in New York, and hardly anyone is doing anything about it. We think Co-op City, and the form it has taken, should be examined as the product of certain forces—social, economic, political, and technical—which architects will have to understand before they can do better, or even as well. We are *not* saying it is the only solution for housing in New York, far from it, but it is one of a set of possible solutions which relates to location, land values, and the needs of the people in a certain way. It obviously has strength, because it's been done, and it seems to be needed and used. So we cannot afford to ignore it. Then we ask, "Can we positively like it?" We started looking at it, and we noticed that it is very direct in certain respects, particularly in the use of brick, and in its fenestration. Then we began to make criticisms, for example, of the skins around

8–12. Guild House. Sign at entrance.

the parking structures. We also questioned the siting. We thought some small changes in the siting could make views of and from buildings more pleasant. We also looked for something frankly pretty and couldn't find it. The housing foundation was not prepared to commercialize their riverside, and use the money to provide the pretty objects that they wanted people to see from their windows. So we began to criticize Co-op City on its own terms. On the other hand, we felt critics should not say that there is or will be social pathology in the housing without proving it. We should not say that Co-op City is an environmental failure and will therefore cause social failure. There is no proof for this claim in the sociological literature. Nevertheless, Co-op City can be human as well as superhuman.

HK: What would have made it human?

DSB: It hasn't made too bad a start, as we suggested, but alterations in the siting to improve the view, and the use of frankly pretty, imageful, and symbolic objects at ground level, would help.

HK: These things are normally skipped in the budget. They are considered to be superfluous.

RV: Modern architects don't approve of them, either. They're adornment, if not immorality.

DSB: They wanted to do something, but they had no money. We suggested that they use the river commercially and not ask the government for the money—sell hamburgers and boat trips to get enough money for fountains and sculptures.

HK: The clients are normally satisfied with the building itself; therefore, they consider symbolic ornament, the message-giver, superfluous. There is a problem in the way you separate the ornament from the building. In your proposal for a Football Hall of Fame building [*Fig. 8–11*], the billboard, the façade, is separate from the building.

DSB: It's very easy for the client to say, "Now cut off the ornament."

RV: Architects deserve this reaction, because it is they who have indoctrinated the clients in saying ornament is evil, or immoral, or superficial. But these architects end by distorting the whole building into ornament. But that is more expensive and irresponsible than just making a billboard façade.

DSB: We did fear that the Guild House sign [*Fig. 8–12*], the big letters over the entrance, might be removed. I think we should consider ways to do the ornament so that it cannot be easily removed. Maybe colored brick and tile, rather than appliqué.

HK: As long as the billboard says, "I'm a cinema," it's all right. But if the billboard says, "I am Boston City Hall," it is not accepted. Even an apartment for elderly people may not be ready for its name to be broadcast.

JC: When you are defending the existing environment, like the Las Vegas Strip, or the new South Street Project [*Fig. 8–13*] in Philadelphia, you must run into political problems.

DSB: Our work on South Street combines social concerns, social analysis, and aesthetics. We were asked by a primarily black citizens' group if we would be their architects and planners, to help them keep the expressway off South Street. With their help, and upon their instruction, we produced an image of what South Street could be. A ring system of expressways threatens the existence of South Street. One realizes that the solution of pushing an expressway through low-cost ghetto land in center city is not only not a solution, but is also an immoral act. Producing a picture for the citizens of South Street which was evocative and imageful turned out to be an astute political move. And we know it was, because the chief antagonist, the Chamber of Commerce, was therefore impelled to produce a counterimage.

It was important to us that we were approached by a group of planners already working with the citizens' committee, who

8–13. South Street. Philadelphia, Pa.

8–14. South Street store front.

said, "If you can like the Las Vegas Strip, we trust you not to neaten up South Street at the expense of its citizens." I think that there's a strong connection between social ideas and formal ideas in this case, a connection we would like very much to maintain.

There's an irony in both the Las Vegas and South Street projects: There is no money. In South Street, we have had to work all along for no money because there just wasn't any. We finally got some for Las Vegas, but, when we first tried for the Las Vegas project, we were told that it didn't have enough social concern, and, at the same time, our request was turned down for the South Street project because it was "too political." So, we feel we fall between two stools.

Again, we feel that South Street, with all its restrictions, is where you need your very best imagination as an architect. Mostly, the problem is to rehabilitate existing beautiful old stores and housing in a way which will be economically viable [*Fig. 8–14*]. Where something new was to be added, we found the less architecture the better. And that calls for, I think, a high level of architectural sophistication. In architecture of social concern, it seems to me, our formal concerns, aesthetic concerns, and imagination are all called for.

GLOSSARY

architrave: In post-and-beam construction, the molded or flat beam resting on and extending between columns.

brise-soleil: A sun shield or grill to provide shade.

cantilever: An extended self-supporting projection (canopy, balcony, beam) of a structural member.

colonnade: A row of columns with entablatures.

dumbbell plan: A ground plan in the shape of a dumbbell: two large areas connected by a narrow straight element.

megastructure: An over-scaled, colossal, multi-unit architectural mass.

mullion: Supporting and dividing elements within a window.

pilaster: A shallow pier or column projecting slightly from a wall.

pilotis: The legs or stilts that support a building with a raised first floor.

plinth: The projecting base or pedestal of a column or wall.

portal jamb: The straight vertical supporting side of a doorway.

post-and-beam: An ancient construction method in which horizontal elements (beams) are made to rest on vertical supports (posts or columns).

postament: A classical base support.

risalet: An extended architectural section that alters the mass of the building.

slip-form construction: The use of a moving form for poured-in-place concrete. The form "slips" to the next construction stage after the previous pour has set.

socle: A base or pedestal; a foundation block.

spandrel: Traditionally, the space between the curve of two arches, or between the arch and its frame.

step-pyramid: A pyramid shape with stepped surfaces.

travertine: A cream-colored, porous Italian marble used as facing material in construction.

venturi action: Air-passage control.

window jamb: The straight, vertical supporting side of a window.

INDEX

Italic page numbers refer to illustrations.

A. S. Beck Shoe Store, New York (Lapidus), 151, *151*
Aalto, Alvar, 73, 232
Abramovitz, Max, 33
Afrikanerstrasse, Berlin (Mies van der Rohe), 35
Alfred Newton Richards Medical Research Laboratories, University of Pennsylvania, Philadelphia (Kahn), 23, 210, *211*, 215
Allen, Roy, 154
American Broadcasting Company Building, New York (Goldberg), *139*, 139–40, *140*, 142, 146
American Embassy Building, New Delhi, India (Stone), 198
Americana Hotel, Bal Harbour, Florida (Lapidus), 153, *154*
Amon Carter Museum, Fort Worth, Texas (Johnson), *20*, 21*n*, 29
Anderson, Beckwith & Haible, 94
Andrews, John, 51
Ansonia Shoe Store, New York (Lapidus), 159, *160*
Art and Architecture Building, Yale University, New Haven, Connecticut (Rudolph), 82, 91–94, *93*, 96–100, *97*, *98*, *100*, 119–20, 244, 255
Asia House, New York (Johnson), *30*, 31, *31*, 34
Astor Tower, Chicago (Goldberg), 134, 135
Autogerechte Stadt, Die (Rostow), 106

Barbonne, Peter, 102
Barcelona Pavilion (Mies van der Rohe), 26, 43, 149
Bauhaus Book, The (Oud), 28
Becton Engineering and Applied Science Center, Yale University, New Haven, Connecticut (Breuer), 255, *256*
Behrens, Peter, 22
Beinecke Rare Book and Manuscript Library, Yale University, New Haven, Connecticut (Bunshaft), 255, *255*
Boston City Hall, Boston, Massachusetts (Kallmann, McKinnell, and Knowles), 101, *101*, 249, 251, 253
Boston Government Service Center, Massachusetts, 100, 101, *114*, 115, 119
Boston Police Station, Precinct 1, Boston, Massachusetts (Shepley, Bulfinch, Richardson, and Abbott), 115, *115*
Boston Public Library, 23, 24
Breuer, Marcel, 27, 171, 256

Brody, Davis, 238, 239
Bronfman, Sam, 40
Brubeck, Dave, 236
Bundy, McGeorge, 71
Bunshaft, Gordon, 31, 32, 34, 35, 255

Casa Fascismo, Como, Italy, 36
CBS Building, New York (Eero Saarinen and Associates), 13, *14*, 15, *15*, 16, *16*, 141
Chalk, Warren, 134–35, 192
Chandigarh (Le Corbusier), 110
Charles Moore's House, *244*, 244–46, *245*, *246*
Chicago School of Architecture, The (Condit), 123*n*
Chorley Elementary School (*see* John W. Chorley Elementary School)
Christian Science Center, University of Illinois, Urbana (Rudolph), 101
Chrysler Building, New York (Van Alen), 166, 172, 173
Church Street South, New Haven, Connecticut (Moore, Lyndon, Turnbull, and Whitaker), 219–23, *220*, *221*, *222*, 227, 229, 236, *239*
Clark, Gerold, 260
Clark and Beuttler, 224
Clark University Library, Worcester, Massachusetts (Johansen), 45
Citizen's Federal Savings Bank, San Francisco, California (Moore, Lyndon, Turnbull, and Whitaker), 224–25, *225*
Complexity and Contradiction (Venturi), 248
Condit, Carl W., 123
Congress Hall, Venice, Italy (Kahn), *202*, 202–3
Constitution Plaza, Hartford, Connecticut, 25*n*
Co-op City, New York (Jessor), *54*, 55, 136, 262, 263, 264
Cope & Lippincott, 261
Corbet, Harvey Wiley, 149
Coronado Island Condominium Project, Coronado, California (Moore), *230*, 231, 233
Crawford Manor, Housing for the Elderly, New Haven, Connecticut (Rudolph), 46, 79, *118*, 119, 120
Creighton, Tom, 152
Crown Hall, Illinois Institute of Technology, Chicago (Mies van der Rohe), 30

Desmond and Lord, 92
Dinkeloo, John, 72, 85
Doubleday Doran Book Shop, Detroit, Michigan (Lapidus), *165*
Drexler, Arthur, 29

Eden Roc Hotel, Miami Beach, Florida (Lapidus), 157, *157*
Edison, Thomas, 131
Eero Saarinen and Associates, 14
Eliot, T. S., 260, 261
Endo Laboratories, Garden City, New York (Rudolph), 101
Erdmann Dormitory Complex, Bryn Mawr College, Bryn Mawr, Pennsylvania (Kahn), 195, *195*, 206, 206–7, *207*, 208–9, *209*

Faculty Club, University of California, Santa Barbara (Moore, Lyndon, Turnbull, and Whitaker), *233*, 234, *234*, 235, *237*, 238, *238*, 241
Farnsworth House (Mies van der Rohe), 16
Federal Reserve Bank, New York (Roche), 57–64, *58*, *59*, *60*, *61*, *62*, *63*, *64*, 76, 170
Fernandez, José A., 164
Field, Erastus Salisbury, 134
First Church of Christ Scientist, Berkeley, California (Maybeck), *232*, 233
First Unitarian Church, Rochester, New York (Kahn), 189, *189*
Fontainebleau Hotel, Miami Beach, Florida (Lapidus), *148*, 150, 155, 156, *156*, 157, 158, *159*, 167, 168, 173, 174, 175
Football Hall of Fame, New Brunswick, New Jersey (Venturi and Rauch), *263*, 265
Ford Foundation Building, New York (Kevin Roche, John Dinkeloo, and Associates), 23, 57, 66, *66*, *68*, 68–72, *70*, *71*
Fort Worth Museum (*see* Amon Carter Museum)
Foster, Richard, 12
Friedrichstrasse Building, Berlin (Mies van der Rohe), 45, *45*, 46
Fry, Maxwell, 73
Fuller, Buckminster, 51, 212

Gage Building, Chicago, Illinois (Sullivan), 34
Gans, Herbert, 252
Gaudí, Antonio, 13, 34
Gebrauchsgrafik (magazine), 161–62, 164
Giedion, Sigfried, 151
Glass House, New Canaan, Connecticut (Johnson), 14, *14*, 15, 16, 21, 23–27, 44
Goff, Bruce, 235
Goldberg, Bertrand (b. 1913), 121, 122–46, 259
Government Center of Bangladesh, Dacca (Kahn), 178, *180*, *193*, *194*, 195, *197*, 235
Grand's Restaurant, Philadelphia, Pennsylvania (Venturi and Rauch), 241, *241*
Graphic Arts Center, New York (Rudolph), *108*, 109, 110, 111, *112*, 113, 114
Greene, Charles, 232
Greene, Henry, 232
Griswold, Whitney, 21

Gropius, Walter, 27, 35, 73, 95, 108, 148, 261
Guaranty Building, Buffalo, New York (Adler & Sullivan), 34
Guild House, Philadelphia, Pennsylvania (Venturi and Rauch; Cope & Lippincott), *261*, 262, *264*, 265

Habitat, Montreal, Canada, 131
Haight, Charles, 257
Häring, Hugo, 204, 232
Harkness Tower, New Haven, Connecticut (James Gamble Rogers), 79
Harrison, Wallace K., 33, 154, 158
Harrison and Abramovitz, 33
Hebrew Academy, Miami Beach, Florida (Lapidus), *176*, 177
Herbert's Home of the Blue White Diamonds, New York (Lapidus), *163*, 164
Hilliard Center (*see* Raymond Hilliard Center)
Hitchcock, Henry-Russell, 27, 34, 52
Hood, Raymond, 149
Housing Project, Orono, Maine (Moore, Lyndon, Turnbull, and Whitaker), *228*, 228–30, *229*, 230
Huxtable, Ada Louise, 171

Indian Institute of Management, Ahmedabad, India (Kahn), *194*, 195, *196*, 197, *198*, 199–202, *200*, *201*
Intellectual vs. the City, The (White and White), 136
International Style, The (Hitchcock and Johnson), 52

Jefferson, Thomas, 136
Jenney, Le Baron, 122
Jessor, Herman, 54
Jewett Arts Center (*see* Mary Cooper Jewett Arts Center)
Jewish Community Center, New Haven, Connecticut (Moore), 225
Jewish Community Center, Trenton, New Jersey (Kahn), *213*, *214*, 214–15, *215*, 216
Johansen, John, 32, 45
John Deere Building, Moline, Illinois (Kevin Roche, John Dinkeloo, and Associates), 72
John Hancock Building, Chicago, Illinois (Skidmore, Owings, and Merrill), 131
John W. Chorley Elementary School, Middletown, New York (Rudolph and Barbonne), *102*, 103, 104
Johnson, Philip (b. 1906), 11–51, 52, 53, 74, 79, 83, 90, 96, 106, 116, 223, 224, 256
Johnson House (*see* Reverdy Johnson House)
Johnson Wax Company Research Tower, Racine, Wisconsin (Wright), 123

Kahn, Louis (b. 1901), 23, 32, 50, 90, 178–217, 235, 241, 243, 252

INDEX 269

Kallmann, McKinnell, and Knowles, 101
Kansas City Office Building, Missouri (Kahn), 190, 191, *191, 192,* 193
Kennedy Center, Washington, D.C. (Stone), 92
Ketchum, Morris, 164
Kevin Roche, John Dinkeloo, and Associates, 58, 65, 72, 81, 103, 220, 223
Kikutake, Kiyonori, 133–34
Kline Biology Tower, Yale University, New Haven, Connecticut (Johnson and Foster), 11, *12, 13,* 17, 18, *20,* 21, 22, *22,* 24, 43, 44, 46, 47, 49, *50,* 79, 116, 257
Knights of Columbus Building, New Haven, Connecticut (Kevin Roche, John Dinkeloo, and Associates), 23, 65, *65,* 66, *66,* 75–78, *76, 77, 80,* 81, 85, *222,* 223, 225
Kump, Ernie, 237

Laboratory of Epidemiology and Public Health, Yale University, New Haven, Connecticut (Johnson and Orr), 36, *36,* 45, 46
Ladenbau (magazine), 164
Lapidus, Alan (b. 1936), 147–77
Lapidus, Morris (b. 1902), 89, 147–77, 243, 253
Le Corbusier, 24, 28, 31, 34, 38, 109, 110, 138, 139, 143, 148, 187, 249, 253
Leet Oliver Building (Haight), *257,* 257–59
Lescaze, William, 162
Lichtenstein, Roy, 236
Lincoln Center, New York (Johnson design), 32, *32*
Lincoln Center Complex, New York, 32–34, 100, 157–58
Lower Manhattan Expressway, New York (Rudolph), *104,* 105, 106, 109, 111
Luckman, Charles, 234
Lyndon, Don, 231, 233, 234

McKim, Mead, and White, 23
Mankiewicz, Joseph L., 158
Marina City Towers, Chicago, Illinois (Goldberg), 122, 123, 124, *124,* 125, 127–29, *127,* 131–33, *132,* 134–39, 141, 143, 146
Marseilles Building (Le Corbusier), 24
Mary Cooper Jewett Arts Center, Wellesley College, Wellesley, Massachusetts (Rudolph; Anderson, Beckwith & Haible), 94, *94*
Mathematics Building, Yale University, New Haven, Connecticut (Venturi and Rauch), *254,* 254–59, *257, 258, 259, 260*
Maybeck, Bernard, 232
Mellon Center (*see* Paul Mellon Center for British Art and British Studies)
Mendelsohn, Erich, 28, 161
Metropolitan Opera House, New York (Harrison), *33,* 158
Meyer, Hannes, 38

Mies van der Rohe, Ludwig, 12, 16, 18, 19, 22, 23, 24, 26, 27, 30, 32, 34, 35, 37, 43, 45, 46, 50, 51, 72–75, 108, 109, 121, 122, 123, 129, 130, 141, 148, 149, 150, 159, 162, 173, 174, 181, 204, 212, 219, 223, 239
Moore, Charles (b. 1925), 78, 218–46
Moore, Lyndon, Turnbull, and Whitaker, 220, 225, 233, 245
Mumford, Lewis, 51, 136
Municipal Building, New York (McKim, Mead, and White), 23

Nebraska Museum (*see* Sheldon Memorial Art Gallery)
Nervi, Pier Luigi, 142
New Canaan Art Gallery, Connecticut (Johnson), *27, 29*
New York Central Building, New York, 150
New York State Theater, New York (Johnson), *33,* 34, 116
New York University Library (Johnson and Foster), 23, 24
Niemeyer, Oscar, 174, 175
Novak, Ben, 152
Nuclear Reactor, Rehovet, Israel (Johnson), 48, *48,* 49, *49*

Oakland Museum, California (Kevin Roche, John Dinkeloo, and Associates), 67, *67,* 85–88, *87*
Olympic Building, New York (Lapidus), *168,* 168–73, *169, 170*
Oriental Masonic Gardens Apartments, New Haven, Connecticut (Rudolph), 113, *113*
Orr, Douglas, 36
Otto, Frei, 51
Oud, J. J. P., 28, 243

Palladio, Andrea, 139
Pampulha Casino, Brazil (Niemeyer), 175, *175*
Parisian Bootery, New York (Lapidus), *149,* 150, 164
Paul Mellon Center for British Art and British Studies, Yale University, New Haven, Connecticut (Kahn), 204, *205*
Pavilion, Philip Johnson estate, New Canaan, Connecticut (Johnson), *17, 20,* 21, 29, 34, 43, 51
Pei, I. M., 100
Perret, Auguste, 41
Pevsner, Nikolaus, 154
Philadelphia City Plan (Kahn), *184,* 184–86, *185*
Philharmonic Hall, Berlin (Scharoun and Weber), 203, *203*
Philharmonic Hall, New York (Abramovitz), *33,* 34

Philip Johnson estate, 26
Plug-in Living Unit Circular Tower, London (Chalk), *134*, 134–35, 192
Ponte Vecchio, Florence, Italy, 110

Rauch, John, 260
Raymond Hilliard Center, Chicago, Illinois (Goldberg), 121, 122, 124–27, *125*, *126*, *127*, 129, *133*, 137, 138, 143, *143*, *144*, *145*, 146
Reverdy Johnson House, Sea Ranch, Gualala, California (Moore, Lyndon, Turnbull, and Whitaker), *233*, 234
Richard C. Lee High School, New Haven, Connecticut (Kevin Roche, John Dinkeloo, and Associates), 103, *103*
Richards Laboratory (*see* Alfred Newton Richards Medical Research Laboratories)
Richardson, Henry Hobson, 23, 47, 151
Robert Taylor Housing, Chicago, Illinois (Shaw, Metz & Associates), 124, 125, 137
Robert Wiley House, New Canaan, Connecticut (Johnson), 15, *16*, 23
Robertson, Jacquelin, 39
Roche, Kevin (b. 1922), 22, 23, 52–89, 104, 116, 170
Rosenblum, Robert, 245
Ross-Frankel, 167
Rudolph, Paul (b. 1918), 32, 46, 79, 82, 83, 90–121, 242, 244, 248

Saarinen, Eero, 13–16, 32, 74, 85, 141, 142
Saarinen, Eliel, 149
Sanders, Morris, 162
Sans Souci Hotel, Miami Beach, Florida (France/Lapidus), 151, 152
Sarasota Senior High School, Florida (Rudolph), 94–95, *95*
Scarborough College, Toronto, Canada (John Andrews), 51
Scharoun, Hans, 203, 232
Schinkel, Karl Friedrich, 23
Schwobilt Clothing Store, Tampa, Florida (Lapidus), *165*
Scott Brown, Denise (b. 1931), 247–66
Scully, Vincent, 79–80, 175
Seagram Building, New York (Mies van der Rohe and Johnson), 12, *12*, 16, 17, 18, *18*, 19, *19*, 21, 94, 173
Seagram's Private Bar in Chrysler Building, New York (Lapidus), 166, *166*, 167, 168
Sheldon Memorial Art Gallery, Lincoln, Nebraska (Johnson), *20*, 21, 29, 30, 31
Shepley, Bulfinch, Richardson, and Abbott, 115
Skidmore, Owings, and Merrill, 36, 55, 56, 131*n*, 169*n*
Smith, David, 72
Smithson, Alison, 24, 106

Smithson, Peter, 24, 106
Soleri, Paolo, 235
South African Administrative Center, Capetown (Skidmore, Owings, and Merrill), 55, 56
South Street, Philadelphia, Pennsylvania, *265*, 265–66, *266*
Southeastern Massachusetts Technological Institute, North Dartmouth, Massachusetts (Rudolph; Desmond and Lord), 91, *92*, 100
Space, Time, and Architecture (Giedion), 151
Spence, Sir Basil, 154
Stafford Harbor, Virginia (Rudolph), 91, *91*, 104
Stirling, James, 28
Stone, Edward Durell, 23, 82, 90, 92, 198
Strip, The, Las Vegas, Nevada, 250, *250*, 254, 265, 266
Sullivan, Louis, 34, 121, 122, 236
Summit Hotel, New York (Lapidus), *148*, 150, 155, 174
Swank Jewelry, New York (Lapidus), *163*, 164

Temple Judea, Coral Gables, Florida (Lapidus), 153, *153*
Temple Street Parking Garage, New Haven, Connecticut (Rudolph), 117, *117*, 242
Tower City, Tokyo, Japan (Kikutake), *133*, 134
Tracey Towers, New York (Rudolph), 119, *119*, 120
Tribune Tower, Chicago, Illinois (Hood), 149
Tugendhat House, Brno, Czechoslovakia (Mies van der Rohe), 26, 150
TWA Terminal at Kennedy International Airport, Long Island, New York (Eero Saarinen and Associates), 123, 142, 158, *158*

Unité, Marseilles, France (Le Corbusier), 24, 187
Universal Atlas Cement Company, New York (Kahn), 179, *182*, 190
Urban Structure (Smithson and Smithson), 106

Venturi, Robert (b. 1925), 209, 210, 230, 235, 236, 240, 241, 247–66
Venturi and Rauch, 254, 257, 261
Vivian Beaumont Theater, New York (Bunshaft), 34
Vreeland, Tim, 241

Warhol, Andy, 252, 262
Warren and Whetmore, 150
Washington Monument, Washington, D.C., 116
Weber, Werner, 203

INDEX 271

Welfare Island Project, New York (Johnson), 106
White, Lucia, 136*n*
White, Morton, 136*n*
Wiley House (*see* Robert Wiley House)
Woolworth Building, New York (Cass Gilbert), 149
Worcester County National Bank, Worcester, Massachusetts (Kevin Roche, John Dinkeloo, and Associates), *81,* 81–82, *84*
Wright, Frank Lloyd, 17, 23, 24, 28, 46, 51, 122, 123, 130, 136, 155
Wurster, William, 232

Yale University Art Gallery, New Haven, Connecticut (Kahn), 32*n,* 179, *181,* 210–12, *211*